Rape and Society

CRIME & SOCIETY

Series Editor   John Hagan, University of Toronto

Rape and Society: Readings on the Problem of Sexual Assault,
edited by Patricia Searles and Ronald J. Berger

Alternatives to Imprisonment: Intentions and Reality,
Ulla V. Bondeson

Inequality, Crime, and Social Control, *edited by*
George S. Bridges and Martha A. Myers

FORTHCOMING

Poverty, Ethnicity, and Violent Crime,
James F. Short

Great Pretenders: A Study of Property Offenders,
Neal Shover

Youth and Social Justice: Toward the Twenty-first Century,
Nanette J. Davis and Suzanne E. Hatty

Crime, Justice, and Revolution in Eastern Europe,
Joachim J. Savelsbert

Crime, Justice, and Public Opinion,
Julian Roberts and Loretta Stalans

The White-Collar Offender, *Michael Benson*
and Francis T. Cullen

Rape and Society

*Readings
on the Problem
of Sexual Assault*

edited by

Patricia Searles
and Ronald J. Berger

University of Wisconsin–Whitewater

Westview Press

Boulder • San Francisco • Oxford

Crime & Society

Copyright © 1995 by Westview Press, Inc.

Published in 1995 in the United States of America by Westview Press, Inc., 5500 Central Avenue, Boulder, Colorado 80301-2877, and in the United Kingdom by Westview Press, 12 Hid's Copse Road, Cumnor Hill, Oxford OX2 9JJ

Library of Congress Cataloging-in-Publication Data
Rape and society : readings on the problem of sexual assault / edited
by Patricia Searles and Ronald J. Berger.
    p.   cm.—(Crime & society)
    Includes bibliographical references.
    ISBN 0-8133-8823-6.—ISBN 0-8133-8824-4 (pbk.)
    1. Rape.   2. Sex crimes.   I. Searles, Patricia.   II. Berger,
Ronald J.   III. Series: Crime & society (Boulder, Colo.)
HV6558.R335   1995
364.1'532—dc20   94-40409
                                                                        CIP

Printed and bound in the United States of America

The paper used in this publication meets the requirements
of the American National Standard for Permanence of Paper
for Printed Library Materials Z39.48-1984.

10   9   8   7   6   5   4   3   2   1

Contents

Preface

THE CONTEMPORARY WOMEN'S MOVEMENT emerged from the general social dis-content and protests of the 1960s to become a major political force in the United States. Margarita Papandreou (1988:xii) described the women's movement as "a loosely knit federation of women's organizations, working in resistance to humiliation, inequality, and injustice." One major focus of this movement has been the problem of violence against women, which includes several conceptually distinct yet overlapping concerns, including rape, incest, battering, sexual harassment, pornography, sexual slavery, and sexual murder.

There has been a virtual explosion of books and articles on violence against women, many of them written from a feminist perspective. Rape was the first such subject to receive extensive examination. Beginning with Susan Griffin's classic 1971 article, "Rape: The All-American Crime," and books by Susan Brownmiller (*Against Our Will*, 1975), Diana Russell (*The Politics of Rape*, 1975), Lorenne Clark and Debra Lewis (*Rape: The Price of Coercive Sexuality*, 1977), Lynda Lytle Holmstrom and Ann Wolbert Burgess (*The Victim of Rape: Institutional Reactions*, 1978), and Susan Griffin (*Rape: The Power of Consciousness*, 1979), rape became the point of departure for an ongoing investigation of the subordination of women and of their experiences of sexual victimization. These works, along with the consciousness-raising movement of the 1970s, enabled women to move "from the discovery that sexual assault was not just an individual and unique experience to the realization that rape, as an issue, was a means of analyzing the psychological and political structures of oppression in our society" (New York Radical Feminists 1974:3).

Since the 1980s, incest, battery, and pornography have come to the forefront of investigators' concerns, and feminist scholars have increasingly analyzed the interrelationship among the various forms of sexual coercion. This book returns to the original focus on rape and falls within the feminist tradition of examining "rape as a paradigm for sexism in society" (Bart 1979). Although the book highlights rape, we have selected articles to show the interconnections among the many forms of violence against women. Hence selections on sexual abuse, incest, battery, pornography, and sexual murder are also included. Represented as well are the experiences of women of diverse backgrounds and lifestyles.

We attempt to provide a comprehensive treatment of the problem of sexual assault by drawing from writers and researchers across a range of social and behavioral sciences and the humanities. We believe this interdisciplinary anthology will be an important resource for academics and professionals who work in the area of sexual assault as well as a valuable text for undergraduate and graduate courses in women's studies, psychology, sociology, and criminology. The readings are drawn from scholarly journals, books, anthologies, and magazines. The selections provide a range of orientations to the topic: theoretical, empirical, literary, and experiential. The academic articles, although sophisticated in theory and method, remain accessible to students and provide excellent vehicles for instructors who wish to demonstrate the value of incisive analyses and carefully designed research. The literary and experiential pieces, which are both moving and thought provoking, sensitize readers to the personal and emotional dimensions of the problem and impress upon them the beauty and power of the written word. From our own teaching experience, we know that these readings are especially effective in provoking and encouraging classroom discussion.

The book is divided into five topical sections. Part 1, "Feminist Foundations for the Study of Rape and Society," introduces readers to a feminist perspective on rape through personal experience, feminist analyses, and survey research data. The authors in Part 2, "Why Men Rape," further examine the reasons men rape through feminist analyses of rapists' accounts, the clinical literature on sex offenders, and the contribution of pornography to the creation of rape culture. Part 3, "Varieties of Rape and Sexual Assault," exposes readers to the continuum of sexual violence in chapters on child sexual abuse, date and acquaintance rape, marital rape, sexual murder, and rape in war. The chapters in Part 4, "Rape and the Legal System," focus on the treatment of rape in the criminal justice system and the legal criteria that govern state interventions in matters of sexual violation. In Part 5, "Surviving and Preventing Rape," the authors offer personal accounts of coping with the aftermath of sexual assault and consider community efforts to help survivors and prevent victimization.

Although the subject matter of this book is disturbing and some of the selections are graphic, we believe that reading and talking about these issues are essential steps in recognizing and confronting the reality of living in a violent society. The chapters may bring back painful memories or bring forth fear, anger, and sadness. Readers may be tempted to distance themselves from these feelings, this reality. But we, women and men, have all been touched by this ungentle world. As Ellen Bass (1983:53) has so eloquently written, "I was not sexually abused. Yet I was sexually abused. We were all sexually abused. The images and attitudes, the reality we breathe in like air, it reaches us all. It shapes and distorts us, prunes some of our most tender, trusting, lovely and loving branches. We learn that this is who a woman is. This is what men think of women. This is what we are taught to think about ourselves. ... We are all wounded. We all need healing."

We offer this book, these readings, as a step toward this healing. It is our hope that exposing rape-supportive attitudes and traditions and the institutionalization of violence against women and children will help us understand how to transform values, how to tear at the social fabric that harms us all. It is our hope that listening to the impassioned voices herein, their anger and pain and hopefulness, will move us to envision and to create a more gentle, more humane, more life-affirming world.

We would like to thank Dean Birkenkamp and the staff of Westview Press for their support of this project. Special thanks go to Diana Luykx and Jill Rothenberg for their helpful suggestions and guidance through the course of developing the manuscript.

Patricia Searles
Ronald J. Berger

Part One

Feminist Foundations for the Study of Rape and Society

FEMINISTS BEGAN THEIR INQUIRY into the problem of sexual assault at a time when the predominant assumption in society, the criminal justice system, and criminology was that women were to blame for their victimization. For instance, Menachem Amir wrote in 1971 that "the victim is the one who is acting out, initiating the interaction between her and the offender, and by her behavior ... generates the potentiality for criminal behavior of the offender or triggers this potentiality, if it existed before" (p. 259). Amir suggested that "victim precipitated" rape occurs in situations where the victim's behavior is interpreted by the offender as directly inviting or signaling availability for sexual contact. Included here are such situations as those in which a woman agrees to sexual relations but changes her mind, fails to strongly resist sexual overtures, accepts a drink from a stranger, or uses "indecent" language and gestures. According to Amir, victim precipitation is also assumed if a woman has a "bad" reputation, is believed to be promiscuous, or has previously engaged in sexual relations with the offender.

From a feminist perspective, however, Amir represented a way of thinking about rape that perpetuated "rape myths." Rape myths are presumptions that women are tempting seductresses who invite sexual encounters, that women secretly want to be raped, that women eventually relax and enjoy rape, and that men have urgent sexual needs that prevent them from controlling their behavior (Berger et al. 1986; Burt 1980). These myths constitute biases that have been reproduced in the legal system, making it difficult for women to achieve justice and to hold men responsible for the harms they have perpetrated.

In the first chapter in this section, "The Trauma of Rape: The Case of Ms. X," Diana Russell presents an interview with a rape survivor, a moving account of a woman who was attacked in her home by a stranger, held prisoner for two days, and repeatedly raped and brutalized. It conveys the deep and long-lasting trauma often associated with rape and shows how rape myths can compound the shame and humiliation rape survivors may feel, keeping them locked in a prison of silence.

The second chapter, Stevi Jackson's "The Social Context of Rape: Sexual Scripts and Motivation," is one of the earliest critiques of the traditional view that rape is an aberrant act of a "sick" individual. Jackson articulates what has become a classic feminist view that rape is an extension or exaggeration of conventional sexual relations and power differentials between women and men. She analyzes the means by which everyday sexual scripts provide vocabularies of motives and techniques of neutralization that rapists use to justify their conduct.

Jackson views sexual assault as a form of socially conditioned sexual aggression that stems from traditional gender-role socialization and sexual learning, not as a biological inevitability. Supporting this view are cross-cultural studies that categorize some societies as "rape prone" and some as relatively "rape free" and that find more rape in societies characterized by male dominance, gender-role rigidity, and glorification of warfare (Sanday 1981a; McConahay and McConahay 1977). The more male-dominated or patriarchal the society, the more social relations between the sexes are hierarchically organized to appropriate women's sexuality (including their procreative capacities) for the use of males. Violence against women is maintained through the institutionalization of dichotomous dominant masculine and subordinate feminine roles and by sexual scripts that promote sexual coercion as culturally normative behavior and a source of sexual pleasure for men and, to some extent, women. Under these conditions, male dominance is normative and even eroticized. As Susan Griffin (1981:78) observed, "In our culture male eroticism is wedded to power. Not only should a man be taller and stronger than a female in the perfect love-match, but he must also demonstrate his superior strength in gestures of dominance which are perceived as amorous." Sexual coercion becomes commonplace, and women's sexual lives are fraught with danger and abuse. Rape and the fear of rape come to be "a daily part of every woman's consciousness" and a means by which men as a group intimidate, control, and keep women "in their place" (Griffin 1979:4; Brownmiller 1975). Thus rape serves as "an unofficial buttress of the *status quo*" (Jackson 1978:37).

In order to facilitate recognition of rape as a serious offense, it has become customary for feminists to emphasize that rape is a crime of violence, not a crime of sexual passion or an uncontrollable expression of a biological need. When viewed this way, rape seems to be a distortion of an otherwise natural human sexuality, a "displacement of power based on physical force onto sexuality" (MacKinnon 1983:646). But according to Catharine MacKinnon, rape is no less sexual because it is violent. In the third chapter, "Sex and Violence: A Perspective," MacKinnon suggests that analysts who define rape—along with battery, harassment, and pornography—as forms of "violence against women" often set up a false dichotomy beween sex and violence. She argues that it is a *male* point of view to sharply distinguish between rape and intercourse, sexual harassment and ordinary sexual initiation, and pornography and erotica because in women's experience rape, sexual harassment, and pornography are not so clearly distinguishable from normal everyday interactions. MacKinnon reminds us that although these violations are often collectively referred to as "violence against women," they all involve a fusion of dominance with sexuality. As she says, "If women as gender female are defined as sexual beings, and violence is eroticized, then men violating women has a sexual component."

Liz Kelly (1987:48) developed a concept she called the "continuum of sexual violence" to help us understand that all sexual violations have a "common character": They all involve men's use of "a variety of forms of abuse, coercion and force in order to control women." Although the continuum concept enables naming and documenting a range of abuses, Kelly argued that women's experiences cannot be placed into "clearly defined and discrete analytic categories" because women's experiences and how they subjectively define them "shade into and out of" particular categories (p. 48). For example, the category of sexual harassment includes looks, gestures, and comments, as well as acts that could also be defined as rape or assault. Kelly pointed out that women do not necessarily "share the same definition of a particular incident" and warned that it is inappropriate to use the concept of continuum to create a hierarchy of offenses based on the "seriousness" of abuse (p. 52). As she said, "The effects on women cannot be read off simplistically from the form of sexual violence" experienced (p. 49).

The "continuum of sexual violence" is also useful for linking particular forms of sexual violation to "more common everyday male behaviour" (Kelly 1987: 51). Elizabeth Stanko (1985:10) suggested that "women who feel violated and intimidated by typical male behaviour have no way of specifying how or why typical male behaviour feels like aberrant male behaviour" because their experience of men's violence is filtered through a perception that men's behavior is *either* typical (hence unharmful) *or* aberrant (hence harmful). The ability to view men's behavior on a continuum helps women "locate and name their own experiences" (p. 51). Kelly found that women experienced heterosexual sex not as an either/or (that is, as consensual sex or as rape), but on a continuum moving from choice to pressure to coercion to force.

Deborah Cameron and Elizabeth Frazer (1987:164) further extended the analysis of the common character of all sexual violations. They said that all violations entail "similar assumptions about male sexuality and women's relation to it." All presume that "men need and feel entitled to have unrestricted sexual access to women, even—sometimes especially—against women's will." In addition, all "collectively function as a threat to women's autonomy," undermine women's self-esteem, and limit women's freedom of action. Hence women must live with the fear of sexual violation (since men's sexuality is presumed to be "naturally" aggressive and predatory), and women must monitor their behavior (since they are responsible for preventing their violation). If they are unsuccessful, women may be blamed for their victimization, and their suffering may be ignored, questioned, or trivialized.

Cameron and Frazer helped us see the *functional* similarity of very different kinds of violations. For instance, they pointed out that both flashing (exhibitionism) and rape are "acts which men do in order to reassure themselves of their power and potency; both include, as a crucial factor in that reassurance, the fear and humiliation of the female victims" (1987: 164). Thus the range of functionally similar violations includes both violent acts (e.g., rape and battery) as well as nonviolent sexual intimidation (e.g., flashing and obscene phone calls). Acts of nonviolent sexual intimidation, the common everyday "verbal, visual, and physical intrusions, ... serve to remind women and girls that they are at risk and vulnerable to male aggression just because they are female" (Sheffield 1989:483–84).

Complementing feminist theoretical analyses of rape and sexual assault are studies that attempt to measure the prevalence of rape (the *proportion* of a group of females that has been victimized) and the incidence of rape (the *frequency* of victimization in a group of females). But the measurement of rape is fraught with methodological difficulties. For example, official crime statistics underrepresent the extent of violence against women because women often fail to report their victimization to the police.[1] Women avoid coming forward because they feel humiliated and embarrassed, fear retaliation by the offender, fear being subjected to hostile questioning, or worry they won't be believed. In fact, it is not uncommon for police to label a woman's complaint "unfounded" (Estrich 1987; Russell 1984).

Victimization surveys, which bypass police reports and ask victims directly about their experiences, attempt to remedy the problem of underreporting. Although these surveys uncover more rapes than official statistics do, they are not valid indicators of rape either (Eigenberg 1990). For instance, the most commonly cited survey is the annual National Crime Survey, which gathers information on a variety of crimes. Until quite recently,[2] the NCS has asked "whether someone has tried to take something from them, rob them, beat them, attack them with a weapon, or steal things from them. *None of these questions asks whether someone has tried to rape them.* The question that is supposed to elicit rape reads: 'Did anyone TRY to attack you in some other way?' " (p. 657).

More in-depth victimization surveys that focus specifically on rape, such as the one conducted by Mary Koss, have uncovered higher rates of victimization than those reported in either police or NCS studies. In the final chapter in this section, "Hidden Rape: Sexual Aggression and Victimization in a National Sample of Students in Higher Education," Koss documents the prevalence and incidence of sexual victimization and sexual aggression in a large sample of college women and men across the country. She found that the majority of women and men whose experiences met legal definitions of rape did not label themselves as rape victims or offenders.[3]

That women may not define what is legally rape as "rape" is not so surprising if we remember MacKinnon's observation that rape is not necessarily very different from what might be for women rather typical experiences of intercourse. MacKinnon (1983) believes that when male initiative and dominance constitute the normative pattern of sexual interaction, the whole notion of "consent" becomes problematic. When, for the most part, women's consent is granted under conditions of dominance and inequality and men are socialized not to take women's "no" seriously (e.g., to presume "no" means "maybe" or "in a little while"), it becomes hard to assess just how much resistance is required to communicate to men either that consent has not been granted or that it has been withdrawn. Hence women may perceive no alternative but to acquiesce. They may, in fact, prefer acquiescence to the risk of bodily injury or to the "humiliation of a lost fight" (p. 650); or perhaps they have learned to eroticize male dominance so as not to feel "forced." Under these conditions, MacKinnon argued, true consent is absent, and the lack of physical force does not guarantee a freely given agreement. Thus women may not define the encounter as rape, although they experienced it as unwanted and nonconsensual. And men, failing to distinguish acquiescence and consent, may not either.

Notes

1. When several news organizations broke with tradition and publicized the name of the woman who accused William Kennedy Smith of rape in 1991, many feminists were outraged. They argued that public exposure subjected survivors to additional trauma and decreased the likelihood that women would come forward in the future. In fact, a *Newsweek* poll conducted after this incident found that 86 percent of those surveyed believed that disclosure would discourage women from reporting rape (Kantrowitz 1991). Other feminists, however, argued that secrecy heightens the shame of rape and that regularly publicizing names would help change social attitudes. In spite of the fact that rape is something one shouldn't have to hide or feel ashamed of, forced exposure may reincite feelings of powerlessness and undermine recovery. Hence most feminists believe that no one should be "outed" or coerced into making their identity public. Nevertheless, only a few states have laws preventing news organizations from disclosing survivors' names without their consent.

2. As a result of these criticisms, the Bureau of Justice Statistics recently redesigned the survey questions to obtain more accurate information about rape (Jensen and Karpos 1993).

3. Williams and Holmes (1981) found that white women are more likely than African American and Hispanic women to hold "feminist" definitions of rape. That is, they are more likely to define rape as sex without the woman's consent and less likely to qualify their definition of rape according to the woman's activities or reputation, the offender's use of force, the victim-offender relationship, and so on. See Neuman (1992) for a discussion of race-by-race differences in definitions of sexual harassment.

Rape Poem

Marge Piercy

There is no difference between being raped
and being pushed down a flight of cement steps
except that the wounds also bleed inside.

There is no difference between being raped
and being run over by a truck
except that afterward men ask if you enjoyed it.

There is no difference between being raped
and being bit on the ankle by a rattlesnake
except that people ask if your skirt was short
and why you were out alone anyhow.

There is no difference between being raped
and going head first through a windshield
except that afterward you are afraid
not of cars
but half the human race.

The rapist is your boyfriend's brother.
He sits beside you in the movies eating popcorn.
Rape fattens on the fantasies of the normal male
like a maggot in garbage.

Fear of rape is a cold wind blowing
all of the time on a woman's hunched back.
Never to stroll alone on a sand road through pine woods,
never to climb a trail across a bald
without that aluminum in the mouth
when I see a man climbing toward me.

Never to open the door to a knock
without that razor just grazing the throat.
The fear of the dark side of hedges,
the back seat of the car, the empty house
rattling keys like a snake's warning.
The fear of the smiling man
in whose pocket is a knife.
The fear of the serious man
in whose fist is locked hatred.

All it takes to cast a rapist is seeing your body
as jackhammer, as blowtorch, as adding-machine-gun.
All it takes is hating that body
your own, your self, your muscle that softens to flab.

All it takes is to push what you hate,
what you fear onto the soft alien flesh.
To bucket out invincible as a tank
armored with treads without senses
to possess and punish in one act,
to rip up pleasure, to murder those who dare
live in the leafy flesh open to love.

The Trauma of Rape:
The Case of Ms. X

Diana E.H. Russell

THIS IS THE CASE of Ms. X, a fifty-five-year-old white woman who teaches elementary school.[1] Ms. X refused to give her name even to the interviewer. Her insistence on total anonymity highlights her continuing fears about being identified as a rape victim. Interestingly, however, Ms. X said that it was a great relief to have the opportunity to talk to someone about her experience and she hoped that other women might learn from her experience to protect themselves better.

... Ms. X was forty-eight when she was raped seven years ago. In all these years, she had previously told only one person about the experience.

MS. X: My boys were in the army, my girl was at college, and I lived alone. I live in the mountains at the end of a road which is completely blind. None of my neighbors can see up that road, so someone could park up there, and no one would ever know it. Apparently the man who raped me had been following me and watching my habits for a long time. He had probably tried the door on several occasions, but fortunately it was locked.

It was a Sunday morning around noon. I had gone up the road to get the newspaper and had come back into the house and was reading the paper. Then I went into the bathroom. I opened the door to the bathroom from my bedroom, and he was standing there with a gun. I just froze. I went into shock.

He kept me prisoner for two nights and two days. With a gun at my head, he made me call my school district on Monday to tell them I was sick. I tried to get out of the bathroom window once, but he caught me. When he slept he kept a tight grip on me so that if I just moved he would arouse and hit me for trying to escape. The first night I didn't sleep at all.

INTERVIEWER: Could you describe him?

MS. X: He looked like he had been a boxer, a professional fighter. He had scars on his eyebrows, his cheekbones, and his nose. He had very little hair on his body. I think he was probably part American Indian. But he had a lot of white blood too. I imagine he was in his forties. He was not well educated, but he had a very quick clever intelligence.

He was very sadistic. His sexual assaults went on constantly, and I was forced into perverse activities—the whole ugly mess—gagging, choking, vomiting. He cleverly didn't black my eyes or leave marks. There were some bruises from where he threw me into furniture, but mainly he would twist my arm and choke me. I found that if I fought him very hard, he came to orgasm more quickly, and it was over for a while, which shows his sadism. I was wondering, "What can I do to get out of this horror?" I would try to submit, thinking, maybe that would get it over with, but I found that it infuriated him if I submitted without fighting him.

INTERVIEWER: So did you fight?

MS. X: Yes, I did.

INTERVIEWER: Did he tell you anything about himself?

MS. X: Not a thing. But he kept threatening to kill me if I did certain things, like if I got to the phone, or tried to escape. He said he had to do what he had to do. He kept saying that, "I have to do this." With my background in psychology, I thought, here's a real sexual psychopath.

He said, "I don't want to kill you, but if you do these things, I'll have to kill you." He said that several times.

INTERVIEWER: Did he ask you any questions?

MS. X: No. I tried to talk to him, but he would not talk. And I found that he didn't have any wallet, so that I couldn't get his license or any other kind of identification. I couldn't do anything! He made me feed him what I had in the house. I had very little, and I had no money, but he wasn't interested in money apparently.

INTERVIEWER: Do you think he'd done this before with other women?

MS. X: I'm sure he had. He was so expert at immobilizing a woman. He knew exactly what to do. Up until this time, I had believed that rape was impossible if a woman didn't want to be raped, that it could only happen to a woman who submits. But I found out how a woman can be totally immobilized. He was a heavy man. He was probably two hundred pounds, and very strong. He would lie on one side of my body, pinning down one leg and one arm, and he'd get his other arm up under my knee, and he'd be twisting my other arm, so that I just couldn't move. He would do it three or four, maybe five times, and then he would sleep. I did escape once from his grip, and I got some clothes on, and I was heading out of a window as quietly as I could, but he caught me.

INTERVIEWER: What was going through your head?

MS. X: I felt that I was outside my body, watching this whole thing, that it wasn't happening to me, it was happening to somebody else. It was a strange feeling, absolutely unreal. I was terrorized, but it's very hard to describe the shock of what was happening. At first, I went into a state of shock where I just shook and shook and shook and shook and shook. And I was freezing cold. Just freezing cold. And he kept the gun on me all the time. He showed me the bullets in case I should think it unloaded.

Then after two days, he was gone. I didn't even know he was gone. Monday night he disappeared as quickly as he came.

INTERVIEWER: Had you ever seen him before?

MS. X: Never.

INTERVIEWER: Do you think he had been drinking?

MS. X: Not at all, although he looked for liquor in the house. I didn't have any. When I realized he was gone, I wanted to pour Lysol all over me. I wanted to be cleansed. I took a bath, and then I thought about calling the police. And I thought no, I can't do that. It's too much of a horror story. People would look at me differently. If it's so horrible to *me*, it must be horrible to other people. I don't want anybody to know what happened to me. I thought that they would see me differently if they knew about it.

INTERVIEWER: Why?

MS. X: Because I thought that other people thought the way I had thought, that this couldn't happen to a woman who didn't want it, or allow it.

INTERVIEWER: You really felt that a woman couldn't be raped?

MS. X: Yes. Can you imagine? I really believed that. So I assumed that if I told people, they would think I had consented, because they would think as I had thought before I had the experience. Also, I remember reading something that stuck in my head about how you have to press charges, and you have to go to court, and you have to do all this stuff. I just couldn't do it. I'm basically a rather retiring person, and the thought that I would have to be in a roomful of people who knew what had happened to me made me sick.

INTERVIEWER: Were there any other reasons you didn't want to report the rape?

MS. X: Well, I think prison would be no place for a man of that age, a psychopath. I don't think psychiatric care could help a man like that.

It would have been marvelous had I known a woman police officer I could talk to, if I had known that it would be confidential, and that I would be treated like a person who did not want to be raped. I never flirted with men, I didn't act seductive in any way. I wasn't interested at the time. I was trying to survive financially, pouring myself into my work, and if I had known I'd be treated like a decent human being, I would have been happy to report it.

...

INTERVIEWER: So, what did you do next?

MS. X: I called my friend, because I knew I couldn't go to school the next day. I didn't know how long it would be before I could face people. She came up to the house and stayed with me, and I poured the whole thing out to her, and we cried together, and held each other. She never told her husband because she said she knew his attitude toward me would change. He also thought a woman couldn't be raped.

After I had called my friend, I said, "Will you stay here and answer my phone, so that if anybody calls from the school department and wants to know how I am, you can say I have the flu, and that you're taking care of me." Then I went straight down to the nearest town, and into the sporting goods store, and I bought a forty sentinel gun and a small Browning automatic. Incidentally, I told the man who raped me that I was going to do this. I told him that I would kill him if he ever came back, and I know I would. And that was a shock to me, to know that this peaceful person who had never known anything but love was capable of killing a human being. But I knew that I could. I know I would kill him.

INTERVIEWER: Did you ever see him again?

MS. X: I was sitting in the living room one night about six months later. There's nothing out there, so I don't draw the drapes. I was sitting there watching television, and something caught my eye, a flash like a match on the steps outdoors. It was very dark, and I looked at it, and then I saw the glow of a cigarette, and I watched it. And I thought, he's there. I felt that it was he.

So I went and got my forty sentinel pistol. It's a large one, and I set it in a very obvious place right beside me on the couch. And I thought, if I act afraid, I'm dead. I'm going to let him know I'm not afraid, and then I'll kill him. And then he left. He never tried to get into the house.

INTERVIEWER: What were your feelings when sitting there with your gun?

MS. X: I was frightened inside. My heart was pounding, but I was very cool in appearance. I acted unconcerned. I think he might have thought he could pull the whole scene again, but since I was well armed, I think he was afraid. On a couple of occasions later, I saw cigarettes that had been stamped out on the steps, and at that time I didn't smoke at all. Throughout the following year, whenever I worked in the garden, I had a little holster, and I kept a gun on my hip. I was so afraid of being surprised again.

INTERVIEWER: You didn't move?

MS. X: No. I guess I'm stubborn. I decided this man isn't going to drive me away from the environment I love. I'm not going to let this thing that happened to me change my life that much, that I have to lose what I worked for and love.

INTERVIEWER: Would you have liked to kill him?

MS. X: No, I wouldn't like to kill him. But I *would* kill him if he attacked me again. I wouldn't like to kill any human being.

INTERVIEWER: So what did you do after talking to your friend?

MS. X: I stayed home and kind of healed. Then I went to school Friday. It was very hard. Very hard.

INTERVIEWER: Did you have bad dreams after the rape?

MS. X: Oh, yes. And I would relive it. It became almost an obsession. I thought I was being punished for something. And I kept wondering, why did this happen to me? What have I done that this thing would happen?

INTERVIEWER: Did you blame yourself?

MS. X: I was trying to find ways to blame myself. Trying to think, what did I do? What brought this on? Later I knew that this was ridiculous, because I hadn't done anything, and it had just happened.

INTERVIEWER: Did you have to take tranquilizers?

MS. X: Oh, yes.

INTERVIEWER: Did you go to a doctor?

MS. X: Yes, but it wasn't until weeks later. I didn't want to go to my own doctor because he was a personal friend of mine. So I couldn't go to him. I asked one of the teachers that I had known in the district. She didn't work in my school, but she had lived a more worldly life than I had, and was more experienced in many ways. So I asked her about a doctor I could go to for a VD check, and she recommended one. I wasn't worried about pregnancy or anything like that, because I was unable to be pregnant.

The rape was a trauma in so many ways, I can't tell you. He injured me so badly. There was blood, lots of blood, all the time.

All through the time he was there, and then afterwards, there was a heavy discharge, a bloody discharge, and that's what scared me. I thought, gee, maybe I have venereal disease. I went to a doctor who I never saw before or since, and he made a joke of it as though I was a really hot number. He acted as though I was a swinger or a prostitute. I didn't tell him I'd been raped. I just said that I had had relations with a man I didn't know, and that I was worried.

He really thought it was hilarious. He was joking, "Wow! You must be something else!" It made me sick. It made me even sicker when he said, "No, you don't have any venereal disease, but stay away from those rough ones." Another bad thing was that he examined me without the presence of a nurse. The nurse went out, and he shut the door, which was very odd. That's never happened to me before. Also, he acted seductive.

INTERVIEWER: Could you tell me more about him?

MS. X: I imagine he was in his fifties. He belonged to the American Medical Association and was supposed to be respectable. So this experience made me glad I hadn't told anybody else about it. It reinforced all my fears. The only relief was that I didn't have VD.

In talking with friends and people after it happened, I tried to find out their attitudes toward rape, and it too reinforced what I had previously thought. They all think that rape isn't really possible. So there was no way to break out of the guilt.

INTERVIEWER: Did you seek counseling?

MS. X: I wanted to so badly! I was *so* tempted! I knew some good counselors, and I would even be on the phone sometimes to call a counselor, but I never was able to do it. I would come so close, because I badly wanted to talk it out, but I couldn't do it. I'd just say, deal with it yourself. Cope with it in your own way. I found out that I am very strong, which surprised me. I wondered if all the protective, loving bringing up that I had had made me strong.

I learned to cope with the obsession by myself. I'd start to fall asleep at night, and the whole thing would come back. Also, I had a number of headaches. Tranquilizers don't do much for me but depress me, so I just took simple medicine. But I would get so discouraged. Sometimes I would get very depressed. I'd think, I'm never going to get this out of my head. When is this garbage going to get out of my head? Because I could be in the most harmonious situation, and bang, there it was again. It was like a flash, and then I'd have to just wrench it away again.

INTERVIEWER: Did it affect your attitude toward men?

MS. X: I'm afraid it did. About three years later I was approached by a professor at X College, and he wanted to take me out. I knew he was a wonderful, fine man, but I was so nervous that I shook the whole time. I was a lousy date because I was so tense. I just couldn't be with a man. The only men I could be with and be comfortable were my sons and my son-in-law.

Dealing with men, even on a business level, was very difficult. Finally, I got to be very objective, and I got over most of it, but if I was alone with a man or he came to the house to pick me up for a date, I was really shaky. I kept telling myself, why, you idiot, why are you like this? Stop it. Relax. But I couldn't.

INTERVIEWER: Did you ever tell anybody else?

MS. X: No. Just that one woman friend. And I never mentioned it to her again. Strangely, it embarrassed her. I tried one time to bring it up again when I was feeling that I wanted to talk it out again, and I could see that it embarrassed her, so I shut up. I thought, well, I'm not going to lay all this heavy stuff on her again. It isn't fair to her.

INTERVIEWER: So you never told your children?

MS. X: No. But I'm fine now. I can relate to men easily now, and I don't get uptight. I haven't had any sexual relationships since that time. But I think I could now.

...

INTERVIEWER: ... What are some other ways in which the rape affected you?

MS. X: I couldn't lock myself into the car I had at that time, and so I carried this little Browning automatic whenever I drove. It made me feel guilty and frightened, and I swore that when I got another car, I'd be sure I'd get one that I could lock on the driver's side. Otherwise, when you stop at a stop sign at night it's risky.

We have a joke in my family and with my friends about how I lock everybody in. I lock myself in, and I've done it so much that it's a habit now, an absolute habit. I do it automatically, so when somebody tries to go out to the car to get something, the door's locked. And they say, "Oh, mother locks in her guests. Once you get into this house, you never get out. She doesn't want anybody to leave," and we just laugh about it.

Before, the only time I locked up was at night, and when I was ready for bed, I checked all the doors. But that's really silly, because if you're there alone, anybody can walk in at other times, which I found out. That man was clever. He had watched me to find out what my patterns were. And he saw me go up and get the paper, and he knew that the door wasn't locked.

I went through a bad period where I was too paranoid. I was carrying the gun, and I knew I couldn't always live with a gun on my hip whenever I was working in the yard, so I decided to be very careful about locking doors. I still have a gun at home, and it's loaded, and I will always have a gun.

...

Notes

1. Ms. X was interviewed by Cameron Smith, a doctoral student at the University of California at Santa Cruz, for a study that she did on rape victims.

2

The Social Context of Rape:
Sexual Scripts and Motivation

Stevi Jackson

THE SUBJECT OF RAPE has provided the raw material for propaganda, jokes and pornography. It has been used as an ideological weapon in times of war, to inject an element of humour into otherwise dull lectures on law and criminology, has fed the erotic fantasies of men and inspired fear in women. Yet it is a subject which ... remains shrouded in myths. ...

Rape is a complex issue. It is both a sexual act and an act of aggression; it has been viewed as a crime against the person and as a crime against property and, more recently, as a political crime (Medea and Thompson, 1974; Brownmiller, 1975). From the victim's perspective it is more than a sexual crime, more than simple physical assault: it is an attack on her mind as well as her body, an attack on her whole person, undermining her will and self-esteem.

The Stranger in the Dark Alley:
Misconceptions of Rapist and Victim

The perpetrators of this act are not the rapists of the popular imagination, psychopaths lurking in dark alleys waiting to pounce on any likely victim and inflict their uncontrollable desires upon her. This is just one of the many widely-believed myths about rape. ...

...

... Rape occurs in a wide variety of contexts and locations. ... All the evidence suggests that Mr. Average rapes Ms. Average.

The idea that both rapist and victim are in some way different from other members of society is based on the assumption that rape is very different from normal sexual acts, an idea that persists despite the great difficulty our laws have in distinguishing between them. There is an element of double-think here: the belief in rape as something apart from everyday expressions of sexuality exists side by side with the notion that rape is impossible, that it doesn't happen at all, that the victim is a woman who has 'changed her mind afterwards'. It is simultaneously thought of as both a heinous crime and as a normal sexual encounter mislabelled criminal. In practice, these apparently contradictory beliefs are used to distinguish the 'real' rapes, involving a brutal madman and an innocent victim, from the fakes. This confusion as to the nature of rape serves to disguise its affinity with normal sexual behaviour.

> 'There is a convenient notion of rape that places it at a vast distance from anything which may be commonly experienced. … The popular view is that, if the rapist cannot be labelled "fiend" or "monster" or "maniac", then he probably isn't a rapist at all' (Toner, 1977:47).

It is the contention of this paper that a close relationship exists between rape and more conventional modes of sexual expression. It is therefore not an aberration nor a particularly unusual occurrence. If rape is to be understood, then it must be placed within the context of the patterns of sexual relationships typical of our society. Explanations for rape are not to be sought for within the individual psyche of rapist or victim but within our accepted sexual mores, for it is these which condition interaction in rape settings and which provide vocabularies of motive for the rapist.

> 'A sociological conception of motives … translates the question of "why" into a "how" that is answerable in terms of a situation and its typical vocabularies of motives, i.e. those which conventionally accompany that type of situation and function as cues and justifications for normative actions in it' (Mills, 1940:440).

Rather than asking *why* some men rape we should ask *how* rape is possible within certain situations, how features of conventional sexual scenes create the potential for rape.

Sexual Scripts, Motives and Neutralization

A framework for analysis of rape in terms of conventional sexual behaviour is provided by Gagnon and Simon's (1974) work on sexual scripts. Rejecting theories of sexuality predicated on the assumption of inbuilt sexual drives, they conceptualize it as the outcome of a complex process of learning whereby the individual develops a capacity to interpret and enact sexual scripts. These scripts serve to organize both internal states and outward behaviour, enabling us to interpret emotions and sensations as sexually meaningful, and providing us with methods of recognizing potential sexual situations and acting effectively within them.

'Scripts are involved in learning the meaning of internal states, organizing the sequences of specifically sexual acts, decoding novel situations, setting the limits on sexual responses, and linking meanings from non-sexual aspects of life to specifically sexual experience' (Gagnon and Simon, 1974:19).

It is these scripts which provide the motivations for sexual conduct. As Mills (1940) has argued, motives are not merely inner states of mind but cultural creations governed by some delineated vocabulary by which individuals anticipate the outcome of their actions. Hence sexual behaviour is not an expression of inner drives but is structured by an accepted vocabulary of motives pertaining to the erotic. Sexual desire is not aroused through a simple stimulus-response mechanism but through the attribution of sexual meanings to specific stimuli and desire alone will not produce sexual behaviour unless the actor is able to define the situation as one in which such conduct is appropriate.

The same scripts which motivate 'normal' sexual behaviour also provide a potential vocabulary of motives for the rapist. It is a mistake to assume that those who engage in acts perceived as deviant necessarily subscribe to a morality at variance with that of non-deviant members of society, or that their motives for engaging in deviant acts are qualitatively different from those that govern conformist behaviour. The moral prescriptions and proscriptions that define the limitations of acceptable conduct may well contain escape clauses allowing behaviour that would generally be considered immoral to be seen as justifiable under certain conditions. These extenuating circumstances, or neutralizations (Sykes and Matza, 1957), are not mobilized only after the act in order to enable the offender to beg our pardon: knowledge of acceptable justifications may control conduct. By absolving himself of guilt in advance, an individual may break or bend rules of conduct.

Like the juvenile delinquents whose behaviour Sykes and Matza (1957) sought to explain, the rapist does not invent techniques of neutralization, but derives them from generally accepted cultural norms. Indeed, some of them are acceptable in the courts as pleas for defence or mitigation. When overlaid by the motives and meanings incorporated into sexual scripts, neutralization techniques become specifically applicable to rape, providing the potential rapist with a positive evaluation of his projected action. Hence the vocabularies of motive appropriate to conventional situations are extended, enabling the rapist to see his acts as acceptable.

Setting the Scene for Rape: Actors, Scripts and Motives

Sexual scripts do not exist in a vacuum, but are bound up with cultural notions of femininity and masculinity. It is gender identity which provides the framework within which sexuality is learnt and through which erotic self-identity is created. Thus men and women learn to be sexual in different ways, to enact different roles in the sexual drama, to utilize different vocabularies of motive. The attributes of masculinity and femininity, learnt from the beginning of childhood and incorporated into expectations of sexual behaviour, provide the motivational and interactional basis of rape.

In the first place, conventional sexual scenes are scripted for an active male and a passive female, activity and passivity being defining characteristics of masculinity and femininity respectively. From the beginning boys learn to be independent, to seek success actively through their own efforts and abilities while girls are encouraged to be dependent, to seek success passively through pleasing others. It is hardly surprising that when they learn of the erotic implications of relationships between them they should express their sexuality this way. The man becomes the seducer, the woman the seduced, he the hunter, she the prey. It is he who is expected to initiate sexual encounters and to determine the direction in which they develop; her part is merely to acquiesce or refuse. Aggression is part of man's activity. He is not only expected to take the lead but to establish dominance over the woman, to *make* her please him, and his 'masculinity' is threatened if he fails to do so. Sexual conquest becomes an acceptable way of validating masculinity, of demonstrating dominance of and superiority over women.

> 'Rape is in this sense a mirror-image of our ordinary sex folkways. Two basic beliefs of these folkways are the natural sexual aggressiveness of man and man's natural physical superiority over women. Put these two beliefs together, set up a competition for masculine prowess such as we have today and no-one should be surprised at the incidence of rape' (Herschberger, 1970:15).

If sexuality was not bound up with power and aggression, rape would not be possible.[1] When these attributes of masculinity are accentuated, as in war, rape reaches epidemic proportions.

Male sexual aggression is also popularly believed to be uncontrollable. Once a man's sexual response has been set in motion, he is supposed to be totally at the mercy of his desires.

> 'One of the most pervasive myths which feed our distorted understanding of rape is the belief in the urgent sexual potency of men. Men are believed to have a virtually uncontrollable sexual desire, which once awakened must find satisfaction regardless of the consequences' (Smart, 1976:95).

This places the responsibility for setting limits on sexual activity in the hands of the woman. She must take care not to arouse him too much lest she fails to control the powerful forces she has unleashed.

It is this belief in the urgency of male sexual drives which provides the first technique of neutralization available to the rapist: denial of responsibility. If a man attributes this to himself, perceives himself as a helpless slave to his desire, then he will be less inclined to curb himself in the face of a woman's refusal and more inclined to resort to force to attain his ends.

The male's supposedly uncontrollable sexual aggression is, moreover, backed by conceptions of female sexuality and the feminine character which conveniently rationalize away any protests a woman might make. The vocabularies of motive of conventional sexual scripts not only provide the rapist with an acceptable account of his actions in terms of his own desires, but also in terms of his perspective on his victim. Where he denies responsibility, he neutralizes the immorality of his behaviour without reference to that of his victim, where he denies injury or denies the victim, it is her actions which are being called to account.

Denial of injury rests on a common misconception of sexual relations which tends to overestimate the effects of male sexual potency and underestimate female sexual autonomy so that a woman's satisfaction is assumed to be dependent on male activity. It is supposed that women need some degree of persuasion before they will engage in sexual activity, but that once their inhibitions have been overcome or their sense of propriety demonstrated, they will respond. A popular belief of the male culture is that what matters in success with women is not attractiveness *per se,* but an ability to apply techniques of seduction, cleverness in countering a woman's objections and persistence in overcoming her resistance (Toner, 1976). This manipulation is a more subtle manifestation of power than brute force. It may not be that rape is forced seduction but that seduction is a subtler form of rape.

The masterful male and yielding female form a common motif of our popular culture. In countless books and films the male hero is portrayed overcoming the anger or indifference of a woman by means of a passionate embrace, which she at first resists and then returns with equal fervour. Sex is seen as a means of forcing a woman into loving submission. Ruth Herschberger suggests that this is a large part of the appeal of the male rape fantasy:

> 'When the man turns to the sensational image of rape he learns of an act which, if effected with any unwilling woman, can force her into a sexual relationship with him. She can be forced into a psychological intimacy with him ... the unwilling woman magically becomes willing, her sensory nerves respond gratefully, stubborn reflexes react obediently, and the beautiful stranger willy-nilly enters into a state of sexual intimacy with her aggressor' (Herschberger, 1970:24).

This view of female sexuality, given added credibility by the Freudian premise of woman's masochism, leads on to the myth that all women secretly want to be raped and that the best course of action for them to take should the fantasy become reality is to 'lie back and enjoy it'. Where the rapist denies injury it is not inconceivable that he thinks that he is doing his victim a favour: rapists have been known to ask to see their victim again.

These ideas also, of course, cast doubt on the credibility of the victim. In part this is a result of a perceived ambivalence towards sex on the part of women.

They will say 'no' but apparently mean 'yes' since they ultimately consent, or rather relent. But this may not represent real ambivalence. Female passivity often results in women participating in sexual acts against their will. They are supposed to control the pace at which the encounter proceeds, but they are supposed to do so gently. Being conditioned to please, to bolster up a man's ego, to refrain from hurting him, a woman's gentle protestations are no match for a determined male with distorted ideas of his own sexuality and sexual capabilities. In some instances women may be too confused or embarrassed to know how to react. Either way the man will see her resistance as a pretence and hence reinforce his beliefs in the efficacy of his seduction techniques and his conviction that women will consent if only he tries hard enough.

A rapist may deny that his victim is a victim at all. But even if he does not delude himself as to the extent of her participation in the act he might see her as a *legitimate* victim (Weiss and Borges, 1973).[2] For denial of the victim to operate as a motive for rape the victim must be seen as being in some way responsible for her fate. The principle that governs this is that, while rape is wrong, some women *deserve* to be raped. The victim is seen as a 'cock-teaser', the cruel woman who leads men on only to reject them. She has acted provocatively and can hardly expect any other response, she 'had it coming'. The provocation may be slight or non-existent from the point of view of the victim. It is enough, insofar as accounting for the rapist's motives is concerned, that he is capable of construing her actions in this way. It is possible for a man to see his prey as a legitimate victim even where no sexual invitation is perceived, where, for instance, a woman is too aloof and refuses to respond to sexual overtures. Medea and Thompson (1974) report an incident at a rape conference where a man expressed this view, saying that women who are raped are those who are 'too good to talk to'. They comment:

'... women are damned both ways—they seem to be looking for it or they are too good for it, they are touchable or they are untouchable. Either way they are candidates for rape' (Medea and Thompson, 1974:5).

Denial of the victim may also incorporate a notion of revenge. Here rape is explicitly used as a weapon, a method of punishing a woman. When it is said of the victim that she 'had it coming', it may mean that she is perceived as having provoked rape as an act of aggression rather than as a sexual act. In this case rape becomes a stark expression of male domination. It has been argued that it has this effect, whether intended or not:

'Rape operates as a social control mechanism to keep women in their 'place' or put them there. The fear of rape, common to most women, socially controls them as it limits their ability to move about freely. As such, it establishes and maintains the woman in a position of subordination' (Weiss and Borges, 1973:94).

This rationale for rape gains additional significance in situations of conflict or war. Here women become doubly legitimate victims by virtue of being members of some despised race, class or nation as well as being female. Rape may be used as a weapon not only against women, but against the social group of which they are members. Eldridge Cleaver's comments on his career as a rapist are illustrative:

> 'Rape was an insurrectionary act. It delighted me that I was defying and trampling on the white man's law, upon his system of values, and that I was defiling his women—and this point, I believe, was the most satisfying to me because I was very resentful over the historical fact of how the white man had used black women. I felt I was getting revenge' (Cleaver, 1970:26).

This statement reveals a great deal about the attitude of the rapist in this type of situation and about rape in general. Cleaver's vengeance is directed towards white *men,* but it is through white women that it is realized. He is simply establishing a right of access to their bodies as he has already done with black women—whom he used as practice targets until he considered himself 'smooth' enough to 'cross the tracks'. His concern with the usage of black women by white men is not with the humiliation, degradation and pain suffered by those women, but for the deprivation of sexual rights suffered by black men. When he repents, he does so because of his own dehumanization through rape, not that of his victims—black or white.

This tendency to discount the feelings of the victim is by no means a personal quirk of Cleaver's. It is quite commonplace in everyday theorizing about rape and is often expressed in justifications of it. These justifications arise out of our sexual scripts and are easily mobilized before the event as techniques of neutralization such that any sexual encounter involving the exercising of male domination may culminate in rape.

Barter and Theft

The possibility of rape is heightened by the incorporation into our sexual scripts of nonsexual motives. Sexuality for men is a means of validating their masculinity as well as being a source of pleasure. For women it is also a means to other ends, in particular a way of earning the love, support and protection of a man. In this game, where each player has different expectations and desires different outcomes, the woman's sexuality assumes the status of a commodity. It is not simply that she is regarded as a sexual object to be acted upon, but that she objectifies her own sexuality in utilizing it as an object of barter. She attempts to extract the highest price possible, marriage, while the man is hoping for a bargain. The objectification of female sexuality which is implied in this form of exchange exposes women to the risk of rape. If something may be bought and sold, it can also be stolen; what can be given can also be taken by force.

Sexual barter creates further ambiguities in the enactment of sexual scripts for it creates the possibility of differential evaluation of the commodity to be exchanged, for there is no fixed price. This problem is even more evident now that women are no longer expected to be as chaste as they once were. Where once 'good' women only traded sex in exchange for marriage, they are now often prepared to settle for a lower price (McCall, 1966). Rape may occur where the man has paid the amount he thinks is appropriate while the woman defines the situation with reference to a different system of values. She may then easily find herself short-changed.

Competing definitions of the situation are a constant source of misinterpretation and misunderstanding in the unfolding of the sexual drama. Where the woman is the passive partner, when selling herself depends on being attractive but not too eager, her methods of communicating desire must be subtle. The man has to rely on successfully decoding the gestural and verbal cues which she provides and it is therefore possible for him to perceive a sexual invitation where none was intended. It is also possible that the woman might not realize that he has defined a situation in sexual terms when she has not. This ambiguity may provide a pretext for the mobilization of the appropriate techniques of neutralization. If the man does not reassess his initial definition of the situation and proceeds to interpret all that transpires within its terms, the likely outcome is rape.

'The stereotypic notions of male and female roles and their relationship to conceptions of masculine and feminine sexuality, coupled with a situation which is fraught with ambiguous expectations, provide the ingredients for systematically socialized actors who can participate in the drama of rape' (Weiss and Borges, 1973:86).

Undercurrents: Negativity and Hostility

The motivations for rape have so far been considered in mainly sexual terms. But rape is not simply a sexual act, it is also an act of aggression and hostility.

'It is a vain delusion that rape is the expression of uncontrollable desire or some kind of compulsive response to overwhelming attraction ... The act is one of murderous aggression, spawned in self-loathing and enacted upon the hated other' (Greer, 1970:251).

Rape frequently involves many forms of humiliation apart from the straightforward sexual act. The degree of violence employed may be far more extreme than is necessary to force the woman into submission, and she may also be further degraded. Victims are often subjected to such treatment as repeated intercourse, forced fellatio, objects being thrust into the vagina or rectum, and being excreted upon (Amir, 1971).

This, like rape itself, is not a manifestation of personal pathology, but of the undercurrent of hostility that runs through our sexual scripts. The divergent goals and expectations held by men and women with regard to sexual relationships, the elements of exploitation that are thus brought into them, the ambivalence and ambiguity surrounding them are bound to create tensions. Add to this the overall inferior status of women and the derisive attitude of many men towards them, and hostility becomes an ever-present threat.

There is, moreover, a great deal of guilt written into sexual scripts. Learning about sex in our society involves learning about guilt, indeed children learn taboos associated with sexuality before they are made aware of the scripts within which they operate (Gagnon and Simon, 1970). The association between sex and dirtiness is still with us despite the so-called 'sexual revolution' and our supposedly 'permissive' society. Children still learn about sex through dirty jokes and whispered clandestine secrets and find the taboo nature of sexuality confirmed by the evasive or negative attitudes of adults towards it. It would be surprising if some of this did not stay with them through adulthood.

If a man regards sex as a necessity, sees himself as being at the mercy of his powerful sexual drives while at the same time viewing the act as distasteful, he may displace his guilt onto the object of his desire, woman.

> 'The man regards her as a receptacle into which he has emptied his sperm, a kind of human spittoon, and turns from her in disgust. As long as man is at odds with his own sexuality and as long as he keeps woman as a solely sexual creature, he will hate her, at least some of the time' (Greer, 1970:254).

There is, in the minds of many men, a strong association between women, sex and filth; many still see sexuality as part of our 'animal' nature in contradistinction to our higher human or humane nature. And this animality has been ascribed to women. This has been a constant theme in theology and latterly in psychology. The witch-hunters of the sixteenth century operated on the assumption that women were more corruptible than men as a result of their insatiable lust, upon which Satan capitalized (Szasz, 1973). Freud picked up the same theme when he argued that women were closer to the instinctual, less fully human than men because of their inability to develop a strong super-ego (Freud, 1973). This tradition is carried on today and finds its expression in our sexual argot and the non-sexual meanings which it has acquired. As Kate Millet argues:

> '... the four-letter word derives from a puritanical tradition which is vigorously antisexual, seeing the act as dirty etc. This in turn derives from a conviction that the female sex is therefore both dirty and inferior to intellectual and rational and therefore "masculine" higher nature of humanity' (Millett, 1970:325).

It is interesting that so many words which originally applied to sexual acts and to female sexual organs have now become terms of abuse.

Thus woman-as-sexual object is paradoxically thought of as asexual and as totally sexual. Denied sexual self-determination she is nonetheless held responsible for the debasement of mankind through her sexuality. If men regard women as somehow less than human, believing the while in their own superiority and are trapped in the assumption of the irresistibility of their sexual urges, it is only to be expected that an explosive alliance between sex and violence should exist within our culture and find its outlet in rape.

'... our highly repressive and puritan tradition has almost hopelessly confused sexuality with sadism, cruelty and that which is in general inhumane and anti-social' (Millett, 1970:326).

Even if this degree of hostility towards women were unusual, some degree of negativity is necessary to explain the ease with which the typical motives are avowed by the rapist or ascribed to him, since these involve either implicating the victim or discounting her. These attitudes underpin motives for rape, are a more constant, less immediate contributory factor than techniques of neutralization, providing the background for their mobilization.[3]

Motives, Action and Interaction

The battery of motivations in the rapist's armoury are continuously available to him. Once he has mobilized one or other or a combination of them, neutralizing his guilt in advance, he is then morally free to act. There is no deterministic link between motives and action; neutralization simply transforms a constant possibility into a specific probability. Having found himself in a state of drift, on a form of 'moral holiday' where he feels rape is justifiable, the rapist must summon the will to act and be able to act. Situational and interactional features of the setting intervene between motivation and action and condition the eventual outcome. The sequence of events need not occur in this order. The rapist may want to act, have selected his victim and planned the action before he employs the techniques of neutralization which render him morally capable of rape. Rape is not always a spontaneous act: there is evidence to suggest that it is often planned.[4] In the case where the rapist lays his plans and motivates himself in advance, interaction between rapist and victim has little significance as a contributory factor to rape. In other cases, however, situations may occur where interaction between participants will itself bring techniques of neutralization into play and may provide the opportunity to translate motives into action. Where the rapist, being motivated in advance, is in a state of drift, interaction between him and a potential victim may increase or decrease the probability of rape occurring.

Explanations or motivation are, then, necessary but not sufficient to account for rape. The eventual outcome of a potential rape situation will depend on how the actors define that situation and the interaction which arises out of their definitions. Here again sexual scripts come into play, for these not only provide possible motives for rape but shape the process of sexual negotiation. No situation is sexual in itself; whether it becomes so depends on interpretations of it.

'Without the proper elements of a script that defines the situation, names the actors and plots the behaviour, nothing sexual is likely to happen. One can easily conceive of numerous social situations in which all or almost all of the ingredients of a sexual event are present, but that remain non-sexual in that not even sexual arousal occurs. Thus combining such elements as desire, privacy and a physically attractive person of the appropriate sex, the probability of something sexual happening will, under normal circumstances, remain exceedingly small until either one or both actors organize these behaviours into an appropriate script' (Gagnon and Simon, 1974:19).

Circumstances may not, however, remain normal and, since there are no hard and fast rules for determining whether or not a situation may be defined as sexual, it is possible that one actor may perceive that sexual scripts are applicable while the other does not. It is possible that, insofar as men evaluate women almost exclusively in terms of their potential as sexual actors, they are capable of applying sexual scripts and becoming sexually motivated in a far wider range of situations than are women. Hence the interactional context in which motives for rape arise and which mediate between motives and action is governed by the same scripts in which those motives themselves originate, those which govern conventional sexual behaviour.

Conclusion: A Note on Rape and Sexual Politics

Rape is more than an attack on a specific victim. The sexual divisions of our society create a situation where rape is a constant threat to all women. In the course of their psychosexual development, men and women learn the typical vocabularies of motive of rapist and victim respectively. In enacting sexual scripts they enter into prescribed forms of interaction from which rape may emerge. The risk of being raped is one every woman takes not only when she walks along dark streets at night, but every time she negotiates a socio-sexual relationship, or indeed any time she participates in interaction with men. Sexual behaviour is social behaviour: though it may appear to be a private matter, something uniquely personal, each sexual relationship is structured by the cultural values of the society in which it takes place.

'Coitus can scarcely be said to take place in a vacuum; although of itself it appears a biological and physical activity, it is set so deeply within the larger context of human affairs that it serves as a charged microcosm of the variety of attitudes and values to which culture subscribes. Among other things it may serve as a model of sexual politics on an individual or personal plane' (Millett, 1972:23).

Sexual relationships are built around sexual inequalities, are scripted for actors whose roles have been predefined as subordinate and superordinate, and hence involve the exercise of power which may be manifested in the sexual act itself, as well as in other aspects of the relationship.

Rape, then, is simply an extreme manifestation of our culturally accepted patterns of male-female relationships. It is, in effect, an unofficial buttress of the *status quo*. It may be argued that it not only demonstrates male dominance but serves to preserve it:

'A world without rapists would be a world in which women moved freely without fear of men. That *some* men rape provides a sufficient threat to keep all women in a state of intimidation, forever conscious of the knowledge that the biological tool must be held in awe for it may turn to weapon with a swiftness borne of harmful intent. Myrmidons to the cause of male dominance ... rapists have performed their duty well, so well in fact that the true meaning of their acts has largely gone unnoticed. Rather than society's aberrants or 'spoilers of purity', men who commit rape have served in effect as front-line masculine shock troops, terrorist guerillas in the longest sustained battle the world has ever known' (Brownmiller, 1975:209).

Notes

1. This is borne out by the most famous example of a society where rape is unknown— the Mountain Arapesh of New Guinea. Not only do the Arapesh conceive of sex as dangerous, even between consenting partners, but the whole notion of sexual aggression is alien to them. Either sex may initiate sexual acts and the emphasis is on mutual preparedness and ease. Any form of compulsion, even within marriage, would be abhorrent to them. There is then, no element in their sexual scripts which could create the possibility of rape (Mead, 1963).

2. Weiss and Borges comment that members of low-status groups are frequently cast in the role of legitimate victim. Possibly the mere fact of his victim being female and therefore of no account is enough to motivate some rapists.

3. In this sense the undercurrents of hostility and negativity may be analogous to 'the condemnation of the condemners' cited by Sykes and Matza as a technique of neutralization in their original paper (Sykes and Matza, 1957), but later reshaped by Matza and seen as an attitude underlying the subculture of delinquency, rather than a specific technique of neutralization (Matza, 1964). If the possible condemners of the rapist are women in general, condemnation of them is a constant feature of the male (rapist) subculture.

4. Amir's data suggests that 71 per cent of rapes are planned, but this may possibly be inaccurate since it is based on official statistics (Amir, 1971).

3

Sex and Violence: A Perspective

Catharine A. MacKinnon

I WANT TO RAISE some questions about the concept of this panel's title, "Violence against Women," as a concept that may coopt us as we attempt to formulate our own truths. I want to speak specifically about four issues: rape, sexual harassment, pornography, and battery. I think one of the reasons we say that each of these issues is an example of violence against women is to reunify them. To say that aggression against women has this unity is to criticize the divisions that have been imposed on that aggression by the legal system. What I see to be the danger of the analysis, what makes it potentially cooptive, is formulating it—and it *is* formulated this way—these are issues of violence, *not* sex: rape is a crime of violence, not sexuality; sexual harassment is an abuse of power, not sexuality; pornography is violence against women, it is not erotic. Although battering is not categorized so explicitly, it is usually treated as though there is nothing sexual about a man beating up a woman so long as it is with his fist. I'd like to raise some questions about that as well.

I hear in the formulation that these issues are violence against women, not sex, that we are in the shadow of Freud, intimidated at being called repressive Victorians. We're saying we're *op*pressed and they say we're *re*pressed. That is, when we say we're against rape, the immediate response is, "Does that mean you're against sex?" "Are you attempting to impose neo-Victorian prudery on sexual expression?" This comes up with sexual harassment as well. When we say we're against sexual harassment, the first thing people want to know is, "What's the difference between that and ordinary male-to-female sexual initiation?" That's a good question. ... The same is also true of criticizing pornography. "You can't be against erotica?" It's the latest version of the accusation that feminists are anti-male. To distinguish ourselves from this, and in reaction to it, we call these abuses violence. The attempt is to avoid the critique—we're not against sex—and at the same time retain our criticism of these practices. So we rename as violent those abuses that have been seen to be sexual, without saying that we have a very different perspective on violence and on sexuality and their relationship. I also think a reason we call these experiences violence is to avoid being called lesbians, which for some reason is equated with being against sex. In order to avoid that, yet retain our opposition to sexual violation, we put this neutral, objective, abstract word *violence* on it all.

To me this is an attempt to have our own perspective on these outrages without owning up to having one. To have our point of view but present it as *not* a particular point of view. Our problem has been to label something as rape, as sexual harassment, as pornography in the face of a suspicion that it might be intercourse, it might be ordinary sexual initiation, it might be erotic. To say that these purportedly sexual events violate us, to be against them, we call them not sexual. But the attempt to be objective and neutral avoids owning up to the fact that women do have a specific point of view on these events. It avoids saying that from women's point of view, intercourse, sex roles, and eroticism can be and at times are violent to us as women.

My approach would claim our perspective; we are not attempting to be objective about it, we're attempting to represent the point of view of women. The point of view of men up to this time, called objective, has been to distinguish sharply between rape on the one hand and intercourse on the other; sexual harassment on the one hand and normal, ordinary sexual initiation on the other; pornography or obscenity on the one hand and eroticism on the other. The male point of view defines them by distinction. What women experience does not so clearly distinguish the normal, everyday things from those abuses from which they have been defined by distinction. Not just "Now we're going to take what *you* say is rape and call it violence"; "Now we're going to take what *you* say is sexual harassment and call it violence"; "Now we're going to take what *you* say is pornography and call it violence." We have a deeper critique of what has been done to women's sexuality and who controls access to it. What we are saying is that sexuality in exactly these normal forms often *does* violate us. So long as we say that those things are abuses of violence, not sex, we fail to criticize what has been made of *sex*, what has been done to us *through* sex, because we leave the line between rape and intercourse, sexual harassment and sex roles, pornography and eroticism, right where it is.

I think it is useful to inquire how women and men (I don't use the term *persons*, I guess, because I haven't seen many lately) live through the meaning of their experience with these issues. When we ask whether rape, sexual harassment, and pornography are questions of violence or questions of sexuality, it helps to ask, to whom? What is the perspective of those who are involved, whose experience it is—to rape or to have been raped, to consume pornography or to be consumed through it. As to what these things *mean* socially, it is important whether they are about sexuality to women and men or whether they are instead about "violence,"—or whether violence and sexuality can be distinguished in that way, as they are lived out.

The crime of rape—this is a legal and observed, not a subjective, individual, or feminist definition—is defined around penetration. That seems to me a very male point of view on what it means to be sexually violated. And it is exactly what heterosexuality as a social institution is fixated around, the penetration of the penis into the vagina. Rape is defined according to what men think violates women, and that is the same as what they think of as the *sine qua non* of sex. What women experience as degrading and defiling when we are raped includes as much that is distinctive to us as is our experience of sex. Someone once termed penetration a "peculiarly resented aspect" of rape—I don't know whether that meant it was peculiar that it was resented or that it was resented with heightened peculiarity. Women who have been raped often do resent having been penetrated. But that is not all there is to what was intrusive or expropriative of a woman's sexual wholeness.

I do think the crime of rape focuses more centrally on what men define as sexuality than on women's experience of our sexual being, hence its violation. A common experience of rape victims is to be unable to feel good about anything heterosexual thereafter—or anything sexual at all, or men at all. The minute they start to have sexual feelings or feel sexually touched by a man, or even a woman, they start to relive the rape. I had a client who came in with her husband. She was a rape victim, a woman we had represented as a witness. Her husband sat the whole time and sobbed. They couldn't have sex anymore because every time he started to touch her, she would flash to the rape scene and see his face change into the face of the man who had raped her. That, to me, is sexual. When a woman has been raped, and it is sex that she then cannot experience without connecting it to that, it was her sexuality that was violated.

Similarly, men who are in prison for rape think it's the dumbest thing that ever happened. ... It isn't just a miscarriage of justice; they were put in jail for something very little different from what most men do most of the time and call it sex. The only difference is they got caught. That view is nonremorseful and not rehabilitative. It may also be true. It seems to me we have here a convergence between the rapist's view of what he has done and the victim's perspective on what was done to her. That is, for both, their ordinary experiences of heterosexual intercourse and the act of rape have something in common. Now this gets us into intense trouble, because that's exactly how judges and juries see it who refuse to convict men accused of rape. A rape victim has to prove that it was not intercourse. She has to show that there was force and she resisted, because if there was sex, consent is inferred. Finders of fact look for "more force than usual during the preliminaries." Rape is defined by distinction from intercourse—not nonviolence, intercourse. They ask, does this event look more like fucking or like rape? But what is their standard for sex, and is this question asked from the *woman's point of view?* The level of force is not adjudicated at her point of violation; it is adjudicated at the standard of the normal level of force. Who sets this standard?

In the criminal law, we can't put everybody in jail who does an ordinary act, right? Crime is supposed to be deviant, not normal. Women continue not to report rape, and a reason is that they believe, and they are right, that the legal system will not see it from their point of view. We get very low conviction rates for rape.[1] We also get many women who believe they have never been raped, although a lot of force was involved. They mean that they were not raped in a way that is legally provable. In other words, in all these situations, there was not *enough* violence against them to take it beyond the category of "sex"; they were not coerced enough. Maybe they were forced-fucked for years and put up with it, maybe they tried to get it over with, maybe they were coerced by something other than battery, something like economics, maybe even something like love.

What I am saying is that unless you make the point that there is much violence in intercourse, as a usual matter, none of that is changed. Also we continue to stigmatize the women who claim rape as having experienced a deviant violation and allow the rest of us to go through life feeling violated but thinking we've never been raped, when there were a great many times when we, too, have had sex and didn't want it. What this critique does that is different from the "violence, not sex" critique is ask a series of questions about normal, heterosexual intercourse and attempt to move the line between heterosexuality on the one hand—intercourse—and rape on the other, rather than allow it to stay where it is.

Having done that so extensively with rape, I can consider sexual harassment more briefly. The way the analysis of sexual harassment is sometimes expressed now (and it bothers me) is that it is an abuse of power, not sexuality. That does not allow us to pursue whether sexuality, as socially constructed in our society through gender roles, is *itself* a power structure. If you look at sexual harassment as power, not sex, what is power supposed to be? Power is employer/employee, not because courts are marxist but because this is a recognized hierarchy. Among men. Power is teacher/student, because courts recognize a hierarchy there. Power is on one side and sexuality on the other. Sexuality is ordinary affection, everyday flirtation. Only when ordinary, everyday affection and flirtation and "I was just trying to be friendly" come into the context of *another* hierarchy is it considered potentially an abuse of power. What is not considered to be a hierarchy is women and men—men on top and women on the bottom. That is not considered to be a question of power or social hierarchy, legally or politically. A feminist perspective suggests that it is.

When we have examples of coequal sexual harassment (within these other hierarchies), worker to worker on the same level, involving women and men, we have a lot of very interesting, difficult questions about sex discrimination, which is supposed to be about gender difference, but does not conceive of gender as a social hierarchy. I think that implicit in race discrimination cases for a brief moment of light was the notion that there is a social hierarchy between Blacks and whites. So that presumptively it's an exercise of power for a white person to do something egregious to a Black person or for a white institution to do something egregious systematically to many Black people. Situations of coequal power—among coworkers or students or teachers—are difficult to see as examples of sexual harassment unless you have a notion of male power. I think we lie to women when we call it not power when a woman is come onto by a man who is not her employer, not her teacher. What do we labor under, what do we feel, when a man—any man—comes and hits on us? I think we require women to feel fine about turning down male-initiated sex so long as the man doesn't have some *other* form of power over us. Whenever—every and any time—a woman feels conflicted and wonders what's wrong with her that she can't decline although she has no inclination, and she feels open to male accusations, whether they come from women or men, of "why didn't you just tell him to buzz off?" we have sold her out, not named her experience. We are taught that we exist for men. We should be flattered or at least act as if we are—be careful about a man's ego because you never know what he can do to you. To flat out say to him, "You?" or "I don't want to" is not *in* most women's sex-role learning. To say it is, is bravado. And that's because he's a man, not just because you never know what he can do to you because he's your boss (that's two things—he's a man and he's the boss) or your teacher or in some other hierarchy. It seems to me that we haven't talked very much about gender *as* a hierarchy, as a division of power, in the way that's expressed and acted out, primarily I think sexually. And therefore we haven't expanded the definition according to women's experience of sexuality, including our own sexual intimidation, of what things are sexual in this world. So men have also defined what can be called sexual about us. They say, "I was just trying to be affectionate, flirtatious and friendly," and we were just all felt up. We criticize the idea that rape comes down to her word against his—but it really *is* her perspective against his perspective, and the law has been written from *his* perspective. If he didn't mean it to be sexual, it's not sexual. If he didn't see it as forced, it wasn't forced. Which is to say, only male sexual violations, that is, only male ideas of what sexually violates us as women, are illegal. We buy into this when we say our sexual violations are abuses of power, not sex.

Just as rape is supposed to have nothing against intercourse, just as sexual harassment is supposed to have nothing against normal sexual initiation (men initiate, women consent—that's mutual?), the idea that pornography is violence against women, not sex, seems to distinguish artistic creation on the one hand from what is degrading to women on the other. It is candid and true but not enough to say of pornography, as Justice Stewart said, "I know it when I see it."[2]

He knows what he thinks it is when he sees it—but is that what *I* know? Is that the same "it"? Is he going to know what I know when I see it? I think pretty much not, given what's on the newsstand, given what is not considered hard-core pornography. Sometimes I think what is obscene is what does *not* turn on the Supreme Court—or what revolts them more. Which is uncommon, since revulsion is eroticized. We have to admit that pornography turns men on; it is therefore erotic. It is a lie to say that pornography is not erotic. When we say it is violence, not sex, we are saying, there is this degrading to women, over here, and this erotic, over there, without saying to whom. It is overwhelmingly disproportionately men to whom pornography is erotic. It is women, on the whole, to whom it is violent, among other things. And this is not just a matter of perspective, but a matter of reality.

Pornography turns primarily men on. Certainly they are getting something out of it. They pay incredible amounts of money for it; it's one of the largest industries in the country. If women got as much out of it as men do, we would buy it instead of cosmetics. It's a massive industry, cosmetics. We are poor but we have *some* money; we are some market. We spend our money to set ourselves up as the objects that emulate those images that are sold as erotic to men. What pornography says about us is that we enjoy degradation, that we are sexually turned on by being degraded. For me that obliterates the line, as a line at all, between pornography on one hand and erotica on the other, if what turns men on, what men find beautiful, is what degrades women. It is pervasively present in art, also, and advertising. But it is definitely present in eroticism, if that is what it is. It makes me think that women's sexuality as such is a stigma. We also sometimes have an experience of sexuality authentic somehow in all this. We are not allowed to have it; we are not allowed to talk about it; we are not allowed to speak of it or image it as from our own point of view. And, to the extent we try to assert that we are beings equal with men, we have to be either asexual or virgins.

To worry about cooptation is to realize that lies make bad politics. It is ironic that cooptation often results from an attempt to be "credible," to be strategically smart, to be "effective" on existing terms. Sometimes you become what you're fighting. Thinking about issues of sexual violation as issues of violence not sex could, if pursued legally, lead to opposing sexual harassment and pornography through morals legislation and obscenity laws. It is actually interesting that this theoretical stance has been widely embraced but these legal strategies have not been. Perhaps women realize that these legal approaches would not address the subordination of women to men, specifically and substantively. These approaches are legally as abstract as the "violence not sex" critique is politically abstract. They are both not enough and too much of the wrong thing. They deflect us from criticizing everyday behavior that is pervasive and normal and concrete and fuses sexuality with gender in violation and is not amenable to existing legal approaches. I think we need to think more radically in our legal work here.

Battering is called violence, rather than something sex-specific: this is done to women. I also think it is sexually done to women. Not only in where it is done—over half of the incidents are in the bedroom.[3] Or the surrounding events—precipitating sexual jealousy. But when violence against women is eroticized as it is in this culture, it is very difficult to say that there is a major distinction in the level of sex involved between being assaulted by a penis and being assaulted by a fist, especially when the perpetrator is a man. If women as gender female are defined as sexual beings, and violence is eroticized, then men violating women has a sexual component. I think men rape women because they get off on it in a way that fuses dominance with sexuality. (This is different in emphasis from what Susan Brownmiller says.)[4] I think that when men sexually harass women it expresses male control over sexual access to us. It doesn't mean they all want to fuck us, they just want to hurt us, dominate us, and control us, and that *is* fucking us. They want to be able to have that and to be able to say when they can have it, to *know* that. That is in itself erotic. The idea that opposing battering is about saving the family is, similarly, abstracted, gender-neutral. There are gender-neutral formulations of all these issues: law and order as opposed to derepression, Victorian morality as opposed to permissiveness, obscenity as opposed to art and freedom of expression. Gender-neutral, objective formulations like these avoid asking *whose* expression, from whose point of view? Whose law and whose order? It's not just a question of who is free to express ourselves; it's not just that there is almost no, if any, self-respecting women's eroticism. The fact is that what we do see, what we are allowed to experience, even in our own suffering, even in what we are allowed to complain about, is overwhelmingly constructed from the male point of view. Laws against sexual violation express what men see and do when they engage in sex with women; laws against obscenity center on the display of women's bodies in ways that men are turned on by viewing. To me, it not only makes us cooptable to define such abuses in gender-neutral terms like violence; when we fail to assert that we are fighting for the affirmative definition and control of our own sexuality, of our own lives as women, and that these experiences violate *that,* we have already been bought.

Notes

1. Robin, 1977; Clark and Lewis, 1977.
2. Jacobellis v. Ohio, 378 U.S. 184, 197 (1964), Justice Stewart dissenting.
3. Dobash and Dobash, 1979, pp. 14–21.
4. Brownmiller, 1975.

Hidden Rape: Sexual Aggression and Victimization in a National Sample of Students in Higher Education

Mary P. Koss

OFFICIALLY, 87,340 RAPES occurred in 1985 (Federal Bureau of Investigation [FBI] 1986). However, this number greatly underestimates the true scope of rape since it includes only instances that were reported to the police. Because many victims never tell even their closest friends and family about their rape (Koss 1985), it is unrealistic to expect that they would report the crime to the police. Government estimates suggest that for every rape reported to police, 3–10 rapes are not reported (Law Enforcement Assistance Administration [LEAA] 1975).

Victimization studies such as the annual National Crime Survey (NCS) are the major avenue through which the full extent of crime is estimated (e.g., Bureau of Justice Statistics [BJS] 1984). In these studies, the residents of a standard sampling area are asked to indicate those crimes of which they or any other household members have been victims during the previous six months. The survey results are then compared to the number of reported crimes in the area, and the rate of unreported crime is estimated. On the basis of such research, the authors of the NCS have observed rape is an infrequent crime (LEAA 1974, 12) and is the most rare of NCS measured violent offenses (BJS 1984, 5). Women's chances of being raped have been described as a small fraction of 1% (Katz and Mazur 1979).

However, the accuracy of these conclusions and the validity of the research on which they are based must be examined closely, as the perceived severity of rape influences the social and economic priority it is accorded.

Several features of the NCS approach (e.g., BJS 1984) may lead to under-reporting of rape, including the use of a screening question that requires the subject to infer the focus of inquiry, the use of questions about rape that are embedded in a context of violent crime, and the assumption that the term *rape* is used by victims of sexual assault to conceptualize their experiences.

In an effort to extend previous research on rape (e.g., Koss and Oros 1982; Koss 1985) to a national sample, the *Ms.* Magazine Project on Campus Sexual Assault was undertaken. Because the FBI definition of rape (used in victimization studies such as the NCS) limits the crime to female victims (BJS 1984) and because women represent virtually 100% of reported rape victims (LEAA 1975), the project focused on women victims and male perpetrators.

Previous Research

Several recently reported estimates of the prevalence of sexual victimization have been reported that were based on studies designed specifically to gauge the extent of sexual assault. Kilpatrick and colleagues (Kilpatrick, Veronen, and Best 1984; Kilpatrick et al. 1985) conducted a victimization survey via telephone of 2,004 randomly selected female residents of Charleston County, South Carolina. In their sample, 14.5% of the women disclosed one or more attempted or completed sexual assault experiences, including 5% who had been victims of rape and 4% who had been victims of attempted rape. Of the women who had been raped, only 29% reported their assault to police. Russell found that 24% of a probability sample of 930 adult women residents of San Francisco described experiences that involved "forced intercourse or intercourse obtained by physical threat(s) or intercourse completed when the woman was drugged, unconscious, asleep, or otherwise totally helpless and unable to consent" (Russell 1984, 35). Only 9.5% of these women reported their experience to police.

Many studies of the prevalence of rape and lesser forms of sexual aggression have involved college students however. There are scientific as well as pragmatic reasons to study this group. College students are a high risk group for rape because they are in the same age range as the bulk of rape victims and offenders. The victimization rate for females peaks in the 16–19 year age group, and the second highest rate occurs in the 20–24 year age group. These rates are approximately four times higher than the mean for all women (BJS 1984). In addition, 47% of all alleged rapists who are arrested are individuals under age 25 (FBI 1986). Approximately 25% of all persons age 18–24 are attending school (U.S. Bureau of Census 1980). Finally, a substantial proportion of rape prevention efforts take place under the auspices of educational institutions and are targeted at students.

Kanin and his associates (Kanin 1957; Kirkpatrick and Kanin 1957; Kanin and Parcell 1977) found that 20–25% of college women reported forceful attempts by their dates at sexual intercourse during which the women ended up screaming, fighting, crying, or pleading and that 26% of college men reported making a forceful attempt at sexual intercourse that caused observable distress and offense in the woman. Rapaport and Burkhart (1984) reported that 15% of a sample of college men acknowledged that they had obtained sexual intercourse against their dates' will. Koss and colleagues (Koss 1985; Koss and Oros 1982; Koss et al. 1985) administered the self-report sexual experiences survey to a sample of 2,016 female and 1,846 male Midwestern university students. They found that 13% of the women experienced a victimization that involved sexual intercourse as a result of actual force or threat of harm; and 4.6% of the men admitted perpetrating an act of sexual aggression that met legal definitions of rape.

All of these prevalence studies suggest that rape is far more extensive than reported in official statistics. However, reported prevalence rates for rape vary from 5% (Kilpatrick et al. 1985) to 20–25% (Kanin 1957; Russell 1984). Unfortunately these different figures are not easy to reconcile as the studies involved both relatively small and geographically diverse samples and different data collection techniques.

Methods

The *Ms.* Magazine Project on Campus Sexual Assault involved administration of a self-report questionnaire to a sample of 6,159 students enrolled in 32 institutions of higher education across the United States. The following is an overview of the project's methodology, described more fully elsewhere (Koss, Gidycz, and Wisniewski 1987).

...

Subjects

The final sample consisted of 6,159 students: 3,187 females and 2,972 males. The female participants were characterized as follows: mean age = 21.4 years; 85% single, 11% married, and 4% divorced; 86% white, 7% black, 3% Hispanic, 3% Asian, and 1% native American; and 39% Catholic, 38% Protestant, 4% Jewish, and 20% other or no religion. The male participants were characterized as follows: mean age = 21.0 years; 90% single, 9% married, 1% divorced; 86% white, 6% black, 3% Hispanic, 4% Asian, and 1% native American; and 40% Catholic, 34% Protestant, 5% Jewish, and 22% other or no religion.

...

Survey Instrument

The data on the incidence and prevalence of sexual aggression were obtained through the use of the ten-item sexual experiences survey (Koss and Oros 1982;

Koss and Gidycz 1985). This survey is a self-report instrument designed to reflect various degrees of sexual aggression and victimization. During survey administration, separate wordings were used for women and for men. The text of all ten items (female wording) can be found in table [4].1. Descriptive data were obtained through the use of closed-ended questions administered subsequent to the survey. The survey booklet instructed all respondents who described any level of experience with sexual aggression or victimization to turn to a section of questions about the characteristics of the most serious incident in which they were involved.

...

Scoring Procedures

The groups labeled rape ("yes" responses to items 8, 9, and/or 10 and any lower-numbered items) and attempted rape ("yes" responses to items 4 and/or 5 but not to any higher-numbered items) included individuals whose experiences met broad legal definitions of these crimes. The legal definition of rape in Ohio (Ohio Revised Code 1980), similar to many states, is the following:

> Vaginal intercourse between male and female, and anal intercourse, fellatio, and cunnilingus between persons regardless of sex. Penetration, however slight, is sufficient to complete vaginal or anal intercourse. ... No person shall engage in sexual conduct with another person ... when any of the following apply: (1) the offender purposely compels the other person to submit by force or threat of force, (2) for the purpose of preventing resistance the offender substantially impairs the other person's judgment or control by administering any drug or intoxicant to the other person.

The group labeled sexual coercion ("yes" responses to items 6 and/or 7 but not to any higher-numbered items) included subjects who engaged in/experienced sexual intercourse subsequent to the use of menacing verbal pressure or misuse of authority. No threats of force or direct physical force were used. The group labeled sexual contact ("yes" responses to items 1, 2, and/or 3 but not to any higher-numbered items) consisted of individuals who had engaged in/experienced sexual behavior (such as fondling or kissing) that did not involve attempted penetration, subsequent to the use of menacing verbal pressure, misuse of authority, threats of harm, or actual physical force.

Results

Prevalence of Sexual Aggression/Victimization

Prevalence rates indicate the total number of persons who report experiences with sexual aggression or victimization during a specified time period, which in

Table [4].1

Frequencies of Individual Sexual Experiences Reported by Postsecondary Students: Prevalence Since Age 14

		Sex				
	Women			Men		
Sexual Behavior	%	M	SD	%	M	SD
1. Have you given in to sex play (fondling, kissing, or petting, but not intercourse) when you didn't want to because you were overwhelmed by a man's continual arguments and pressure?	44	3.2	1.5	19	2.9	1.5
2. Have you had sex play (fondling, kissing, or petting, but not intercourse) when you didn't want to because a man used his position of authority (boss, teacher, camp counselor, supervisor) to make you?	5	2.7	1.7	1	2.5	1.5
3. Have you had sex play (fondling, kissing, or petting, but not intercourse) when you didn't want to because a man threatened or used some degree of physical force (twisting your arm, holding you down, etc.) to make you?	13	2.1	1.5	2	2.3	1.5
4. Have you had a man attempt sexual intercourse (get on top, attempt to insert his penis) when you didn't want to by threatening or using some degree of force (twisting your arm, holding you down, etc.), but intercourse *did not* occur?	15	2.0	1.4	2	2.0	1.2
5. Have you had a man attempt sexual intercourse (get on top, attempt to insert his penis) when you didn't want to by giving you alcohol or drugs, but intercourse *did not* occur?	12	2.0	1.4	5	2.2	1.4
6. Have you given into sexual intercourse when you didn't want to because you were overwhelmed by a man's continual arguments and pressure?	25	2.9	1.6	10	2.4	1.4
7. Have you had sexual intercourse when you didn't want to because a man used his position of authority (boss, teacher, camp counselor, supervisor) to make you?	2	2.5	1.7	1	2.0	1.4
8. Have you had sexual intercourse when you didn't want to because a man gave you alcohol or drugs?	8	2.2	1.5	4	2.5	1.5
9. Have you had sexual intercourse when you didn't want to because a man threatened or used some degree of physical force (twisting your arm, holding you down, etc.) to make you?	9	2.2	1.5	1	2.3	1.5
10. Have you had sexual acts (anal or oral intercourse or penetration by objects other than the penis) when you didn't want to because a man threatened or used some degree of physical force (twisting your arm, holding you down, etc.) to make you?	6	2.2	1.6	1	2.5	1.5

Notes: The sample size was 3,187 women and 2,972 men. All questions were prefaced with instructions to refer to experiences "from age 14 on." Sexual intercourse was defined as "penetration of a woman's vagina, no matter how slightly, by a man's penis. Ejaculation is not required."

Table [4].2
Prevalence Rates for Five Levels of Sexual Aggression and Sexual Victimization

Sexual Aggression/Victimization (Highest Level Reported)	Women (%)		Men (%)	
	Weighted	Unweighted	Weighted	Unweighted
No sexual aggression/victimization	46.3	45.6	74.8	75.6
Sexual contact	14.4	14.9	10.2	9.8
Sexual coercion	11.9	11.6	7.2	6.9
Attempted rape	12.1	12.1	3.3	3.2
Rape	15.4	15.8	4.4	4.6

Notes: The sample size was 3,187 women and 2,972 men. Prevalence rates include sexual experiences since age 14.

this study was since the age of 14. The unweighted response frequencies for each item of the Sexual Experiences Survey are presented in table [4].1. The frequencies of victimization ranged from 44% (women who reported having experienced unwanted sexual contact subsequent to coercion) to 2% (women who reported having experienced unwanted sexual intercourse subsequent to the offender's misuse of authority). The frequency with which men reported having perpetrated each form of sexual aggression ranged from the 19% who said that they had obtained sexual contact through the use of coercion to the 1% who indicated that they had obtained oral or anal penetration through the use of force. Those respondents who had engaged in/experienced sexually aggressive acts indicated that each act had occurred a mean of 2.0–3.2 times since age 14.

However, the data on the individual sexually aggressive acts are difficult to interpret, because persons may have engaged in/experienced several different sexually aggressive acts. Therefore, respondents were classified according to the highest degree of sexual victimization/aggression they reported (see table [4].2). With weighted data correcting for regional disproportions, 46.3% of women respondents revealed no experiences whatsoever with sexual victimization, while 53.7% of women respondents indicated some form of sexual victimization. The most serious sexual victimization ever experienced was sexual contact for 14.4% of the women, sexual coercion for 11.9% of the women, attempted rape for 12.1% of the women, and rape for 15.4% of the women. Weighted data for males indicated that 74.8% of men had engaged in no forms of sexual aggression, whereas 25.1% of the men revealed involvement in some form of sexual aggression. The most extreme level of sexual aggression perpetrated was sexual contact for 10.2% of the men, sexual coercion for 7.2% of the men, attempted rape for 3.3% of the men, and rape for 4.4% of the men. Examination of these figures reveals that the effect of weighting was minimal and tended to reduce slightly the prevalence of the most serious acts of sexual aggression.

The relationship of prevalence rates to the institutional parameters used to design the sample was examined via chi-square and analysis of variance (ANOVA). Due to the large sample size, differences that have no real practical significance could reach statistical significance. Therefore, effect sizes were calculated using Cohen's method (w for chi-square and f for F) to gauge the importance of any significant differences (1977). ... The prevalence of sexual victimization as reported by women did not differ according to the size of the city where the institution of higher education was located, ... the size of the institution, ... the type of institution, ... or whether the minority enrollment of the institution was above or below the national mean. ... However, rates of sexual victimization did vary by region ... and by the governance of the institution. ... The rate at which women reported having been raped was twice as high in private colleges (14%) and major universities (17%) as it was at religiously affiliated institutions (7%). Victimization rates were also slightly higher in the Great Lakes and Plains states than in other regions.

The prevalence of reported sexual aggression by men also did not differ according to city size, ... institution size, ... minority enrollment, ... governance, ... and type of institution. ... However, the percent of men who admitted perpetrating sexual aggression did vary according to the region of the country in which they attended school. ... Men in the Southeast admitted rape twice as often (6%) as in the Plains states (3%) and three times as often as in the West (2%).

Finally, the relationships between the prevalence rates and individual subject demographic variables were also studied and included income, religion, and ethnicity. The rate at which women reported experiences of sexual victimization did not vary according to subject's family income ... or religion. ... The prevalence rates of victimization did vary according to ethnicity. ... For example, rape was reported by 16% of white women ($N = 2655$), 10% of black women ($N = 215$), 12% of Hispanic women ($N = 106$), 7% of Asian women ($N = 79$), and 40% of native American women ($N = 20$).

The number of men who admitted acts of sexual aggression did not vary according to subject's religion ... or family income. ... However, the number of men who reported acts of sexual aggression did differ by ethnic group. ... For example, rape was reported by 4% of white men ($N = 2484$), 10% of black men ($N = 162$), 7% of Hispanic men ($N = 93$), 2% of Asian men ($N = 106$), and 0% of native American men ($N = 16$).

Incidence of Sexual Aggression/Victimization

Incidence rates indicate how many new episodes of an event occurred during a specific time period. In this study, respondents were asked to indicate how many

Table [4].3

Frequencies of Individual Sexual Experiences Reported by Postsecondary Student: One-Year Incidence

	Sex			
	Women		Men	
Sexual Experience	Victims	Incidents	Perpetrators	Incidents
Sexual contact by verbal coercion	725	1716	321	732
Sexual contact by misuse of authority	50	97	23	55
Sexual contact by threat or force	111	211	30	67
Attempted intercourse by force	180	297	33	52
Attempted intercourse by alcohol/drugs	143	236	72	115
Intercourse by verbal coercion	353	816	156	291
Intercourse by misuse of authority	13	21	11	20
Intercourse by alcohol/drugs	91	159	57	103
Intercourse by threat or force	63	98	20	36
Oral/anal penetration by threat or force	53	96	19	48

Note: The sample size was 3,187 women and 2,972 men.

times during the previous year they had engaged in/experienced each item listed in the survey. To improve recall, the question referred to the previous academic year from September to September, time boundaries that are meaningful to students. Some subjects reported multiple episodes of sexual aggression/victimization during the previous year. Therefore, the incidence of sexual aggression/victimization was calculated two ways. First, the number of people who reported one or more episodes during the year was determined. Second, the total number of sexually aggressive incidents that were reported by women and by men was calculated.

The incidence rate for rape during a 12-month period was found to be 353 rapes involving 207 different women in a population of 3,187 women. Comparable figures for the other levels of sexual victimization were 533 attempted rapes (323 victims), 837 episodes of sexual coercion (366 victims), and 2,024 experiences of unwanted sexual contact (886 victims). The incidence data for the individual items used to calculate these rates are found in table [4].3.

Incidence rates for the sexual aggression admitted by men also were calculated. Responses to the three items that characterize rape for the 12-month period preceding the survey indicate that 187 rapes were perpetrated by 96 different men. Comparable incidence rates during a 12-month period for the other levels of sexual aggression were 167 attempted rapes (105 perpetrators), 854 episodes of unwanted sexual contact (374 perpetrators), and 311 situations of sexual coercion (167 perpetrators). The incidence data for the individual items that were used to calculate these rates also are presented in table [4].3.

From these data, victimization rates can be calculated. If the total number of all the women who during the previous year reported a sexual experience that met legal definitions of rape and attempted rape is divided by two (to obtain a six-month basis) and set to a base number of 1,000 women (instead of the 3,187 women actually surveyed), the victimization rate for the surveyed population of women was 83/1,000 women during a six-month period. However, the FBI definition of rape (i.e., forcible vaginal intercourse with a female against consent by force or threat of force, including attempts) on which the NCS is based is narrower than the state laws (i.e., oral, anal, or vaginal intercourse or penetration by objects against consent through threat, force, or intentional incapacitation of the victim via drugs) on which the groupings in this study were based (BJS 1984). Therefore, the victimization rate was also calculated in conformance with the FBI definition. Elimination of all incidents except those that involved actual or attempted vaginal sexual intercourse through force or threat of harm resulted in a victimization rate of 38/1,000 women during a six-month period.

Perpetration rates were also determined using data from the male subjects. When all unwanted oral, anal, and vaginal intercourse attempts and completions were included in the calculations, a perpetration rate of 34/1,000 men was obtained. Use of the FBI definition resulted in a perpetration rate of 9/1,000 college men during a six-month period.

Descriptive Profile of Sexual Aggression/Victimization

To develop a profile of the sexual aggression/victimization experiences that were reported by postsecondary students, researchers used inferential statistics descriptively.

Women's Vantage Point. Women were asked detailed questions about the most serious victimization, if any, that they had experienced since the age of 14. These criterion variables were analyzed by chi-square analysis for dichotomous data and ANOVA for continuous data by the five levels of the sexual victimization factor. ...

From the data ... the following profile of the rapes reported by women students emerge. (All items were scored on a 1 [not at all] to 5 [very much] scale unless otherwise indicated.) The victimizations happened 1–2 years ago when the women were 18–19 years old ($M = 18.5$); 95 % of the assaults involved one offender only; 84% involved an offender who was known to the victim; 57% of offenders were dates. The rapes happened primarily off campus (86%), equally as often in the man's house or car as in the woman's house or car. Most offenders (73%) were thought to be drinking or using drugs at the time of the assault, while the victim admitted using intoxicants in 55% of the episodes. Prior mutual intimacy had occurred with the offender to the level of petting above the waist (M = 3.52 on a 1–6 scale). However, the victims believed that they had made their nonconsent to have sexual intercourse "quite" clear (M = 4.05). Typically, the victim perceived that the offender used "quite a bit" of force (M = 3.88), which involved twisting her arm or holding her down. Only 9% of the rapes involved hitting or beating, and only 5% involved weapons. Women rated their amount of resistance as moderate (M = 3.80). Forms of resistance used by many rape victims included reasoning (84%) and physically struggling (70%). Many women (41%) were virgins at the time of their rape. During the rape, victims felt scared (M = 3.66), angry (M = 3.97), and depressed (M = 3.93). Rape victims felt somewhat responsible (M = 2.80) for what had happened, but believed that the man was much more responsible (M = 4.29).

Almost half of victimized women (42%) told no one about their assault. Just 8% of the victims who told anyone reported to police (equivalent to 5% of all rape victims), and only 8% of the victims who told anyone visited a crisis center (again equivalent to 5% of all rape victims). Those who reported to police rated the reaction they received as "not at all supportive" (M = 1.02). On the other hand, family (M = 3.70) and campus agency (M = 4.00) reaction were seen as supportive.

Surprisingly, 42% of the women indicated that they had sex again with the offender on a later occasion, but it is not known if this was forced or voluntary; most relationships (87%) did eventually break up subsequent to the victimization. Many rape victims (41%) stated that they expected a similar assault to happen again in the future, and only 27% of the women whose experience met legal definitions of rape labeled themselves as rape victims.

Although these analyses demonstrated statistically significant differences between the situational characteristics of the rapes reported by women compared with the lesser degrees of sexual victimization, the effect sizes of these differences were generally small. Thus, the descriptive profile of the rapes reported by college women is applicable to a great extent to the lesser degrees of sexual victimization as well. With the effect sizes for guidance, the following large and important differences between rapes and other forms of sexual victimization can be noted. Rapes were less likely to involve dating partners than other forms of sexual victimization. While 70–86% of lesser forms of victimization involved dating couples, only 57% of the rapes did. Men who raped were perceived by the victims as more often drinking (73%) than men who engaged in lesser degrees of sexual aggression (35–64%). Rapes, as well as attempted rapes, were more violent. More than half of rape victims (64%) and attempted rape victims (41%) reported that the offender used actual violence, such as holding them down, while fewer than 10% of other victims reported actual force. Likewise, the use of physical resistance was reported by many more victims of rape (70%) and attempted rape (52%) than by victims of lesser degrees of sexual assault (26–33%). Finally, rape victims (27%) were much more likely than any other group (1–3%) to see their experience as a rape.

Men's Vantage Point. Men were asked detailed questions about the most serious sexual aggression, if any, that they had perpetrated since the age of 14. These criterion variables also were analyzed by chi-square analysis for dichotomous data and ANOVA for continuous data by the five levels of the sexual aggression factor. ...

With these data, characteristics of the rapes perpetrated by college men can be determined. The rapes happened one to two years ago when the men were 18–19 years old ($M = 18.5$); 84% of the assaults involved one offender only; 84% involved an offender who was known to the victim; 61% of offenders were dates. The rapes happened primarily off campus (86%), equally as often in the man's house or car as in the woman's house or car. Most men who raped (74%) said they were drinking or using drugs at the time of the assault, and most (75%) perceived that their victims were using intoxicants as well. Men believed that mutual intimacy had occurred with the victim to the level of petting below the waist ($M = 4.37$), and they felt that the victims' nonconsent to have sexual intercourse was "not at all" clear ($M = 1.80$).

Typically, men who raped perceived that they were "somewhat" forceful ($M = 2.85$) and admitted twisting the victim's arm or holding her down. Only 3% of the perpetrators of rape said that they hit or beat the victim, and only 4% used weapons. They perceived victims' resistance as minimal ($M = 1.83$). Forms of resistance that assailants observed included reasoning, which was used by 36% of the rape victims, and physically struggling, which was used by 12%. Few men (12%) were virgins at the time they forced a woman to have sexual intercourse.

During the assault, offenders felt minimal negative emotions, including feeling scared ($M = 1.52$), angry ($M = 1.45$), or depressed ($M = 1.59$). Instead, perpetrators of rape were more likely to feel proud ($M = 2.27$). Although they felt mildly responsible ($M = 2.43$) for what had happened, rapists believed that the woman was equally or more responsible ($M = 2.85$). Half of the men who reported an act that met legal definitions of rape (54%) told no one at all about their assault, and only 2% of them were reported to police by the victim. Among the men, 55% indicated that after the assault they had had sex with the victim again, but it is not known if this was forced or voluntary. A substantial number of men who raped (47%) stated that they expected to engage in a similar assault at some point. Most men (88%) who reported an assault that met legal definitions of rape were adamant that their behavior was definitely not rape.

Although these analyses demonstrated statistically significant differences between the assault characteristics reported by men who raped compared with men who perpetrated lesser degrees of sexual aggression, the effect sizes of these differences were generally small. Thus, the descriptive profile of the rapes reported by male college students generally is applicable to the lesser degrees of sexual aggression as well. With the effect sizes for guidance, the following large and important differences between rapes and other forms of sexual aggression can be noted. Men who raped were more often drinking (74%) than men who engaged in lesser degrees of sexual aggression (33–67%). They perceived that the victim was more often drinking (75%) than was perceived by men who perpetrated lesser degrees of sexual aggression (31–65%). Men who reported behavior that met legal definitions of rape were less likely to be virgins at the time of their assault (12%) than other sexually aggressive men (24–48%). Men who perpetrated rape and sexual coercion were more likely to have sex with the victim again (64% and 55% respectively) than other perpetrators (32–37%). In addition, men who raped reported sexual intercourse with a larger number of partners since the assaultive episode than was reported by less sexually aggressive men.

Discussion

In this study, behaviorally specific items regarding rape and lesser forms of sexual aggression/victimization were presented in a noncrime context to an approximately representative national sample of college students. The results indicate that 15.4% of women reported experiencing and 4.4% of men reported perpetrating, since the age of 14, an act that met legal definitions of rape. Because virtually none of these victims or perpetrators had been involved in the criminal justice system, their experiences qualify as "hidden rape," which is not reflected in official crime statistics such as the *Uniform Crime Reports* (e.g., FBI 1985).

As mentioned earlier, a victimization rate for women of 38/1,000 was calculated. This rate is 10–15 times greater than rates based on the NCS (BJS 1984), which are 3.9/1,000 for women age 16–19 and 2.5/1,000 for women age 20–24. Even men's rate of admitting to raping (9/1,000) is two to three times greater than NCS estimates of the high risk of rape for women between the ages of 16–24. At least among students in higher education, it appears that official surveys (such as the NCS) fail to describe the full extent of sexual victimization.

However, NCS rates are based on representative samples of all persons in the U.S. in the 16–24-year-old group, whereas the present sample represents only the 25% of persons age 18–24 who attend college. Using other available data for guidance, one can speculate how the victimization rates among postsecondary students might compare with the rates among nonstudents in the same age group. Although the data do not suggest a direct relationship between level of education and rape victimization rates, the rates are related to family income. Thus, nonstudents, who are likely to come from poorer families than students enrolled in higher education, might show even higher incidence rates than those found in the study sample. However, only when empirical data on young persons not attending school become available can the victimization rates reported in the NCS for persons age 18–24 be fully analyzed.

The characteristics of the rapes described by study respondents differ from the characteristics of rapes described by official statistics (e.g., BJS 1984). For example, 60–75% of the rapes reported in the NCS by women age 16–24 involved strangers, and 27% involved multiple offenders (i.e., group rapes). Study respondents, most of whom were between the ages of 18–24, did report stranger rapes (16%) and group rapes (5%), but the vast majority of incidents were individual assaults (95%) that involved close acquaintances or dates (84%).

The differences between the kinds of rape described in official reports and in this study suggest that it is episodes of intimate violence that differentiate between the results. Either the wording of screening questions or the overall crime context-questioning of the NCS may fail to elicit from respondents the large number of sexual victimizations that involve close acquaintances.

The findings of this study demonstrate that men do not admit enough sexual aggression to account for the number of victimizations reported by women. Specifically, 54% of women claimed to be sexually victimized, but only 25% of men admitted any degree of sexually aggressive behavior. However, the number of times that men admitted perpetrating each aggressive act is virtually identical to the number of times women reported experiencing each act. Thus, the results fail to support notions that a few sexually active men could account for the victimization of a sizable number of women. Clearly, some of the victimizations reported by college women occurred in earlier years and were not perpetrated by the men who were surveyed. In addition, some recent victimizations may have involved community members who were not attending college. Future research must determine the extent to which these explanations account for the sizable difference in rates.

The data on validity suggest that those sexual experiences reported by the women did, in fact, occur, while additional relevant sexual experiences may not have been reported by men. Men may not be intentionally withholding information, but rather may be perceiving and conceptualizing potentially relevant sexual experiences in a way that was not elicited by the wording of the sexual experiences survey. Scully and Marolla (1982) studied incarcerated rapists who denied that the incident for which they were convicted was a rape. Many of these men, although they used physical force and injured their victims, saw their behavior as congruent with consensual sexual activity. It may be that some men fail to perceive accurately the degree of force and coerciveness that was involved in a particular sexual encounter or to interpret correctly a woman's consent or resistance.

This hypothesis is supported by the descriptive differences between men's and women's perceptions of the rape incidents. Although there were many points of agreement between men and women (e.g., the proportion of incidents that involved alcohol and the relationship of victim and offender), victims saw their nonconsent as clearer and occurring after less consensual intimacy than offenders. Victims perceived their own resistance and the man's violence as much more extreme than the offenders did. Future research might compare consent, violence, and resistance attributions among sexually aggressive and sexually nonaggressive men. If differences were found, the line of inquiry would lead to a new focus for rape prevention programs—educating vulnerable men to perceive accurately and communicate clearly.

The results of the study have additional implications for clinical treatment and research. The extent of sexual victimization uncovered by the national survey suggests that clinicians should consider including questions about unwanted sexual activity in routine intake interviewing of women clients and that they more frequently should consider sexual victimization among the possible etiological factors that could be linked to presenting symptoms. Of course, the study sample consisted of students, whereas many psychotherapy seekers are adults. However, it is not unusual for symptoms of post-traumatic stress disorder, which victims of rape may experience, to emerge months or even years after the trauma (American Psychiatric Association 1980).

For researchers, these results in combination with the work of others begin to describe the full extent of rape and suggest how reported statistics on rape reflect only those rapes reported to police (i.e., 5%), rapes acknowledged as rape by the victim (i.e., 27%), and those for which victim assistance services are sought (i.e, 5%), rather than reflecting rapes that have not been revealed (i.e., 42%). Future research must address the traumatic cognitive and symptomatic impact of rape on victims who do not report, confide in significant others, seek services, or even identify as victims. It is possible that the quality of many women's lives is reduced by the effects of encapsulated, hidden sexual victimization and the victims' subsequent accommodation to the experience through beliefs and behavior (Koss and Burkhart 1986).

Statistically significant regional and ethnic differences in the prevalence of sexual aggression/victimization were found. Unfortunately, the meaning of these results cannot be fully interpreted, as ethnicity and region were confounded (i.e., minority students are not distributed randomly across the regions of the country). However, effect sizes calculated on the variables of region and ethnicity indicate that their impact on prevalence rates is small. In the future, researchers will need to analyze the effect of ethnicity by controlling for region (and vice versa). As a result, other data available on the subjects, including personality characteristics, values, beliefs, and current behavior, can be used to attempt to account for any remaining differences.

Overall, the prevalence rates for sexual victimization/aggression were robust and did not vary extensively from large to small schools; across types of institutions; or among urban areas, medium-sized cities, and rural areas. The ubiquity of sexual aggression and victimization supports Johnson's observation that "the locus of violence rests squarely in the middle of what our culture defines as 'normal' interaction between men and women" (Johnson 1980, 146). As the editors of the *Morbidity and Mortality Weekly Report,* issued by the Centers for Disease Control in Atlanta, have noted, there is an "… increasing awareness in the public health community that violence is a serious public health problem and that nonfatal interpersonal violence has far-reaching consequences in terms of morbidity and quality of life" (Centers for Disease Control 1985, 739). Future research needs to devote attention to the preconditions that foster sexual violence.

Within the rape epidemiology literature are studies that have differed in methodology and have reported varying prevalence rates. Although the Ms. project involved a set of self-report questions whose validity and reliability have been evaluated, each data-collection method has advantages and disadvantages and cannot be fully assessed without reference to the special requirements of the topic of inquiry, the target population, and practical and financial limitations. Future epidemiological research must define how much variation in rates is due to the method of data collection or the screening question format and how much is due to sample differences. Nevertheless, the most important conclusion suggested by this entire line of research is that rape is much more prevalent than official statistics suggest.

…

Part Two

Why Men Rape

PART 1 INTRODUCED THE FOUNDATIONS for a feminist inquiry into the problem of rape and sexual assault. The authors highlighted the feminist challenge to the traditional view of rape as a pathological aberration and emphasized the importance of social and cultural factors that contribute to rape. Numerous surveys have documented the widespread acceptance of rape-supportive attitudes among American males (see Berger et al. 1986; Fonow, Richardson, and Wemmerus 1992; Lundberg-Love and Geffner 1989). A correlation between attitudes and behavior has also been demonstrated. Traditional attitudes toward gender roles, a game-playing orientation toward sexual relationships,[1] a belief in rape myths, and a view of sexual aggression as normal male behavior have all been associated with higher levels of self-reported sexual aggression among college men. Furthermore, research indicates that 20 to 30 percent of college men show substantial sexual arousal when viewing depictions of rape in which the woman is *not* portrayed as aroused by the rape, and 50 to 60 percent show some degree of arousal when the woman *is* portrayed as aroused (Malamuth 1985; Russell 1988). In addition, 25 to 35 percent of college men report there is a likelihood they would rape if they thought they could get away with it (Malamuth 1981; Russell 1988).

Timothy Beneke argued that it is common for men to "regard sex as an achievement, ... as gaining possession of a valued commodity" (1982:15). As he said, "Not every man is a rapist, but every man who grows up in America ... learns all too much to think like a rapist, to structure his experience of women and sex in terms of status, hostility, control, and dominance" (p. 16). The first chapter in this section, "Jay: An 'Armchair' Rapist," presents Beneke's interview with a man who "thinks like a rapist." Jay does not believe that he *could* rape, but he *wants* to when he sees a "hot" and sexy woman he presumes is flaunting her sexuality to tease him. Beneke argued that men often think of rape as a "counterattack" when a woman has attacked a man with her "weapon," that is,

51

her "provocative beauty" (p. 31). Beneke said that as long as "a woman's appearance is viewed as a weapon and sexual feeling is believed to make one helpless, women will be blamed for rape" (p. 32).

In the second chapter, " 'Riding the Bull at Gilley's': Convicted Rapists Describe the Rewards of Rape," Diana Scully and Joseph Marolla analyze interviews with incarcerated rapists to explain the objectives men have when they rape. Scully and Marolla found that rape serves as a means of revenge and punishment, a means of gaining access to unwilling or unavailable women, an added bonus to burglary or robbery, an adventurous recreational activity, and an exciting form of impersonal sex that allows men to avoid intimacy and feel powerful. They conclude that "some men rape because they have learned that in this culture sexual violence is rewarding."

In the third chapter, "Considering Sex Offenders: A Model of Addiction," Judith Lewis Herman argues that feminist sociocultural theory has not adequately explained "the wide variability among men whose attitudes and behavior would otherwise identify them as likely to rape." She combines the insights of psychological analyses with feminist analyses of sexual violence[2] to develop an "addiction" model of sex offending and discusses the implications of considering sexual assault as potentially addictive. Herman argues that efforts to eliminate sexual violence must include preventive education, improved strategies for the early identification, control, and treatment of sex offenders, and "stricter and more effective regulation of the organized sex industry."

Herman's concern with the "extreme and outrageous incitements to sexual violence" contained in pornography is echoed in the last chapter in this section, "Pornography as Sex Discrimination." Here Catharine MacKinnon argues that pornography is "at the center of a cycle of abuse" that cannot be interrupted until "the pornography that is its incentive, product, stimulus, and realization" is eliminated. As she says, "As long as pornography exists as it does now, women and children will be used and abused to make it, as they are now. And it will be used to abuse them, as it is now." MacKinnon analyzes why contemporary obscenity law has not prevented pornography from flourishing and proposes an alternative "civil rights" approach designed to empower women by giving them the option of civil suit against those whose involvement with pornography causes harm.[3]

In response to feminist assertions that pornography causes and perpetuates acts of sexual violence against women, creates a social climate in which sexual assault and abuse are tolerated, and objectifies, dehumanizes, and degrades women, a number of social psychologists have attempted to experimentally assess whether pornography has harmful effects (see Berger, Searles, and Cottle 1991). Researchers have shown that even brief exposure to sexually violent pornography can "increase the viewer's acceptance of rape myths, ... increase the willingness of a man to say that he would commit a rape, increase aggressive behavior against women in a laboratory setting and decrease one's sensitivity to rape and the plight of the rape victim" (Donnerstein 1984:53). Although it is obviously not possible to examine experimentally "the relationship between pornography and *actual* sexual aggression" (p. 53), Neil Malamuth (1985:405), one of the leading researchers in the field, interpreted the experimental evidence as strongly supporting the view that at least some pornography contributes "to a cultural climate that is more accepting of aggression against women."

Diana Russell (1988:49), a feminist sociologist, hypothesized that pornography "predisposes some men to want to rape women, ... intensifies the predisposition in other men already so predisposed, ... [and] undermines some men's internal inhibitions ... and ... some men's social inhibitions against acting out their desire to rape." She reviewed not only the experimental findings but also data from questionnaires, interviews, and testimonials and concluded that the data, when considered as a whole, strongly support the view that pornography plays a "causative role in some sexual assaults." She also suggested that pornography is used "to try to *persuade* a woman or a child to engage in certain acts, to legitimize the acts, and to undermine resistance, refusal, or disclosure" (p. 63).

Although the experimental research on the effects of pornography has received much attention and can be used to support claims about the harms of pornography, a conclusion that pornography is harmful is not dependent on this research. Some feminists are critical of the fact that the experimental research, generally involving males studying males, has higher prestige than the evidence of harm taken from the testimony of victims of pornography or contained in the pictures of abuse themselves (Dworkin 1984; MacKinnon 1986). Experimental research also has higher prestige than both social science surveys that reveal women's negative experiences with pornography and clinical evidence provided by professionals (e.g., therapists and district attorneys) who work with victims or with convicted and self-reported sex offenders. Cheryl Champion (1986:24), for instance, estimated that about 40 percent of clinical sex-offender cases involve perpetrators who use pornography, typically in a very compulsive and obsessive manner, "for masturbation, fantasy contemplation, and actual acting out of their scenarios on their victims." The experimenters say they cannot determine whether pornography "causes" rape, and some critics question laboratory studies for their artificiality and lack of correspondence to the real world; but the testimony of "women, men and children who have been abused because of pornography" is often discounted or dismissed as anecdotal (Bart 1986:105). In MacKinnon's compelling chapter, which concludes this section, she implores us to hear this testimony and recognize that for many survivors the connection between pornography and sexual exploitation is real indeed.

Notes

1. This attitude is illustrated in the nationally publicized case of the Spur Posse, a clique of high school males from Lakewood, California, who waged a competition to see who could have intercourse with the most females (Gelman 1993).

2. Other research that attempts to join psychological and feminist analyses found that rapists' fathers are more likely to be physically and emotionally distant and, to a lesser extent, physically abusive toward their sons (Lisak 1991; Lisak and Roth 1990). Father-distant child rearing may, in psychoanalytic terms, lead to a reaction formation involving hypermasculine behavior.

3. The "civil rights" approach was first presented as an ordinance in Minneapolis. This ordinance was passed twice by the city council and vetoed twice by the mayor. A similar ordinance passed in Indianapolis was ruled unconstitutional in an opinion by Federal District Court judge Sarah Evans Barker. Judge Barker's decision was affirmed in an opinion by Seventh Court of Appeals judge Frank Easterbrook and affirmed without an opinion by the U.S. Supreme Court (American Booksellers Association, Inc. v. Hudnut, 598 F. Supp. 1316 [1984]; 771 F.2d 323 [1985]; 106 S. Ct. 1664 [1986]). For further discussion of the ordinance and the court decisions, see Berger, Searles, and Cottle (1991).

Jay: An "Armchair" Rapist

Timothy Beneke

HE IS TWENTY-THREE, *grew up in Pittsburgh, and works as a file clerk in the financial district of San Francisco.*

Where I work it's probably no different from any other major city in the U.S. The women dress up in high heels, and they wear a lot of makeup, and they just look really *hot* and really sexy, and how can somebody who has a healthy sex drive not feel lust for them when you see them? I feel lust for them, but I don't think I could find it in me to overpower someone and rape them. But I definitely get the feeling that I'd like to rape a girl. I don't know if the actual act of rape would be satisfying, but the *feeling* is satisfying.

These women look so good, and they kiss ass of the men in the three-piece suits who are *big* in the corporation, and most of them relate to me like "Who are *you?* Who are *you* to even *look* at?" They're snobby and they condescend to me, and I resent it. It would take me a lot longer to get to first base than it would somebody with a three-piece suit who had money. And to me a lot of the men they go out with are superficial assholes who have no real feelings or substance, and are just trying to get ahead and make a lot of money. Another thing that makes me resent these women is thinking, "How could she want to hang out with somebody like that? What does that make her?"

I'm a file clerk, which makes me feel like a nebbish, a nurd, like I'm not making it, I'm a failure. But I don't really believe I'm a failure because I know it's just a phase, and I'm just doing it for the money, just to make it through this phase. I catch myself feeling like a failure, but I realize that's ridiculous.

What exactly do you go through when you see these sexy, unavailable women?

Let's say I see a woman and she looks really pretty and really clean and sexy, and she's giving off very feminine, sexy vibes. I think, "Wow, I would love to make love to her," but I know she's not really interested. It's a tease. A lot of times a woman knows that she's looking really good and she'll use that and flaunt it, and it makes me feel like she's laughing at me and I feel *degraded.*

I also feel dehumanized, because when I'm being teased I just turn off, I cease to be human. Because if I go with my human emotions I'm going to want to put my arms around her and kiss her, and to do that would be unacceptable. I don't like the feeling that I'm supposed to stand there and take it, and not be able to hug her or kiss her; so I just turn off my emotions. It's a feeling of humiliation, because the woman has forced me to turn off my feelings and react in a way that I really don't want to.

If I were actually desperate enough to rape somebody, it would be from wanting the person, but also it would be a very spiteful thing, just being able to say, "I have power over you and I can do anything I want with you," because really I feel that *they* have power over *me* just by their presence. Just the fact that they can come up to me and just melt me and make me feel like a dummy makes me want revenge. They have power over me so I want power over them. ...

Society says that you have to have a lot of sex with a lot of different women to be a real man. Well, what happens if you don't? Then what are you? Are you half a man? Are you still a boy? It's ridiculous. You see a whiskey ad with a guy and two women on his arm. The implication is that real men don't have any trouble getting women.

How does it make you feel toward women to see all these sexy women in media and advertising using their looks to try to get you to buy something?

It makes me hate them. As a man you're taught that men are more powerful than women, and that men always have the upper hand, and that it's a man's society; but then you see all these women and it makes you think, "Jesus Christ, if we have all the power how come all the beautiful women are telling us what to buy?" And to be honest, it just makes me hate beautiful women because they're using their power over me. I realize they're being used themselves, and they're doing it for the money. In *Playboy* you see all these beautiful women who look so sexy and they'll be giving you all these looks like they want to have sex so bad; but then in reality you know that except for a few nymphomaniacs, they're doing it for the money; so I hate them for being used and for using their bodies in that way.

In this society, if you ever sit down and realize how manipulated you really are it makes you pissed off—it makes you want to take control. And you've been manipulated by women, and they're a very easy target because they're out walking along the streets, so you can just grab one and say, "Listen, you're going to do what I want you to do," and it's an act of revenge against the way you've been manipulated.

I know a girl who was walking down the street by her house, when this guy jumped her and beat her up and raped her, and she was black and blue and had to go to the hospital. That's beyond me. I can't understand how somebody could do that. If I were going to rape a girl, I wouldn't hurt her. I might *restrain* her, but I wouldn't *hurt* her. ...

The whole dating game between men and women also makes me feel degraded. I hate being put in the position of having to initiate a relationship. I've been taught that if you're not aggressive with a woman, then you've blown it. She's not going to jump on *you,* so *you've* got to jump on *her.* I've heard all kinds of stories where the woman says, "No! No! No!" and they end up making great love. I get confused as hell if a woman pushes me away. Does it mean she's trying to be a nice girl and wants to put up a good appearance, or does it mean she doesn't want anything to do with you? You don't know. Probably a lot of men think that women don't feel like real women unless a man tries to force himself on her, unless she brings out the "real man," so to speak, and probably too much of it goes on. It goes on in my head that you're complimenting a woman by actually staring at her or by trying to get into her pants. Lately, I'm realizing that when I stare at women lustfully, they often feel more threatened than flattered.

"Riding the Bull at Gilley's": Convicted Rapists Describe the Rewards of Rape

Diana Scully and Joseph Marolla

OVER THE PAST SEVERAL DECADES, rape has become a "medicalized" social problem. That is to say, the theories used to explain rape are predicated on psychopathological models. They have been generated from clinical experiences with small samples of rapists, often the therapists' own clients. Although these psychiatric explanations are most appropriately applied to the atypical rapist, they have been generalized to all men who rape and have come to inform the public's view on the topic.

Two assumptions are at the core of the psychopathological model; that rape is the result of idiosyncratic mental disease and that it often includes an uncontrollable sexual impulse (Scully and Marolla, 1985). For example, the presumption of psychopathology is evident in the often cited work of Nicholas Groth (1979). While Groth emphasizes the nonsexual nature of rape (power, anger, sadism), he also concludes, "Rape is always a symptom of some psychological dysfunction, either temporary and transient or chronic and repetitive" (Groth, 1979:5). Thus, in the psychopathological view, rapists lack the ability to control their behavior; they are "sick" individuals from the "lunatic fringe" of society.

In contradiction to this model, empirical research has repeatedly failed to find a consistent pattern of personality type or character disorder that reliably discriminates rapists from other groups of men (Fisher and Rivlin, 1971; Hammer and Jacks, 1955; Rada, 1978). Indeed, other research has found that fewer than 5 percent of men were psychotic when they raped (Abel et al., 1980).

Evidence indicates that rape is not a behavior confined to a few "sick" men but many men have the attitudes and beliefs necessary to commit a sexually aggressive act. In research conducted at a midwestern university, Koss and her coworkers reported that 85 percent of men defined as highly sexually aggressive had victimized women with whom they were romantically involved (Koss and Leonard, 1984). A recent survey quoted in *The Chronicle of Higher Education* estimates that more than 20 percent of college women are the victims of rape and attempted rape (Meyer, 1984). These findings mirror research published several decades earlier which also concluded that sexual aggression was commonplace in dating relationships (Kanin, 1957, 1965, 1967, 1969; Kirkpatrick and Kanin, 1957).[1] In their study of 53 college males, Malamuth, Haber and Feshback (1980) found that 51 percent indicated a likelihood that they, themselves, would rape if assured of not being punished.

In addition, the frequency of rape in the United States makes it unlikely that responsibility rests solely with a small lunatic fringe of psychopathic men. Johnson (1980), calculating the lifetime risk of rape to girls and women aged twelve and over, makes a similar observation. Using Law Enforcement Assistance Association and Bureau of Census Crime Victimization Studies, he calculated that, excluding sexual abuse in marriage and assuming equal risk to all women, 20 to 30 percent of girls now 12 years old will suffer a violent sexual attack during the remainder of their lives. Interestingly, the lack of empirical support for the psychopathological model has not resulted in the de-medicalization of rape, nor does it appear to have diminished the belief that rapists are "sick" aberrations in their own culture. This is significant because of the implications and consequences of the model.

A central assumption in the psychopathological model is that male sexual aggression is unusual or strange. This assumption removes rape from the realm of the everyday or "normal" world and places it in the category of "special" or "sick" behavior. As a consequence, men who rape are cast in the role of outsider and a connection with normative male behavior is avoided. Since, in this view, the source of the behavior is thought to be within the psychology of the individual, attention is diverted away from culture or social structure as contributing factors. Thus, the psychopathological model ignores evidence which links sexual aggression to environmental variables and which suggests that rape, like all behavior, is learned.

Cultural Factors in Rape

Culture is a factor in rape, but the precise nature of the relationship between culture and sexual violence remains a topic of discussion. Ethnographic data from pre-industrial societies show the existence of rape-free cultures (Broude and Green, 1976; Sanday, 1979), though explanations for the phenomena differ.[2]

Sanday (1979) relates sexual violence to contempt for female qualities and suggests that rape is part of a culture of violence and an expression of male dominance. In contrast, Blumberg (1979) argues that in pre-industrial societies
women are more likely to lack important life options and to be physically and
politically oppressed where they lack economic power relative to men. That is, in
pre-industrial societies relative economic power enables women to win some
immunity from men's use of force against them.

Among modern societies, the frequency of rape varies dramatically, and the
United States is among the most rape-prone of all. In 1980, for example, the rate
of reported rape and attempted rape for the United States was eighteen times
higher than the corresponding rate for England and Wales (West, 1983). Spurred
by the Women's Movement, feminists have generated an impressive body of theory regarding the cultural etiology of rape in the United States. Representative of
the feminist view, Griffin (1971) called rape "The All American Crime."

The feminist perspective views rape as an act of violence and social control
which functions to "keep women in their place" (Brownmiller, 1975; Kasinsky,
1975; Russell, 1975). Feminists see rape as an extension of normative male behavior, the result of conformity or overconformity to the values and prerogatives
which define the traditional male sex role. That is, traditional socialization encourages males to associate power, dominance, strength, virility and superiority
with masculinity, and submissiveness, passivity, weakness, and inferiority with
femininity. Furthermore, males are taught to have expectations about their level
of sexual needs and expectations for corresponding female accessibility which
function to justify forcing sexual access. The justification for forced sexual access is buttressed by legal, social, and religious definitions of women as male
property and sex as an exchange of goods (Bart, 1979). Socialization prepares
women to be "legitimate" victims and men to be potential offenders (Weiss and
Borges, 1973). Herman (1984) concludes that the United States is a rape culture
because both genders are socialized to regard male aggression as a natural and
normal part of sexual intercourse.

Feminists view pornography as an important element in a larger system of
sexual violence; they see pornography as an expression of a rape-prone culture
where women are seen as objects available for use by men (Morgan, 1980; Wheeler, 1985). Based on his content analysis of 428 "adults only" books, Smith (1976)
makes a similar observation. He notes that, not only is rape presented as part of
normal male/female sexual relations, but the woman, despite her terror, is always depicted as sexually aroused to the point of cooperation. In the end, she is
ashamed but physically gratified. The message—women desire and enjoy
rape—has more potential for damage than the image of the violence *per se.*[3]

The fusion of these themes—sex as an impersonal act, the victim's uncontrollable orgasm, and the violent infliction of pain—is commonplace in the actual accounts of rapists. Scully and Marolla (1984) demonstrated that many convicted rapists denied their crime and attempted to justify their rapes by arguing

that their victim had enjoyed herself despite the use of a weapon and the infliction of serious injuries, or even death. In fact, many argued, they had been instrumental in making *her* fantasy come true.

The images projected in pornography contribute to a vocabulary of motive which trivializes and neutralizes rape and which might lessen the internal controls that otherwise would prevent sexually aggressive behavior. Men who rape use this culturally acquired vocabulary to justify their sexual violence.

Another consequence of the application of psychopathology to rape is it leads one to view sexual violence as a special type of crime in which the motivations are subconscious and uncontrollable rather than overt and deliberate as with other criminal behavior. Black (1983) offers an approach to the analysis of criminal and/or violent behavior which, when applied to rape, avoids this bias.

Black (1983) suggests that it is theoretically useful to ignore that crime is criminal in order to discover what such behavior has in common with other kinds of conduct. From his perspective, much of the crime in modern societies, as in pre-industrial societies, can be interpreted as a form of "self help" in which the actor is expressing a grievance through aggression and violence. From the actor's perspective, the victim is deviant and his own behavior is a form of social control in which the objective may be conflict management, punishment, or revenge. For example, in societies where women are considered the property of men, rape is sometimes used as a means of avenging the victim's husband or father (Black, 1983). In some cultures rape is used as a form of punishment. Such was the tradition among the puritanical, patriarchal Cheyenne where men were valued for their ability as warriors. It was Cheyenne custom that a wife suspected of being unfaithful could be "put on the prairie" by her husband. Military confreres then were invited to "feast" on the prairie (Hoebel, 1954; Llewellyn and Hoebel, 1941). The ensuring mass rape was a husband's method of punishing his wife.

Black's (1983) approach is helpful in understanding rape because it forces one to examine the goals that some men have learned to achieve through sexually violent means. Thus, one approach to understanding why some men rape is to shift attention from individual psychopathology to the important question of what rapists gain from sexual aggression and violence in a culture seemingly prone to rape.

In this paper, we address this question using data from interviews conducted with 114 convicted, incarcerated rapists. Elsewhere, we discussed the vocabulary of motive, consisting of excuses and justifications, that these convicted rapists used to explain themselves and their crime (Scully and Marolla, 1984).[4] The use of these culturally derived excuses and justifications allowed them to view their behavior as either idiosyncratic or situationally appropriate and thus it reduced their sense of moral responsibility for their actions. Having disavowed deviance, these men revealed how they had used rape to achieve a number of objectives. We find that some men used rape for revenge or punishment while, for others, it was an "added bonus"—a last minute decision made while committing another crime. In still other cases, rape was used to gain sexual access to women who were unwilling or unavailable, and for some it was a source of power and sex without any personal feelings. Rape was also a form of recreation, a diversion or an adventure and, finally, it was something that made these men "feel good."

Methods[5]

Sample

During 1980 and 1981 we interviewed 114 convicted rapists. All of the men had been convicted of the rape or attempted rape (n = 8) of an adult woman and subsequently incarcerated in a Virginia prison. Men convicted of other types of sexual offense were omitted from the sample.

In addition to their convictions for rape, 39 percent of the men also had convictions for burglary or robbery, 29 percent for abduction, 25 percent for sodomy, 11 percent for first or second degree murder and 12 percent had been convicted of more than one rape. The majority of the men had previous criminal histories but only 23 percent had a record of past sex offenses and only 26 percent had a history of emotional problems. Their sentences for rape and accompanying crimes ranged from ten years to seven life sentences plus 380 years for one man. Twenty-two percent of the rapists were serving at least one life sentence. Forty-six percent of the rapists were white, 54 percent black. In age, they ranged from 18 to 60 years but the majority were between 18 and 35 years. Based on a statistical profile of felons in all Virginia prisons prepared by the Virginia Department of Corrections, it appears that this sample of rapists was disproportionately white and, at the time of the research, somewhat better educated and younger than the average inmate.

All participants in this research were volunteers. In constructing the sample, age, education, race, severity of current offense and past criminal record were balanced within the limitations imposed by the characteristics of the volunteer pool. Obviously the sample was not random and thus may not be typical of all rapists, imprisoned or otherwise.

All interviews were hand recorded using an 89-page instrument which included a general background, psychological, criminal, and sexual history, attitude scales and 30 pages of open-ended questions intended to explore rapists' own perceptions of their crime and themselves. Each author interviewed half of the sample in sessions that ranged from three to seven hours depending on the desire or willingness of the participant to talk.

Validity

In all prison research, validity is a special methodological concern because of the reputation inmates have for "conning." Although one goal of this research was to understand rape from the perspective of men who have raped, it was also necessary to establish the extent to which rapists' perceptions deviated from other descriptions of their crime. The technique we used was the same others have used in prison research; comparing factual information obtained in the interviews, including details of the crime, with reports on file at the prison (Athens, 1977; Luckenbill, 1977; Queen's Bench Foundation, 1976). In general, we found that rapists' accounts of their crime had changed very little since their trials. However, there was a tendency to understate the amount of violence they had used and, especially among certain rapists, to place blame on their victims.

How Offenders View the Rewards of Rape

Revenge and Punishment

As noted earlier, Black's (1983) perspective suggests that a rapist might see his act as a legitimized form of revenge or punishment. Additionally, he asserts that the idea of "collective liability" accounts for much seemingly random violence. "Collective liability" suggests that all people in a particular category are held accountable for the conduct of each of their counterparts. Thus, the victim of a violent act may merely represent the category of individual being punished.

These factors—revenge, punishment, and the collective liability of women—can be used to explain a number of rapes in our research. Several cases will illustrate the ways in which these factors combined in various types of rape. Revenge-rapes were among the most brutal and often included beatings, serious injuries, and even murder.

Typically, revenge-rapes included the element of collective liability. That is, from the rapist's perspective, the victim was a substitute for the woman they wanted to avenge. As explained elsewhere, (Scully and Marolla, 1984), an upsetting event, involving a woman, preceded a significant number of rapes. When they raped, these men were angry because of a perceived indiscretion, typically related to a rigid, moralistic standard of sexual conduct, which they required from "their woman" but, in most cases, did not abide by themselves. Over and over these rapists talked about using rape "to get even" with their wives or other significant woman.[6] Typical is a young man who, prior to the rape, had a violent argument with his wife over what eventually proved to be her misdiagnosed case of venereal disease. She assumed the disease had been contracted through him, an accusation that infuriated him. After fighting with his wife, he explained that he drove around "thinking about hurting someone." He encountered his victim, a stranger, on the road where her car had broken down. It appears she accepted his offered ride because her car was out of commission. When she realized that rape was pending, she called him "a son of a bitch," and attempted to resist. He reported flying into a rage and beating her, and he confided,

> I have never felt that much anger before. If she had resisted, I would have killed her … The rape was for revenge. I didn't have an orgasm. She was there to get my hostile feelings off on.

Although not the most common form of revenge rape, sexual assault continues to be used in retaliation against the victim's male partner. In one such case, the offender, angry because the victim's husband owed him money, went to the victim's home to collect. He confided, "I was going to get it one way or another." Finding the victim alone, he explained, they started to argue about the money and,

> I grabbed her and started beating the hell out of her. Then I committed the act,[7] I knew what I was doing. I was mad. I could have stopped but I didn't. I did it to get even with her and her husband.

Griffin (1971:33) points out that when women are viewed as commodities, "In raping another man's woman, a man may aggrandize his own manhood and concurrently reduce that of another man."

Revenge-rapes often contained an element of punishment. In some cases, while the victim was not the initial object of the revenge, the intent was to punish her because of something that transpired after the decision to rape had been made or during the course of the rape itself. This was the case with a young man whose wife had recently left him. Although they were in the process of reconciliation, he remained angry and upset over the separation. The night of the rape, he met the victim and her friend in a bar where he had gone to watch a fight on TV. The two women apparently accepted a ride from him but, after taking her friend home, he drove the victim to his apartment. At his apartment, he found a note from his wife indicating she had stopped by to watch the fight with him. This increased his anger because he preferred his wife's company. Inside his apartment, the victim allegedly remarked that she was sexually interested in his dog, which he reported, put him in a rage. In the ensuing attack, he raped and pistol-whipped the victim. Then he forced a vacuum cleaner hose, switched on suction, into her vagina and bit her breast, severing the nipple. He stated:

> I hated at the time, but I don't know if it was her (the victim). (Who could it have been?) My wife? Even though we were getting back together, I still didn't trust her.

During his interview, it became clear that this offender, like many of the men, believed men have the right to discipline and punish women. In fact, he argued that most of the men he knew would also have beaten the victim because "that kind of thing (referring to the dog) is not acceptable among my friends."

Finally, in some rapes, both revenge and punishment were directed at victims because they represented women whom these offenders perceived as collectively responsible and liable for their problems. Rape was used "to put women in their place" and as a method of proving their "manhood" by displaying dominance over a female. For example, one multiple rapist believed his actions were related to the feeling that women thought they were better than he was.

Rape was a feeling of total dominance. Before the rapes, I would always get a feeling of power and anger. I would degrade women so I could feel there was a person of less worth than me.

Another, especially brutal, case involved a young man from an upper middle class background, who spilled out his story in a seven-hour interview conducted in his solitary confinement cell. He described himself as tremendously angry, at the time, with his girl friend whom he believed was involved with him in a "storybook romance," and from whom he expected complete fidelity. When she went away to college and became involved with another man, his revenge lasted eighteen months and involved the rape and murder of five women, all strangers who lived in his community. Explaining his rape-murders, he stated:

> I wanted to take my anger and frustration out on a stranger, to be in control, to do what I wanted to do. I wanted to use and abuse someone as I felt used and abused. I was killing my girl friend. During the rapes and murders, I would think about my girl friend. I hated the victims because they probably messed men over. I hated women because they were deceitful and I was getting revenge for what happened to me.

An Added Bonus

Burglary and robbery commonly accompany rape. Among our sample, 39 percent of rapists had also been convicted of one or the other of these crimes committed in connection with rape. In some cases, the original intent was rape and robbery was an after-thought. However, a number of the men indicated that the reverse was true in their situation. That is, the decision to rape was made subsequent to their original intent which was burglary or robbery.

This was the case with a young offender who stated that he originally intended only to rob the store in which the victim happened to be working. He explained that when he found the victim alone,

> I decided to rape her to prove I had guts. She was just there. It could have been anybody.

Similarly, another offender indicated that he initially broke into his victim's home to burglarize it. When he discovered the victim asleep, he decided to seize the opportunity "to satisfy an urge to go to bed with a white woman, to see if it was different." Indeed, a number of men indicated that the decision to rape had been made after they realized they were in control of the situation. This was also true of an unemployed offender who confided that his practice was to steal whenever he needed money. On the day of the rape, he drove to a local supermarket and paced the parking lot, "staking out the situation." His pregnant victim was the first person to come along alone and "she was an easy target." Threatening her with a knife, he reported the victim as saying she would do anything if he didn't harm her. At that point, he decided to force her to drive to a deserted area where he raped her. He explained:

I wasn't thinking about sex. But when she said she would do anything not to get hurt, probably because she was pregnant, I thought, 'why not.'

The attitude of these men toward rape was similar to their attitude toward burglary and robbery. Quite simply, if the situation is right, "why not." From the perspective of these rapists, rape was just another part of the crime—an added bonus.

Sexual Access

In an effort to change public attitudes that are damaging to the victims of rape and to reform laws seemingly premised on the assumption that women both ask for and enjoy rape, many writers emphasize the violent and aggressive character of rape. Often such arguments appear to discount the part that sex plays in the crime. The data clearly indicate that from the rapists' point of view rape is in part sexually motivated. Indeed, it is the sexual aspect of rape that distinguishes it from other forms of assault.

Groth (1979) emphasizes the psychodynamic function of sex in rape arguing that rapists' aggressive needs are expressed through sexuality. In other words, rape is a means to an end. We argue, however, that rapists view the act as an end in itself and that sexual access most obviously demonstrates the link between sex and rape. Rape as a means of sexual access also shows the deliberate nature of this crime. When a woman is unwilling or seems unavailable for sex, the rapist can seize what isn't volunteered. In discussing his decision to rape, one man made this clear.

> All the guys wanted to fuck her ... a real fox, beautiful shape. She was a beautiful woman and I wanted to see what she had.

The attitude that sex is a male entitlement suggests that when a woman says "no," rape is a suitable method of conquering the "offending" object. If, for example, a woman is picked up at a party or in a bar or while hitchhiking (behavior which a number of the rapists saw as a signal of sexual availability), and the woman later resists sexual advances, rape is presumed to be justified. The same justification operates in what is popularly called "date rape." The belief that sex was their just compensation compelled a number of rapists to insist they had not raped. Such was the case of an offender who raped and seriously beat his victim when, on their second date, she refused his sexual advances.

> I think I was really pissed off at her because it didn't go as planned. I could have been with someone else. She led me on but wouldn't deliver ... I have a male ego that must be fed.

The purpose of such rapes was conquest, to seize what was not offered.

Despite the cultural belief that young women are the most sexually desirable, several rapes involved the deliberate choice of a victim relatively older than the assailant.[8] Since the rapists were themselves rather young (26 to 30 years of age on the average), they were expressing a preference for sexually experienced, rather than elderly, women. Men who chose victims older than themselves often said they did so because they believed that sexually experienced women were more desirable partners. They raped because they also believed that these women would not be sexually attracted to them.

Finally, sexual access emerged as a factor in the accounts of black men who consciously chose to rape white women.[9] The majority of rapes in the United States today are intraracial. However, for the past 20 years, according to national data based on reported rapes as well as victimization studies, which include unreported rapes, the rate of black on white (B/W) rape has significantly exceeded the rate of white on black (W/B) rape (LaFree, 1982).[10] Indeed, we may be experiencing a historical anomaly, since, as Brownmiller (1975) has documented, white men have freely raped women of color in the past. The current structure of interracial rape, however, reflects contemporary racism and race relations in several ways.

First, the status of black women in the United States today is relatively lower than the status of white women. Further, prejudice, segregation and other factors continue to militate against interracial coupling. Thus, the desire for sexual access to higher status, unavailable women, an important function in B/W rape, does not motivate white men to rape black women. Equally important, demographic and geographic barriers interact to lower the incidence of W/B rape. Segregation as well as the poverty expected in black neighborhoods undoubtedly discourages many whites from choosing such areas as a target for housebreaking or robbery. Thus, the number of rapes that would occur in conjunction with these crimes is reduced.

Reflecting in part the standards of sexual desirability set by the dominant white society, a number of black rapists indicated they had been curious about white women. Blocked by racial barriers from legitimate sexual relations with white women, they raped to gain access to them. They described raping white women as "the ultimate experience" and "high status among my friends. It gave me a feeling of status, power, macho." For another man, raping a white woman had a special appeal because it violated a "known taboo," making it more dangerous, and thus more exciting, to him than raping a black woman.

Impersonal Sex and Power

The idea that rape is an impersonal rather than an intimate or mutual experience appealed to a number of rapists, some of whom suggested it was their preferred form of sex. The fact that rape allowed them to control rather than care encouraged some to act on this preference. For example, one man explained,

> Rape gave me the power to do what I wanted to do without feeling I had to please a partner or respond to a partner. I felt in control, dominant. Rape was the ability to have sex without caring about the woman's response. I was totally dominant.

Another rapist commented:

> Seeing them laying there helpless gave me the confidence that I could do it. ... With rape, I felt totally in charge. I'm bashful, timid. When a woman wanted to give in normal sex, I was intimidated. In the rapes, I was totally in command, she totally submissive.

During his interview, another rapist confided that he had been fantasizing about rape for several weeks before committing his offense. His belief was that it would be "an exciting experience—a new high." Most appealing to him was the idea that he could make his victim "do it all for him" and that he would be in control. He fantasized that she "would submit totally and that I could have anything I wanted." Eventually, he decided to act because his older brother told him, "forced sex is great, I wouldn't get caught and, besides, women love it." Though now he admits to his crime, he continues to believe his victim "enjoyed it." Perhaps we should note here that the appeal of impersonal sex is not limited to convicted rapists. The amount of male sexual activity that occurs in homosexual meeting places as well as the widespread use of prostitutes suggests that avoidance of intimacy appeals to a large segment of the male population. Through rape men can experience power and avoid the emotions related to intimacy and tenderness. Further, the popularity of violent pornography suggests that a wide variety of men in this culture have learned to be aroused by sex fused with violence (Smith, 1976). Consistent with this observation, recent experimental research conducted by Malamuth et al. (1980) demonstrates that men are aroused by images that depict women as orgasmic under conditions of violence and pain. They found that for female students, arousal was high when the victim experienced an orgasm and *no* pain, whereas male students were highly aroused when the victim experienced an orgasm and pain. On the basis of their results, Malamuth et al. (1980) suggest that forcing a woman to climax despite her pain and abhorrence of the assailant makes the rapist feel powerful; he has gained control over the only source of power historically associated with women, their bodies. In the final analysis, dominance was the objective of most rapists.

Recreation and Adventure

Among gang rapists, most of whom were in their late teens or early twenties when convicted, rape represented recreation and adventure, another form of delinquent activity. Part of rape's appeal was the sense of male camaraderie engendered by participating collectively in a dangerous activity. To prove one's self capable of "performing" under these circumstances was a substantial challenge and also a source of reward. One gang rapist articulated this feeling very clearly:

> We felt powerful, we were in control. I wanted sex and there was peer pressure. She wasn't like a person, no personality, just domination on my part. Just to show I could do it—you know, macho.

Our research revealed several forms of gang rape. A common pattern was hitchhike-abduction rape. In these cases, the gang, cruising an area, "looking for girls," picked up a female hitchhiker for the purpose of having sex. Though the intent was rape, a number of men did not view it as such because they were convinced that women hitchhiked primarily to signal sexual availability and only secondarily as a form of transportation. In these cases, the unsuspecting victim was driven to a deserted area, raped, and in the majority of cases physically injured. Sometimes, the victim was not hitchhiking; she was abducted at knife or gun point from the street usually at night. Some of these men did not view this type of attack as rape either because they believed a woman walking alone at night to be a prostitute. In addition, they were often convinced "she enjoyed it."

"Gang date" rape was another popular variation. In this pattern, one member of the gang would make a date with the victim. Then, without her knowledge or consent, she would be driven to a predetermined location and forcibly raped by each member of the group. One young man revealed this practice was so much a part of his group's recreational routine, they had rented a house for the purpose. From his perspective, the rape was justified because "usually the girl had a bad reputation, or we knew it was what she liked."

During his interview, another offender confessed to participating in twenty or thirty such "gang date" rapes because his driver's license had been revoked making it difficult for him to "get girls." Sixty percent of the time, he claimed, "they were girls known to do this kind of thing," but "frequently, the girls didn't want to have sex with all of us." In such cases, he said, "It might start out as rape but, then, they (the women) would quiet down and none ever reported it to the police." He was convicted for a gang rape, which he described as "the ultimate thing I ever did," because unlike his other rapes, the victim, in this case, was a stranger whom the group abducted as she walked home from the library. He felt the group's past experience with "gang date" rape had prepared them for this crime in which the victim was blindfolded and driven to the mountains where, though it was winter, she was forced to remove her clothing. Lying on the snow, she was raped by each of the four men several times before being abandoned near a farm house. This young man continued to believe that if he had spent the night with her, rather than abandoning her, she would not have reported to the police.[11]

Solitary rapists also used terms like "exciting," "a challenge," "an adventure," to describe their feelings about rape. Like the gang rapists, these men found the element of danger made rape all the more exciting. Typifying this attitude was one man who described his rape as intentional. He reported:

It was exciting to get away with it (rape), just being able to beat the system, not women. It was like doing something illegal and getting away with it.

Another rapist confided that for him "rape was just more exciting and compelling" than a normal sexual encounter because it involved forcing a stranger. A multiple rapist asserted, "it was the excitement and fear and the drama that made rape a big kick."

Feeling Good

At the time of their interviews, many of the rapists expressed regret for their crime and had empirically low self-esteem ratings. The experience of being convicted, sentenced, and incarcerated for rape undoubtedly produced many, if not most, of these feelings. What is clear is that, in contrast to the well-documented severity of the immediate impact, and in some cases, the long-term trauma experienced by the victims of sexual violence, the immediate emotional impact on the rapists is slight.

When the men were asked to recall their feelings immediately following the rape, only eight percent indicated that guilt or feeling bad was part of their emotional response. The majority said they felt good, relieved or simply nothing at all. Some indicated they had been afraid of being caught or felt sorry for themselves. Only two men out of 114 expressed any concern or feeling for the victim. Feeling good or nothing at all about raping women is not an aberration limited to men in prison. Smithyman (1978), in his study of "undetected rapists"—rapists outside of prison—found that raping women had no impact on their lives nor did it have a negative effect on their self-image.

Significantly a number of men volunteered the information that raping had a positive impact on their feelings. For some the satisfaction was in revenge. For example, the man who had raped and murdered five women:

> It seems like so much bitterness and tension had built up and this released it. I felt like I had just climbed a mountain and now I could look back.

Another offender characterized rape as habit forming: "Rape is like smoking. You can't stop once you start." Finally one man expressed the sentiments of many rapists when he stated,

> After rape, I always felt like I had just conquered something, like I had just ridden the bull at Gilley's.

Conclusions

This paper has explored rape from the perspective of a group of convicted, incarcerated rapists. The purpose was to discover how these men viewed sexual violence and what they gained from their behavior.

We found that rape was frequently a means of revenge and punishment. Implicit in revenge-rapes was the notion that women were collectively liable for the rapists' problems. In some cases, victims were substitutes for significant women on whom the men desired to take revenge. In other cases, victims were thought to represent all women, and rape was used to punish, humiliate, and "put them in their place." In both cases women were seen as a class, a category, not as individuals. For some men, rape was almost an after-thought, a bonus added to burglary or robbery. Other men gained access to sexually unavailable or unwilling women through rape. For this group of men, rape was a fantasy come true, a particularly exciting form of impersonal sex which enabled them to dominate and control women, by exercising a singularly male form of power. These rapists talked of the pleasures of raping—how for them it was a challenge, an adventure, a dangerous and "ultimate" experience. Rape made them feel good and, in some cases, even elevated their self-image.

The pleasure these men derived from raping reveals the extreme to which they objectified women. Women were seen as sexual commodities to be used or conquered rather than as human beings with rights and feelings. One young man expressed the extreme of the contemptful view of women when he confided to the female researcher.

> Rape is a man's right. If a woman doesn't want to give it, the man should take it. Women have no right to say no. Women are made to have sex. It's all they are good for. Some women would rather take a beating, but they always give in; it's what they are for.

This man murdered his victim because she wouldn't "give in."

Undoubtedly, some rapes, like some of all crimes, are idiopathic. However, it is not necessary to resort to pathological motives to account for all rape or other acts of sexual violence. Indeed, we find that men who rape have something to teach us about the cultural roots of sexual aggression. They force us to acknowledge that rape is more than an idiosyncratic act committed by a few "sick" men. Rather, rape can be viewed as the end point in a continuum of sexually aggressive behaviors that reward men and victimize women.[12] In the way that the motives for committing any criminal act can be rationally determined, reasons for rape can also be determined. Our data demonstrate that some men rape because they have learned that in this culture sexual violence is rewarding. Significantly, the overwhelming majority of these rapists indicated they never thought they would go to prison for what they did. Some did not fear imprisonment because they did not define their behavior as rape. Others knew that women frequently do not report rape and of those cases that are reported, conviction rates are low, and therefore they felt secure. These men perceived rape as a rewarding, low risk act. Understanding that otherwise normal men can and do rape is critical to the development of strategies for prevention.

We are left with the fact that all men do not rape. In view of the apparent rewards and cultural supports for rape, it is important to ask why some men do not rape. Hirschi (1969) makes a similar observation about delinquency. He argues that the key question is not "Why do they do it?" but rather "Why don't we do it?" (Hirschi, 1969:34). Likewise, we may be seeking an answer to the wrong question about sexual assault of women. Instead of asking men who rape "Why?", perhaps we should be asking men who don't "Why not?"

Notes

1. Despite the fact that these data have been in circulation for some time, prevention strategies continue to reflect the "lunatic fringe" image of rape. For example, security on college campuses, such as bright lighting and escort service, is designed to protect women against stranger rape while little or no attention is paid to the more frequent crime—acquaintance or date rape.

2. Broude and Green (1976) list a number of factors which limit the quantity and quality of cross-cultural data on rape. They point out that it was not customary in traditional ethnography to collect data on sexual attitudes and behavior. Further, where data do exist, they are often sketchy and vague. Despite this, the existence of rape-free societies has been established.

3. This factor distinguishes rape from other fictional depictions of violence. That is, in fictional murder, bombings, robbery, etc., victims are never portrayed as enjoying themselves. Such exhibits are reserved for pornographic displays of rape.

4. We also introduced a typology consisting of "admitters" (men who defined their behavior as rape) and "deniers" (men who admitted to sexual contact with the victim but did not define it as rape). In this paper we drop the distinction between admitters and deniers because it is not relevant to most of the discussion.

5. For a full discussion of the research methodology, sample, and validity, see Scully and Marolla (1984).

6. It should be noted that significant women, like rape victims, were also sometimes the targets of abuse and violence and possibly rape as well, although spousal rape is not recognized in Virginia law. In fact, these men were abusers. Fifty-five percent of rapists acknowledged that they hit their significant woman "at least once," and 20 percent admitted to inflicting physical injury. Given the tendency of these men to under-report the amount of violence in their crime, it is probably accurate to say, they under-reported their abuse of their significant women as well.

7. This man, as well as a number of others, either would not or could not bring himself to say the word "rape." Similarly, we also attempted to avoid using the word, a technique which seemed to facilitate communication.

8. When asked towards whom their sexual interests were primarily directed, 43 percent of rapists indicated a preference for women "significantly older than themselves." When those who responded, "women of any age" are added, 65 percent of rapists expressed sexual interest in women older than themselves.

9. Feminists as well as sociologists have tended to avoid the topic of interracial rape. Contributing to the avoidance is an awareness of historical and contemporary social injustice. For example, Davis (1981) points out that fictional rape of white women was used in the South as a post-slavery justification to lynch black men. And LaFree (1980a) has demonstrated that black men who assault white women continue to receive more serious sanctions within the criminal justice system when compared to other racial combinations of victim and assailant. While the silence has been defensible in light of historical racism,

continued avoidance of the topic discriminates against victims by eliminating the opportunity to investigate the impact of social factors on rape.

10. In our sample, 66 percent of black rapists reported their victim(s) were white, compared to two white rapists who reported raping black women. It is important to emphasize that because of the biases inherent in rape reporting and processing, and because of the limitations of our sample, these figures do not accurately reflect the actual racial composition of rapes committed in Virginia or elsewhere. Furthermore, since black men who assault white women receive more serious sanctions within the criminal justice system when compared to other racial combinations of victim and assailant (LaFree, 1980a), B/W rapists will be overrepresented within prison populations as well as overrepresented in any sample drawn from the population.

11. It is important to note that the gang rapes in this study were especially violent, resulting in physical injury, even death. One can only guess at the amount of hitchhike-abduction and "gang-date" rapes that are never reported or, if reported, are not processed because of the tendency to disbelieve the victims of such rapes unless extensive physical injury accompanies the crime.

12. It is interesting that men who verbally harass women on the street say they do so to alleviate boredom, to gain a sense of youthful camaraderie, and because it's fun (Benard and Schlaffer, 1984)—the same reason men who rape give for their behavior.

7

Considering Sex Offenders:
A Model of Addiction

Judith Lewis Herman

IN THE PAST DECADE, feminist consciousness-raising and political action have changed the definition of sexual violence from a private event to a public issue. The testimony of victims, first in consciousness-raising groups, then in public speakouts, and finally in formal survey research, has documented the high prevalence of all forms of sexual assault. The best currently available data indicate that for women, the risk of being raped is approximately one in four, and that for girls, the risk of sexual abuse by an adult is greater than one in three.[1] Boys appear to be at lower, but still substantial, risk for sexual assault by older boys or men.[2] The findings that most victims are female and that the vast majority of offenders are male have been reproduced in every major study. They are not artifacts of reporting, and in any case reporting is extremely low; probably less than 10 percent of all sexual assaults are reported to police, and less than 1 percent result in arrest, conviction, and imprisonment of the offender.[3]

In bringing sexual assault to public awareness, feminist thinkers have offered not only documentation but also a social analysis in which sexual assault is intrinsic to a system of male supremacy. Feminist theorists have called attention to the social legitimacy of many forms of sexual assault, including glorification of sexual violence in the dominant culture. If, as some feminists argue, the normative social definition of sexuality involves the erotization of male dominance and female submission, then the use of coercive means to achieve sexual conquest might represent a crude exaggeration of prevailing norms, but not a departure from them.[4] Moreover, feminist theorists have suggested that sexual assault serves a political function in preserving the system of male dominance through terror, thus benefiting all men whether or not they personally commit assaults.[5]

An alternative set of concepts for understanding sexual assault has been developed within the mental health professions, where traditionally, sexual assault has been understood as deviant and unusual. Explanations have focused on the psychopathology of the individual offender, his victim, or his family. Explanations based on a model of psychopathology suffer from a weak empirical base; however, unlike feminist explanations, they are consistent with conventional and widely shared beliefs. They appeal to the commonsense notion that men who commit sex crimes must be "sick." Moreover, they offer the possibility of understanding the enormous range and variability of behaviors included under the term "sexual assault."

Feminist Social Theory

There is an overwhelming amount of evidence to support a sociocultural analysis of sexual assault. In the past decade, feminist social theorists have generated a vast quantity of new research and have successfully predicted the salient factors associated with sexually assaultive behavior. Cross-cultural studies have shown that a high prevalence of rape is associated with male dominance. Rape is common in cultures where only a male creator/deity (rather than a couple or a female creator/deity) is worshipped, where warfare is glorified, where women hold little political or economic power, where the sexes are highly segregated, and where care of children is an inferior occupation.[6]

In our own culture, where all of these conditions obtain, rape-supportive attitudes and beliefs are widely held. Literature for a predominantly male mass audience—that is, pornography[7]—and the writings of lionized literary figures contain particularly articulate expressions of such attitudes.[8] The popularity of this literature offers indirect evidence of rape-supportive attitudes; more direct evidence is provided by attitudinal survey research.[9] Large-scale surveys conducted primarily with high school and college students indicate that a majority of students consider the use of force acceptable to achieve sexual relations in certain circumstances (e.g., if a woman is "getting a man sexually excited"). Though students of both sexes endorse these attitudes, males embrace them more heartily than females.[10] Moreover, a considerable minority of male students (35 percent) admit to some hypothetical likelihood of committing rape if guaranteed immunity from detection or punishment.[11]

A significant proportion of the male population not only endorses rape-supportive attitudes and finds the fantasy of rape agreeable, but also becomes sexually aroused by depictions of rape. The most widely appealing scenario appears to be one in which a female victim, after being subdued, becomes sexually excited by the rape. In one study, a majority of college males found this scenario as arousing as a portrayal of nonviolent, consensual intercourse, while a significant minority found the coercion scenario *more* arousing. It also appears to be the case that those who are aroused by depictions of sexual violence are more likely to hold rape-supportive attitudes and describe themselves as likely to commit rape.[12]

It is possible that the attitudes and patterns of sexual arousal documented in these studies are characteristic only of adolescents and that a mature male population might exhibit less hostility to women in general, and less enthusiasm for rape in particular. However, at the very least, these findings suggest that adolescent male subculture provides a powerful indoctrination in sexual violence. If the effects of this socialization were limited to attitudes and masturbatory fantasies, it might be possible to await the supposed maturation process with equanimity. However, there is strong reason to believe that adolescence is a critical period in the development of sexually assaultive behavior. Clinical studies of habitual sex offenders consistently document the occurrence of the first sexual assault in adolescence.[13] Studies of reported rape consistently indicate that about 25 percent of rapists are under eighteen.[14] Large-scale surveys of nonclinical populations indicate that before reaching adulthood, a significant number of young men have already committed a sexual assault. In a national probability survey of adolescents, Suzanne Ageton found that 1 percent of the boys acknowledged an attempted or completed rape in the previous year.[15] Extrapolating to the number of years at risk yields a rough estimate that between 1 and 7 percent of boys attempt or complete a sexual assault while still in their teens. Mary Koss, C. Gidycz, and N. Wisniewski, in a national survey of male college students (average age twenty-one), found that 4.4 percent acknowledged having committed rape in a dating situation, and another 3.3 percent acknowledged attempting rape. In the same study, Koss described a spectrum of sexual behaviors reported by the participants, ranging from unaggressive to highly aggressive. While the majority of young men (74.8 percent) reported that they have had exclusively consensual sexual relations, one in four (25.1 percent) acknowledged using some form of coercion to achieve sexual relations with an unwilling partner.[16] Similar results have been obtained in two other studies.[17]

Both the adolescent and college student studies demonstrate a strong association between social attitudes and sexually aggressive behavior. In Ageton's study, boys who committed sexual assaults were also likely to belong to a peer group that accepted all forms of interpersonal violence. Almost half of the young offenders told their peers about their exploits, and most of their friends approved of their behavior. Very few (14 percent) expressed any feelings of guilt. (By contrast, 40 percent of adolescent sexual assault victims felt guilty.)[18] In a study by Koss et al., the young men who acknowledged an attempted or completed rape were also those most likely to endorse rape-supportive attitudes.[19] A third study has demonstrated that young men who had committed sexual assaults differed markedly from their peers on a "rape arousal inventory," a self-report measure of arousal to a fantasized rape scenario.[20]

While measures of attitudes and arousal prove to be strongly correlated with actual assaultive behavior, standard psychological measures prove useless as predictors. No significant differences between the sexually assaultive men and their peers can be demonstrated on standard projective-test and screening measures of psychopathology. The young rapists in the college-student surveys were demonstrably sexist, but not demonstrably "sick."[21] Similarly, major ethnic or class differences have not so far been observed. The attitudes and behaviors of male dominance appear to vary surprisingly little across class and racial lines.

In summary, a large body of recent data describes a broad range of sexual attitudes and behavior, from nonaggressive to highly aggressive, among the American male population. This research demonstrates the interrelationship of rape-supportive attitudes, arousal to violent pornography, self-reported likelihood of committing a sexual assault, and actual assaultive behavior. These data suggest that attitudinal or arousal measures may be meaningful indicators in identifying those males likely to commit sexual assaults.

The major weakness of feminist sociocultural theory and research is that this work does not explain the wide variability among men whose attitudes and behavior would otherwise identify them as likely to rape. John Briere et al., for example, identify a population of college men who espouse rape-supportive beliefs, become aroused to rape scenarios, and describe themselves as likely to rape if promised immunity from punishment, but who do not acknowledge ever having committed a sexual assault. It is not clear whether these men simply have not yet raped and will probably do so in the future, whether they have in fact already committed assaults that they do not acknowledge, or whether some as yet unidentified inhibitory factors distinguish this apparently dangerous group from those who have already committed rape. Furthermore, within the group who already admit to sexual assaults, there is no present way to distinguish those who are unlikely to repeat their offense from those who have already developed or will develop a compulsive pattern of sexually assaultive behavior.

More specifically, in most of this research "sexual assault" is defined in terms that concentrate on middle range violent acts against the most socially legitimate victims: adolescent girls or adult women. Research on the range of attitudes and behaviors regarding assaults against men or children, or extremely violent sexual assaults against women, is currently at a very early stage of development. Indirect evidence from content and market analyses of pornographic literature indicates that there is a small but growing and economically significant consumer market for these types of materials.[22] Direct studies of sexual arousal to scenarios in which a male or child victim is shown or in which extreme violence is depicted have been limited to identified sex offender populations, where specific patterns of arousal have been associated with the offender's preferred mode of sexual aggression.[23] The degree to which such patterns of arousal are present in the general male population is as yet unknown. One study

indicates that pictures of girls begin to evoke detectable sexual arousal responses in a population of heterosexual men when the subjects in the photographs are six to eight years old.[24] Preliminary findings from a nationwide, random sample telephone survey indicate that 4–17 percent of the male population
acknowledge having molested a child.[25] Further research is clearly indicated in
this area.

Psychological Theories

Psychological study of sex offenders is hampered greatly by the difficulty of
identifying a representative population for study. Although victims of sex crimes
increasingly have been willing to testify about their experiences, offenders have
not. Most clinical studies to date focus on sex offenders whose crimes have been
reported to police, a group probably comprising less than 10 percent of all offenders; many studies are restricted to incarcerated offenders, a group representing perhaps 1 percent of the total. The processes of reporting, criminal prosecution, conviction, and sentencing shape the research population and limit the
general applicability of study findings. For example, sexual assaults are much
more likely to be reported to police when the offender is unknown to the victim,
when he belongs to a minority ethnic group, or when the assault is very violent.
Similar selection processes are likely to operate at each stage of criminal proceedings. Thus, the group of sex offenders who become ensnared in the criminal
justice system cannot be considered a representative population. Generaliza-
tions regarding the psychology of offenders based on clinical studies of reported
or convicted criminals are therefore highly questionable.

Psychological studies of convicted sex offenders have uniformly failed to
demonstrate any association between psychiatric diagnosis and sexually assaultive behavior. The great majority of convicted offenders do not suffer from psychiatric conditions (psychotic disorders or severe mental retardation) that might
be invoked to diminish criminal responsibility.[26] Alcoholism is frequently cited
as a contributing factor in sex offenses, not least by offenders themselves who, if
they admit their behavior, often attribute it to alcohol intoxication.[27] In several
studies, a significant proportion of convicted sex offenders have been observed
to be alcohol abusers: estimates range from 25 to 50 percent.[28] However, since
these studies generally lack appropriate comparison groups, it is not clear
whether this extent of alcohol abuse is characteristic of sex offenders specifically, of a general prison population, or of a demographically similar population
of men who have not committed crimes. Alcohol abuse is very common in the
general male population, with estimates ranging from 11 to 60 percent, depending on the definition employed.[29]

The role of alcohol can probably best be understood as a facilitating one: intoxication may aid in overcoming inhibitions for those already predisposed to

commit sexual assaults. Interestingly, it appears that a placebo may be as effective as alcohol in dissolving inhibitions. In one ingenious study, G. Terrence Wilson and David M. Lawson show that young men who had drunk alcohol, and those who had not but believed that they had, become equally aroused by violent rape pornography. Both groups were more aroused than a comparison group who believed they were sober.[30] Thus, the social meaning of drunkenness, with its implied exemption from ordinary behavioral limits, may play a more significant role than the pharmacological effects of alcohol in the behavior of an offender.

Though the majority of convicted sex offenders do not suffer from major psychiatric disorders, many do meet the diagnostic criteria for the so-called personality disorders. Sociopathic, schizoid, paranoid, and narcissistic personality disorders are all frequently described in criminally identified offenders.[31] All of these disorders involve a preoccupation with one's own fantasies, wishes, and needs, a lack of empathy for others, and a desire to control and dominate others rather than to engage in mutual relationships. As in the case of alcoholism, it is unclear whether such disorders are any more common in convicted sex offenders than in other prisoners: the one adequately controlled study in the literature indicates that they are not.[32] Moreover, there is no evidence whatsoever that these personality disorders are more common in an undetected offender population than they are in the male population at large.

The most striking characteristic of sex offenders, from a diagnostic standpoint, is their apparent normality. Most do not qualify for any psychiatric diagnosis.[33] One psychiatrist who has extensive experience in treating undetected (that is, unreported) offenders in the community characterizes them in these words: "These paraphiliacs are not strange people. They are people who have one slice of their behavior that is very disruptive to them and to others; behavior they cannot control. But the other aspects of their lives can be pretty stable. We have executives, computer operators, insurance salesmen, college students, and people in a variety of occupations in our program. They are just like everyone else, except they cannot control one aspect of their behavior."[34]

Another therapist with extensive experience treating offenders describes her perception of them as follows: "I look at the case file and then I look at the offender and the two don't connect. The offenders are often bright, attractive, they take care of themselves, they have lots of social skills, and they can appear very competent or they can appear pathetic and hurt. My first reaction on meeting a new offender is always "there must be some mistake. He couldn't have done what his record says he did."[35]

Failing to find any readily apparent mental disorder that characterizes sex offenders, psychological investigators have increasingly focused on aspects of their developmental histories that might offer clues to understanding their behavior. The hypothesis most frequently entertained is that sex offenders were themselves sexually victimized in childhood or adolescence. The sexual offense is thus a reenactment of the trauma or an attempt to overcome it through the mechanism of "identification with the aggressor." Proponents of this theory often invoke the concept of a "cycle of abuse," or of "generational transmission," whereby the sexually victimized children of one generation become the victimizers of the next.

The "cycle of abuse" concept is extremely popular. It is commonly invoked to explain most crimes of violence occurring in the private sphere, such as wife-beating and child abuse. It is generally accepted for several reasons: first, most experienced clinicians have seen cases that do indeed illustrate a multigenerational pattern of violence and abuse. These are among the most difficult, complex, and memorable cases that clinicians encounter. Second, the concept is intellectually satisfying: it is congruent with well-documented clinical observations of reenactment of trauma and heightened aggression in abused children.[36] These short-term observations are simply projected unmodified into the future and the transformation of victim to offender is readily imaginable. Third, the concept is emotionally satisfying: it permits clinicians to empathize with offenders and also offers the comforting assurance that their behavior is an understandable result of a pathological history. Finally, such a concept is politically advantageous for the mental health professions. Expenditures for treatment of offenders are more easily justified to a punitive and economy-minded public if the mental health professions can claim that treatment will interrupt the cycle of abuse and prevent the development of the next generation of offenders.

Indeed, the only serious problem with the "cycle of abuse" concept is its lack of empirical validity.[37] When the theory is applied to sexual assault, its most glaring weakness is its inability to explain the virtual male monopoly on this type of behavior. Since girls are sexually victimized at least twice or three times more commonly than boys, this theory would predict a female rather than a male majority of sex offenders. Unable to account for this contradiction, proponents of the cycle of abuse theory are sometimes reduced to denying reality: it is among adherents of this theory that one still encounters assertions that large undetected reserves of female offenders are yet to be discovered.[38]

More commonly, proponents implicitly recognize the effects of profound gender differences in the socialization of sex and aggression, differences that may in fact be amplified by the effects of victimization.[39] Thus modified, the cycle of abuse concept would predict that sexually abused boys grow up to be sex offenders, and abused girls grow up to be their wives, girlfriends, and victims.

No long-term study following abused children into adulthood has ever been done. Nor would it be possible, from an ethical standpoint, to do such a study without intervening to stop the abuse. Therefore, there is no way presently to document what proportion of abused children grow up to become offenders,

and what proportion do not, or to compare their fates with those of children who were never abused. The best available evidence documenting a connection between childhood abuse and sexually assaultive behavior comes from retrospective studies of identified sex offenders. Most of these studies are unrepresentative of the general (unreported) offender population. Moreover, most lack appropriate comparison groups, and many are vague in their definition of childhood sexual abuse. Nicholas Groth, for example, in a widely quoted study, defines sexual abuse as "any sexual activity witnessed and/or experienced that is emotionally upsetting or disturbing."[40] Few people are fortunate enough to reach adulthood without being upset by a sexual experience. Thus, the validity of the findings in such studies seems highly questionable.

Despite the general weakness of the cycle of abuse concept, some points of consensus do emerge from this work. Estimates of the correlation between an abuse history and sexually assaultive behavior vary widely depending on the type of population studied: the more deviant the population, the greater the likelihood that prior abuse histories will be discovered. For example, two community-based programs for adolescent offenders report that their patients do not appear to have abuse histories significantly more often than the general population.[41] By contrast, a maximum security, "end of the road" institution for very violent juvenile offenders reports that 100 percent of their inmates have been sexually assaulted.[42] In the largest available studies of criminally and medically identified offender populations, the figure seems to hover between 25 and 40 percent.[43] Thus many offenders do seem to have an abuse history, but apparently the majority do not.

Histories of abuse do appear to be particularly common in pedophiles who prefer boy victims. The members of this group have a number of characteristics that distinguish them from other sex offenders. Their deviant behavior often has an early onset, they may lack any significant interest in consenting sexual relations with adults (this is the group that Groth describes as "fixated" offenders),[44] their behavior is often extremely compulsive and resistant to treatment,[45] and they tend to have many victims. In one series, a group of 146 homosexual pedophiles at large in the community had committed an average of 279 assaults *each*.[46] Impressionistic reports from several treatment programs indicate that while psychiatric diagnoses of any kind are uncommon in this group, sexual abuse histories are particularly common, ranging from 40 to 60 percent.[47] In one outpatient treatment program, the staff estimated that 55 percent of the child molesters had been victimized, most commonly by male babysitters. They further observed that young men who raped women did not appear to have unusually frequent abuse histories, but that young men who raped men were almost uniformly victims of sexual abuse.[48] Taken together, these data suggest the possibility that childhood sexual trauma in boys may be a particularly significant risk factor for the development of sexually abusive behavior *directed at males*. The cycle of abuse theory may turn out to have some prediction power for this population.

At best, however, if the cycle of abuse theory is fully borne out by future research, it can only demonstrate that boyhood sexual victimization is one among many factors that increase the risk for the later development of sexually abusive behavior. It is highly unlikely that the concept will prove applicable to the majority of sex offenders. At this point, based on the best available research data, we have to assume that most sexually abused boys do not become sex offenders, and that most offenders themselves were not abused as boys.

Failing to demonstrate obvious psychopathology or a pathogenic history in most offenders, many clinicians have moved away from the unrewarding and difficult study of the offender himself in order to concentrate on the more accessible aspects of his family and social environment. In many psychopathological explanations of the sex offender's behavior, the offender himself tends to disappear, while attributes of his parents, wife, or victim are cited.[49] Father-daughter incest, for example, is frequently described as a symptom of a dysfunctional family system, in which all family members are implicated.[50] The father's sexual exploitation of his daughter is explained on the basis of situational stresses, sexual deprivation, or marital conflict. The mother's role is often described as pivotal: she is held responsible for creating a "role reversal" with her daughter and for driving her husband to seek gratification elsewhere by withholding sex and nurturance.[51] The compulsive quality of the incestuous father's sexual interest in children is implicitly ignored or explicitly denied—this in spite of the fact that numerous studies indicate that one-third to one-half of incestuous fathers repeat their offenses with more than one child.[52] Direct behavioral studies of such fathers, however, indicate that their sexual preoccupation with children is not necessarily confined to the immediate family situation and, by implication, is likely to persist regardless of changes in family structure.[53]

If the offender does not disappear entirely in psychopathological formulations, his sexual offense often does. Most psychodynamic explanations tend to minimize the sexual component of the offender's behavior and to reinterpret the assault as an ineffectual attempt to meet ordinary human needs. This renders the behavior more comprehensible (and, presumably, more accessible to psychotherapy) and the offender more sympathetic. The victimizer becomes a victim, no longer an object of fear but of pity. Groth, for example, describes a type of "power rapist" who commits his crimes "in an effort to combat deep-seated feelings of insecurity and vulnerability." The offense is described as an expression of the offender's wishes for "virility, mastery, and dominance." Groth describes the rapist as a man who "does not have his life under control and experiences adult life demands and responsibilities as overwhelming," and who "finds adult sexuality threatening for it confronts him with his unadmitted doubts about his masculine adequacy."[54] Elsewhere, Groth describes the child molester in similar terms: "an immature individual whose pedophilic behavior serves to compensate for his relative helplessness in meeting adult bio-psycho-social life demands. ... Through sexual involvement with a child, the offender attempts to fulfill his psychological needs for recognition, acceptance, validation, affiliation, mastery, and control."[55] Emphasizing these "needs" for power and dominance, Groth minimizes the sexual motivation for the offenses, sometimes calling them "pseudo-sexual acts." The compulsive, repetitive quality of the sexual assaults is attributed not to the fact that they are pleasurable, but to the fact that they are emotionally disappointing. This, in spite of considerable testimony from rapists and other offenders that the sexual assault often produces an intense "high."[56]

The effect of this euphemistic reformulation of the offender's behavior is to detoxify it, to make it more acceptable. The offender's craving for sexual domination is reinterpreted as a longing for human intimacy. His wish to control others is reinterpreted as an ordinary masculine need for "mastery." Since normative concepts of manhood do to some extent include the domination of women and children, the offender's desire to share in adult male prerogatives is validated; his choice of means is considered unfortunate. Since the gratification obtained from the sexual assault itself is minimized, this sort of explanation offers the promise that the assaultive behavior will be readily given up if the offender can learn other, more socially acceptable ways of achieving "masculine adequacy."

Such psychodynamic formulations do make it possible to empathize with the offender, a prerequisite for any rehabilitative effort, and they do offer the hope that psychological treatment may be effective. The danger in these formulations, however, is inextricable from their advantages. In attempting to establish an empathic connection with the offender, the would-be therapist runs the risk of credulously accepting the offender's rationalizations for his crimes (as well as supplying him with new ones). Moreover, such formulations allow attention to be diverted from the troubling sexual offense to other problems more amenable to ordinary psychotherapy.

Treatment models based on these psychodynamic concepts tend to focus on the offender's general social attitudes and relationships or on his own experiences as a victim, but not on the concrete details of his sexual fantasies and behavior. For example, a prison-based program described by Groth has proliferated into ten discussion-group components including such topics as sex education, relationships to women, management of anger, stress reduction, and communication skills, but it has no method for monitoring the offender's continued arousal to fantasies of sexual assault.[57] Another outpatient treatment program for incest offenders developed by a nationally famous sex therapist includes social skills training, stress management, couple therapy, sex therapy, and family therapy, but again, no particular focus on the offender's sexual desire for children. The patient is required to sign a contract stating that he will not reoffend while in treatment; but it is not clear how compliance with this "contract" is monitored or enforced, other than by asking the offender to report on himself.[58]

The validity of psychodynamic formulations of sexual assault, and the treatment models generated from them, are not merely matters of academic interest. There are serious risks in having overconfident expectations of the efficacy of treatment. Since no long-term follow-up studies of treatment have been done, and since the difficulties in carrying out such studies are great, most treatment programs rely on self-evaluation of their own effectiveness. The greater the effort invested in offender treatment, the greater the motivation of the treating professionals to believe in the success of treatment and to overlook evidence to the contrary. When a treatment program minimizes the importance of the actual sexual behavior and does not provide any concrete method for monitoring it, failures are likely to go unrecognized, sometimes with disastrous consequences. In one extreme documented case, a young man mandated to psychiatric treatment after committing a rape at age fourteen subsequently committed six additional rapes and five rape-murders *while in treatment.* His psychiatrist was entirely unaware of these crimes and could apparently detect no clues to their occurrence in the material offered by the patient in his treatment sessions.[59]

Such dramatic treatment failures may, in fact, be unusual, but disasters of this kind serve as reminders that our current understanding of the psychology of sex offenders is very crude, any treatment must be considered entirely experimental, and claims for therapeutic success should be offered with great caution and received with healthy skepticism.

A Model of Addiction

An incestuous father writes: "Once I started it continued, there was no stopping point for me. I told myself it would pass, but it did not, and as my daughters grew and became women I would fondle and touch them. I became addicted to their favors, and with addiction they lost a father. It was just terrible."[60] Clinicians who work closely with sex offenders often describe them as addicts. As one author puts it: "We suggest that you consider sexual deviants as special types of junkies. Self-control will in every case be a full-time job, every waking hour for the rest of their lives."[61]

Though the analogy of addiction is commonly invoked by offenders and clinicians alike, the implications of an addiction model are rarely elaborated, either in the feminist social analysis of sexual violence or in the psychological literature on offenders. Yet the concept of addiction offers a point of intersection for the observations developed by psychologists and those of social theorists. A model of addiction also offers clear guidelines for the development of offender treatment programs, for preventive educational work, and for legal and regulatory strategies.

It is known that sociocultural factors play a major role in creating a climate of risk for addiction. Alcoholism, for example, flourishes in cultures that do not allow children to learn safe drinking practices (i.e., moderate alcohol consumption integrated with social and family life), and that glorify or excuse adult drunkenness.[62] By analogy, compulsive, exploitative sexual behavior may be fostered in cultures that do not permit children to learn safely about sex, and that glorify or excuse sexual violence. American culture, in which sex education for children is generally lacking and in which sexual violence is often admired, would qualify as a high-risk culture. Some subcultures might be particularly likely to produce sex offenders if childhood sexual curiosity is severely punished or if high levels of interpersonal violence are tolerated. This would explain the frequent presence of extreme religious fundamentalism and rigidly punitive sexual attitudes in the backgrounds of sex offenders.[63] Similarly, this would explain the findings that associate membership in a violent peer group with commission of sexual assaults in adolescence.[64]

The virtual male monopoly on sexually assaultive behavior is also congruent with a model of addiction. In most, if not all, compulsive antisocial behaviors (alcoholism, drug dependency, gambling), men consistently outnumber women by a ratio of at least three to one.[65] The greater social latitude and tolerance accorded to antisocial behavior in males undoubtedly fosters addictions. Another contributing factor may be the impoverishment in male development of the emotional resources of intimacy and interdependence. Lacking these resources, men may be more susceptible to developing dependence on sources of gratification that do not require a mutual relationship with a human being: the bottle, the needle, or the powerless, dehumanized sexual object.[66]

The concept of addiction is also useful in identifying a spectrum of behaviors within a population at risk. In our culture, for example, although social exposure to alcohol is almost universal, the range of drinking behavior is very broad, encompassing abstainers, social drinkers, and alcohol abusers. The line of demarcation between heavy social drinking and alcohol abuse is unclear, and drinking patterns vary even among problem drinkers. Alcohol abuse may be situational, appearing only transiently in response to particular cultural demands (adolescent initiation rituals, for example); it may be episodic, as in the case of "binge" drinkers; or it may become compulsive and relentlessly progressive at any time in the life cycle, from adolescence onward.

A similar spectrum of behaviors exists in the general population with regard to sexual assault. As Koss, Gidycz, and Wisniewski demonstrated in their college student survey, a small group of young men abstained from sexual relations, the majority engaged in socialized, consensual relations, and a considerable minority engaged in coercive or frankly violent sexual activities. The line of demarcation between socially acceptable and abusive sexual behavior was unclear in the minds of their informants: for example, a considerable number of the young men who had achieved sexual relations by force or threat of force did not label their behavior as rape, nor did many of their victims.[67]

Not all offenders develop an addictive pattern of sexually coercive behavior (nor, conversely, is all addictive sexual behavior criminal or coercive). An addiction model of sexual assault would predict a range of behaviors from the opportunistic to the highly compulsive. Some offenders might commit assaults only in response to peer pressure in a male-bonding situation where the social rules permit or encourage such behavior (e.g., a fraternity party or military adventure); others might develop a "binge" pattern of episodic assaults; and a third group might develop a repetitive or escalating pattern of sexual violence relatively uninfluenced by the social setting. This range of behaviors is evident in the clinical literature.[68]

Both alcohol abusers and sex offenders rarely run afoul of the law. The harmful effects of a compulsive drinking pattern are generally felt first by the drinker's family, detected somewhat later at his workplace, and even later by his physician. An arrest for an alcohol-related offense (most commonly driving while intoxicated) seldom occurs until the alcoholism is fairly advanced and the alcoholic has been driving drunk for a considerable period of time. Similarly, most sex offenders who do get arrested have already developed a well-established compulsive pattern. Because they are rarely detected until they have reached an advanced stage of addiction, we know very little about the early and middle stages in the development of the pattern of sexual assault. Retrospective reconstructions by apprehended offenders commonly reveal histories of sexual offenses beginning in adolescence, or even before puberty.[69] The existing clinical data suggest that early onset of abusive behavior indicates a syndrome that is extremely tenacious and resistant to change, while later onset may be associated with a more episodic course.[70] Unfortunately, assaults committed by juveniles are often cavalierly dismissed either as adolescent experimentation (in the case of child molestation, date rape, or gang rape), or insignificant nuisance activities (in the case of peeping, exhibitionism, obscene phone-calling, or fetishism). Early signs of an addictive (that is, repetitive and progressive) process are generally denied or overlooked under the assumption that these behaviors will be outgrown.

Because so little attention has been paid to the early stages of compulsive sexual behavior, at present we have no reliable criteria for distinguishing between men who commit situational sex crimes, which are truly unlikely to be repeated, and men who are likely to develop a repetitive pattern of sexual assault. Current clinical attempts to codify recidivism risk in young offenders focus mainly on assessing the degree to which clear symptoms of compulsive behavior are already apparent.[71]

Sex offenders subjectively describe a cyclical pattern of altered mood and behavior that appears relatively impervious to conscious control. Environmental or internal stimuli may trigger sexual fantasies that develop into a compelling craving to carry out the fantasied act. A trance-like excitement builds, heightened by risk and danger as the offender stalks and secures access to his victim. An intense "high" during anticipation and completion of the act may be followed by fear, disgust, depression, and remorse, coupled with a short-lived resolve never to repeat the act. This dysphoria is relieved by increasing preoccupation with sexual fantasies, and the cycle is repeated. The behavior develops a repetitive, compulsive quality which is only transiently interrupted by internal inhibitions. Some offenders describe a progressive pattern in which increasingly risky or violent assaults are required to produce the desired "high." In the words of one child molester, "It's like drugs. After you lose the effect of one drug, you go on to a different one. If I hadn't been in this program ... I'm pretty sure I would have gone up to rape."[72]

The offender clearly does retain some capacity for self-control, but he uses it only when he perceives that external controls are present, in order to avoid detection or other adverse consequences to himself. It is this partial loss of internal control that makes the offender so confusing and difficult to understand. Is he in control of his behavior or is he not? Is his a moral or a medical problem? Does he lack will power or is he suffering from a "disease"? Such questions have been debated about alcoholics and other addicts in every historical epoch, without clear resolution or the development of a public consensus.[73]

Behavioral as well as subjective descriptions of sex offenders suggest that they share many of the characteristics of alcoholics or other addicts. The offender behaves as though his primary attachment is to the mood-altering addictive activity. All other relationships are sacrificed or manipulated in the service of this activity. An elaborate defensive structure develops, the purpose of which is the protection and preservation of the addiction.[74] Denial is the primary defensive mode employed, but in addition, an extensive body of paranoid defenses and rationalizations may be developed. If the addict acknowledges his behavior at all, he generally blames other people for it. An unhappy childhood, stormy marriage, or frustrating job provides the justification and the excuse for the addiction. The rapist's cry and the alcoholic's are one and the same: "She drove me to it!"[75]

In the case of alcoholism, these rationalizations no longer have credibility in the professional literature. Early childhood trauma, marital conflict, depression, and situational stress were once thought to be causative factors in the genesis of alcoholism. With the advent of more sophisticated research, however, such notions have been discredited. The inadequacies and personality defects commonly observed in alcoholics are now understood to be a result of addiction rather than their cause. Whatever the alcoholic's history or preexisting personality structure may have been, once he becomes addicted he develops a personality disorder and generally recalls his childhood as miserable. Furthermore, alcohol abuse is likely to lead to depression, marital dissatisfaction, and situational stresses.[76] As in the case of now discredited theories of the etiology of alcoholism, psychodynamic formulations of the psychology of sex offenders are unlikely to be borne out by well-designed research in the general population of offenders.

The concept of sexual assault as a potentially addictive behavior has major implications for treatment and social rehabilitation of offenders. The first implication is that at present, the commission of one sexual assault cannot be dismissed as "adolescent curiosity" or any other benign, self-correcting problem. In the absence of well-documented criteria for distinguishing situational offenders from early addicts, it would seem prudent to consider all offenders potential addicts.

The second implication is that when dealing with a sex offender, one cannot assume that he has any reliable internal motivation for change. The offender may have lost effective control of his behavior, though he has not lost moral or legal responsibility for it. External motivation for change must therefore be provided. Legal sanctions and careful, sustained supervision (e.g., intensive probation or parole, and in some cases incarceration) are the appropriate source of external motivation. Professionals who attempt treatment must ally and cooperate with law-enforcement authorities and obtain a waiver of confidentiality from the patient. Though such measures may seem punitive or antitherapeutic, they are both therapeutic and necessary when a patient represents a clear danger to himself or others. Sex offenders are dangerous. They cannot be treated or rehabilitated unless their behavior is effectively controlled.

The third implication is that the primary focus of any therapeutic effort must be on changing the addictive behavior itself. For alcoholics, this means that the central focus of treatment is on drinking. For sex offenders, this means that treatment must focus in concrete detail on the unacceptable sexual behavior. The offender's patterns of sexual fantasy and arousal, his modus operandi for securing access to his victims and evading detection, his preferred sexual activities, and his system of excuses and rationalizations must be painstakingly documented, and changes must be closely monitored. The offending sexual behaviors cannot be wished away by describing them as attempts to meet nonsexual "needs" for mastery or nurturance. Some experienced therapists require that a statement from the victim describing the offender's crime and its impact on her life be made available in the record before any form of treatment is attempted. Frequent review of this document is necessary to counteract the tendencies toward denial and minimization of the offense which both patient and therapist may share.

The minimum components of a potentially successful therapeutic program for sex offenders would include a behavior modification component directly focused on the unacceptable sexual activities, a reliable method of monitoring the offender's continuing interest in sexual assault independent of his own self-report, and a supervision structure that reliably and swiftly provides sanctions for repeated offenses. Various operant conditioning methods have been shown to be at least transiently effective in changing patterns of sexual arousal,[77] and the penile strain-gauge, used for measuring arousal to sexual stimuli, has shown promise as a monitoring device.[78] Further research is needed to develop the most effective and practical methods of behavior modification. Some programs, for example, employ the technique of masturbatory satiation, encouraging repetitions of deviant fantasies until the patient is thoroughly bored with them,[79] while other programs forbid pornography, discourage masturbation, and rely mainly on aversive conditioning techniques.[80] The relative value of these different approaches has not been systematically evaluated.

Psychopharmacologic methods have also been used in an attempt to change addictive behavior and motivation. For example, some alcoholism programs rely heavily on daily administration of disulfiram, a medication that changes the patient's metabolism so that ingestion of alcohol produces extremely unpleasant symptoms. In the treatment of sex offenders, antiandrogenic hormones have been used experimentally to decrease sexual arousal. The particular object of the offender's desire is unchanged, but the intensity of the desire is reportedly weakened.[81] Of course, the patient's motivation to comply with treatment cannot be taken for granted. Alcoholics who relapse frequently discontinue their daily dose of disulfiram; similarly, recidivist sex offenders may discontinue their medroxyprogesterone. An effective pharmacologic agent alone does not constitute a treatment program.

The treatment of addiction begins with a focus on the negative consequences of the behavior, but it does not end there. An addicted person is not likely to give up the central gratification of his life in response to negative sanctions only. Strong positive inducements must be offered as well. Studying the recovery process in alcoholics and heroin addicts, George Vaillant identified four factors associated with achievement of stable abstinence. The first is a constant reminder of the negative consequences of the addiction. The remaining three are a substitute addiction, a new source of hope and self-esteem, and social support.[82]

Highly structured group treatment and self-help programs appear to be the most successful approach to the social rehabilitation of addicts, including sex offenders. A group of peers who are reliably available on demand and who are committed to the goal of recovery through abstinence fulfills all four of these criteria. A constant reminder of the negative consequences of addiction is found in the testimony of group members; a substitute addiction and social support are available in the activities of the group itself; a new source of hope is provided by the testimony of group members who have changed their lives; and a new source of self-esteem is provided by the structure of a program which requires acknowledgment of the harm done but offers an opportunity for restitution and service to others.

Some form of structured group process has evolved in almost every existing treatment program for sex offenders.[83] Most programs also explicitly or implicitly define stages of recovery analogous to the twelve steps of Alcoholics Anonymous (AA).[84] In particular, the first, fifth, ninth, and twelfth steps defined by AA seem to have particular relevance for sex offenders. The first step involves acknowledgment of powerlessness over the addiction. For the sex offender, this means the breaking of secrecy, the admission of previously denied or rationalized behavior, and the acceptance of the need for others in order to control it. The fifth step, which follows a searching self-examination, involves admission "to God, to ourselves, and to another human being the exact nature of our wrongs." For sex offenders, this means full disclosure of the number and type of assaults committed and a beginning recognition of the harm done to others. The ninth step involves making amends to the persons who have been harmed. For sex offenders, this step often involves a ritualized apology to the victim, especially if she is a family member or otherwise involved in an ongoing relationship with the offender.[85]

Finally, the twelfth step involves the validation of recovery by sharing the experience in some public forum. It is this mobilization of altruism that provides for the offender the possibility of restored self-esteem and social rehabilitation. Only when his experience is offered in service to others can his crime be expiated. Grass roots treatment programs for offenders have often developed creative ways of involving offenders in public service. In one program, incarcerated offenders staff a well-publicized "hotline," counseling men who feel tempted to commit sexual assaults.[86] In another, offenders in outpatient treatment consent to have their group therapy observed by professionals in training. The group meetings take place in a courtroom, and the observers sit in the jury box.[87] In another outpatient program, treatment is not completed until the offender has participated in a public education forum or helped to orient a new patient just entering the program.[88] All of these can be considered variants of the twelfth step of AA: "Having had a spiritual awakening as a result of these steps, we tried to carry the message to others."

The use of religious terminology in descriptions of the recovery process is not coincidental. Relinquishing an addiction represents a profound psychological change, analogous to religious conversion. When the addiction has resulted in the commission of crimes, the destruction of social bonds is so extensive that sometimes a religious framework may offer the only hope of reconnection. This is not to say that religious conversion guarantees recovery (a sex offender who announces that he has been "born again" is not thereby cured), but rather that something analogous may be an important part of the recovery process. That such conversions are rare and difficult to predict is a reminder that any claims for therapeutic success with sex offenders should be offered with great modesty.

A final implication of the addiction model for treatment of sex offenders involves the prognosis for rehabilitation. Significant recovery from any addiction takes time. Addiction interferes with normal maturation and destroys social relationships. These problems remain even after the compulsive behavior is given up. Indeed, it is only after reliable limits have been placed on the addictive behavior that the addict faces the degree to which his abilities and his relationships with others have deteriorated. In recovery from alcoholism, for example, full rehabilitation (i.e., achievement of a level of functioning equal to the best level attained prior to the onset of the addiction), has been shown to require at least three years of sustained abstinence.[89] A similar time frame should be anticipated for recovery even with cooperative, well-motivated sex offenders. Current claims of successful treatment outcome after twelve weeks[90] or six months[91] are unlikely to be borne out with careful follow-up.

Even after the achievement of full recovery, some ongoing maintenance activity may be required indefinitely to prevent relapse.[92] Once an addiction has become established, it must be considered a lifelong process. An addict may achieve abstinence; he does not achieve cure. In the words of one experienced therapist:

> We only talk about *controlling* sexual deviancies, about *reducing* them to minimal levels. Our long-range goal is to eliminate them, but we don't expect realistically to meet that goal. ... The closest parallel—it is a good, but not a 100 percent analogy—is alcoholism. You don't talk about "ex-alcoholics," because if someone describes himself as an ex-alcoholic you are going to worry about him. And we do not talk about ex–sex offenders. We talk about alcoholics who don't drink any more—sober alcoholics. And we talk about sex offenders who do not offend any more. The conditioning patterns are ingrained in adult clients. We try to educate them to be aware of that, that it is really going to be a lifelong process. If someone in our program tells us "I'll never do it again," we say, "Hey, you are not ready to leave this program."[93]

Viewing sexual assault as a potentially addicting behavior means coming to terms with the fact that the problem is complex and tenacious, and that promises of rapid solution are not likely to be fulfilled. Treatment and rehabilitation of offenders is an ambitious undertaking, requiring constancy of purpose and sustained mobilization of social resources on a large scale. The required degree of cooperation between the criminal justice and mental health systems has rarely been achieved, even for short periods of time. Yet nothing less is likely to be at all effective.

If the implications for treatment are somewhat discouraging, the addiction concept offers considerable hope for the efficacy of preventive measures. Because patterns of addiction are so highly sensitive to social risk factors, preventive intervention aimed at decreasing known risk factors or at protecting populations known to be at high risk should result in a significant lowering of the rate of sexual assault.

In practical terms, this means that sex education for all children remains a valuable aspect of primary prevention. However, the existing sex-education establishment, which generally advocates a male-oriented, libertarian position, cannot be counted on to implement an acceptable program. Ideally, educational efforts must combine full presentation of accurate information, respect for individual privacy and choice, and an articulated vision of socially responsible conduct. Issues of power and exploitation must be addressed explicitly. Boys and young men might be considered a priority for preventive work, especially where they are organized in groups that foster traditional sexist and rape-supportive attitudes. Target populations might include, for example, athletic teams, college fraternities, and the military. Primary prevention work with groups at high risk for victimization or for offending behavior may also result in early disclosure of sexual assaults that have already occurred, increasing the possibility for early intervention and treatment of both victim and offender.

Vigorous enforcement of existing criminal laws prohibiting sexual assault might also be expected to have some preventive effect, since both compulsive and opportunistic offenders are keenly sensitive to external controls. The reforms in rape legislation and women's presence in the criminal justice system should result in an increased willingness to hold offenders publicly accountable for their crimes. Prosecution is particularly important in cases where traditional cultural standards legitimate and condone sexual assault (for example, in marital or date rape or the rape of prostitutes). In these cases, prosecution serves an educational function, exposing and challenging traditional rape-supportive attitudes.

Further research is required to identify those factors which seem to protect high-risk boys and men from becoming offenders and to distinguish one-time offenders from those who go on to develop an habitual pattern of sexual assault. For instance, the influence of pornography in consolidating sexual fantasy and violent behavior is not yet fully understood. If pornography is understood to be a definitive ideological expression of male supremacy and it is shown to play a role in conditioning masturbatory fantasy and sexual response, then a link between violent pornography and sexual violence becomes apparent.[94] Indeed, recent research indicates that repeated exposure to violent pornography amplifies sexist and rape-supportive attitudes in men (not in women). Of great concern is the finding that the most pronounced effects of violent pornography are seen in men who already have highly adversarial and callous attitudes toward women and admit to a high likelihood of committing rape.[95]

The effect of the outcome of the first assault on further assaults is another topic that merits attention: Judith Becker, for example, believes that an addictive pattern is powerfully reinforced when the first assault meets with no adverse consequences.[96] Public exposure of the attacker may prove to be an important deterrent to the commission of repeated crimes. The goal of research in this area should be the identification of a group of "early warning signals" and "early intervention strategies" for use in widespread public prevention campaigns.

Social Consensus and Change

For the past hundred years and more, feminist thinkers and organizers have struggled with the problem of addiction. Though most addicts have been men, women and children have suffered the consequences of their addictions. One hundred years ago, the formation of the Women's Christian Temperance Union organized the entrance of women into the political arena on an unprecedented scale. The cause of temperance was strongly linked to other progressive social reforms, most particularly to women's suffrage. The women of the temperance movement saw the male saloon culture as the destroyer of home and family, and attributed male violence against women and children to the corrupting effects of the traffic in alcohol. Their attack on intemperance was also an attack on the male attitude of privilege and entitlement of antisocial behavior.[97] The political forces arrayed against the temperance movement were essentially those who advocated male supremacy and unrestricted individualism both in social conduct and in economic life.[98]

The organized efforts of the first wave of feminism ultimately resulted in the passage of two constitutional amendments, one year apart. The nineteenth amendment, passed in 1920, enfranchised women as citizens; the eighteenth amendment, passed in 1919, prohibited the manufacture or sale of alcohol.

In the absence of a well-established social consensus against drinking, Prohibition proved legally unenforceable and was repealed after little more than a decade. A large proportion of the population continued to drink in defiance of the law. Rather than eliminating the traffic in alcohol, prohibition fostered the development of a powerful, criminally organized alcohol industry, which was passively tolerated by law enforcement officials (when they did not actively collude in it).

Because of the ultimate failure (and resultant disrepute) of the prohibitionist legal strategy, the social and cultural successes of the temperance movement have often been overlooked. Alcohol production and consumption actually *were* reduced during Prohibition,[99] and deaths from complications of alcoholism also declined.[100] Moreover, following repeal, alcohol consumption increased slowly but has never returned to the very high levels that preceded the temperance movement.[101] The legalized alcohol industry that emerged after repeal did submit to a greater degree of regulation, including partial advertising censorship and restrictions on distribution of alcohol to minors. The industry also accepted token responsibility for public education on responsible drinking and for alcoholism research and treatment. The temperance movement also permanently influenced public attitudes about drinking to some degree. While the majority consensus today rejects governmental suppression of alcohol, it does generally support some restrictions in recognition of alcohol's potential dangerousness to public health and social order. Finally, the temperance movement in many stages of its history was instrumental in organizing self-help and medical treatment for alcoholism.

The existence of a national and international traffic in women and children as sexual objects is well documented by feminist writers both in the past and in the present.[102] Just as heroin addicts have their pushers, sexual addicts have their pornographers, pimps, and sex rings. At present, the industry of sexual exploitation has both a nominally criminalized component (prostitution, child sex rings, child and hard-core pornography) and a "legitimate" component (soft-core pornography, men's magazines). Both the legal and illegal components of the industry operate with little social restriction and increasing audacity. The pornography industry, in particular, has significantly increased its portrayal of explicitly violent sexual assault in the past decade.[103] Such depictions are also increasingly common in the general mass media and advertising. An effective strategy for eliminating sexual violence thus must include not only a strategy for early identification, control, and treatment of offenders, not only a strategy for preventive education, but also a strategy for engagement with the organized sex industry. The experience of the temperance movement would suggest that abolition of the industry in its entirety is a goal that must await completion of a feminist revolution. In a culture where individual liberty is valued far more than social responsibility, some form of the sex and pornography industry is likely to be tolerated (even by puritanical conservatives, and even by liberal feminists), just as other addiction industries that injure the public health are tolerated (tobacco subsidized as well as legalized, alcohol legalized, and narcotics largely under prohibition).

Within the scope of a short-term reform strategy, the greatest hope for development of a public regulatory consensus may be found on the issue of sexual violence. The recent attempt legally to redefine pornography as the subordination of women and to seek civil rather than criminal remedies represents an important conceptual advance.[104] Direct action and boycott strategies, reminiscent of the "women's crusade" against saloons a century ago, have also proven effective against pornographers and advertisers when their materials include blatant sexual violence.[105]

To a considerable degree, the feminist movement in the last decade has succeeded in changing the public view of victims of sexual violence and in mobilizing public support in favor of more active prosecution of sex offenders. The final step in this stage of consciousness-raising involves the development of a new consensus in favor of stricter and more effective regulation of the organized sex industry, with particular focus on curtailing the most extreme and outrageous incitements to sexual violence.

A more long-range goal requires effecting a profound change in the general climate of sexual attitudes and socialization, so that no form of sexually exploitative behavior is excused or tolerated. The feminist movement, which in the last two decades has brought the issue of sexual violence into public consciousness, remains the only social force committed to and capable of bringing about such change. It is possible to envision a society whose practices in this regard are exactly the opposite of our own: one which freely permits children to learn safely about sex, but which firmly and consistently rejects any form of sexually exploitative behavior. Such a society should produce few customers for those who traffic in human flesh, few sexual addicts, and few sex offenders.

Notes

1. Russell, 1984.
2. Finkelhor, 1979.
3. Russell, 1984.
4. New York Radical Feminists, 1974; MacKinnon, 1983, pp. 635–658; Herman, 1981; Bart, 1983; Bart and O'Brien, 1985.
5. Griffin, 1971, pp. 26–35; Brownmiller, 1975.
6. Sanday, 1981b.
7. Dworkin, 1981.
8. Millett, 1970b.
9. Burt, 1980, pp. 217–30.
10. Goodchilds and Zellman, 1984.
11. Malamuth, 1981, pp. 138–57.
12. Malamuth, 1984.
13. Groth, Longo, and McFadin, 1982, pp. 102–6.
14. U.S. Department of Justice, 1981.
15. Ageton, 1983.
16. Koss, Gidycz, and Wisniewski, 1987, pp. 162–70.
17. Rapaport and Burkhart, 1984; Briere, Corne, Runtz, and Malamuth, 1984.
18. Ageton, 1983.
19. Koss, Leonard, Beezley, and Oros, 1985, pp. 981–92.
20. Briere et al., 1984.
21. Koss et al., 1985.
22. Dietz and Evans, 1982, pp. 1493–95.

23. Quinsey and Marshall, 1983, Earls and Marshall, 1983.

24. Freund, McKnight, Langevin, and Cibiri, 1972, pp. 119–33.

25. Finkelhor and Lewis, 1987.

26. Gebhard et al., 1965; Henn, 1978; Groth, 1979; Knight, Rosenberg, and Schneider, 1985.

27. Scully and Marolla, 1984, pp. 530–44.

28. Rada et al., 1978, pp. 296–300; Knight et al., 1985.

29. Vaillant, 1983.

30. Wilson and Lawson, 1976, pp. 587–94.

31. Knight et al., 1985.

32. Karacon, Williams, and Guerraro, 1974, pp. 19–26.

33. Abel, Rouleau, and Cunningham-Rather, 1985.

34. Abel, quoted in Knopp, 1984, p. 9.

35. Georgia Green, Bridgewater Special Treatment Center, Maximum Security Prison, Bridgewater, Mass. (personal communication, April 1986).

36. Green, 1983, pp. 231–37; Goodwin, 1986; Terr, 1983, pp. 1543–50.

37. Pagelow, 1984; Kaufman and Zigler, 1987, pp. 186–92.

38. Groth, 1979; Justice and Justice, 1979.

39. Carmen, Rieker, and Mills, 1984, pp. 378–83.

40. Groth, 1979, p. 98.

41. Lutheran Social Service of Minnesota, 1982; Becker, Cunningham-Rather, and Kaplan, 1986, pp. 431–45.

42. Closed Adolescent Treatment Center, Denver, Colo., cited in Knopp, 1982, p. 119.

43. Groth, 1979; Abel, Becker, and Skinner, 1983.

44. Groth, Hobson, and Gary, 1982.

45. Becker (1985), e.g., reports that pedophiles who prefer boy victims are one of the most treatment-resistant groups in her program. This group also has an early onset of compulsive behavior (72% by age 19) and has a very high average number of victims (76 victims per offender).

46. Abel, Mittleman, and Becker, 1983.

47. Groth, Hobson, and Gary (1982) claim that the "majority" of their patients were sexually abused as children but offer neither numerical data nor a description of the methodology by which they obtained this information; see also Seghorn, Boucher, and Cohen, 1983.

48. University of Washington Hospital, Adolescent Clinic, Juvenile Sex Offender Program, cited in Knopp, 1982.

49. Connell and Wilson, 1974; Brownmiller, 1975.

50. Kempe and Kempe, 1978; Justice and Justice, 1979.

51. See MacIntyre, 1981, pp. 462–66; Myers, 1985, pp. 47–58.

52. Herman, 1981.

53. Abel et al., 1983. In this study, 44% of the incestuous fathers had also abused girls outside the family.

54. Groth and Hobson, 1983, pp. 165–66.

55. Groth, Hobson, and Gary, 1982, p. 137.

56. Smithyman, 1978; Scully and Marolla, 1985b.

57. Groth et al., 1982.

58. Schwartz and Masters, 1985.

59. Ressler, Burgess, and Douglas, 1983, pp. 36–40.

60. From an anonymous personal communication, 1984.

61. Laws and Osborne, 1983.

62. Vaillant, 1983; Greely and McReady, 1980; Pittman and Snyder, 1962.

63. Gebhard et al., 1965; Goldstein, Kant, and Hartman, 1974; Summit and Kryso, 1978, pp. 237–51.

64. Ageton, 1983.

65. Robins and Smith, 1980.

66. Lewis, 1976.

67. Koss et al., 1987.

68. Carnes, 1983.

69. Abel, Mittelman, and Becker, 1985.

70. Groth, Hobson, and Gary, 1982.

71. Knopp, 1982.

72. Knopp, 1982, p. 26.

73. Lender and Martin, 1982.

74. Carnes, 1983.

75. Scully and Marolla, 1984.

76. McCord and McCord, 1960; Vaillant, 1983.

77. Knopp, 1984; Becker and Abel, 1985; Quinsey and Marshall, 1983.

78. Earls and Marshall, 1983.

79. Abel, Becker, Cunningham-Rather, 1984; Laws and O'Neil, 1981, pp. 111–36.

80. Silver, 1976, pp. 134–40.

81. Berlin, 1983.

82. Vaillant, 1983.

83. Knopp, 1982.

84. Carnes, 1983.

85. Giaretto, 1982.

86. Brecher, 1978.

87. Mary Devlin, personal communication, Brockton, Mass., 1982.

88. Peter Coleman, personal communication, Tacoma, Wash., 1977.

89. Vaillant, 1983.

90. Schwartz and Masters, 1985.

91. Giaretto, 1982.

92. Pithers, Marques, and Gibat, 1983.

93. Robert Wolfe, quoted in Knopp, 1982, p. 19.

94. See Bart, 1986, pp. 103–5; Diamond, 1980; Malamuth and Donnerstein, 1984.

95. Malamuth, 1984.

96. Becker, 1985.

97. Pleck, 1987.

98. Lender and Martin, 1982.

99. Haggard and Jellinek, 1942; Burnham, 1968, pp. 51–68.

100. Terris, 1967, pp. 2076–88.

101. Lender and Martin, 1982.

102. Rush, 1980; Barry, Bunch, and Castley, 1984; Burgess, Groth, and McCausland, 1981, pp. 110–19.

103. Malamuth and Donnerstein, 1982.

104. MacKinnon and Dworkin, 1984.

105. Lederer, 1980; Penrod and Linz, 1984.

8

Pornography as Sex Discrimination

Catharine A. MacKinnon

OVER TIME, THIS GOVERNMENT has tried various approaches to the problem of pornography. The 1970 president's commission found that, although pornography may outrage sensibilities and offend tastes and morals, it was harmless.[1] In the face of these findings, the Supreme Court nonetheless decided that when materials violate community standards, appeal to the prurient interest, are patently offensive, and are otherwise worthless, they may be prohibited as obscenity. State and local legislatures have tried confining obscenity by zoning it, defining it as a moral nuisance, hiding it behind opaque covers in secret rooms, or by paying the pornographers to get out of town.

Despite these attempts, the pornography industry has flourished. I think that obscenity law may be part of the reason why. In order to find that something appeals to the prurient interest, for example, a finder of fact must admit to arousal by the material. The more violent the material, the less likely this becomes, because people do not tend to want to admit publicly that they are sexually aroused by violent materials. Similarly, to be patently offended by materials, it is necessary to not be desensitized to them. People are neither aroused nor offended by materials to which they are desensitized, so that the more pornography one sees, the less offensive it becomes. Taken together, the tests of prurient interest and patent offensiveness have a built-in bind. Finders of fact are required to admit both that the materials arouse them sexually and that the materials offend them patently. That which turns them on, they must also reject as revolting. This may begin to clarify why pornography is perhaps the last thing obscenity law has been used to address.

Perhaps an even more fundamental problem is that pornography is so profitable—sexually to its users and financially to its pushers—that it effectively sets community standards. The more pornography exists in a community, the more likely it is that community standards will *de facto* come to correspond to it. ... Consumer preferences escalate toward the more violent materials—a dynamic which means that new markets, hence greater profits, are created through creating community standards that tolerate more and more violating materials.[2]

Primarily, though, pornography has been allowed to flourish because its real harm has been legally and socially obscured. I mean the violation of women and children that is essential to its making and inevitable through its use. This harm *could* be overlooked, and *has* been overlooked, because the pornographers, who are pimps, take people who are already powerless, who begin socially powerless—the poor, the young, the innocent, the used, the already used up, the desperate, the female—and deepen their invisibility and their silence. Pornography deepens their invisibility and their silence through making their subjection the sexually enjoyable, the sexually enjoyed, sex itself. Women are coerced to perform for pornography and are made to act as if they are enjoying themselves.[3] This pornography then is forced on women who are forced to act it out, to correspond to the way the pornography uses and presents the women in it. It then becomes possible to point to the world pornography has created and say that it truthfully expresses women's nature, because it corresponds to their reality. This process has succeeded in making the victims of pornography so invisible as victims that through years of inquiry, including the 1970 commission, the only harm this government could see was sex it disapproved of seeing, rather than its most powerless citizens being hurt. Pornography has made its victims so silent that until the hearings on the proposed civil rights antipornography ordinance in Minneapolis in December of 1983, no official body heard them scream, far less speak.[4]

The United States Supreme Court recently admitted that the obscenity doctrine had missed something, someone actually, for whose injuries the law had therefore been inadequate. When it recognized in the *Ferber* case that child pornography is a form of child abuse—over the opposition of the ACLU, I might add—and whether or not the materials are obscene is beside the point, the Court found that pornography made using children could be criminally banned consistent with the first amendment.[5] With many others, Andrea Dworkin and I have been working to expose the specific atrocities to women that have also been hidden, and for which existing law remains inadequate. These abuses were documented here in Minneapolis in December, 1983, for the first time in the history of the world to our knowledge—which is an appalling fact in itself. The abuses that were spoken in public include coercion to perform for pornography, the pervasive forcing of pornography on individuals, assaults directly caused by specific pornography, and the targeting for rape, battery, sexual harassment,

sexual abuse as children, forced prostitution, and the civil denigration and inferiority characteristic of a second class civil status that is endemic to this traffic in
female sexual slavery.

Pornography makes women what Andrea Dworkin has called "the sexual disappeared of this society."[6] Because these injuries are disproportionally inflicted
on women; because they are inflicted on everyone who is victimized by them on
the basis of their sex; because virtually nothing is being done about it; and because women matter—this seems to be the real sticking point—we proposed a
new approach: that pornography be civilly actionable by its victims as sex discrimination and recognized as a violation of human rights.

...

The harm of pornography begins with the women in it. In pornography, you
see women being bound, battered, tortured, humiliated, and sometimes killed—
or merely taken and used. For every act you see in the visual materials, a woman
actually had to be tied or cut or burned or gagged or whipped or chained, hung
from a meat hook or from trees by ropes, as in *Penthouse,* December, 1984, uri-
nated on or defecated on, forced to eat excrement, penetrated by eels or rats or
knives or pistols, raped deep in the throat with penises, smeared with blood,
mud, feces, and ejaculate. Or merely—and this includes the glossy legitimate
men's entertainment magazines—taken through every available orifice or
posed, presented, displayed as though that were her fondest wish in life. Penis
into vagina intercourse, by the way, is a minority theme.

Pornography sexualizes women's inequality. It makes the inequality of women
sexy. It sexualizes, most broadly speaking, dominance and submission. Every
kind of woman is used, each one's particular inequalities exploited as deemed
sexually exciting.

Asian women are bound so they are not recognizably human, so inert they
could be dead. Black women play plantation, struggling against their bonds.
Jewish women orgasm in reenactments of Auschwitz. Pregnant women and
nursing mothers are accessible, displayed. Women are splayed across hoods of
cars, trussed like dead prey. Amputees and other disabled or ill women's injuries
or wounds or stumps are proffered as sexual fetishes. Retarded girls are gratify-
ingly compliant. Adult women are infantilized as children, children are adult
women, interchangeably fusing vulnerability with the sluttish eagerness said to
be natural to women of all ages, beginning at age one. So-called lesbians, actually women sexually arranged with other women for the purpose of being
watched and claimed, are bought and sold with the rest.

The point is, because the profit from these mass violations counts and women
do not, because these materials are valued and women are not, because the
pornographers have credibility and rights and powerful friends to front for their
interests and women do not, the products of these acts are protected and
women are not. So these things are done so that pornography can be made of

them. All of you who have been looking for a "direct causal link" between pornography and harm might consider this one.

The pornography industry is largely an organized crime industry in which overt force is standard practice. Yet the question persists, are these women there because they like it? Pimps are known for their violence, yet the question persists, are these women there as an expression of pure freedom? In a society whose opportunities for women are so limited that prostitution is many women's best economic option, even when explicit violence is not used, as often it is, the compulsion of poverty, of drugs, of the street, of foreclosed alternatives, or of fear of retribution for noncooperation can be enforcement enough.

Every act that is exacted from the women in the pornography, who are typically made to act as though they are enjoying themselves, is acted out on yet more women integral to the pornography's consumption. Such women are given no choice about seeing the pornography or about performing the sex. The pornography is forced on them to destroy their self-respect and their resistance to sexual aggression, to terrorize them into compliance or silence as a sex act in itself, or to instruct and season them for exact replication of the scripts and postures and scenes. Our testimony shows that rapes are thereby stimulated, inspired, fantasized, planned, and actualized. We have women held down while the pornography is held up; women turned over as the pages are turned over.

The evidence is consistent across social studies, clinicians who work with victims and perpetrators, battered women's shelters, rape crisis centers, groups of former and current prostitutes, incest survivors and their therapists, court cases, and police.[7] The most direct evidence, typically given the low value of those who provide it, comes from the victims themselves, used on one end of pornography or the other. This evidence, together with the laboratory tests in controlled experiments on what are termed non-predisposed normals (meaning men) and some recent correlational results, support the conclusion that exposure to pornography increases attitudes and behaviors of aggression and discrimination, specifically by men against women. This conclusion is particularly supported by this evidence if you see that administering electric shock is a behavior, and if you see that not seeing an account of a rape as an account of a rape, is a form of discrimination. The increment of increase in aggression due to exposure varies according to the type of pornography, but it varies only in degree.

I think these results occur because sex and violence are inextricably interwoven in the harm of pornography. They are interwoven in the material itself. Pornography makes sex into a violation and makes rape and torture and intrusion into sex. The sex and the violence are interwoven on every other level of the pornography's social existence as well. Over time and exposure, many viewers respond sexually to violence against women whether it is presented in a sexualized context or not. It therefore *is* sex, behaviorally speaking. Too, violence is used to coerce women to perform for materials that *show* violence, but violence is also used to coerce women to perform for materials which are sexually explicit, are subordinating, but do *not* show the violence it took to make them. The violence that is recognized as violence occurs off screen, except perhaps for the bruises the make-up fails to cover. Women are also forcibly compelled to consume pornography until they acquiesce without further complaint or resistance in sex that violates their personal dignity, their desires, their bodies, not to mention their sexual preferences, without the need for further violence.

Pornography is an icon of male supremacy, the fusion of those twin icons, sex and speech. Thus legitimized, it neither appears nor needs to be violent at all times. Subjection is always violating, but it is not always violent; even less often it is perceived as such.

Further effects of exposure to pornography include the trivialization and objectification of women, increased acceptance of rape myths, desensitization to sexual force, and spontaneous rape-fantasy generation. These are the so-called attitudes, so far from being considered violence to some that they are not even considered behavior. Sexual arousal is the only thing that does not seem to desensitize, so long as the materials escalate, yet nobody seems very sure whether it is an attitude or a behavior. But the only thing we cannot yet predict with exactness, although some of our colleagues are working on it, is which individual woman will be next on which individual man's list and for what specific expression of his escalated misogyny. We do know that such acts will occur. We do know that these materials, through the arousal they *do* cause, will contribute to these acts of misogyny, causally to many. We also know that the more pornography is consumed in the society, the less harmful these acts will socially be perceived as being. We also know that such acts will typically occur in contexts traditionally regarded as consensual, if not intimate, giving the aura of consent to the acts themselves: in marriages and families, on dates, among acquaintances, on the job, in churches, in schools, in doctors' offices, in prostitution. Rarely between strangers. Almost always between women and men.

On the basis of this analysis of its social reality, we have concluded that pornography, not alone but crucially, institutionalizes a subhuman victimized second class status for women in particular. If a person can be denigrated, and doing that is defended and legalized as freedom; if one can be tortured and the enjoyment of watching it is considered entertainment protected by the Constitution; if the pleasure that other people derive from one's pain is the measure of one's social worth, one isn't worth much, socially speaking.

Our legal argument is simple: tolerance of such practices is inconsistent with any serious mandate of equality and with the reasons speech is protected. The civil rights approach to pornography is based on the notion that this remains true even when the means are words and pictures, the enjoyment and pleasure are sexual and economic, and even when—again, this seems to be the difficult part—the victims are women.

Based on empirical investigation of the materials actually available now in this country that do this damage, our law defines pornography as the graphic sexually explicit subordination of women through pictures and words that also includes women being sexually used and abused, for example being dehumanized as sexual objects who enjoy pain, humiliation or rape, bound, mutilated, bruised, dismembered, in postures of servility or submission or display, or penetrated by objects or animals. Men, children, or transsexuals, all of whom are sometimes violated in these same ways in and through pornography, can sue for similar treatment.[8]

...

Just the fact that [materials that fit the definition of harm] exist, however, does not make them actionable. Only alleged victims of specific activities of coercion into pornography, of forcing pornography on a person, of assault caused by specific pornography, and of trafficking—which is production, sale, exhibition, or distribution of provable subordination—can sue. Some people believe that most if not all of these acts are already illegal. No existing law adequately reaches the materials which provide the incentive, the actualization, and the realization of these harms. And so long as the materials are protected and profitable, as they *are,* it will be effectively impossible to reach any of the included acts. As things stand, all you have to be able to do is to *do* them, to get away with them.

There is also a built-in perversity in enforcing existing criminal laws while leaving the materials untouched. Not only does it require that the acts *already be done* before anything can be done about them; it provides an incentive to murder. Pornography is already an incentive to rape a woman and run. But the more likely it is that the perpetrator will be criminally prosecuted, the greater incentive there is to do away with the evidence. Another prostitute O.D.'d in an alley, so what. Also, murdering women for the camera creates snuff films, which actually show women and children being murdered, a very profitable form of pornography, which also ensures that the victim is not a witness. This is one reason why it is so important that women *other* than those in the pornography can also bring civil claims.

...

... Pornography as defined in our law undermines sex equality—a compelling state interest and a legitimate concern of government—by harming people, differentially women. Under current first amendment law, exceptions are recognized. Speech interests are sometimes outweighed by other interests. The most common reason is harm. Compared with existing exceptions and counterbalances to the first amendment, the harm that this law recognizes meets a higher standard than any of them have met or have been required to meet, from the weakest to the strongest.

...

... If speech interests can become comparatively less valued for constitutional purposes when the materials are false, obscene, indecent, lewd, racist, provocative, dangerous, coercive, threatening, intrusive, inconvenient, or inaesthetic, we believe they should be able to be civilly actionable when they can be proven to be coerced, assaultive, and discriminatory.

... Pornography is at the center of a cycle of abuse that cannot be reached or stopped without reaching and stopping the pornography that is its incentive, product, stimulus, and realization.

...

The bottom line of all the resistance we encounter to this law is that a lot of people, people who matter, enjoy pornography. That is why they defend it. That is also why there is so much hysteria and distortion over the civil rights approach. The worry is not that it would misfire, but that it would fire at all. The fear is, it would work.

The fact that some people like pornography does not mean it does not hurt other people. As in any instance of a conflict of rights, the side you take is a choice. We know that so long as pornography exists as it does now, women and children will be used and abused to make it, as they are now. And it will be used to abuse them, as it is now. ...

Notes

1. Report of the Commission on Obscenity and Pornography, 1970.

2. Donnerstein, 1986.

3. Lovelace, 1980; Gershel, 1985; Baldwin, 1984.

4. Public Hearings on Ordinances to Add Pornography as Discrimination Against Women: Before the Minneapolis City Council Gov't Operations Comm., 1st Sess. 4-12 (Dec. 12, 1983).

5. New York v. Ferber, 458 U.S. 742 (1982).

6. Effect of Pornography on Women and Children: Hearings Before the Subcomm. on Juvenile Justice of the Comm. of the Judiciary, 98th Cong. 2d. Sess. 227-55 (1984), testimony of Andrea Dworkin.

7. Public Hearings (see note 4); Malamuth and Donnerstein, 1984; MacKinnon, 1985.

8. Indianapolis, Ind., City-County General Ordinance 35 (June 11, 1984).

Part Three

Varieties of Rape
and Sexual Assault

RAPE HAS TRADITIONALLY been conceptualized rather narrowly. The sexual violations that have been most likely to be seen as rape are those that Linda Williams
(1984) labeled "classic rape." These rapes, which are those most likely to be reported to the police and treated seriously by the criminal justice system (see
Part 4), include cases in which a woman is raped by a stranger, is threatened
with or subjected to a high degree of force, is seriously injured, is raped in public, is abducted from a public place, is attacked in her car, or is attacked after her
home has been broken into. This book began with an example of a classic rape,
"The Case of Ms. X." In this section we offer readings designed to broaden understanding of the range of sexual violations that constitute the problem of rape
and sexual assault and that are part of the continuum of sexual violence.

In "Child Sexual Abuse," an excerpt from a groundbreaking anthology of writings of child sexual abuse survivors, Ellen Bass discusses the reality and impact
of child sexual abuse. Bass maintains that the "basic inequality of power, understanding, … [and] freedom between a child and an adult" means that there is
coercion whenever a child is sexually used by an adult, even if there is no physical force. Bass argues that societal messages not only condone but even subtly
and overtly encourage men to violate children and that "the condoning of this
violence is not simply a contemporary perversion but part of an ancient and
pervasive worldwide tradition" (see Heise 1989). In biblical times, under both
Talmudic and Christian law, sex between men and young girls was actually
sanctioned.[1]

The betrayal and damage the abused child experiences is illustrated in the
second chapter in this section, Maggie Hoyal's "These Are the Things I Remember." In this moving personal portrayal of dysfunctional family life, Hoyal traces
the progression of her childhood molestation and rape and shows how her father attempted to justify his conduct and gain her compliance by arguing that

he knew what was best for her—that he was teaching her about sexuality and trying to prevent her from turning out "cold like [her] mother."

According to Judith Herman (1981:4), father-daughter incest is the most frequently reported type of incest as well as "a paradigm of female sexual victimization." In this gross misuse of power, "the father, in effect, forces the daughter to pay with her body for affection and care that should be freely given." This, she says, "destroys the protective bond between parent and child" and is always destructive to the child.

Herman found in her study of forty women who had experienced father-daughter incest that incestuous families often appeared quite conventional to outsiders. They were frequently churchgoing, financially stable, and able to maintain "a facade of respectability" (p. 71). These families, however, adhered rigidly to traditional gender roles. The fathers were "perfect patriarchs" who commanded absolute, unquestioning authority from other family members and often asserted this authority with force. Typically, they exercised "minute control over the lives of their wives and daughters," frequently isolating them from the outside world (p. 73). The mothers were generally full-time home-workers, and even those who weren't lacked "the working skills or experience that would have made independent survival a realistic option" for them (p. 72). The mothers often experienced some disabling condition—depression, alcoholism, or other psychiatric or medical problems—and were generally "in no position to challenge their husbands' domination or to resist their abuses" (p. 78). The mothers conveyed a message to their daughters "that a woman is defenseless against a man, that marriage must be preserved at all costs, and that a wife's duty is to serve and endure." At a very early age the daughters were "pressed into service as 'little mothers' within the family," caring for younger siblings and taking on responsibility for household chores and keeping "Daddy happy" (p. 79). The daughters sensed correctly that they could not rely on their mothers to protect them and hence bore "the incestuous relationship in silence, biding their time until they were old enough to leave home" (p. 90).[2]

The third chapter in this section highlights another common nonstranger violation, that is, acquaintance or date rape. In Diana Russell's "White Man Wants a Black Piece: The Case of Sonia Morrell," a young African American woman describes her experience of sexual coercion by a white man determined to prove he was man enough "to satisfy a black woman."[3] In this account we see that Sonia's date, Bob, endorses many of the traditional notions that contribute to date rape—for instance, a sense of entitlement to a "payoff" for having shown one's date a good time; a view of sex as a conquest, an achievement that validates one's masculinity and elevates one's status; an assumption that women really want sex in spite of their protests and that they eventually come to enjoy it. We see that Sonia initially blames herself for what happened because she agreed to accompany Bob to a party at his fraternity house but that over time she comes to recognize that rape is not just "a man coming out of the bushes and attacking you"—that this experience of nonconsensual intercourse was, in fact, rape. We also see the intersection of racist and sexist attitudes in Bob's treatment of Sonia[4] and how racism exacerbates the power of rape myths to silence the victimized woman.[5] As Sonia says, "I felt that they would believe him, because he was white ... and I was just this black girl."

Although many rapes, like Sonia's, occur in fraternity houses, Patricia Yancey Martin and Robert Hummer argue that little research has analyzed fraternities as "rape-prone contexts." Research on the situational context of rape, they say, has more frequently focused on the "potential risk factors for individuals."[6] In "Fraternities and Rape on Campus," Martin and Hummer analyze how "fraternities create a sociocultural context in which the use of coercion in sexual relations with women is normative and in which mechanisms to keep this pattern in check are minimal at best and absent at worst." They show how fraternity norms and practices condition members to view women as sexual objects and to consider sexual coercion a contest or game. This contest, they say, "is played not between men and women but between men and men. Women are the pawns or prey in the interfraternity rivalry game."

Marital rape is another form of acquaintance rape that has often gone unrecognized. In the fifth chapter, "Types of Marital Rape," David Finkelhor and Kersti Yllo argue that most people view forced marital sex as "an unpleasant, but not particularly serious, marital squabble." Just as Sonia Morrell did not initially define her acquaintance rape as rape, most people do not see marital rape as "real rape." Finkelhor and Yllo analyze three types of marital rape (i.e., battering rape, force-only rape, and obsessive rape) and show how the public's "sanitized stereotype" masks how abusive and traumatizing marital rape really is.[7]

The three types of marital rape Finkelhor and Yllo distinguish parallel the types of rape (i.e., anger rape, power rape, and sadistic rape) that A. Nicholas Groth (1979) discovered in his studies of incarcerated rapists. Anger rapes, like battering rapes, "are committed primarily to express hostility toward women, to retaliate against them, and to humiliate and hurt them" (Finkelhor and Yllo 1985:47). Power rapes, like force-only rapes, "are committed primarily to assert dominance and control over women" in order to compensate for underlying feelings of inadequacy (p. 47). Sadistic rapes, like obsessive rapes, have "a bizarre or ritualistic quality" to them (Groth 1979:44). In sadistic rapes, "aggression itself becomes eroticized."

Sexual abuse and sexual assault (of children and adults, of strangers, acquaintances, and intimates) may go hand in hand with physical violence—spankings, beatings, sustained battery, sometimes torture and mutilation, even murder.[8] In "The Sexual Politics of Murder," Jane Caputi argues that not only is rape "a direct expression of sexual politics, a ritual enactment of male domination," but so is sexual murder. Caputi sees sexual murder as "the ultimate expression of sexuality as a form of power." What is political about sexual murder is often overlooked when a murder is dismissed as only a *sex* murder (what the FBI also labels "recreational murder"), but to Caputi sexual murder is "rooted in a system of male supremacy in the same way that lynching is based in white supremacy. … [It is] a form of patriarchal terrorism."

Deborah Cameron and Elizabeth Frazer (1987) extended the analysis of what is political about sexual murder. Like other forms of violence against women, Cameron and Frazer maintained that it "expresses not purely individual anger and frustration but a collective, culturally sanctioned misogyny which is important in maintaining the collective power of men" (p. 164). Sexual killing, they said, is "male violence taken to its logical extreme, where humiliation becomes annihilation. Death is the ultimate negation of autonomy," and the mutilation of breasts and genitals common in sexual murder "is the ultimate violation of the female sex and body" (pp. 164–65).[9]

When Cameron and Frazer discussed the "reign of terror" of Peter Sutcliffe, the Yorkshire Ripper, we understood the meaning of the phrase "sexual terrorism" and why Susan Brownmiller (1975:15) characterized rape as a "process of intimidation by which *all men* keep *all women* in a state of fear."

> Any man could have been the killer. … The whole weight of the culture colluded in the terror that affected women's existence in the North of England: the police who insisted we stay off streets, the commentators who so callously devalued the lives of prostitutes, the football crowds who chanted and made jokes about the Ripper, those men, who under cover of protecting frightened women found a golden opportunity to threaten and assault us. (Cameron and Frazer 1987:16)

Cameron and Frazer pointed out that although some sexual murderers kill males rather than females, what is constant is "the gender of the *killer*" (1987:167). They argued that "there is more to sexual killing than misogyny and terror" (p. 166), that the common denominator is the social construction of masculine sexuality as transcendence over others. Cameron and Frazer described the motifs of masculine sexuality as performance, penetration, and conquest. They analyzed how sexual acts and desires that transgressed religious or social norms came over time to be seen as "forms of transcendence, thus becoming the source of both power and pleasure and paving the way for that male sexual sadism which becomes, at its most extreme, the lust to kill" (p. 169). The connection between sex and violence, they argued, is pervasive in our culture, "contributing to a taken-for-granted stereotype of masculine sexuality as intrinsically sadistic, intrinsically desiring to take the Other by force. In a culture which thus conflates sex, power and death, the sexual killer is hardly an exile" (p. 68).

Neither is the sexual killer an exile in war, in spite of the fact that rape is considered a criminal act under contemporary international rules of war. As General George Patton said about World War II, "There would unquestionably be some raping" (quoted in Brownmiller 1975:31). Susan Brownmiller, in her 1975 groundbreaking book on rape, put it this way:

> It has been argued that when killing is viewed as not only permissible but heroic be-
> havior sanctioned by one's government or cause, the distinction between taking a
> human life and other forms of impermissible violence gets lost, and rape becomes
> an unfortunate but inevitable by-product of the necessary game called war. Women,
> by this reasoning, are simply regrettable victims—incidental, unavoidable casual-
> ties—like civilian victims of bombing, lumped together with children, homes, per-
> sonal belongings, a church, a dike, a water buffalo, or next year's crop. But rape in
> war is qualitatively different from a bomb that misses its military target, different
> from impersonal looting and burning, different from deliberate ambush, mass mur-
> der or torture during interrogation, although it contains elements of all of the above.
> Rape is more than a symptom of war or evidence of its violent excess. Rape in war is
> a familiar act with a familiar excuse. (p. 32)[10]

Whereas Martin and Hummer describe women as pawns in men's "interfraternity rivalry game," Susan Brownmiller described the body of a woman raped in war as "a ceremonial battlefield, a parade ground, for the vic-
tors' trooping of the colors" (1975, p. 38).[11] In "Making Female Bodies the Battle-
field," Brownmiller updates her classic treatise with a discussion of rape and ethnic cleansing in the former Yugoslavia. Here we come to understand how the horror of rape in war does not end when the assault is over. For "if she survives the assault, what does the victim of wartime rape become to her people? Evidence of the enemy's bestiality. Symbol of her nation's defeat. A pariah. Dam-
aged property. A pawn in the subtle wars of international propaganda." The meaning of objectification becomes painfully clear.

In the final chapter in this section, "Dispatch from Boznia-Herzegovina: A Seventeen-Year-Old Survivor Testifies to Systematic Rape," Mirsada, a young Muslim woman, describes the nightmare of living in a war-torn country where rape, battery, mutilation, and murder are commonplace, where "girls [are] slaughtered ... like cattle." Although Balkan women and girls, whatever their religious and ethnic backgrounds, have been victimized in the former Yugoslavia, most reports have focused on the atrocities committed on Muslims and Cro-
atians by Serbian soldiers. Catharine MacKinnon (1993) argued that there is evi-
dence that mass rapes are Serbian military policy, ordered for "Serbian morale," and that pornography is used to sexualize ethnic hatred (p. 27). Atrocities are ar-
ranged so other soldiers can watch, and they are filmed in "rape theatre[s]" to prime even more soldiers in the genocidal campaign of ethnic cleansing (p. 24). As she said, "Xenophobia and misogyny merge here; ... bigotry becomes orgasm. Whatever this rape does for the rapist, the pornography of the rape mass-
produces. The materials become a potent advertisement for a war, a perfect motivator for torturers, who then do what they are ordered to do and enjoy it. Yes, it improves their morale" (p. 27).

Notes

1. Recent statistics indicate that 10 to 23 percent of religious leaders in the United States today have engaged in inappropriate sexual contact or sexual behavior with congregants, clients, or employees (Bonavoglia 1992). Although abuse has been charged against religious leaders of many faiths, Annie Laurie Gaylor found that 40 percent of abuse charges involved Catholic priests, who make up just 10 percent of U.S. clergy (cited in Conklin 1992). On the whole, however, "religious institutions have chosen to protect their offending clergy—and themselves—rather than the ... victims" (p. 41). Abuse has often been ignored or denied, and even when blame has been appropriately placed, sanctions have frequently not been applied. According to Father Gregory Coiro, the preferred approach has been "rehabilitation, reconciliation, and healing, rather than suspension or dismissal" (cited in Bonavoglia 1992:45).

Peter Rutter (1989) argued that a "forbidden zone" exists not only in the professional relationship between the clergyperson and congregant but also in that between therapist and client, doctor and patient, lawyer and client, teacher and student, and mentor and protégée. He holds that professionals "have moral, legal, and ethical responsibilities not to allow themselves to become sexually involved" with clients no matter how consenting those clients appear to be, because in professional relationships "factors of power, trust, and dependency ... can render a [client] unable to *withhold* consent" (pp. 21, 28). Thus any sexual behavior by the professional is "inherently exploitative" (p. 24).

The Hippocratic oath and the ethics codes of the American Medical Association and American Psychiatric Association explicitly forbid sex between doctor and patient, but these professions have traditionally been reluctant to investigate and punish abuse, although disciplinary action has become more common in recent years. Studies have found that 13 percent of physicians and 6 to 10 percent of psychiatrists have had sexual contact with their patients (Rutter 1989).

2. Concerning the question of the mother's responsibility, Herman says: "Even by patriarchal standards, the mother in the incestuous family is unusually oppressed. More than the average wife and mother, she is extremely dependent upon and subservient to her husband. ... Rather than provoke her husband's anger or risk his desertion, she will capitulate. If the price of maintaining the marriage includes the sacrifice of her daughter, she will raise no effective objections. Her first loyalty is to her husband, regardless of his behavior. She sees no other choice. Maternal collusion in incest, when it occurs, is a measure of maternal powerlessness. ... The lack of a strong, competent, and protective mother does seem to render girls more vulnerable to sexual abuse. ... But no degree of maternal absence or neglect constitutes an excuse for paternal incest" (p. 49).

3. The interview of Sonia Morrell provides an example of interracial rape, but according to Harlow's (1991) analysis of victimization survey data (1973–1987), rape is generally an *intraracial* phenomenon. In cases of single-offender rapes, Harlow found that 90 percent of black women and 78 percent of white women were raped by assailants of their own race. In cases of multiple-offender rapes, 85 percent of black women and 63 percent of white women were raped by assailants of their own race.

4. Angela Davis (1981:177) argued that "racism has always drawn strength from its ability to encourage sexual coercion. While Black women and their sisters of color have been the main targets of ... racist-inspired acts, ... once white men were persuaded that they could

commit sexual assaults against Black women with impunity, their conduct toward women of their own race could not have remained unmarred. Racism has always served as a provocation to rape, and white women in the United States have necessarily suffered the ricochet fire of their attacks. This is one of the many ways in which racism nourishes sexism."

5. In her analysis of the aftermath of the highly publicized New Bedford rape case, in which a woman was sexually assaulted by several Portuguese men on a pool table in a neighborhood bar, Lynn Chancer (1987) demonstrated how ethnic oppression can exacerbate sexist prejudice. Many men and women in the local Portuguese community expressed sympathy for the accused rapists and responded with hostility to the Portuguese victim, blaming her for the ethnic prejudice that erupted after the rape. Chancer argued that proclaiming the culpability of the rapists was, to the Portuguese community of New Bedford, tantamount to indicting the entire ethnic group and proving that the prejudice against immigrants was justified.

6. The presence of power differentials associated with dating rituals has been identified as a "risk factor" in date rape (Harney and Muehlenhard 1991; Lundberg-Love and Geffner 1989). For example, when a male pays all the expenses of a date, he is more likely to expect sex in return. Women also appear to be more vulnerable when they go to the man's apartment rather than their own, for in his territory the woman is more isolated and the man feels in greater control. Similarly, when women are without transportation they have less freedom to extricate themselves from an uncomfortable situation before it gets out of hand. Parking, parties, and other disinhibiting situations involving alcohol also increase women's vulnerability to rape.

Research also indicates that females who are abused as children have a greater risk of being revictimized as adults (Russell 1986). The incest survivor, for instance, has typically "experienced the inappropriate pairing of love and attention with sexual exploitation and coercion" and is thus more "vulnerable to the exploitive manipulations of the date rapist" (Lundberg-Love and Geffner 1989:176).

7. Although Finkelhor and Yllo (1985:89) defined as marital rape only those circumstances involving "actual or threatened physical force," they recognized that marital rape exists on a continuum with other forms of coercive sex. In particular, they described *social coercion* as the pressure to have sex that women feel "as a result of social expectations or conventions" (p. 86), for example, a belief that intercourse is their "wifely duty" or their religious obligation. They labeled it *interpersonal coercion* "when a woman has sex with her husband in the face of threats that are not violent in nature" (p. 87), for example, when she fears he will become angry or unpleasant or withhold money or assistance if she doesn't comply. Finkelhor and Yllo argued that sexual compliance in response to social or interpersonal coercion can be very distressing, as well as damaging to one's dignity and self-esteem.

8. Parental violence continues to be a leading cause of death of children under three years of age (Strong and DeVault 1992), and each year 30 percent of all women murdered are killed by their husbands or lovers (FBI 1987).

9. Sexual murder is sometimes narrrowly defined as murder following rape or sexual assault, but this definition is problematic because some serial murderers are necrophiliacs rather than rapists and some are sexually aroused by the mutilation of the victim's genitals or by the killing itself. Cameron and Frazer (1987) argued that "rape and sex-

ual assault are neither necessary nor sufficient to make a murder 'sexual.' What is important is the eroticization of the act of killing in and for itself" (p. 18).

10. Recently, the Tailhook scandal revealed American military personnel's proclivity to abuse women within their own ranks. Naval fighter pilots, "the 'fair-haired sons' of the Navy," have been known for their heavy alcohol consumption, unruly behavior, intolerance of women, and "a mindset among some that fighter pilots were so special they were exempt from rules of good order and discipline" (Pope 1993:303). At the 1991 convention of the Tailhook Association for retired and active naval aviators, the first gathering including Persian Gulf War pilots, at least 83 women (including 22 officers and 61 civilians) were sexually assaulted. They were "physically fondled, caressed, and had hands up their dresses and down their blouses; some were bitten on the buttock, as they were physically picked up and passed down a gauntlet of drunken naval aviators" (p. 304).

11. Brownmiller's assertion that the "military effect" of rape in war is "intimidation and demoralization for the victims' side" (1975, p. 37) parallels Davis's (1981) analysis of the function of the rape of female slaves in American history. "It would be a mistake to regard the institutionalized pattern of rape during slavery as an expression of white men's sexual urges. ... Rape was a weapon of domination, a weapon of repression, whose covert goal was to extinguish slave women's will to resist, and in the process to demoralize their men" (pp. 23–24).

Child Sexual Abuse

Ellen Bass

...

THE SEXUAL ABUSE OF CHILDREN spans all races, economic classes, and ethnic groups. Even babies are its victims—hospitals treat three-month-old infants for venereal disease of the throat. Sexually abused children are no more precocious, pretty, or sexually curious than other children. They do not ask for it. They do not want it. Like rape of women, the rape and molestation of children are most basically acts of violation, power, and domination.

Parents United, a self-help support group for people who have been involved with child molestation, estimates that one out of four girls and one out of seven boys will be sexually abused. ... At least 97 percent of child molesters and rapists are men; 75 percent are family members, men well known to the child (Butler 1978; Brownmiller 1975; Rush 1980). These are statistics. Because the majority of abuses are not reported, exact figures are impossible to obtain. The true numbers may be greater. But even these show clearly that the sexual abuse of children is common; that the abusers are men—not exceptional, but average; that the victims are mostly girls—not exceptional, but ordinary. This is violence by men against children, and although there can be individual explanations, individual resolution, and though there is always individual pain, individual wounding, scarring, the issue is not an individual issue but a societal one. We live in a society where men are encouraged to do violence to women and children, subtly and overtly.

...

... There can be no equality of power, understanding, or freedom in sex between adults and children. Children are dependent upon adults: first, for their survival; then for affection, attention, and an understanding of what the world in which they live is all about.

Though there may be no physical force involved, every time a child is sexually used by a man, there is coercion. A child submits to sex with a man for many reasons: She is afraid to hurt the man's feelings; she wants and needs affection and this is the only form in which it's being offered; she is afraid that if she resists, the man will hurt her or someone else; she is afraid that if she resists, the man will say she started it and get her in trouble; she is taken by surprise and has no idea what to do; the man tells her it's okay, the man says he's teaching her, the man says everybody does it; she has been taught to obey adults; she thinks she has no choice.

Children trust the adults in their lives, even when the adults are untrustworthy, because they have no choice. When that trust is betrayed, they learn the world is not dependable.

By actions as well as by words, adults teach children what to fear, what to trust, what is good, bad, shameful, safe, possible. Children either accept our definitions or, if their experience is radically different (as it is for children who are molested), they are thrown into conflict, confusion, insecurity, and anguish.

When a man sexually uses a child, he is giving that child a strong message about her world: He is telling her that she is important because of her sexuality, that men want sex from girls, and that relationships are insufficient without sex. He is telling her that she can use her sexuality as a way to get the attention and affection she genuinely needs, that sex is a tool. When he tells her not to tell, she learns there is something about sex that is shameful and bad; and that she, because she is a part of it, is shameful and bad; and that he, because he is a part of it, is shameful and bad. She learns that the world is full of sex and is shameful and bad and not to be trusted, that even those entrusted with her care will betray her; that she will betray herself.

Although sometimes a child is able to say no, most children are not able to say no even when they desperately want to. Fortunately, programs are being developed to teach children how to refuse sexual advances, unwanted touching, and other invasions of their persons, but even though these programs are immensely valuable, there is no way to equalize the basic inequality of power, understanding, or freedom between a child and an adult.

...

People are becoming alarmed, and rightly so, about the extent of child abuse in general and child sexual abuse specifically. The taboo against speaking about this abuse is being torn open. But ... it is important to understand that the phenomenon of violence against women and children and the condoning of this violence is not simply a contemporary perversion but part of an ancient and pervasive worldwide tradition.

In biblical times, sex was sanctioned between men and young girls (Rush 1980:16–47). Under talmudic law, the sexual use of girls over the age of three was permissible, provided the girl's father consented and appropriate moneys were transferred. Sexual intercourse was an acceptable means of establishing be-trothal, and the use of both women and girls was regulated by a detailed set of laws reflecting the property status of females. Women and girls were owned, rented, bought, and sold as sexual commodities. As long as these transactions were conducted with proper payment to the males, rabbis and lawmakers ap-proved.

The sexual use of girls under the age of three was not regulated legally, as these children were considered too young to be legal virgins, and were therefore without monetary value. Sex with girls under the age of three was not subject to any restrictions. As in hunting, it was open season. Boys under the age of nine were also fair game. Though sex between adult men was severely punished, men could—and did—use young boys at will.

The advent of Christianity did not change things substantially. Canon law held that sexual intercourse established possession, and popes through the cen-turies upheld rape as an indissoluble means of contracting a marriage. However, Christian law raised the age for legally valid sex from three to seven, making sex-ual intercourse with girls over seven binding and sexual intercourse with girls under seven of no consequence to the authorities. In the thirteenth century, the concept of statutory rape was introduced. Its enforcement was not impressive, however, as the clergy itself infamously exploited girls sexually—in the confes-sional and in the convent schools.

...

[Today,] advertisements, the media, and pornography encourage acceptance of the sexual use of children. By blurring the distinction between woman and girl-child, these omnipresent images sometimes leave the message that chil-dren, as well as women, can be—and should be—sexually consumed. Women are photographed in seductive poses dressed in ankle socks, holding lollipops and teddy bears. Adolescent and preadolescent girls are photographed soft-fo-cus in and out of lacy, ribboned lingerie.

...

[Such images] confuse adult women with children; vulnerability with sexual invitation; masculinity with aggression; yes with no; women with their genitals; and both women and children with property, owned by men.

Men are taught to equate power and violence with a sense of well-being. Many seek this sense of well-being so desperately, so recklessly, that they are willing to look for it even in the bodies of children. Their concern for the child is too weak to check them, their desire for domination too strong.

In a world that is polluted, possibly beyond recovery, and in which the health of future generations is mortgaged for cars and electrical appliances, it is per-fectly consistent that so many men foul the lives of children. It reflects a deep selfishness, an insistence that their desires be met, at whatever cost to others, even to their own children.

The sexual abuse of children is part of a culture in which violence to life is condoned. Our forests, our rivers, our oceans, our air, our earth, this entire biosphere, all are invaded with poison—raped, just as our children are raped. It is very possible that in fifty years or less, life as we know it will not exist on earth. Nuclear war could kill us all. Even without an explosion, the radiation emitted in the various phases of mining, milling, and constructing nuclear power plants and weapons is already so abundant that the continuation of our species is in grave danger (Caldicott 1981). It is not odd that men whose desire for profit has superseded their own instinct for survival should so abuse their young. To stunt a child's trust in people, in love, in her world, to instill a fear that may take a lifetime to overcome, may never be overcome, to force one's body into the body of a child, of a baby, to desecrate children so is consistent for people who desecrate all life and the possibility of future life.

...

These Are the Things I Remember

Maggie Hoyal

> *"Because I could never talk about what had happened to me, it dominated my life. Then, through my writing, I discovered that I have an intellect that is not stupid but unstretched, a heart which can feel more than pain, a body that once again belongs to me."*

...

WE WERE ASLEEP WHEN IT STARTED. It was mama's voice that woke me up. I had never heard it sound like that, hard and biting.

"It won't work this time," she said.

"Don't you say that," daddy said.

"I told you, Dick, if it happened again I was going to leave you."

"That's your damn English talking."

"It's not right what you do to her!"

I sucked in my breath. What was mama saying?

"She didn't wake up. She doesn't even have to know it happened," he said.

"For God's sake, you promised to stop."

"I will, I will. Just say you won't leave me."

"There is something wrong with you, Dick. It's not safe for the children to be—"

It was then that he struck her, cutting off the words with a hard slap. "You're never taking my kids away from me."

I wanted this not to be happening. I got out of bed and walked soundlessly to the door. I tried to stop shaking. When I looked through the cracked opening into the living room, I could see mama holding the side of her face and tears coming down.

He grabbed her arm and dragged her into the bathroom and threw her to the floor. "No one's ever taking my kids. I'll see 'em dead first."

That was when mama screamed and I started out the door and halfway into the living room. His back was to me, but I could see him put his hands around her throat and squeeze. I tried to scream, but the sound wouldn't come out of my throat. When he stood up, mama was lying in a limp heap upon the bathroom floor. He just stood there looking down at her.

I thought she was dead. He brought his arms up and started rubbing his hands like they were tired. It scared me. I thought any minute he was going to turn on me, so I ran softly into the bedroom and closed the door back the way it was.

If my brothers were awake, they never said so. I never talked about it to anyone.

*   *   *

One morning mama was gone. We kept waiting for her to come home. But when daddy came in from work that night, he brought a lady with him and he told us mama was gone for good and this was our new mama. That night I was alone in my small bed on the far side of the room. My brothers slept in the army bunk beds that rested against the other wall. The lady that was not our mother had tucked us in and kissed our cheeks. Before the light snapped off, I noticed she had wrong-colored hair, and afterward there was only the silence of the house, empty of mother.

I cried quietly at first, not wanting my brothers to hear, but then it took over, the crying, and I didn't care anymore. I hoped the darkness would hide me, and the silence. Muffled footsteps came into the room and the light ruined my face, exposed it, swollen-eyed and smeared with tears that wouldn't stop even then.

"Are you okay, honey?" the lady that was not our mother asked.

Dickie pushed himself up on an elbow and brushed the hair out of his eyes. "Aw, she's just crying about our mother. Don't worry about her. We like you fine."

"Yeah, we think you're prettier, too," Bobbie stuck in, "and anyway she's just bein' a baby."

"You miss your mama, honey, is that it?"

I cut off the woman's words, pushed them away in my mind and kept repeating over and over my brother's words.

"You're a baby, you're a baby."

I knew if I kept thinking on those words I could stop crying. I could push the pain behind the anger and hide it there until the lady was gone and it was safe again in the darkness.

"That's right. See, you've stopped crying like a good girl. You go on back to sleep now."

When the light went off, I pushed my face hard into the pillow and let the sob come, but this time there was no sound, just the wetness growing in a circle around my face.

*   *   *

I don't remember the day mother came back, I only know that something ended between us.

I came to her only because there was no one else. I was eight years old, but I remember, even in that first vision of St. Lucia, walking across the island sand, which shone white even in the darkness that was undisturbed by cities. I remember thinking how beautiful the world was. The wind sweeping in from the ocean. I remember thinking nothing ugly could happen here.

It was the first motel built on the island, and dad had been the foreman on the job. Instead of the promised bonus for finishing the job early, we were all guests in the motel.

We were on our way to supper at the motel dining room. It was the first time we had to dress in our best clothes before we could go and eat. Mom and dad went first, quietly talking, my brothers following behind like two hungry dogs at their heels. I was walking behind the others, not wanting to ruin the beauty, the sounds of the night, with words. I saw the shadow first as it crossed mine in the white sand—the dark husk of a man before me in the sand—and I jumped. I had been warned about the native men, but then I realized it was only dad.

He began to speak in hushed, urgent tones. "It will be different here," he said.

"What?"

"There won't be anyone to disturb us. ... Oh, don't pretend," he continued. "You know what I'm talking about."

It hit me, what he meant. I had thought it was over. I had thought it couldn't happen here. I'd put it out of my mind as if it had never happened at all. Him hanging on my door when I got undressed at night, the back-door touching whenever mom was at work. Whenever no one was there to go to, to stop him. I couldn't think of anything to say. I felt tired, and all the beauty of the island was defeated in that moment. Now it was a dangerous place, isolated and lawless.

"Don't worry. I'll take care of your mother so she'll never know."

"But—"

"Don't worry. I'll take care of everything."

He walked away then.

Even if I had thought of anything to say, it was too late.

A few days later, when mother was shopping and the boys were scouting out the island, it began. I heard it in his voice when he called my name. I didn't answer, but he knew I was in my room. After calling a second time, he became angry and yelled for me to come.

I still didn't move.

He walked into my room, but instead of being angry like I thought he would be, he was smiling.

"Take down your pants," he said.

"What'd I do?" I said.

He was still smiling, as if he were in a dream.

"Why?" I answered in a small voice.

He moved toward me.

"It's wrong," I said.

"Your damn mother and her Victorian morals. There's no place for them here. I'm not going to let you turn out cold like your mother."

"I'll tell her."

He grabbed my arms and held them to my sides. His hand slipped down between my legs. His voice was soothing then. He didn't notice that I struggled.

I could feel myself against his hand. I wanted to cry, but I couldn't. I couldn't do anything. I felt the same as when I tried to jump across a mud flat next to a creek and landed short. I started sinking in, and when I pulled at one foot, the other went in deeper. That's what it felt like, sinking.

He pulled his hand out of my pants and spit on his fingers and rubbed them together. He didn't even seem aware of me. The sound of his spitting made me sick. Then he put his hand back down my pants and started to say something in that singsong voice he used.

The front screen door slammed and his hand ripped out of my pants like it was burned. Then he turned on me and whispered harshly, "Don't you say anything to your mother ever. If you do, you'll be sorrier than you've ever been in your life."

I made the bathroom and locked the door. Something that always made my father angry. He used to tease me mean about it, saying I was a prude, like it was something stupid to be. I pulled my pants down and took soap and water and washed off the spit. When I came out, my brothers were there eating sandwiches. The day went on like nothing had ever happened.

At dinner, mom said, "You're awfully quiet, you sick?"

I just shook my head and looked down at my plate. She got up and came over to feel my head.

"You don't feel warm, but you'd better get to bed early just the same."

"Don't baby the girl, she's probably just sulking."

"Just the same, Dick, she don't look right. It wouldn't hurt to be careful."

"There's not a damn thing wrong with her."

"You're probably right."

"Damn right I'm right. You might be a smart little RN and gone to college, but you don't know half of nothing."

"I'm sorry, I didn't mean anything."

"Why, your mother didn't even know how to cook when I married her. I had to teach her. And she sure didn't know anything about being a mother, or a woman, for that matter! Still don't know how to be."

"I been trying, Dick."

"Well, just don't try and tell me I don't know what I'm talking about."

My mother nodded silently and got up to start the dishes.

When dad went off to work the next day, I tried to get my mother alone. Her friends were visiting from the other side of the island, and she made coffee and served little cakes.

I had always been quiet; it was hard for me to talk when other people were around, and I knew that mom would be annoyed at being disturbed.

"Mom, I have to talk to you," I said.

The other people in the room stopped talking and looked at me.

"Oh, is that your daughter?" one woman said. "Why, she looks just like you."

I remember grimacing.

"What do you want?" mom said.

"I want to talk to you alone."

"Oh, this is silly. Excuse me, Marsha, I'll be back in a minute."

When we got in the room, she turned to me impatiently and said, "What's wrong, Molly, are you sick?"

"No ..."

When anyone looked upset, that was the first thing my mother asked. She always looked disappointed when it wasn't that one thing she knew how to fix.

"Then what is it? You interrupted our guests."

"It's about dad. He's ... he's doing things."

"What things?"

"He makes me let him look at me and ... he touches me."

"Where? Where does he touch you?"

All I could do was look down in embarrassment.

"It's wrong, isn't it?" I said. "It's wrong what he does."

Mother didn't answer.

"Doesn't it say it's wrong to do that in the Bible? Doesn't it?"

"Yes, yes, of course it does."

"Will you make him stop?"

I heard the sound of laughter coming from the other room. Mother heard it, too. I could hear it in her voice, I could see it in the way her eyes were already darting back and forth toward the door. It was as if my mother were caught and wanted to get away. Back to the safety of polite conversation and meaningless laughter.

"Now, listen, I have to go, they will be wondering, but I'll talk to your father and none of this will ever happen again." As she started to leave the room, she turned back, her face directed toward me but not looking at my eyes. "If it does, you let me know."

I stood alone in the room, staring at the door as it closed after her.

*   *   *

When I was fourteen, my parents were divorced and I went with my father and my brother Bob. We were living at the Pine Grove Apartments in Miami. My brother was gone a lot because he was dating a girl my father didn't like. I didn't hear from my mother, but I knew about where it was she lived.

I was going to school and taking care of all the household chores—washing, shopping, and cooking. It was awkward because I had so much to do and I was so afraid to make a mistake. My father thought everything should be perfect. I remember I had just brought the groceries in. I walked to the store and carried the two large bags the five blocks back home. I had just set them down on the counter and collapsed into a chair when my father came barging through the door.

"What are you doing on your butt? The groceries aren't even put away."

I jumped up and headed toward the kitchen.

"Hurry up and make dinner, I'm hungry—no, fix me a drink first."

There was something about his voice that worried me. It was the old feeling of something crawling up the back of my neck.

"You know those clothes you bought last week?"

The question took me by surprise and I didn't answer right away.

"You know who bought those clothes? Me! You just show the little card and think everything is for free. It's not free, I pay for it. And now you have to pay for it."

I hadn't had new clothes in three years and it was dad who'd said I couldn't go around looking the way I did. "I don't want no ragamuffin for a daughter. Take the card and plan to spend about a hundred dollars."

By the time I got through the underwear and the bras and a few skirts and blouses, that was it. I was amazed at how fast it went.

"Now you have to pay for it," he said. "That was the deal."

Dad had said I would be happier I had chose him 'cause he would make me be something, not like mother. She was ruining Dickie by taking him away from discipline, spoiling him.

"He'll be just like all my brothers and sisters, failures. Not one of 'em any good except maybe Pauline, but she's more like a man than a woman should be."

That was the worst thing anyone could be when we were growing up. A failure.

I guess that's some of the reason I went with dad. It didn't seem like there was a choice. Mom never contradicted him about it, and though dad was strict, nothing ugly had happened in several years and I thought that was over. Mom and I were always at odds then and the only thing I felt from her besides annoyance was a void. That frightened me even more than dad did. With dad, at least I felt it mattered that I existed.

But it was like that. Spaces of years where the molesting seemed like a bad nightmare that had happened once to someone else—and then, out of nowhere, there it was.

"What do you mean, pay for it? I don't have any money. Anyway, you told me to buy the clothes. It was your idea."

"Don't talk stupid. Fix me another drink."

I was afraid and confused.

But then dad sat back and smiled at me like he was proud of me all of a sudden. "You know, I'm going to take you and Bob back with me to St. Lucia. Things could be good there. I'll get my flying license back again, like when I was an officer in the air force, and we'll start our own business. Just the real Muellers—Dickie won't get nothing. He don't deserve to be a Mueller.

"And you—why, you won't even know yourself. Molly, you'll be an independent woman, not like your mother. You'll be free. I'm going to teach you how to fly better than any man, and just you and me we'll make a damn good business jockeying tourists back and forth between the islands. Bob, he'll do all the paper work and keep things going right while we fly our heads off."

It sounded like a dream. I thought about how it would be, flying all alone sometimes, just me and—

"But we have to get this other stuff out of the way first."

"What other stuff?"

"You and me. We have to go through with it and get to the other side. You're getting older now and you know other boys. Maybe some of those rich tourists are going to start dating you. You can't keep feeling the way you do about me. I'm your father, and when you meet some special boy, then you'll find you come to love him like you think you love me now. I know you won't think so now, but someday this will just be a memory in the past."

I felt like I was sinking. I leaned on the counter and tried to think the thing out. *My God. He thinks I want to ... Jesus. He thinks it's me that ...*

It was the first time I really realized he was sick. Before, I had just pushed it all out of my mind. Now I had to face it, to face him. I kept thinking I had to trust myself now. I wondered what he would do if I told him he made me sick.

I thought about it, fucking him. My mind just couldn't keep hold of it. I wondered if I could take that. Then I thought about him. What would it do to him if I told him what I really thought? Would he go crazy? Was he crazy?

The argument wove in and out—first the threat, *you owe me;* and then what was worse, the pleading: *I'm your father, trust me, trust me.* And then, what if I told him he was insane?

I had to decide.

I was so tired of it drilling at me like a tedious argument that would never, never end. I thought, If I do it, maybe then it will be over with for good. He will finally have what he wants and leave me alone.

I thought, Okay, you motherfucker, I'll trust you once.

Maybe I was just tired of fighting, tired of having no one to go to. Tired of wondering who was right. My father had told me that mom already knew everything, and that my brothers knew about it, too.

When I was twelve, Bob had caught me packing to run away and he just laughed at me. "You run away? You don't have it in you. What do you want to go for anyway?"

I had started to cry. I told him about dad. What had been going on. He knew what I meant.

"I have to run away, Bob."

"No, you don't want to go and do that," he said. "Dad must know what he's doing, he's our father—he knows what's best."

After that, I knew there would never be any help from Bob.

My father interrupted my thoughts for the millionth time. "Well ... ?"

"All right, all right, I'll do it. But I have my period now."

Then there was no pretense about teaching me or doing what was good for me.

"When is it going to be over?"

"I don't know," I said sharply.

It was the longest period I ever had, but finally even I knew that it wouldn't work for much longer.

It was in the middle of the afternoon when dad drew the line.

"Now," he said.

"But—"

"I don't believe that period shit. If you still have it, show me your pad."

"Listen, forget it. I never wanted to do it anyway. You keep pushing it and pushing it."

"See? I knew you were lying."

"I wasn't lying. I had my period."

"I knew it, you said 'had.' See? You said 'I *had* my period.' You can't fool me. I knew you were lying. I was just waiting for you to own up to it yourself."

I was trapped. My period had been over for five days. I was caught in a lie that, no matter how inconsequential, seemed to discredit anything I had to say. I couldn't seem to win.

"I know you better than you know yourself, that's why I know what's best for you better than you do, or ever will, for that matter.

"Now," he said, "take off your clothes."

"In the middle of the day? What about Bob?"

"Bob won't be home till later. He's busy, and anyway you don't have to worry about him. Hurry up."

I stood there. My toes seemed to try to crawl under the terrazzo floor. I was looking at the cold white bed. The room was filled with icy air and white light shifting through the pale green curtains. I wanted to say something. I wanted to say no.

"I don't want to," I said.

"That's over with now. It's been decided." His voice was threatening now, dangerous.

"I have to go."

"Go then, but make it short."

My legs were trembling. I looked into the bathroom mirror and laughed softly into it, at the lovely creature, the scared girl, staring out at me.

I had never even gone on a date. I looked like I was ready to attend my first party.

"Come on, get done and get out of there."

"Coming," I yelled back. Even here he won't leave me alone, I thought bitterly.

I thought of locking the door.

There was no lock.

Damned cheap apartments, they can't even afford privacy for the john door. Can't even lock the door on your father when he's crazy and you're scared.

I thought of Bob. A glint of hope that maybe he would come. At the next moment, the door would open and put a stop to the whole miserable thing. Then I laughed again into the mirror, No, no pretending, not now. No, dad was right, Bob was busy. He wouldn't be back till it was too late to matter.

Then I thought I would break down, and the tears stung in my eyes. Bob, how could you leave me here with this crazy man, who doesn't even know what crazy is?

"I'm coming in there to get you if you don't get out of there soon."

I started taking off my blouse, not wanting to undress in front of him. After all this time, my breasts were growing. How I hated them in that moment. My body was late at doing everything. I had thought my breasts would never grow, and now the joy of it, of becoming a woman, was twisted and stolen from me.

"No!" I screamed, but the words never left my mouth.

I took off my skirt and panties. My belly was brown and smooth. I hadn't put on any lazy fat yet. My clothes fell to the floor. I should fold them, I thought, and then wanted to cry again. They were the new clothes I had just bought. They were carelessly pretty in the tight, short style of Miami in the Sixties. City of light. Artificial city where the sun never touches the cold irony of its people, drifting from air-conditioned apartments to neon bars.

I touched the cold sheets. His touch was cold, too, his sloppy groping gestures hidden under the sheets. The touch of his hanging belly on top of mine. The smell of Old Spice and Canadian Club breathing down on me from his sloppy open mouth. He wasn't drunk. He was never drunk, just undignified. He felt my cunt with his fingers and then, like a doctor prescribing a medicine, he said,

"We'll just get some baby oil and then it won't hurt at all. You're lucky I am doing this for you the first time and not some punk in the back seat of a car."

I was beyond thinking and feeling then.

I remember the putrid smell of baby oil and the cold wet oil dripping from my thighs. I remember saying over and over to myself, It will be over soon, it will be over soon, it will be over ...

The shock of the searing pain so deep inside me, I knew no one had a right to that. I pulled away, furiously struggling to get free. I screamed. He looked at me with contempt.

"It doesn't hurt that much. I used the baby oil so I know."

It was then that I started screaming, "No, *get off me! Get off me!*"

He seemed shocked. "Take it easy now. Well, maybe it does hurt the first time a little. Okay, calm down, okay."

His body slid across me like a great lumpy slug.

I closed my eyes for a second to squeeze the tears back.

He went to touch me, but I jerked away.

I crawled from the bed, my cunt aching like it had been sliced open. I walked slowly to the bathroom, a trickle of blood running in a thin, delicate line down my thigh.

White Man Wants a Black Piece: The Case of Sonia Morrell

Diana E.H. Russell

Ms. MORRELL WAS RAPED in Massachusetts when she was twenty years old. She was first interviewed three or four months after it happened and then again, a year later. …

Ms. Morrell's mother is black and her father white. She is very light skinned, and people are sometimes confused about her racial identity. She, however, considers herself black, and that is where her identity lies.

SONIA MORRELL: It was a Friday night, and there was supposed to have been this party on campus. But there wasn't a party, and so about three of my friends and I came back from a God-awful Friday night dinner to the dorm and said, "OK, where are the guys? Where is everybody?" We looked into the living room, and there were these two white guys sitting in there, so we went in, and this girl from our dorm was down there talking to them, and she introduced us to them. It turned out that they were frat guys from X [a prestigious private college].

I was talking to the guy named Vic. The other guy, Bob, was whispering to the girl who introduced us, and they kept looking at me. The girl came over to me and said, "If Bob asked you out, would you go out?" I said, "Who's Bob?" I haven't run into that since high school—where the guy can't even come over and ask you himself.

So he said, "We're having this wine and cheese party tomorrow night at our house. Would you like to come?" I said, "Oh, you have a house?" He said, "Yeah, a fraternity." I thought that my two friends and I could drive to this party, but he said, "Well, I was just inviting you." I said, "Oh, OK." He said, "I'll come and get you and bring you back."

Afterward I panicked, especially considering he was white, and I discussed it with my friends. I have white friends, but never a white fraternity guy. I didn't know how to relate to this guy. Everybody said, "Go, Sonia, because it will be a good experience for you, and you'll learn something." Anyway, it's not every day you get to go to a cheese and wine party, and there was supposed to be a band, so I said, "OK, OK."

Bob came. On the way there we talked about something racial. He said something about this black guy he knew. The way he was talking about him, I really didn't dig it. I thought he's either got a lot of gall or he's ignorant. So I said, "Do you know that I am black?" He said, "Oh, yeah." I figured that the girl he kept talking to the night I met him had told him. I asked her later if she had, and she said that he had asked her, "She's part white, isn't she?"

We arrived, and there were all these white frat people and sorority girls there; everybody there had blond hair. There were no nonwhites there. Just me. The band was really hip. They kept looking at me, and one of the guys in the band turned to me and said, "What are *you* doing here?" I said, "I don't know." He said, "You don't belong in a place like this, because this is the shits." And I said, "What are *you* doing here?" He said, "Well, we're getting paid." I said, "Well, I didn't have anything else to do, so I thought it might be interesting." Then good old Bob came back.

INTERVIEWER: What did he look like?

MS. MORRELL: He was maybe six one. He was pretty tall and in build a little bit overweight. He was really strong. Really! I'm small, so compared to me he was very big. He was between twenty and twenty-two. He came from a wealthy family. I thought he was really handsome, and he seemed nice except for the racial thing.

We danced, and he kept drinking a whole lot of wine. I had one glass of wine, and after that I drank Seven Up, and I ate a lot of cheese. We danced slow, and he said, "Wow, I've never danced with a girl who could follow me before." He started getting chummy, you know, wrapping his arms around me a little bit more, and I said, "Easy, fella."

We went outside. He held my hand and introduced me to his friends, and his friends were very strange and kept saying, "Wow, you're really hip, aren't you? Wow, Bob, she's hip." I was looking at the girls with their blond hair, and their flower pant suits giving me the eye, like, get out of here. It was pretty bad. But it was interesting because I had never experienced anything like this, so it didn't really bother me.

The party was coming to an end. Bob had been drinking a considerable amount of wine, but I was feeling great. I felt a little bit mellow from the one glass of wine. He said, "Do you want to go upstairs to my room?" and I said, "For what?" He said, "Just to talk." I said, "OK." I wanted to make sure everything was cool. He had been pretty nice, and he was interesting to me.

We went to his room, and I sat down in the chair, and he sat down on the bed, and he was telling me about his life when all of a sudden he grabs my arm and tries to pull me up. I just sat there. I didn't want to get up. He said, "Come on, sit over here on the bed with me. It's hard for me to talk to you in this arrangement." I said, "OK," and I got on the bed with him. He came at me immediately. I figured, OK, one kiss was cool. So he kissed me. It was a crummy kiss, and I was thinking, "Oh, I have to leave."

He kissed me once more, and I looked at my watch, and I said, "Oh, wow, I better get back to the dorm soon. I didn't sign out." He said, "I saw it when you signed out. I've taken girls out from your college before. I know all about the signing-in stuff." I said, "But I really do have to get back because it's getting late, and I'm tired, and I have a lot of studying to do tomorrow." He said, "You can stay a little bit longer." I said, "OK. OK. Then I have to go." He said, "OK." So we talked again.

Then he attacked me again. We started to struggle. I was not responding to his kisses. Then he started with my clothes. I had thought that it was just going to be one of those little make-out sessions, but it was something else. It was terrible. I had these knit pants on, and he kept pulling them down, and I kept pulling them up.

He got my shirt unbuttoned. Then I'd start to button it up, then he'd start to pull my pants down, then I'd pull them up, then he'd unbutton my shirt. It was like a perverted movie.

He was rather large and quite strong, but he wasn't violent. He was persistent. It was this struggle, struggle, struggle, back and forth. I was really fighting him off, but it was not doing much good. I said, "I want to go! Please take me back to school." He said, "No." I said, "Please, Bob, please. Take me back to school. I don't know you, and I'm not the kind of girl who likes to go hopping into bed with people. Please take me back." "No," he said.

So I said, "OK, I'm going to leave then." So he grabbed my purse and said, "You won't get far without your purse." I said, "Oh, come on. You can't be this hard up that you want to go through all this stuff. Give me my purse!" I was really mad. He said, "No." So I thought, "Well, I'll call school and have someone come and get me." But I didn't know where the phone was, and I didn't even think about my best friend who was half an hour away from where we were. I said, "Look. You said you'd pick me up, and you said you'd take me back. Please, please take me back." "No," he said.

"I haven't done anything to deserve this," I said.

"Yeah," he said, "but I've shown you a good time, now I want you to show me a good one." I said, "Look, it was a shitty evening. So now I've given you back your shit. Take me back to the dorm." He said, "No. You know you're lying. You had a good time." It was just terrible. He said, "If you'll make love with me, I'll take you home." I said, "No! Take me home now!" So he continued to fight, fight, fight. He got my pants off. I don't know how he managed that. It was about two o'clock in the morning, and I was getting pretty tired. Then he started with my underpants, and that was a huge struggle. It was incredible. He had taken his own pants off, but still had his underpants on. He pulled my underpants down, and he fell down on top of me, his penis was next to my vagina, but still in his underpants. He started blowing in my ear, because he really thought he was turning me on. He started putting his tongue in my ear and blowing in it and thumping against me with his damn penis. Hell!

So I kept trying to push him and push him and push him, and he kept saying, "What's the matter with you? Aren't I pleasing to you?" He had grabbed my breasts like they were two doorknobs, and he was gripping them painfully. I was getting pretty tired, and somehow he got his penis out and pressed himself inside me. He must have been two inches long, because I didn't even feel it. I just felt this thrust, and I realized he was inside me.

I felt like some huge gigantic vagina. I didn't even feel him. He was thumping up and down, and breathing deeply, but I didn't move. My legs were together, but suddenly he grabbed my legs, and he said, "Spread," and threw them apart. Shit! Then he comes flying out of me and turns me around on my stomach, and he grabs me so I'm on my knees and pushes himself into me again. I guess he really thought he was doing a whole lot. I was like a dish rag. I just had had it. And he just went thump, thump, thump.

All I kept thinking about was how I was going to get to leave. Then he threw me on my back again and came into me from the front, and it's bam, bam, bam. Then suddenly he stopped. And I thought, "My God, now he's had a heart attack." I didn't understand what was wrong with him. Then he just rolled over, and I felt wetness, and I figured, "Oh, that's what it is."

When he was making out with me earlier he had said, "I hope you're protected." And I'd said, "What do you mean?" He'd said, "Well, I would use a condom if you weren't." I'd said, "You're not going to get to use a condom." So I guess he assumed that I was protected. So after lying still, he rolled over and asked me, "Do you have your pills in your purse?" I said, "Oh, yeah, sure. I just carry them around with me daily for exciting adventures like this." Then he fell asleep, just like that. Ka-bam. I mean he "came" just like he went to sleep, ka-bam.

I wanted to go to the bathroom, but it was downstairs. And in this frat house with all these perverted frats, I was afraid that if I got up and went outside, they would attack me. So I lay there, and then I woke him up, and I said, "Please, can we leave." Immediately he started in again. Tha-gump, tha-gump, tha-gump, and I just lay there. This time he didn't try all his little positions. He came, bam, fell out, and then he sloshed over me, and went back to sleep again.

I *had* to go to the bathroom, my bladder was bursting. I put on my long sweater, and I go out in the hall. I felt horrible. I kept thinking that I was like a receptacle for his sperm. I wanted to wash. I went to the boys' bathroom, and when I came out this frat guy who was asleep on the stairs woke up and said, "Hey, do you want to ball? Oh, wow, I see you're already here balling somebody else. Out of sight. Out of sight. Well, when you get done with them, why don't you come with me?" This made me scared to leave the place.

I went back into Bob's room. I felt better. I lay down on the bed. It must have been about 5:30 A.M. by that time. I had my sweater on, and my underpants and my bra, and I was just lying there. He woke up, and this claw comes over and attacks my breasts again. I pushed his hand away, and he said, "What's the matter?" I said, "I want to leave." He said, "Why? Didn't you like it? What is it? You don't like white guys? Tell me, what is the difference between black guys and white guys?" I said, "Black guys have rhythm." And he said, "Oh, how do you mean? They move with rhythm?" I said, "Yeah."

So then I guess he had to prove his manhood to me, and he comes flopping on top of me again, and I said, "Hold it, hold it, hold it." I had my underpants on, and here he's going to try to shove himself up through my underpants. I said, "Hold it, hold it, hold it. Forget it. OK? You're an excellent love maker. I want to go home."

He said, "Well, I've made it with a black girl. You know, you're the first one I've ever made it with. I feel so good. I was so afraid that I wouldn't be able to satisfy a black woman. But now I know I can." I felt like throwing up on the bed. I said, "You're really sick!" which was a mistake, because he started on this whole passion thing, that he really dug me, and that he and I could really get it on.

It was day by then, and he said, "Come on. Let's get up and get dressed." He acted like it'd been the love affair of his life. He said, "Come on, I'll take you downstairs, and we'll feed you. You're so skinny." We got down to the little dining room and he said, "OK, what do you want to eat?" I said, "Nothing." "You have to eat something." So I said, "OK, I'll have a cup of coffee." He said, "You've got to have something else." I said, "OK, I'll eat one of these doughnuts." He said, "No, you've got to eat more than that. Take two doughnuts, and you've got to eat some cereal." So I'm eating the stuff, and he's reading the newspaper, and he saw an article. I don't remember what it was, but he made an extremely racist comment. I said, "I'm going to throw up." He got upset. I said, "Don't talk to me, I'm going to throw up. Really. Just leave me alone." I really thought that I was going to lose it any minute. So then he said, "Well, we're going to go."

We got in the car and we're driving along when we saw this girl that I know and that he knows from my school, and so we gave her a ride back. Bob kept putting his hand over and patting my thigh. Back at the dorm he said, "What do you want to do next weekend?" I said, "Anything but be with you!" He said, "Oh, come on!"

INTERVIEWER: Did you see what Bob did as rape?

MS. MORRELL: No, I didn't feel that I had been raped. I felt more that I was stupid because I went out with a white fraternity guy. I had been bothered in high school by white guys wanting to get a black girl to see what they're like. So I blamed myself for going out with him. Also I didn't think of it as rape because I knew him and because I consented to go. At the time I thought rape was a man coming out of the bushes and attacking you, so somebody you knew couldn't rape you.

INTERVIEWER: When did you perceive it differently?

MS. MORRELL: When a rape victim told me about her experience, which was similar to mine, I stopped her and said, "My God, that same thing happened to me."

INTERVIEWER: So when she talked about it in those terms, you agreed with her that it was rape?

MS. MORRELL: Yes. I thought she was absolutely right.

INTERVIEWER: Once you perceived it as rape, did that change how you felt about it?

MS. MORRELL: Oh, hell, yes! I don't feel I'm to blame at all. I have every right in the world to go out with a man, and I have every right in the world to say no, and my no should be respected. Men can go out, and they don't get raped.

INTERVIEWER: Do you think that the experience affected your sexual relationships with men?

MS. MORRELL: The rape was a big blow. With my boyfriend I always felt like I was going through the routine. You know, I'm supposed to do this, and I do it, because I'm supposed to please him. But I didn't feel anymore that I was getting anything out of it. Then right after talking to that other woman who was raped, I started becoming aware that I had rights as a woman. It's funny, because I've always demanded equality economically and in every other sphere, but sexually my demands were absolutely zero, so I started really thinking about that.

I didn't want to think that all white men were like Bob. In the summer I had a white boyfriend, and it was fine. But what I noticed is I have completely rejected traditional ideas of masculinity. I don't want somebody very big or strong, I imagine because of fear. I see a man who's built big, and I immediately become paranoid. And I'm very afraid of older men. Past a certain age, they just really frighten me.

INTERVIEWER: Did your experience affect your attitude toward men in other ways?

MS. MORRELL: Well, I don't trust men. I went on a date a couple of weeks ago and was absolutely petrified. I was pacing the floors about going. I really am afraid, and I have very little desire to go out and meet more men, because I'm afraid of trusting somebody and having them hurt me.

INTERVIEWER: You feel that it was your experience with Bob that caused this?

MS. MORRELL: Oh, yeah. I get very nervous when a man tries to talk to me at a party or something. I'm afraid I'll like him. I'll think he's nice, and then he'll push himself on me. Another thing it did was confirm my belief about men who brag about sex being the shittiest at it!

INTERVIEWER: Did it affect your attitude toward yourself at all?

MS. MORRELL: When it first happened, I thought I was carrying the burden that all black women carry. Now I feel that I'm just taking what all women have to take, but what all women should refuse to take.

INTERVIEWER: Did you find yourself feeling guilty or responsible in any way?

MS. MORRELL: Immediately afterward I did. Now I feel very guilty that I didn't just go out and hit him really hard in the mouth, because I am pretty strong, and I could have done that. That makes me damn mad. I was still following that feminine role that says I wouldn't be able to do anything. Even if I'd just have screamed!

INTERVIEWER: Why didn't you?

MS. MORRELL: Because if I drew attention to what was happening, everyone would blame me and say I was stupid. I felt that they would believe him, because he was white, and he was a fraternity guy, and I was just this black girl. I just thought it was useless.

I believe strongly that a black woman against a white man has got very little chance at all. Generally any woman against a man has little. And then I was really afraid to be stuck on that campus in that area, because it was all fraternity houses, and I didn't know where I was.

INTERVIEWER: Can you remember what your predominant feeling was at the time of the rape?

MS. MORRELL: Well, first I was afraid that he was going to call in his frat brothers and run a train on me, because he said they were in the hall. I remember hearing in high school about girls that had had trains run on them.

INTERVIEWER: That means it's a gang rape?

MS. MORRELL: Yes. One right after the other.

Also, I really felt hurt, because I had trusted him and thought he was nice. But the feelings of anger and disgust were stronger. I said things to him that were really nasty. I kept putting him down, saying he was really a shitty love maker. I'm using the word *love making* now because that's exactly how I thought of it. Like I said, I couldn't accept that he was raping me. I thought that he was making me make love with him. So I wouldn't move, and I kept faking yawns. But then when he went to sleep, I cried all night.

INTERVIEWER: Did you ever see or hear of him again?

MS. MORRELL: Yeah. He called me up to ask me out to a play. I hung up on him. I thought he was out of his mind. I never thought he'd ever mention my name again, but he remembered my whole name and asked one of my friends if I still lived in the same dorm.

INTERVIEWER: So is that the only contact you've had with him afterward, indirectly or directly?

MS. MORRELL: Yeah. Every now and then I think I see somebody who looks like him, and I get really paranoid, and I want to run.

INTERVIEWER: What was your predominant feeling after the rape incident?

MS. MORRELL: I told my close friend, the girl I live with now, what happened.

INTERVIEWER: Was she the first person you told?

MS. MORRELL: Yeah. And this interview is the second. I have never told anyone else. I was embarrassed to tell my friend, but I did because I was so upset. I went into a deep depression for a couple of days. I didn't want to do anything. I stayed in my room and watched television and read. I just couldn't handle it, and then when he called a week later, that was too much.

INTERVIEWER: How did your friend react to it?

MS. MORRELL: She is black, and she reacted by making digs at whites. She said, "All they want is to use us." But she never mentioned the word rape.

INTERVIEWER: Did she blame you at all?

MS. MORRELL: No, because she's my friend. But there was a hint of "you shouldn't have gone." But she felt guilty because she had told me to go!

INTERVIEWER: How long did your feeling of depression last?

MS. MORRELL: I think it lasted about four days. I was getting back to normal and feeling pretty good, and then he called, and then it lasted again for about three days. I had broken up with my boyfriend, but he came to see me a week afterward, and I didn't want him to touch me.

INTERVIEWER: Did you tell him what had happened?

MS. MORRELL: Oh, no. I never would have told him, because I think he would have killed me. Black men are pretty heavy about white men messing with black women. I knew he would blame me and say I was stupid to have gone. I also knew that he'd get his friends, and they'd probably go and beat the hell out of the guy.

INTERVIEWER: And you didn't want that?

MS. MORRELL: No. I didn't want to be reminded of it. I just wanted the whole thing to be buried. I was embarrassed. It wasn't that I thought that my boyfriend would get in trouble, because all the black students down there would've rallied around him, and it would've been cool. But I just decided the easiest thing was to forget it.

INTERVIEWER: Why don't you tell people now?

MS. MORRELL: I don't want my boyfriend to know. I think he would generalize about what happened to me and apply it to all whites. I'm sure he would.

We broke up for a while, and he wanted to know if I'd gone out with anybody, and I said yes. And the first question he asked was, "Well, was he white?" I know it'd hurt him too much to tell him, and there is no sense in that. He can't deal with things like that.

Also, I won't tell my mother, because she would be hurt too much. I don't see any reason to cause her pain, and it's not bothering me anymore.

INTERVIEWER: Could you say anything else about how you perceived your rapist's personality and his motivation?

MS. MORRELL: I definitely think that there was a master-slave thing going on. I think a lot of white men really want to screw a black woman. When I was dancing slow with him, he was making some racial comments, like, "I've always noticed black people dance much better than white people."

He really wanted to be a stud, I think. That's why I started trying to blow his game away. I figured I can't hurt him physically, so mentally I'm going to do him in. I think he believed having a black woman helped him to prove his manhood. Also, I think he knew that if it was somebody white, like most of the girls that he knew from the sororities, he'd just be ruined, because that girl would have more power to do something about it, to cause him trouble. I guess he felt there was no risk with me.

INTERVIEWER: Did he expect you to enjoy it?

MS. MORRELL: Oh, yeah. He kept saying things like, "Do you like this? How's this position? Well, that was really nice, wasn't it?" and, "How do you like this?" or, "Do this. Don't you like this? This is really good, huh?" And I'd say, "Shit," or something, and then he'd get real upset.

INTERVIEWER: What did you think of his expecting you to enjoy it?

MS. MORRELL: I couldn't believe it. I thought he was completely fucked.

INTERVIEWER: What would you say his politics were?

MS. MORRELL: He saw himself as a white liberal, and he thought he was going to help all black people, but he is an extreme racist.

INTERVIEWER: Do you imagine that he had raped other women before you?

MS. MORRELL: I really doubt it. He was really clumsy. I was equally clumsy because I had never been through it before either. It seemed like the first time for both of us. Now, I know what I should have done. And if he had done it before, he would have been a lot more on his toes, a lot quicker.

He took too many risks. I remember there was a pocket knife on the bedside table, and I thought maybe I could kill him. But I decided I really couldn't handle that. But had he been experienced, he wouldn't have left something like that out. And he even got up and went to the bathroom and left me in the room alone. I could have split and called the police, but I didn't have a dime. Still he didn't know that. So I really don't think he had done it before. He probably is one of those smooth make-out men usually. He's got the kind of label that a lot of girls dig. I know the white girls in my dorm thought he was really hot stuff.

INTERVIEWER: What would you do now if you were in the same situation?

MS. MORRELL: I would hit him. I would really hit him. And I really, really feel stupid that I didn't scream, because I should have screamed. The band was still downstairs, and I could have screamed. I should have just busted out of his room and told him to shove my purse up his ass. I should have gone down and said to the band, "Man, you got to get me out of here. That guy has my purse, and he's trying to rape me." And I know that they would have helped me. Then I could have gotten my purse back.

The thing was, I didn't think about it. I was so involved in the struggle that I didn't reason about what I should be doing. By the time I realized what was happening, it was too late. And then that frat guy was sitting out in the hall, drunk, guarding the stairway. I was pretty much overcome with shock at the time.

You have to be prepared for it, and I was not prepared. But I'm prepared now, and somebody would be in for a definite shock if they tried that on me again. I'd really raise hell. ...

    ...

12

Fraternities and Rape on Campus

Patricia Yancey Martin
and Robert A. Hummer

RAPES ARE PERPETRATED on dates, at parties, in chance encounters, and in specially planned circumstances. That group structure and processes, rather than individual values or characteristics, are the impetus for many rape episodes was documented by Blanchard (1959) 30 years ago (also see Geis 1971), yet sociologists have failed to pursue this theme (for an exception, see Chancer 1987). A recent review of research (Muehlenhard and Linton 1987) on sexual violence, or rape, devotes only a few pages to the situational contexts of rape events, and these are conceptualized as potential risk factors for individuals rather than qualities of rape-prone social contexts.

Many rapes, far more than come to the public's attention, occur in fraternity houses on college and university campuses, yet little research has analyzed fraternities at American colleges and universities as rape-prone contexts (cf. Ehrhart and Sandler 1985). Most of the research on fraternities reports on samples of individual fraternity men. One group of studies compares the values, attitudes, perceptions, family socioeconomic status, psychological traits (aggressiveness, dependence), and so on, of fraternity and nonfraternity men (Bohrnstedt 1969; Fox, Hodge, and Ward 1987; Kanin 1967; Lemire 1979; Miller 1973). A second group attempts to identify the effects of fraternity membership over time on the values, attitudes, beliefs, or moral precepts of members (Hughes and Winston 1987; Marlowe and Auvenshine 1982; Miller 1973; Wilder, Hoyt, Doren, Hauck, and Zettle 1978; Wilder, Hoyt, Surbeck, Wilder, and Carney 1986). With minor exceptions, little research addresses the group and organizational context of fraternities or the social construction of fraternity life (for exceptions, see Letchworth 1969; Longino and Kart 1973; Smith 1964).

Gary Tash, writing as an alumnus and trial attorney in his fraternity's magazine, claims that over 90 percent of all gang rapes on college campuses involve
fraternity men (1988, p. 2). Tash provides no evidence to substantiate this claim,
but students of violence against women have been concerned with fraternity
men's frequently reported involvement in rape episodes (Adams and Abarbanel
1988). Ehrhart and Sandler (1985) identify over 50 cases of gang rapes on campus
perpetrated by fraternity men, and their analysis points to many of the conditions that we discuss here. Their analysis is unique in focusing on conditions in
fraternities that make gang rapes of women by fraternity men both feasible and
probable. They identify excessive alcohol use, isolation from external monitoring, treatment of women as prey, use of pornography, approval of violence, and
excessive concern with competition as precipitating conditions to gang rape
(also see Merton 1985; Roark 1987).

The study reported here confirmed and complemented these findings by focusing on both conditions and processes. We examined dynamics associated
with the social construction of fraternity life, with a focus on processes that foster the use of coercion, including rape, in fraternity men's relations with women.
Our examination of men's social fraternities on college and university campuses
as groups and organizations led us to conclude that fraternities are a physical
and sociocultural context that encourages the sexual coercion of women. We
make no claims that all fraternities are "bad" or that all fraternity men are rapists. Our observations indicated, however, that rape is especially probable in fraternities because of the kinds of organizations they are, the kinds of members
they have, the practices their members engage in, and a virtual absence of university or community oversight. Analyses that lay blame for rapes by fraternity
men on "peer pressure" are, we feel, overly simplistic (cf. Burkhart 1989; Walsh
1989). We suggest, rather, that fraternities create a sociocultural context in which
the use of coercion in sexual relations with women is normative and in which
the mechanisms to keep this pattern of behavior in check are minimal at best
and absent at worst. We conclude that unless fraternities change in fundamental
ways, little improvement can be expected.

Methodology

Our goal was to analyze the group and organizational practices and conditions
that create in fraternities an abusive social context for women. We developed a
conceptual framework from an initial case study of an alleged gang rape at Florida State University that involved four fraternity men and an 18-year-old coed.
The group rape took place on the third floor of a fraternity house and ended with
the "dumping" of the woman in the hallway of a neighboring fraternity house.
According to newspaper accounts, the victim's blood-alcohol concentration,

when she was discovered, was .349 percent, more than three times the legal limit for automobile driving and an almost lethal amount. One law enforcement officer reported that sexual intercourse occurred during the time the victim was unconscious: "She was in a life-threatening situation" (*Tallahassee Democrat,* 1988b). When the victim was found, she was comatose and had suffered multiple scratches and abrasions. Crude words and a fraternity symbol had been written on her thighs (*Tampa Tribune*, 1988). When law enforcement officials tried to investigate the case, fraternity members refused to cooperate. This led, eventually, to a five-year ban of the fraternity from campus by the university and by the fraternity's national organization.

In trying to understand how such an event could have occurred, and how a group of over 150 members (exact figures are unknown because the fraternity refused to provide a membership roster) could hold rank, deny knowledge of the event, and allegedly lie to a grand jury, we analyzed newspaper articles about the case and conducted open-ended interviews with a variety of respondents about the case and about fraternities, rapes, alcohol use, gender relations, and sexual activities on campus. Our data included over 100 newspaper articles on the initial gang rape case; open-ended interviews with Greek (social fraternity and sorority) and non-Greek (independent) students (N = 20); university administrators (N = 8, five men, three women), and alumni advisers to Greek organizations (N = 6). Open-ended interviews were held also with judges, public and private defense attorneys, victim advocates, and state prosecutors regarding the processing of sexual assault cases. Data were analyzed using the grounded theory method (Glaser 1978; Martin and Turner 1986). In the following analysis, concepts generated from the data analysis are integrated with the literature on men's social fraternities, sexual coercion, and related issues.

Fraternities and the Social Construction of Men and Masculinity

Our research indicated that fraternities are vitally concerned—more than with anything else—with masculinity (cf. Kanin 1967). They work hard to create a macho image and context and try to avoid any suggestion of "wimpishness," effeminacy, and homosexuality. Valued members display, or are willing to go along with, a narrow conception of masculinity that stresses competition, athleticism, dominance, winning, conflict, wealth, material possessions, willingness to drink alcohol, and sexual prowess vis-à-vis women.

Valued Qualities of Members

When fraternity members talked about the kind of pledges they prefer, a litany of stereotypical and narrowly masculine attributes and behaviors was recited and

feminine or woman-associated qualities and behaviors were expressly de-
nounced (cf. Merton 1985). Fraternities seek men who are "athletic," "big guys,"
good in intramural competition, "who can talk college sports." Males "who are
willing to drink alcohol," "who drink socially," or "who can hold their liquor" are
sought. Alcohol and activities associated with the recreational use of alcohol are
cornerstones of fraternity social life. Nondrinkers are viewed with skepticism
and rarely selected for membership.[1]

Fraternities try to avoid "geeks," nerds, and men said to give the fraternity a
"wimpy" or "gay" reputation. Art, music, and humanities majors, majors in traditional women's fields (nursing, home economics, social work, education), men
with long hair, and those whose appearance or dress violate current norms are
rejected. Clean-cut, handsome men who dress well (are clean, neat, conforming,
fashionable) are preferred. One sorority woman commented that "the top ranking fraternities have the best looking guys."

One fraternity man, a senior, said his fraternity recruited "some big guys, very
athletic" over a two-year period to help overcome its image of wimpiness. His
fraternity had won the interfraternity competition for highest grade-point average several years running but was looked down on as "wimpy, dancy, even gay."
With their bigger, more athletic recruits, "our reputation improved; we're a much
more recognized fraternity now." Thus a fraternity's reputation and status depends on members' possession of stereotypically masculine qualities. Good
grades, campus leadership, and community service are "nice" but masculinity
dominance—for example, in athletic events, physical size of members, athleticism of members—counts most.

Certain social skills are valued. Men are sought who "have good personalities," are friendly, and "have the ability to relate to girls" (cf. Longino and Kart
1973). One fraternity man, a junior, said: "We watch a guy [a potential pledge]
talk to women ... we want guys who can relate to girls." Assessing a pledge's ability to talk to women is, in part, a preoccupation with homosexuality and a conscious avoidance of men who seem to have effeminate manners or qualities. If a
member is suspected of being gay, he is ostracized and informally drummed out
of the fraternity. A fraternity with a reputation as wimpy or tolerant of gays is ridiculed and shunned by other fraternities. Militant heterosexuality is frequently
used by men as a strategy to keep each other in line (Kimmel 1987).

Financial affluence or wealth, a male-associated value in American culture, is
highly valued by fraternities. In accounting for why the fraternity involved in the
gang rape that precipitated our research project had been recognized recently as
"the best fraternity chapter in the United States," a university official said: "They
were good-looking, a big fraternity, had lots of BMWs [expensive, German-made
automobiles]." After the rape, newspaper stories described the fraternity mem-

bers' affluence, noting the high number of members who owned expensive cars (*St. Petersburg Times*, 1988).

The Status and Norms of Pledgeship

A pledge (sometimes called an associate member) is a new recruit who occupies a trial membership status for a specific period of time. The pledge period (typically ranging from 10 to 15 weeks) gives fraternity brothers an opportunity to assess and socialize new recruits. Pledges evaluate the fraternity also and decide if they want to become brothers. The socialization experience is structured partly through assignment of a Big Brother to each pledge. Big Brothers are expected to teach pledges how to become a brother and to support them as they progress through the trial membership period. Some pledges are repelled by the pledging experience, which can entail physical abuse; harsh discipline; and demands to be subordinate, follow orders, and engage in demeaning routines and activities, similar to those used by the military to "make men out of boys" during boot camp.

Characteristics of the pledge experience are rationalized by fraternity members as necessary to help pledges unite into a group, rely on each other and join together against outsiders. The process is highly masculinist in execution as well as conception. A willingness to submit to authority, follow orders, and do as one is told is viewed as a sign of loyalty, togetherness, and unity. Fraternity pledges who find the pledge process offensive often drop out. Some do this by openly quitting, which can subject them to ridicule by brothers and other pledges, or they may deliberately fail to make the grades necessary for initiation or transfer schools and decline to reaffiliate with the fraternity on the new campus. One fraternity pledge who quit the fraternity he had pledged described an experience during pledgeship as follows:

> This one guy was always picking on me. No matter what I did, I was wrong. One night after dinner, he and two other guys called me and two other pledges into the chapter room. He said, "Here, X, hold this 25 pound bag of ice at arms' length 'til I tell you to stop." I did it even though my arms and hands were killing me. When I asked if I could stop, he grabbed me around the throat and lifted me off the floor. I thought he would choke me to death. He cussed me and called me all kinds of names. He took one of my fingers and twisted it until it nearly broke. ... I stayed in the fraternity for a few more days, but then I decided to quit. I hated it. Those guys are sick. They like seeing you suffer.

Fraternities' emphasis on toughness, withstanding pain and humiliation, obedience to superiors, and using physical force to obtain compliance contributes to an interpersonal style that de-emphasizes caring and sensitivity but fosters intragroup trust and loyalty. If the least macho or most critical pledges drop out, those who remain may be more receptive to, and influenced by, masculinist values and practices that encourage the use of force in sexual relations with women and the covering up of such behavior (cf. Kanin 1967).

Norms and Dynamics of Brotherhood

Brother is the status occupied by fraternity men to indicate their relations to each other and their membership in a particular fraternity organization or group. Brother is a male-specific status; only males can become brothers although women can become "Little Sisters," a form of pseudomembership. "Becoming a brother" is a rite of passage that follows the consistent and often lengthy display by pledges of appropriately masculine qualities and behaviors. Brothers have a quasi-familial relationship with each other, are normatively said to share bonds of closeness and support, and are sharply set off from nonmembers. Brotherhood is a loosely defined term used to represent the bonds that develop among fraternity members and the obligations and expectations incumbent upon them (cf. Marlowe and Auvenshine [1982] on fraternities' failure to encourage "moral development" in freshman pledges).

Some of our respondents talked about brotherhood in almost reverential terms, viewing it as the most valuable benefit of fraternity membership. One senior, a business-school major who had been affiliated with a fairly high-status fraternity throughout four years on campus, said:

> Brotherhood spurs friendship for life, which I consider its best aspect, although I didn't see it that way when I joined. Brotherhood bonds and unites. It instills values of caring about one another, caring about community, caring about ourselves. The values and bonds [of brotherhood] continually develop over the four years [in college] while normal friendships come and go.

Despite this idealization, most aspects of fraternity practice and conception are more mundane. Brotherhood often plays itself out as an overriding concern with masculinity and, by extension, femininity. As a consequence, fraternities comprise collectivities of highly masculinized men with attitudinal qualities and behavioral norms that predispose them to sexual coercion of women (cf. Kanin 1967; Merton 1985; Rapaport and Burkhart 1984). The norms of masculinity are complemented by conceptions of women and femininity that are equally distorted and stereotyped and that may enhance the probability of women's exploitation (cf. Ehrhart and Sandler 1985; Sanday 1981, 1986).

Practices of Brotherhood

Practices associated with fraternity brotherhood that contribute to the sexual coercion of women include a preoccupation with loyalty, group protection and secrecy, use of alcohol as a weapon, involvement in violence and physical force, and an emphasis on competition and superiority.

Loyalty, Group Protection, and Secrecy. Loyalty is a fraternity preoccupation. Members are reminded constantly to be loyal to the fraternity and to their brothers. Among other ways, loyalty is played out in the practices of group protection and secrecy. The fraternity must be shielded from criticism. Members are admonished to avoid getting the fraternity in trouble and to bring all problems "to the chapter" (local branch of a national social fraternity) rather than to outsiders. Fraternities try to protect themselves from close scrutiny and criticism by the Interfraternity Council (a quasi-governing body composed of representatives from all social fraternities on campus), their fraternity's national office, university officials, law enforcement, the media, and the public. Protection of the fraternity often takes precedence over what is procedurally, ethically, or legally correct. Numerous examples were related to us of fraternity brothers' lying to outsiders to "protect the fraternity."

Group protection was observed in the alleged gang rape case with which we began our study. Except for one brother, a rapist who turned state's evidence, the entire remaining fraternity membership was accused by university and criminal justice officials of lying to protect the fraternity. Members consistently failed to cooperate even though the alleged crimes were felonies, involved only four men (two of whom were not even members of the local chapter), and the victim of the crime nearly died. According to a grand jury's findings, fraternity officers repeatedly broke appointments with law enforcement officials, refused to provide police with a list of members, and refused to cooperate with police and prosecutors investigating the case (*Florida Flambeau*, 1988).

Secrecy is a priority value and practice in fraternities, partly because full-fledged membership is premised on it (for confirmation, see Ehrhart and Sandler 1985; Longino and Kart 1973; Roark 1987). Secrecy is also a boundary-maintaining mechanism, demarcating in-group from out-group, us from them. Secret rituals, handshakes, and mottoes are revealed to pledge brothers as they are initiated into full brotherhood. Since only brothers are supposed to know a fraternity's secrets, such knowledge affirms membership in the fraternity and separates a brother from others. Extending secrecy tactics from protection of private knowledge to protection of the fraternity from criticism is a predictable development. Our interviews indicated that individual members knew the difference between right and wrong, but fraternity norms that emphasize loyalty, group protection, and secrecy often overrode standards of ethical correctness.

Alcohol as Weapon. Alcohol use by fraternity men is normative. They use it on weekdays to relax after class and on weekends to "get drunk," "get crazy," and "get laid." The use of alcohol to obtain sex from women is pervasive—in other words, it is used as a weapon against sexual reluctance. According to several fraternity men whom we interviewed, alcohol is the major tool used to gain sexual mastery over women (cf. Adams and Abarbanel 1988; Ehrhart and Sandler 1985).

One fraternity man, a 21-year-old senior, described alcohol use to gain sex as follows: "There are girls that you know will fuck, then some you have to put some effort into it. ... You have to buy them drinks or find out if she's drunk enough. ..."

A similar strategy is used collectively. A fraternity man said that at parties with Little Sisters: "We provide them with 'hunch punch' and things get wild. We get them drunk and most of the guys end up with one." "'Hunch punch,'" he said, "is a girls' drink made up of overproof alcohol and powdered Kool-Aid, no water or anything, just ice. It's very strong. Two cups will do a number on a female." He had plans in the next academic term to surreptitiously give hunch punch to women in a "prim and proper" sorority because "having sex with prim and proper sorority girls is definitely a goal." These women are a challenge because they "won't openly consume alcohol and won't get openly drunk as hell." Their sororities have "standards committees" that forbid heavy drinking and easy sex.

In the gang rape case, our sources said that many fraternity men on campus believed the victim had a drinking problem and was thus an "easy make." According to newspaper accounts, she had been drinking alcohol on the evening she was raped; the lead assailant is alleged to have given her a bottle of wine after she arrived at his fraternity house. Portions of the rape occurred in a shower, and the victim was reportedly so drunk that her assailants had difficulty holding her in a standing position (*Tallahassee Democrat,* 1988a). While raping her, her assailants repeatedly told her they were members of another fraternity under the apparent belief that she was too drunk to know the difference. Of course, if she was too drunk to know who they were, she was too drunk to consent to sex (cf. Allgeier 1986; Tash 1988).

One respondent told us that gang rapes are wrong and can get one expelled, but he seemed to see nothing wrong in sexual coercion one-on-one. He seemed unaware that the use of alcohol to obtain sex from a woman is grounds for a claim that a rape occurred (cf. Tash 1988). Few women on campus (who also may not know these grounds) report date rapes, however; so the odds of detection and punishment are slim for fraternity men who use alcohol for "seduction" purposes (cf. Byington and Keeter 1988; Merton 1985).

Violence and Physical Force. Fraternity men have a history of violence (Ehrhart and Sandler 1985; Roark 1987). Their record of hazing, fighting, property destruction, and rape has caused them problems with insurance companies (Bradford 1986; Pressley 1987). Two university officials told us that fraternities "are the third riskiest property to insure behind toxic waste dumps and amusement parks." Fraternities are increasingly defendants in legal actions brought by pledges subjected to hazing (Meyer 1986; Pressley 1987) and by women who were raped by one or more members. In a recent alleged gang rape incident at another Florida university, prosecutors failed to file charges but the victim filed a civil suit against the fraternity nevertheless (*Tallahassee Democrat,* 1989).

Competition and Superiority. Interfraternity rivalry fosters in-group identification and out-group hostility. Fraternities stress pride of membership and superiority over other fraternities as major goals. Interfraternity rivalries take many
forms, including competition for desirable pledges, size of pledge class, size of
membership, size and appearance of fraternity house, superiority in intramural
sports, highest grade-point averages, giving the best parties, gaining the best or
most campus leadership roles, and, of great importance, attracting and displaying "good looking women." Rivalry is particularly intense over members, intramural sports, and women (cf. Messner 1989).

Fraternities' Commodification of Women

In claiming that women are treated by fraternities as commodities, we mean that
fraternities knowingly, and intentionally, *use* women for their benefit. Fraternities use women as bait for new members, as servers of brothers' needs, and as
sexual prey.

Women as Bait

Fashionably attractive women help a fraternity attract new members. As one fraternity man, a junior, said, "They are good bait." Beautiful, sociable women are
believed to impress the right kind of pledges and give the impression that the
fraternity can deliver this type of woman to its members. Photographs of
shapely, attractive coeds are printed in fraternity brochures and videotapes that
are distributed and shown to potential pledges. The women pictured are often
dressed in bikinis, at the beach, and are pictured hugging the brothers of the fraternity. One university official says such recruitment materials give the message:
"Hey, they're here for you, you can have whatever you want," and, "we have the
best looking women. Join us and you can have them too." Another commented:
"Something's wrong when males join an all-male organization as the best place
to meet women. It's so illogical."

Fraternities compete in promising access to beautiful women. One fraternity
man, a senior, commented that "the attraction of girls [i.e., a fraternity's success
in attracting women] is a big status symbol for fraternities." One university official commented that the use of women as a recruiting tool is so well entrenched
that fraternities that might be willing to forgo it say they cannot afford to unless
other fraternities do so as well. One fraternity man said, "Look, if we don't have
Little Sisters, the fraternities that do will get all the good pledges." Another said,
"We won't have as good a rush [the period during which new members are assessed and selected] if we don't have these women around."

In displaying good-looking, attractive, skimpily dressed, nubile women to potential members, fraternities implicitly, and sometimes explicitly, promise sexual access to women. One fraternity man commented that "part of what being in

a fraternity is all about is the sex" and explained how his fraternity uses Little Sisters to recruit new members:

> We'll tell the sweetheart [the fraternity's term for Little Sister], "You're gorgeous; you can get him." We'll tell her to fake a scam and she'll go hang all over him during a rush party, kiss him, and he thinks he's done wonderful and wants to join. The girls think it's great too. It's flattering for them.

Women as Servers

The use of women as servers is exemplified in the Little Sister program. Little Sisters are undergraduate women who are rushed and selected in a manner parallel to the recruitment of fraternity men. They are affiliated with the fraternity in a formal but unofficial way and are able, indeed required, to wear the fraternity's Greek letters. Little Sisters are not full-fledged fraternity members, however; and fraternity national offices and most universities do not register or regulate them. Each fraternity has an officer called Little Sister Chairman who oversees their organization and activities. The Little Sisters elect officers among themselves, pay monthly dues to the fraternity, and have well-defined roles. Their dues are used to pay for the fraternity's social events, and Little Sisters are expected to attend and hostess fraternity parties and hang around the house to make it a "nice place to be." One fraternity man, a senior, described Little Sisters this way: "They are very social girls, willing to join in, be affiliated with the group, devoted to the fraternity." Another member, a sophomore, said: "Their sole purpose is social—attend parties, attract new members, and 'take care' of the guys."

Our observations and interviews suggested that women selected by fraternities as Little Sisters are physically attractive, possess good social skills, and are willing to devote time and energy to the fraternity and its members. One undergraduate woman gave the following job description for Little Sisters to a campus newspaper:

> It's not just making appearances at all the parties but entails many more responsibilities. You're going to be expected to go to all the intramural games to cheer the brothers on, support and encourage the pledges, and just be around to bring some extra life to the house. [As a Little Sister] you have to agree to take on a new responsibility other than studying to maintain your grades and managing to keep your checkbook from bouncing. You have to take time to be a part of the fraternity and support the brothers in all they do. (*The Tomahawk*, 1988)

The title of Little Sister reflects women's subordinate status; fraternity men in a parallel role are called Big Brothers. Big Brothers assist a sorority primarily with the physical work of sorority rushes, which, compared to fraternity rushes, are more formal, structured, and intensive. Sorority rushes take place in the daytime and fraternity rushes at night so fraternity men are free to help. According to one fraternity member, Little Sister status is a benefit to women because it gives them a social outlet and "the protection of the brothers." The gender-stereotypic conceptions and obligations of these Little Sister and Big Brother statuses indicate that fraternities and sororities promote a gender hierarchy on campus that fosters subordination and dependence in women, thus encouraging sexual exploitation and the belief that it is acceptable.

Women as Sexual Prey

Little Sisters are a sexual utility. Many Little Sisters do not belong to sororities and lack peer support for refraining from unwanted sexual relations. One fraternity man (whose fraternity has 65 members and 85 Little Sisters) told us they had recruited "wholesale" in the prior year to "get lots of new women." The structural access to women that the Little Sister program provides and the absence of normative supports for refusing fraternity members' sexual advances may make women in this program particularly susceptible to coerced sexual encounters with fraternity men.

Access to women for sexual gratification is a presumed benefit of fraternity membership, promised in recruitment materials and strategies and through brothers' conversations with new recruits. One fraternity man said: "We always tell the guys that you get sex all the time, there's always new girls. ... After I became a Greek, I found out I could be with females at will." A university official told us that, based on his observations, "no one [i.e., fraternity men] on this campus wants to have 'relationships.' They just want to have fun [i.e., sex]." Fraternity men plan and execute strategies aimed at obtaining sexual gratification, and this occurs at both individual and collective levels.

Individual strategies include getting a woman drunk and spending a great deal of money on her. As for collective strategies, most of our undergraduate interviewees agreed that fraternity parties often culminate in sex and that this outcome is planned. One fraternity man said fraternity parties often involve sex and nudity and can "turn into orgies." Orgies may be planned in advance, such as the Bowery Ball party held by one fraternity. A former fraternity member said of this party:

> The entire idea behind this is sex. Both men and women come to the party wearing little or nothing. There are pornographic pinups on the walls and usually porno movies playing on the TV. The music carries sexual overtones. ... They just get schnockered [drunk] and, in most cases, they also get laid.

When asked about the women who come to such a party, he said: "Some Little Sisters just won't go. ... The girls who do are looking for a good time, girls who don't know what it is, things like that."

Other respondents denied that fraternity parties are orgies but said that sex is always talked about among the brothers and they all know "who each other is doing it with." One member said that most of the time, guys have sex with their girlfriends "but with socials, girlfriends aren't allowed to come and it's their [members'] big chance [to have sex with other women]." The use of alcohol to help them get women into bed is a routine strategy at fraternity parties.

Conclusions

In general, our research indicated that the organization and membership of fraternities contribute heavily to coercive and often violent sex. Fraternity houses are occupied by same-sex (all men) and same-age (late teens, early twenties) peers whose maturity and judgment is often less than ideal. Yet fraternity houses are private dwellings that are mostly off-limits to, and away from scrutiny of, university and community representatives, with the result that fraternity house events seldom come to the attention of outsiders. Practices associated with the social construction of fraternity brotherhood emphasize a macho conception of men and masculinity, a narrow, stereotyped conception of women and femininity, and the treatment of women as commodities. Other practices contributing to coercive sexual relations and the cover-up of rapes include excessive alcohol use, competitiveness, and normative support for deviance and secrecy (cf. Bogal-Allbritten and Allbritten 1985; Kanin 1967).

Some fraternity practices exacerbate others. Brotherhood norms require "sticking together" regardless of right or wrong; thus rape episodes are unlikely to be stopped or reported to outsiders, even when witnesses disapprove. The ability to use alcohol without scrutiny by authorities and alcohol's frequent association with violence, including sexual coercion, facilitates rape in fraternity houses. Fraternity norms that emphasize the value of maleness and masculinity over femaleness and femininity and that elevate the status of men and lower the status of women in members' eyes undermine perceptions and treatment of women as persons who deserve consideration and care (cf. Ehrhart and Sandler 1985; Merton 1985).

Androgynous men and men with a broad range of interests and attributes are lost to fraternities through their recruitment practices. Masculinity of a narrow and stereotypical type helps create attitudes, norms, and practices that predispose fraternity men to coerce women sexually, both individually and collectively (Allgeier 1986; Hood 1989; Sanday 1981, 1986). Male athletes on campus may be similarly disposed for the same reasons (Kirshenbaum 1989; Telander and Sullivan 1989).

Research into the social contexts in which rape crimes occur and the social constructions associated with these contexts illumine rape dynamics on campus. Blanchard (1959) found that group rapes almost always have a leader who pushes others into the crime. He also found that the leader's latent homosexuality, desire to show off to his peers, or fear of failing to prove himself a man are frequently an impetus. Fraternity norms and practices contribute to the approval and use of sexual coercion as an accepted tactic in relations with women. Alcohol-induced compliance is normative, whereas, presumably, use of a knife, gun, or threat of bodily harm would not be because the woman who "drinks too much" is viewed as "causing her own rape" (cf. Ehrhart and Sandler 1985).

Our research led us to conclude that fraternity norms and practices influence members to view the sexual coercion of women, which is a felony crime, as sport, a contest, or a game (cf. Sato 1988). This sport is played not between men and women but between men and men. Women are the pawns or prey in the interfraternity rivalry game; they prove that a fraternity is successful or prestigious. The use of women in this way encourages fraternity men to see women as objects and sexual coercion as sport. Today's societal norms support young women's right to engage in sex at their discretion, and coercion is unnecessary in a mutually desired encounter. However, nubile young women say they prefer to be "in a relationship" to have sex while young men say they prefer to "get laid" without a commitment (Muehlenhard and Linton 1987). These differences may reflect, in part, American puritanism and men's fears of sexual intimacy or perhaps intimacy of any kind. In a fraternity context, getting sex without giving emotionally demonstrates "cool" masculinity. More important, it poses no threat to the bonding and loyalty of the fraternity brotherhood (cf. Farr 1988). Drinking large quantities of alcohol before having sex suggests that "scoring" rather than intrinsic sexual pleasure is a primary concern of fraternity men.

Unless fraternities' composition, goals, structures, and practices change in fundamental ways, women on campus will continue to be sexual prey for fraternity men. As all-male enclaves dedicated to opposing faculty and administration and to cementing in-group ties, fraternity members eschew any hint of homosexuality. Their version of masculinity transforms women, and men with womanly characteristics, into the out-group. "Womanly men" are ostracized; feminine women are used to demonstrate members' masculinity. Encouraging renewed emphasis on their founding values (Longino and Kart 1973), service orientation and activities (Lemire 1979), or members' moral development (Marlowe and Auvenshine 1982) will have little effect on fraternities' treatment of women. A case for or against fraternities cannot be made by studying individual members. The fraternity qua group and organization is at issue. Located on campus along with many vulnerable women, embedded in a sexist society, and caught up in masculinist goals, practices, and values, fraternities' violation of women—including forcible rape—should come as no surprise.

Note

1. Recent bans by some universities on open-keg parties at fraternity houses have resulted in heavy drinking before coming to a party and an increase in drunkenness among those who attend. This may aggravate, rather than improve, the treatment of women by fraternity men at parties.

13

Types of Marital Rape

David Finkelhor and Kersti Yllo

FOR MOST PEOPLE, forced sex in marriage has little to do with what they would call "real" rape. When they think of "real" rape, they think of a stranger, a weapon, an attack, a threat to a woman's life. Forced marital sex, on the other hand, conjures up an unpleasant, but not particularly serious, marital squabble.

This attitude toward marital rape as a rather innocuous event was vividly illustrated when we solicited fictitious descriptions of marital rape from over four hundred university students. Here are some of the typical replies:

He wants to. She doesn't. He says, "That's tough, I'm going to anyway," and he does.

Husband and wife are newly separated. He comes for a short visit and forces her to make love because he really does love her and misses her.

The wife was unwilling to have sex and he forced himself on her.

These images of marital rape constitute what we call the "sanitary stereotype"—marital rape depicted as a petty conflict. People do not regard it as very serious because in their minds the action itself is not very dramatic. To most, it is a disagreement over sex that the husband wins. Their images are very bland: little graphic violence, little pain, little suffering. The coercion involved is abstract; people use neutral phrases like "he forced her" or "he makes her" to describe the rape.

...

To the women we talked to in the course of our study, marital rapes were frightening and brutal events that usually occurred in the context of an exploitative and destructive relationship. This sexual abuse was only peripherally about sex. More often it was about humiliation, degradation, anger, and resentment.

Women were left, if not physically disabled, then psychologically traumatized for a long time. ...

...

The lack of public awareness about the reality of marital rape can be ascribed largely to the secrecy surrounding the problem, a secrecy maintained by most parties to the problem—victims, abusers, and the public at large. Victims are ashamed. Abusers help to keep them quiet and intimidated through threats, emotional blackmail, and a kind of "brainwashing" that makes the victims feel that they are to blame. The rest of us feel awkward, uncomfortable, and helpless to do anything, so we choose not to ask and not to hear.

Many women who have been sexually assaulted by their husbands do not see themselves as having been raped. They tend to view the assault as part of a marital conflict for which they are to blame, wondering if their own inadequacies as wives and partners are at the root of the problem and believing their own sexual problems provoke their husbands. That their husbands are violent is taken by many to be a judgment on themselves: a judgment that they could not maintain a normal marriage or please their partners enough. A marital rape is part of a personal shame that they do not want others to know.

...

Battering Rape

Many marital-rape victims are ... battered wives, and entrapment and terror are part and parcel of their lives. [Their stories illustrate] many of the elements of the classic battering situation: the husband becomes increasingly brutal; his outbursts are capricious and unpredictable; he comes to dominate [his wife's] life and makes threats to deter her from leaving or acting independently.

About half of the women in our sample of marital-rape victims were battered.

...

We noted certain common features in the marital rapes that occurred in battering relationships. First, the sexual violence in these relationships was another aspect of the general abuse. These men hit their wives, belittled them, called them names, took their money, and, as another way of humiliating and degrading them, resorted to sexual violence.

Often the sexual abuse was a continuation of the beatings. Husbands would find a pretext and start to attack. Beatings might last for an hour, or for a day. At some point, usually toward the end of the beating, the husband would either strip his wife or force her to disrobe and then have intercourse. ...

When rapes followed physical assaults, two different patterns occurred. Sometimes, the hitting and the punching would continue throughout the sex, and the sex itself would be full of violence. In other cases, the men would act as though they were finished with the beating and wanted to make up with a little sex. The women, exhausted and in pain from the beating and hardly feeling close to their husbands, would not want to be touched. In these cases, the husbands would roughly push themselves on their exhausted partners or threaten them with more violence unless they complied.

Marital-rape incidents were not isolated episodes in these marriages. In the sanitary stereotype, a marital rape might be a once-in-a-relationship occurrence, something quite rare that happens under unusual circumstances. Exactly 50 percent of the women in our study said they had been sexually assaulted twenty times or more. (In other studies the percentage of repeatedly raped victims runs from 59 percent to 87 percent.[1]) ... For some, assaults were so common they could not remember how often. "It happened half of the time we had sex during those three years," said one woman typical of this group. For most marital-rape victims, rape is a chronic and constant threat, not an isolated problem. The battered women, of course, were the most vulnerable of all to such repeated sexual abuse. Twice as many battered women suffered from chronic rapes (twenty times or more) as the other raped women. ...

One cannot say that the marital rapes of these battered women occurred because of a conflict over sex. Rather, the rapes they suffered were an extension of the other violence. Many times the incidents occurred suddenly, without having anything lead up to them. One woman's husband dragged her off into the bedroom while they were entertaining guests. Another grabbed and raped her when she was on the way to the bathroom. These assaults had much of the same unprovoked character as the battering assaults, which also could occur over nothing more serious than her forgetting to buy his cigarettes or wanting to watch a different television show. The attacks seemed like capricious expressions of anger and resentment. Though they were sexual acts, they were not sparked by sexual disagreements.

What illustrated the basically nonsexual motivation of the rapes we studied is, ironically, that many of the battered wives said that they enjoyed having sex with their husbands when they were approached with genuine desire and affection. But instead of wooing their wives to bed, the husbands would beat them up and then demand sex, or jump them roughly with no preliminaries whatsoever. Such men were not using force because their wives were reluctant to comply. Rather, they were using force because they wanted to frighten, humiliate, punish, and degrade.

...

The conventional stereotype of marital rape disregards the fact that a great many wives are forcibly subjected to a variety of sexual abuses in addition to, or sometimes in lieu of, forced vaginal intercourse. Wives are raped with objects. For instance, one woman's husband tried to rape her with a broomstick and several husbands had their wives insert things in their vaginas and then took pictures of them. Wives are raped anally and their genitals are mutilated. One woman said that her husband would bite her genitals until they bled, and another said she was burned with cigarettes. Wives are forced to have intercourse with their husbands' friends. Two of the women we interviewed said that their assaults had occurred when their husbands ganged up on them with some of their friends. One was able to escape, but the other was not so lucky.

One-third of the women we interviewed mentioned an episode of forced anal intercourse. A fifth told of forced oral sex. Nearly a quarter said they had been subjected to sex in the presence of others—usually their children. These incidents are not disagreements over sexual positions; they are sexual humiliations inflicted on women.

[One woman who experienced "battering rape" was] Gretchen. ... [During her first marriage,] ... she was physically brutalized and sexually abused in a way that has left permanent psychological scars.

...

... [Gretchen's husband] would often beat her and then would want to take her to bed. "I was too afraid to say no. I was afraid I'd get another beating." Sometimes she tried to push him away, but he just persisted until she relented. It got to the point where she was impossibly tense whenever he came near her. At the beginning of the relationship the violence was the worst part, but as the relationship went on, it was the forced sex and the sexual sadism that became the worst. ... "He must have got some satisfaction from hurting me. There wasn't a time when sex with him wasn't violent or painful."

He beat her up and forced her to have sex with him two days before their son was born, and then again two days after. The doctor and nurse wanted to turn him over to the police, but she talked them out of it. "I had just had a baby and I didn't want to raise him by myself." One time she asked her family doctor what was wrong with her husband. "The only thing wrong with him is that he is a sex maniac," the doctor told her. "He needs to have his sexual satisfaction."

"He was possessed," she said in her interview with us, "really possessed. He had this idea that he wanted to pull the insides out of me." He would put his whole hand inside her vagina and try to pull it inside out. Once when he did this he began to hurt her so badly that she kicked him away with her feet. As he pulled away, his fist ripped her vagina, and she started to bleed "like somebody had turned the water on."

A doctor was called, but when he proved unable to stop the bleeding, she was sent to the hospital. As the doctor prepared to sew up the five-to-six-centimeter wound, the husband hit him for touching her genitals ("Nasty as he was, he was jealous, too"). Four blood transfusions later, she recovered, but the doctor told her she had been very, very lucky. Unfortunately, the doctor neither asked about the cause of the injury nor reported it to the police.

...

Force-Only Rape

[Clearly,] battered women are at high risk for marital rape. The kind of man who beats his wife is also more likely to rape her. If he is not deterred by the social conventions against punching and hitting, he will probably not be inhibited by social conventions against forcing sex, either. ...

However, ... in our study we found that marital rape was not by any means limited to women who were battered. It occurred in relationships in which there was little or no other violence. ... We call this second type *force-only rape* because husbands use only as much force as necessary to coerce their wives into sex.

...

... Among the women we interviewed, there were many—about 40 percent—who were victims of force-only rapes. Some had been struck; some remembered nasty, violent episodes; but the violence was unusual. ... These women had not been subjected to the frequent and frightening outbursts that the victims of battering had.

...

... Their husbands did not use more force than was necessary to achieve sexual access; the goal was to accomplish the sex act rather than hurt the woman.

...

... The force-only rapes were not necessarily less humiliating and upsetting, but they less often involved extra violence, and more often involved a specifically sexual grievance.

...

[One woman who experienced "force-only rape" was] Harriet. ... For months, she had been challenging her husband's control over her, rebelling against his refusal to communicate and his refusal to do his share of the work. Because of the unfair division of labor, she says she lost her respect for him and no longer wished to have sex with him. He must have felt her challenge and decided that he would reassert his control. ... To maintain his "ownership" of his wife and his power over her, he raped her.

...

... "We were in bed, on our opposite sides, and he decided that he wanted to have sex. I said, 'Leave me alone.' But he forced himself on me." Carl didn't hit her; he simply rolled her over on her back, pinned her arms behind her, forced her legs apart, and had intercourse with her. "I was trying to push him away and trying to kick at him. But he is a big man—225 pounds, six feet tall—and I'm five feet two, 110 pounds, soaking wet. So I had to give up. He had full advantage of me within ten minutes."

Though he did not abuse her physically or verbally, he told her not to struggle, for it would not do any good. He did not tear off her nightgown, just hoisted it up to her waist. Intercourse lasted about five minutes.

"It wasn't physically painful and I didn't cry. But I was disgusted, angry, and I hated him."

He told her afterward, "You realize that I raped you. You forced me to do it. You didn't want to have sex with me, so I had to force you." ...

Obsessive Rape

In addition to the cases we classified as battering and force-only rapes, we encountered a half dozen that did not fit into either of these categories, that had a bizarre element to them. Sometimes the men in these cases battered their wives, and sometimes they did not. But in all cases, their sexual interests ran toward the strange and the perverse, and they were willing to use force to carry these activities out. We termed this third type *obsessive rape*.

...

[One woman who experienced "obsessive rape" was Melanie.] The first incident of physically forced sex occurred one night after [her husband] had been out drinking. It was late, and Melanie was doing laundry. He came in and flopped down on the bed—passed out, she thought. She went to the next-door building where the laundry room was to put in another load. As she walked back into the apartment, a man jumped out of the closet, grabbed her from behind, and began to rip off her clothes. At first, she did not even realize that it was her husband. Though she screamed and struggled to get away, he used his superior size and weight to overpower her, tear her clothes off, and rape her anally.

...

After that, he became obsessed with anal sex, demanding it more and more often. He also became more and more forceful during regular intercourse. "He would turn ugly so quickly, especially if I showed any sign of enjoying it. He would put a pillow over my face and I would scream quietly," Melanie remembers. He pressured her into doing bizarre things that made her uncomfortable. He would tie her up, for example, insert objects into her vagina, and then want to take pictures of her. "I was humiliated to find out that he had shown a picture of me with a banana in my vagina to a friend of his."

There were also more brutal attacks [which] ... began to occur more frequently toward the end of their six-year marriage. One incident that stood out in Melanie's mind occurred when they were living in a rural area. ... They were having sex one night when they heard a commotion outside and went in their bathrobes to investigate. Discovering that it was just their cats making noise, Melanie began to head back to the house, but her husband stopped her. "Wait there," he told her, "I'll be right back." She was standing in the darkness wondering what he was up to when suddenly he attacked her from behind. "He grabbed my arms behind me and tied them together. He pushed me over the log pile and raped me," she said. Once again, he penetrated her anally.

...

Melanie felt trapped in what she called her husband's "pornographic world." He seemed obsessed with sex. He would talk about it incessantly, evaluating last night's activities at the breakfast table and planning the approaching night at dinner. He was deeply engrossed in all types of pornography: movies, books, magazines. "He read book after book about women being brutalized and victimized." Much of the material was focused on anal sex, she recalls. He was also writing pornographic short stories himself. Melanie once found one in which a woman matching her description was gang-raped. In another story, the same character was murdered by her husband when he came home from work one day.

...

[Once] Melanie came across a file card [on which] ... her husband had written a list of dates corresponding to the forced-sex episodes of the previous few months. Next to each date was a code. "As close as I could figure it, he had graded each rape on some sort of zero-to-ten ranking, depending, I guess, on how good it was." There were other numbers and letters which she suspects indicated the types of acts he committed. "The card totally stunned me. And it opened my eyes to the fact that he wasn't going to change." She had thought that his attacks had been spontaneous, but it became clear that his behavior was calculated. She was not sure whether he had planned the attacks beforehand or just evaluated them afterward, but she knew that his attitude toward the rapes was much more rational than she ever suspected.

...

Melanie's husband shared a number of characteristics with other perpetrators of obsessive rapes. His general preoccupation with sex was typical. Another common characteristic among all these husbands was their interest not only in reading pornography but in creating it as well, usually by taking pictures of their wives.

Melanie's husband also had the customary predilection for unusual sexual activities: practicing anal intercourse, inserting objects into his wife's vagina, tying her up. Though none of these activities was rare among the other rapists of women we interviewed, they were particularly common among this group of obsessive rapists. ...

One thing that stands out strongly in Melanie's story is her husband's apparent relish in activities that caused her torment. The staged rapes aroused him because they frightened her. His taste in pornography ran toward the brutal. This man needed to humiliate his wife in order to enjoy sex. Rape for him was a preferred style of sexual arousal, and he seemed to derive pleasure from inflicting pain. ... Men like him rape their wives in part because the aggression itself is arousing to them. In fact, in some cases, violence may be essential to their sexual arousal. ...

...

... [Other obsessive rapists] did not seem to be aroused by the pain or suffering they caused but actually by the perverse acts in which they forced their wives to engage.

...

We expect that other types of marital rape may be revealed after further studies of the victims and perpetrators of marital rape. However, the major point ... will remain: ... marital rape occurs in different kinds of relationships and takes different forms. To characterize marital rape as the province of battered women alone is not to see its full scope. Unfortunately, as we have shown, marital rape occurs in relationships that give fewer signs of "violence" than most of us would surmise.

Notes

1. See Frieze (1980), Russell (1982), Pagelow (1980), Thyfault (1980), and Shields and Hanneke (1981).

The Sexual Politics of Murder

Jane Caputi

Those of us who are ... so much influenced by violence in the me-
dia, in particular pornographic violence, are not some kind of in-
herent monsters. We are your sons, and we are your husbands,
and we grew up in regular families.

—Ted Bundy (Lamar 1989, p. 34)

IN HER RECENT BOOK, *The Demon Lover: On the Sexuality of Terrorism,* Robin
Morgan (1989) relates an incident that occurred during a civil rights movement
meeting in the early 1960s. A group composed of members of both the Congress
of Racial Equality (CORE) and the Student Nonviolent Coordinating Committee
(with men outnumbering women three to one) had gathered in the wake of the
disappearance of three civil rights workers in Mississippi. The FBI, local police,
and the national guard had been dredging local lakes and rivers in search of the
bodies. During this search, the mutilated parts of an estimated 17 unidentified
bodies were found, all but one of whom were women. Morgan recalls that a male
CORE leader, upon hearing that news, agonized: "There's been a whole god-
damned lynching we never even *knew* about. There's been some brother disappeared who never even got *reported.*" When Morgan asked, why only *one* lynching and what about the other 16 bodies, she was told: "Those were obviously *sex*
murders. Those weren't political" (pp. 223–24).

Twenty years later, that perception still holds sway. For example, in the spring
of 1984, Christopher Wilder raped and murdered a still unknown number of
women. About to be apprehended by the police, he shot himself. The *Albuquer-*
que Tribune (April 14, 1984, p. 2) commented:

Wilder's death leaves behind a mystery as to the motives behind the rampage of death and terror. With plenty of money, soft-spoken charm, a background in photography, and a part-time career on the glamorous sports car racing circuit, Wilder, 39, would have had no trouble attracting beautiful women.

This man not only murdered women but first extensively tortured them. Although the FBI refuses to release all the details of that abuse, it was revealed that Wilder had bound, raped, repeatedly stabbed his victims, and tortured them with electric shocks. One woman (who survived the attack) had even had her eyelids glued shut. Obviously, Wilder did not wish to date, charm, or attract women; his desire was to torment and destroy. From a feminist perspective, there is no mystery behind Wilder's actions. His were sexually political murders, a form of murder rooted in a system of male supremacy in the same way that lynching is based in white supremacy. Such murder is, in short, a form of patriarchal terrorism.

That recognition, however, is impeded by longstanding tradition, for, as Kate Millett (1970) noted in her classic work, *Sexual Politics:*

> We are not accustomed to associate patriarchy with force. So perfect is its system of socialization, so complete the general assent to its values, so long and so universally has it prevailed in human society, that it scarcely seems to require violent implementation. ... And yet ... control in patriarchal societies would be imperfect, even inoperable, unless it had the rule of force to rely upon, both in emergencies and as an ever-present instrument of intimidation. (pp. 44–45)

Early feminist analysts of rape (Brownmiller 1975; Griffin 1983; Russell 1975) asserted that rape is not, as the common mythology insists, a crime of frustrated attraction, victim provocation, or uncontrollable biological urges. Nor is it one perpetrated only by an aberrant fringe. Rather, rape is a direct expression of sexual politics, a ritual enactment of male domination, a form of terror that functions to maintain the status quo. MacKinnon (1982) further maintains that rape is not primarily an act of violence but is a *sexual* act in a culture where sexuality itself is a form of power, where oppression takes sexual forms, and where sexuality is the very "linchpin of gender inequality" (p. 533).

The murders of women and children—including torture and murder by husbands, lovers, and fathers, as well as that committed by strangers—are not some inexplicable evil or the domain of "monsters" only. On the contrary, sexual murder is the ultimate expression of sexuality as a form of power. Sex murder (what the FBI also terms "recreational murder") is part of a tradition that Mary Daly first named as gynocide (1973, p. 73). As further defined by Andrea Dworkin (1976), gynocide is "the systematic crippling, raping, and/or killing of women by men ... the relentless violence perpetrated by the gender class men on the gender class women." She adds that "under patriarchy, gynocide is the ongoing reality of life lived by women" (pp. 16, 19).

It is only through an extraordinary numbing that such a reality can be denied, for the terrible reminders are everywhere: in the ubiquitous posters pleading for information about women who have "disappeared"; in the daily newspaper reports of various public and private atrocities. ...

...

... In myriad ways, the culture regularly doublethinks a distance between itself and sexual violence, denying the fundamental *normalcy* of that violence in a male supremacist culture and trying to paint it as the domain of psychopaths and "monsters" only (Cameron and Frazer 1987; Caputi 1987). The career of sex killer Ted Bundy is especially instructive on this point.

The Boys Next Door

Most men just hate women. Ted Bundy killed them.

—Jimmy McDonough (1984, p. 3)

At some point when I was writing my book, *The Age of Sex Crime* (1987), an analysis of the contemporary phenomenon of serial sex murder, I had a dream that I was back living in the white, middle-class, suburban neighborhood I grew up in and that Ted Bundy had moved in a few houses down. This was but one of several such dreams I had while engaged in the writing. Still it made a deep impression on me. Certainly, it meant that my subject was getting closer and closer to my psyche. But it also was significant that the nightmare figure was Ted Bundy, for Bundy is almost universally hailed as the killer who represented the all-American boy, the boy next door who did not marry but, rather, killed the girl next door.

Ted Bundy committed serial murder, and FBI statistics show that this new type of murder has increased drastically in the United States in the last 20 years. In addition, in 1984, the Justice Department estimated that there were at the very least 35 and possibly as many as 100 such killers roaming the country. Justice Department official Robert O. Heck summed up the general situation:

> We all talk about Jack the Ripper; he killed five people [sic]. We all talk about the "Boston Strangler" who killed 13, and maybe "Son of Sam" who killed six. But we've got people [sic] out there now killing 20 and 30 people and more, and some of them just don't kill. They torture their victims in terrible ways and mutilate them before they kill them. Something's going on out there. It's an epidemic. (Lindsey 1984, p. 7)

Although Heck's statement is superficially correct, his language obscures what actually is going on out there, for the "people" who torture, kill, and mutilate in this way are men, while their victims are characteristically females—women and girls—and to a lesser extent younger males. As this hierarchy indicates, these are crimes of sexually political, essentially *patriarchal*, domination. So hidden is this knowledge, however, that criminologist Steven Egger (1984), after first noting that all known serial killers are male, goes on to observe: "This sexual differentiation may lead researchers to study maleness and its socialization as an etiological consideration. However, the lack of this obvious distinction has apparently precluded such study" (p. 351). Yet most researchers have not yet made that so obvious distinction because to do so would inevitably introduce the issue of sexual politics into sexual murder.

Although sexual force against women is endemic to patriarchy, the twentieth century is marked by a new form of mass gynocide: the mutilation serial sex murder. This "age of sex crime" begins with the crimes of "Jack the Ripper," the still unidentified killer who in 1888 murdered and mutilated five London prostitutes. Patriarchal culture has enshrined "Jack the Ripper" as a mythic hero; he commonly appears as an immortal figure in literature, film, television, jokes, and other cultural products. The function of such mythicization is twofold: to terrorize women and to empower and inspire men.

The unprecedented pattern laid down during the Ripper's original siege is now enacted with some regularity: the single, territorial, and sensationally nicknamed killer; socially powerless and scapegoated victims; some stereotyped feature ascribed in common to the victims (e.g., all coeds, redheads, prostitutes, and so on); a "signature" style of murder or mutilation; intense media involvement; and an accompanying incidence of imitation or "copycat" killings. Ripper-type killers include the "Lipstick Killer," the "Boston Strangler," the "Son of Sam," the "Hillside Strangler," the "Green River Killer," and the "South Side Slayer," to name only a few.

The Ripper myth received renewed attention in 1988, the centennial year of the original crimes. That occasion was celebrated by multiple retellings of the Ripper legend. In England, Ripper paraphernalia, such as a computer game, T-shirts, buttons, and cocktails appeared (Cameron 1988). Retellings included a British-produced massively promoted made-for-TV movie, *Jack the Ripper;* an exploitation thriller, called *Jack's Back,* about a killer of prostitutes in contemporary Los Angeles; and scores of new books on the master killer.

Within months of this anniversary celebration for the mythic father of sexual murder, the focus effortlessly and eerily shifted to a figurative son of that very father—a man who himself was portrayed as a paradigmatic American son, the "handsome," "intelligent," and "charming" Ted Bundy. In 1979, he was convicted of three women's deaths and is suspected of being responsible for perhaps 47 more. Bundy, like "Jack the Ripper," is a sex criminal who has spawned a distinctive legend and been attended by a distinctive revelry. In the days preceding his death, his story dominated the mass media, memorializing and further mythicizing a killer who had already been the subject of scores of articles, five books, and a made-for-TV movie (where he was played by Mark Harmon, an actor whom *People Weekly* once gushed over as the "world's sexiest man"). The atmosphere surrounding his execution was repeatedly described as a "carnival" or "circus." On the morning Bundy went to the electric chair, hundreds (from photographs of the event, the crowd seemed to be composed largely of men) gathered across the street from the prison. Many wore specially designed costumes, waved banners proclaiming a "'Bundy BBQ" or "I like my Ted well done," and chanted songs such as "He bludgeoned the poor girls, all over the head. Now we're all ecstatic, Ted Bundy is dead." A common journalistic metaphor for the overall scene was that of a tailgate party before a big game. Indications of a spreading Bundy cult continue to appear: a student group at the University of New Mexico in April 1989 offered a program showing a tape of Bundy's final interview. The poster advertising that event displayed a likeness of the killer under the headline: "A Man with Vision. A Man with Direction. A Prophet of Our Times. ... Bundy: The Man, The Myth, The Legend."

This sort of spontaneous outpouring of folk sentiment regarding Ted Bundy was not without precedent. In the late 1970s, when he was awaiting trial for the murder of Caryn Campbell in Aspen, Colorado, Bundy managed to escape twice. The first time he was caught and returned to custody; the second time he was successful and traveled to Florida. But upon the news of his escapes (particularly the first) a phenomenal reaction occurred. All observers concur: "In Aspen, Bundy had become a folk hero" (Larsen 1980, p. 182); "Ted achieved the status of Billy the Kid at least" (Rule 1980, p. 255); "Aspen reacted as if Bundy were some sort of Robin Hood instead of a suspected mass murderer. A folklore sprang up out of the thin Rocky Mountain air" (Nordheimer 1978, p. 46). T-shirts appeared reading, "Ted Bundy is a One Night Stand." Radio KSNO programmed a Ted Bundy request hour, playing songs like "Ain't No Way to Treat a Lady." A local restaurant offered a "Bundyburger," consisting of nothing more than a plain roll: "Open it and see the meat has fled," explained a sign. Yet after his second escape, the FBI took Bundy seriously enough to name him to their 10 Most Wanted List, seeking him "in connection with 36 similar-type sexual slayings throughout several Western states."

Just as Bundy's white, young, generally middle-class victims were stereotypically (and with marked racist and classist bias) universalized as "anyone's daughters," Bundy himself was depicted as the fatherland's (almost) ideal son— handsome, intelligent, a former law student, a rising star in Seattle's Republican party. And although that idealization falls apart upon close examination (Bundy's photographs show an ordinary face, and he had to drop out of law school due to bad grades), it provided an attractive persona for purposes of identification. As several feminist analysts (Lacy 1982–83; Millett 1970; Walkowitz 1982) have noted, a recurrent and vivid pattern accompanying episodes of sensationalized sex murder is ordinary male identification with the sex killer, as revealed in "jokes, innuendoes, veiled threats (*I* might be the Strangler, you know)" (Lacy 1982–83, p. 61).

After his first escape, the male identification was with Bundy as an outlaw rebel-hero. But subsequently, Bundy did the supremely unmanly thing of getting caught; moreover, at the last moment he confessed to his crimes and manifested fear of death. No longer qualifying as hero, Bundy was now cast into the alternate role of scapegoat. The "bloodthirsty revelers" outside the prison gates, through their objectification of the victims and lust for death, still mirrored Bundy, but now delightedly demanded that the preeminent patriarchal son die as a token sacrifice for his and their sins.

In the final days before his execution, Bundy spoke directly about his cultural construction as a sex killer, telling James Dobson, a psychologist and religious broadcaster, that since his youth he had been obsessed with pornography. Bundy claimed that pornography inspired him to act out his torture and murder fantasies. Five years earlier, another interviewer (Michaud and Aynesworth 1983) had reported a similar conversation with Bundy:

> He told me that long before there was a need to kill there were juvenile fantasies fed by photos of women in skin magazines, suntan oil advertisements, or jiggly starlets on talk shows. He was transfixed by the sight of women's bodies on provocative display. ... Crime stories fascinated him. He read pulp detective magazines and gradually developed a store of knowledge about criminal techniques—what worked and what didn't. That learning remained incidental to the central thrill of reading about the abuse of female images, but nonetheless he was schooling himself. (p. 117)

Bundy also spoke for himself (although in the third person since he had not yet decided to openly admit his guilt):

> Maybe he focused on pornography as a vicarious way of experiencing what his peers were experiencing in reality. ... Then he got sucked into the more sinister doctrines that are implicit in pornography—the use, the abuse, the possession of women as objects. ... A certain percentage of it [pornography] is devoted toward literature that explores situations where a man, in the context of a sexual encounter, in one way or another engages in some sort of violence toward a woman, or the victim. There are, of course, a whole host of substitutions that could come under that particular heading. Your girlfriend, your wife, a stranger, children—whatever—a whole host of victims are found in this literature. And in this literature, they are treated as victims. (p. 117)

Bundy's self-confessed movement from pornography (reportedly introduced to him at an early age by a grandfather who beat his wife, regularly assaulted other people, and tormented animals) to actual sexual assault is consistent with testimony from other sex offenders, including sex murderers, who claim that viewing pornography affected their criminal behavior (Caputi 1987; Einsiedel 1986).

Diana E. H. Russell (1988) has proposed a theoretical model of the causative role of pornography in violence against women. Russell first distinguishes between pornography and erotica, drawing upon a definition of pornography as "sexually explicit material that represents or describes degrading or abusive sexual behavior so as to endorse and/or recommend the behavior as described" (Longino 1980, p. 44). She defines erotica as "sexual representations premised on equality" (Leidholdt and Russell forthcoming; Russell 1988, p. 46). Using the findings from a range of social research from the past decade, Russell argues that pornography predisposes or intensifies a predisposition in some men to rape women and that it can undermine some men's internal or social inhibitions against acting out sexually violent behavior. Bundy's testimony clearly supports that model.

Bundy's assertions released a wave of scorn, ridicule, and fury in the mainstream press, with some commentators seemingly more angry at his aspersions on pornography than at his crimes. As one columnist (Leo 1989) fulminated: "As Bundy told it, he was a good, normal fellow, an 'all-American boy' properly raised by diligent parents, though one would have liked to hear more about his 'diligent' mother. While nothing of this mother-son relationship is known, a hatred of women virulent enough to claim 50 lives does not usually spring full-blown from the reading of obscene magazines" (p. 53). Once again, normalcy as well as "maleness and its socialization" are vehemently discarded as an etiological consideration for sexual murder; misogynist myth prevails and the finger of blame is pointed unswervingly at a woman. Since Bundy's execution, an extensive article has appeared in *Vanity Fair;* predictably, it absolves pornography and instead condemns Louise Bundy as responsible for the evolution of her son into a "depraved monster" (MacPherson 1989).

A companion chorus of voices suggests that we cannot take Bundy seriously because Dobson, the fundamentalist crusader, led Bundy to his assertions to further his own agenda. Thus, once again, the feminist connection between violence against women and pornography is potentially discredited by its association with fundamentalism. Yet few feminists would agree with the Right that pornography is the sole or root cause of violence against women. Rather, pornography (as well as its diffusions through mainstream culture) is a modern mode for communicating and constructing patriarchy's necessary fusion of sex and violence, for sexualizing torture. Clearly, that imperative has assumed other forms historically: the political operations of military dictatorships, the enslavement of Africans in the "new world," witch-hunting and inquisitions by the Christian church and state, and so on. The basic elements for a gynocidal campaign—an ideology of male supremacy, a vivid imagination of (particularly female) sexual filth, loathing of eroticism, belief in the sanctity of marriage and the family, and the containment of women in male-controlled institutions—structure fundamentalism's very self-serving opposition to pornography.

Finally, it was claimed that Bundy, a characteristic manipulator, was simply manipulating and lying one last time, trying to absolve himself in his eleventh hour by blaming society. Yet a feminist analysis would not accept the equation that to recognize the responsibility of society for sexually political murder is to absolve the murderer. Rather, it would point to the connection between Bundy and his society, naming Bundy as that society's henchman (albeit, like other sex criminals, a freelancer) in the maintenance of patriarchal order through force. Indeed, we might further recognize Bundy as a martyr for the patriarchal state, one who, after getting caught, had to pay for his fervor, the purity of his misogyny, and his attendant celebrity with his life.

Everyone's Sisters

There was wide public attention in the Ted [Bundy] case ... because the victims resembled everyone's [sic] daughter. ... But not everybody relates to prostitution on the Pacific Highway.

—Robert Keppel, member of the Green River
Task Force (Starr 1984, p. 106)

The victims were universally described as runaways, prostitutes, or drug addicts who "deserved" to die because of how they lived. The distorted portrayal of the girls and women could be expected in a city notorious for its racism, but there was a particular sexist turn, because the victims were not only Black, but female.

—Barbara Smith (1981, p. 68; on a 1979
series of murders in Boston)

Some of the victims were prostitutes, but perhaps the saddest part of this case is that some were not.

—Sir Michael Havers, prosecuting counsel at the trial
of Peter Sutcliffe, the "Yorkshire Ripper" (Holloway 1981, p. 39)

There'd be more response from the police if these were San Marino housewives. ... If you're Black and living on the fringe, your life isn't worth much.

—Margaret Prescod, founder of the Black Coalition
Fighting Back Serial Murders (Uehling 1986, p. 28)

Ted Bundy's victims were young white women and were consistently described in the press as "beautiful" with "long, brown, hair." We can recognize some of this description as a fetishization meant to further eroticize the killings for the public. However, while some highly celebrated killers such as Bundy or David Berkowitz, the "Son of Sam," chose victims on the basis of their correspondence to a pornographic, objectifying, and racist ideal, the majority of victims of serial killers are women who, as Steven Egger (1984) noted, "share common characteristics of what are perceived to be prestigeless, powerless, and/or lower socioeconomic groups" (p. 348), that is, prostitute women, runaways, "street women," women of color, impoverished women, single and elderly women, and so on. The Bundy murders consistently aroused not only a unique folklore and ritual revelry but also a public display of mourning because, in the first place, mainstream men could readily identify with Bundy and also because sexual murder, like rape, is understood as a property crime. A far different societal response is forthcoming when the women killed are not white, not "family women," and not middle class. A pattern of police officials waiting an unreasonable amount of time before organizing a concentrated effort to catch a killer, failing to warn a community, refusing to initiate community involvement, prejudicially labeling victims, and ignoring community input has marked nearly all investigations of the murders of "prestigeless" women (Grant 1988a, 1988b; Jones and Wood 1989; Serrano 1989).

In the "Jack the Ripper" crimes, all of the victims were prostitute women. The killer (or, far more likely, someone pretending to be the killer) wrote to the press a letter that not only originated the famous nickname, but also boasted: "I am down on whores and I shan't quit ripping them until I do get buckled." In the late 1970s, a gynocidal killer was active in northern Britain; the first victims were all prostitute women. Perpetuating the myth of the immortal and recurring sex criminal, the men of the press nicknamed him "the Yorkshire Ripper." As in many cases involving the serial murder of prostitute women, including those of the "Green River Killer," the "South Side Slayer," and a current series of murders of "prestigeless" women in San Diego County, a great deal of controversy has attended police handling, or rather, mishandling, of the case (Serrano 1989). In the wake of that controversy in Yorkshire, the British press has claimed that the major problem that the police faced in the early years of that investigation was "apathy over the killing of prostitutes." Police work, it was declared, depends upon public interest, cooperation, and support; and, as the London *Times* noted, "Such was the apathy at the time that it was virtually nil" (Osman and Ford 1981, p. 5). Ironically, in Yorkshire, such open attitudes of hostility to prostitute women and apathy toward their murders were openly expressed not only by the public but also by the police themselves.

Four years after the first mutilation and murder, the killer had begun to target nonprostitute women, and West Yorkshire's Constable Jim Hobson issued an extraordinary statement as an "anniversary plea" to the killer: "He has made it clear that he hates prostitutes. Many people do. We, as a police force, will continue to arrest prostitutes." Here, Hobson matter-of-factly aligns "Ripper" motives and actions to larger social interests as well as police goals. He goes on, shifting voice to a direct appeal to the killer: "But the Ripper is now killing innocent girls. That indicates your mental state and that you are in urgent need of medical attention. You have made your point. Give yourself up before another innocent woman dies" (Smith 1982, p. 11). From such official statements we learn that it is normal to hate prostitute women; the killer is even assured of social solidarity in this emotion. His deeds, it seems, only become socially problematic when he turns to so-called innocent girls. Over in the Americas, one consultant on the "Green River Killer" case, psychiatrist John Liebert, offered his expert opinion that serial murderers either idealize women or degrade them, seeing women as "'angels or whores,' with no sensible middle ground" (Berger 1984, p. 1). Once again, we are at an utter loss in distinguishing the point of view of the ostensibly deviant sex killer from that of his pursuers or his society. Moreover, the notion that this distinction has any abiding reality in the sex killer's mind is both erroneous and dangerous.

In the mid-1980s, at least 17 women, characterized by the police as prostitutes, were murdered within a 40-mile radius in South Central Los Angeles, a primarily African-American neighborhood; all but 3 of the victims were African-Americans. The police waited until 10 women were killed before notifying the public that a serial murderer was operating and then waited until there were 4 more deaths before forming a task force. In response to police and media neglect, Margaret Prescod, a longtime public spokeswoman for US PROS (a national network of women who work in the sex industry and their supporters) founded the Black Coalition Fighting Back Serial Murders. Rachel West (1987) notes:

> The Black Coalition has stated again and again that they are not convinced that all the women murdered were prostitutes and that the police have offered little evidence to support that claim. When the police could not dig up a prostitution arrest record on victim 17, they immediately said, "but she was a street woman." This statement reflects the attitude of the police toward poor women generally, especially if they are black. We all know only too well that any of us at any time can be labeled a prostitute woman, if we dare step out of line in the way we speak and dress, in the hours we keep, the number of friends we have, or if we are "sexual outlaws" of any kind. (p. 285)

West further observes that in many other instances of serial murder, the killer might begin with prostitute women, but then moves on to women of all types (as in the "Hillside Strangler" killings). When the police or press describe the murdered women as prostitutes, it lulls nonprostitute women into a false feeling of safety. It plays upon sexist and frequently racist prejudices to mute the seriousness of the murders, and—most effectively—it diverts the blame to the victim.

In October 1888, Charles Warren, police chief in charge of the "Jack the Ripper" case, pontificated to the press: "The police can do nothing as long as the victims unwittingly connive at their own destruction. They take the murderer to some retired spot, and place themselves in such a position that they can be slaughtered without a sound being heard" (Cameron and Frazer 1987, p. 20). That sentiment was echoed, one century later, in a piece in the *Los Angeles Times* (Boxall 1989) titled, "Prostitutes: Easy Prey for Killers." It portrays "drug-dazed" women, good daughters gone bad, and contains a quote from Commander William Booth of the Los Angeles police department: "I think that's the highest-risk occupation there is. Mercenaries are way behind prostitutes. ... There is nothing that carries the risk with it, in peacetime, as streetwalking prostitution" (p. 1). The same article states: "Police sweeps have greatly reduced streetwalking in Hollywood, police say, leaving the gritty main drags of South-Central the city's streetwalking center. Elsewhere in Los Angeles, prostitution tends to take more sophisticated, expensive and less hazardous forms, such as escort services" (p. 23). Thus we can surmise that police actions have contributed toward creating a more dangerous city for South-Central women; moreover, these women, targeted because of their race and class, are in far greater danger than women in moneyed, white areas. Clearly, the illegality of prostitution and institutionalized harassment by the police contributes to making prostitution such a "high-risk" occupation.

Although, as far as I know, there are no national statistics kept on the number of prostitutes murdered annually, the Los Angeles police claim that there have been 69 murders of prostitute women and 30 women killed in what they call "street murders" in the past four years. Assuredly, those numbers register appalling danger. Yet ... each year 30 percent of all women murdered are killed by their husbands and lovers, about 1,500 women per year (*Uniform Crime Reports*, 1987, p. 11), and *at least* 1.8 million women are beaten by husbands and lovers annually (Summers 1989, p. 54). Despite blandishments directed toward stereotypical "angels" and "good girls," wifehood seems to rank right up there with prostitution as an endemically unsafe occupation. Faced with such statistics, the invidious distinctions collapse, and we realize with Rachel West (1987) that "the rights of prostitute women are the rights of all women" (p. 285).

As I worked on the conclusion to this piece, I listened to a National Public Radio news program ("Morning Edition," June 7, 1989) reporting that nine women (all of whom were described as prostitutes or drug addicts) had been murdered in the past year in New Bedford, Massachusetts, the site of a notorious gang rape (Chancer 1987). Two other women have been missing for months. A serial killer is suspected; "apathy" is said to be the primary response of the mainstream New Bedford community. Obviously, we have heard this story before. Yet the ascription of "apathy," so common in such cases, is really quite misleading. The reigning, though denied, mood is *hatred*, sexually political hatred. A "hate crime" is conventionally defined as "any assault, intimidation or harassment that is due to the victim's race, religion or ethnic background" (Malcolm 1989, p. A12). That definition obviously must be expanded to include gender (as well as sexual preference). Vast numbers of women are now suffering and dying from various forms of hate crime worldwide, including neglect, infanticide, genital mutilation, battering, rape, and murder. What men might call "peacetime," researcher Lori Heise (1989) truthfully names a "global war on women."

15

Making Female Bodies the Battlefield

Susan Brownmiller

"This is all about identity," the TV newscaster said earnestly, attempting to shed some light on the murderous ethnic rage that has torn the former Yugoslavia apart.

Perhaps the newscaster should have amended his analysis to say *male* identity. Balkan men have proved eager to fight and die for their particular subdivision of Slavic ethnicity, which they further define by religious differences. The Serbs are Eastern Orthodox, while their sworn enemies, the Croats, are Roman Catholic. Bosnians, or rather the 44 percent of the population in Bosnia and Herzegovina that is neither Serb nor Croat, are Muslims; they currently side with the Croats. But Balkan women, whatever their ethnic and religious background, and in whatever fighting zone they happen to find themselves, have been thrust against their will into another identity. They are victims of rape in war.

If the Serbs have emerged as the bad guys in world opinion, it is largely because they have been wildly successful in carving a Greater Serbia out of chunks of Croatia and Bosnia and Herzegovina. Serbian land advances have been accomplished in the age-old manner of territorial aggression, with looting, pillage and gratuitous violence that gets lumped under the rubric of atrocity.

So it is heart-rending, but not surprising, to hear of mass rapes committed in Bosnian villages recently overrun by Serbian fighters. Bosnian refugees fleeing to Croatia give horrendous eyewitness accounts. Detention camps have been turned into brothels that the Bosnian foreign minister in Washington calls "rape camps." Pregnant detainees will suffer the additional shame of bearing unwanted children of war. An emotional Bosnian appeal calls the Serbian rapes "unprecedented in the history of war crimes," an organized, systematic attempt "to destroy a whole Muslim population, to destroy a society's cultural, traditional and religious integrity."

Alas for women, there is nothing unprecedented about mass rape in war when enemy soldiers advance swiftly through populous regions, nor is it a precedent when, howling in misery, leaders of the overrun country call the endemic sexual violence a conspiracy to destroy their national pride, their manhood, their honor. When German soldiers marched through Belgium in the first months of World War I, rape was so extensive, and the Franco-Belgian propaganda machine so deft, that The Rape of the Hun became a ruling metaphor. Afterward, the actual cases were dismissed by propaganda analysts as rhetoric designed to whip up British and American support, but if the rapes had not had propaganda value, they wouldn't have surfaced.

Women are raped in war by ordinary youths as casually, or as frenetically, as a village is looted or gratuitously destroyed. Sexual trespass on the enemy's women is one of the satisfactions of conquest, like a boot in the face, for once he is handed a rifle and told to kill, the soldier becomes an adrenaline-rushed young man with permission to kick in the door, to grab, to steal, to give vent to his submerged rage against all women *who belong to other men.*

Sexual sadism arises with astonishing rapidity in ground warfare, when the penis becomes justified as a weapon in a logistical reality of unarmed noncombatants, encircled and trapped. Rape of a doubly dehumanized object—as woman, as enemy—carries its own terrible logic. In one act of aggression, the collective spirit of women *and* of the nation is broken, leaving a reminder long after the troops depart. And if she survives the assault, what does the victim of wartime rape become to her people? Evidence of the enemy's bestiality. Symbol of her nation's defeat. A pariah. Damaged property. A pawn in the subtle wars of international propaganda.

During World War II, when the Germans were on the march again, atrocious rapes were committed on the bodies of Russian and Jewish women in the occupied villages and cities while still more women were dragged off to forcible brothels, or to death. When the tide reversed and the Soviet Army began advancing into German territory on the road to Berlin, it was the turn of German women to experience the use of their bodies as an extracurricular battlefield. In the Pacific, the euphoric Japanese occupation of China's wartime capital in 1937 was accomplished with such freewheeling sexual violence that it became known as The Rape of Nanking. Astounding though it seems, it wasn't until this year that Korean "comfort women" overcame their shame sufficiently to tell of *their* unwilling role in World War II as sexual conscripts for the Japanese Army.

How short is the memory of those who see warfare strictly in terms of national and religious pride. The mass rapes committed by Pakistani soldiers in newly independent Bangladesh were also called "unprecedented" in 1971, when the government of Bangladesh appealed for international aid to help with the after-math. As in Bosnia now, Bengali women were abducted into military brothels and subjected to gang assaults. Although the raped women of Bangladesh were termed Heroines of Independence and permitted to secure abortions, they were ostracized by their own men when they returned to their Muslim villages. And lest this brief overview be accused of its own ethnocentric bias, sporadic cases of gang rape appear in the records of courts-martial for American soldiers in Viet-nam, and further accounts are contained in the Winter Soldier Investigation conducted by Vietnam Veterans Against the War.

The plight of raped women as casualties of war is given credence only at the emotional moment when the side in danger of annihilation cries out for world attention. When the military histories are written, when the glorious battles for independence become legend, the stories are glossed over, discounted as exag-gerations, deemed not serious enough for inclusion in scholarly works.

And the women are left with their shame.

16

Dispatch from Bosnia-Herzegovina: A Seventeen-Year-Old Survivor Testifies to Systematic Rape

Nina Kadić
(Translation by Zoran Minderović)

[Interview with] Mirsada

ON THE MORNING OF MARCH 3, the chetniks [Serbian fighters] arrived in our village, Kaloševic. They wore masks, and White Eagle insignia on their uniforms. I was terribly afraid. We were not allowed to leave our homes. Non-Serbs were not allowed in the streets. We were not able to buy anything. Those who ventured outside never returned. Some of the men hid in the forest, and those who could afford it went abroad. My father and brother managed to join the Bosnia and Herzegovina Territorial Defense; they are somewhere at the front.

I could see from my window how they rounded up people. They dragged my neighbor, a Serb, and his entire family out of the house. As he was not a member of the Serbian militia and had refused to kill Muslims and Croats, they took his 12-year-old sister Zeljka to the camp.

Three chetniks entered our house. They were drunk. One of them hit my mother, cursing and threatening her. He said that we would regret the day we were born. I trembled. My sister Sanela clung to me, crying. When we went out I realized that she had wet herself.

That day they rounded up all the women and girls. As we passed through the village I saw corpses, dead people in their own yards. The chetniks had set some of the houses on fire. It was pandemonium. They looted, they smashed the win-

174

dows of the food market, fighting among themselves for the few bottles of liquor. We left the village crying. A village of fire, blood, and death.

We hiked for more than five hours into the forest, I didn't know where. Finally, we reached the camp. It was very crowded—all women, children, and old men.

It looked like some kind of forest motel. The cabins were used as sentry boxes. The whole area was fenced with barbed wire, and divided into two sections. They separated me from my mother and sister. They told us we would later be together, but I never saw them again. I stayed with the girls and the younger women.

They raped us every night. The White Eagles would come to get us; they would bring us back in the morning. There were nights when more than 20 of them came. They did all kinds of things to us. I don't want to remember.

We had to cook for them, and serve them, naked. They raped and slaughtered some girls right in front of us. Those who resisted had their breasts cut.

There were women from various towns and villages. There were a thousand of us, maybe more. I spent over four months in that camp. It is a nightmare that cannot be described or understood.

One night, Zeljka's brother Rade helped 12 of us escape. They caught two of us. We spent days hiding in the forest, in improvised underground shelters, and we managed to get away.

If it hadn't been for Zeljka's brother, I would not have survived. I would have killed myself, because death is not as horrible as the treatment I suffered. Sometimes I think I will go crazy. Every night in my dreams I see the face of Stojan, the camp guard. He was the most ruthless among them. He even raped ten-year-old girls, as a "delicacy." Most of those girls didn't survive. They murdered many girls, slaughtered them like cattle.

I want to forget everything. I cannot live with these memories. I will go insane.

For a Paralyzed Woman Raped and Murdered While Alone in Her Own Apartment

Leslie A. Donovan

Nights like these
strangeness crouches at the edge of shadows,
even the tv sounds foreign, cold, inhuman—
but there is nothing
though every creak finds my body frightened,
hopeless as the primeval rattle sounding
beneath a rock just stepped on—
I see her alone in that apartment
Chaucer open before her, a desk lamp craning
above the page, its light glinting
off her wheelchair and
I tell myself it's a silly woman these days who
imagines in the dark like a helpless child,
overwhelmed by being alone
still every moment each unshuttered window seems
to beckon forward a dense shape
faceless, full of force—
the neighbors didn't hear her deadbolt
rip clear of the door and the
house is framed in suppressed terror—
the curve of my antique rocker is suddenly
a threat stretched just beyond the corner of my eye
I search my rooms for brass candlesticks
and aerosol cans
considering how ash trays and
hard bound books might be used as weapons—

Chaucer might have helped her if she
had been able to lift it above his thigh.

My collie finds me
by the phone forbidding myself to cry over a busy signal
he leans against me, pretending I am an oak tree
though we both know better
my fingers lose themselves blessedly in his fur
thinking how simple-sweet the relief
of his known body near me
its thickness allows my tears and
his bulk, warm and supportive
and Alexander's Great Horse becomes a shield
acknowledging the vulnerability I would deny
while the terrible strangeness of that other's body
stays with her forever in the helplessness of such nights
and I stay in the dark by the phone
gripping great tufts of fur
as if to hold him between me and
the strangeness of this night, her memories.

Leslie A. Donovan holds a B.A. from the University of New Mexico and was a candidate for the M.A. degree in English Literature there when this poem was written. A mobility-impaired wheelchair-user as a result of severe rheumatoid arthritis, her work has appeared in local and regional publications.

Part Four

Rape and the Legal System

SEVENTEENTH-CENTURY ENGLISH lord chief justice Matthew Hale warned that rape is a charge "easily to be made and hard to be proved, and harder to be defended by the party accused, tho' never so innocent" (cited in Estrich 1987:5). Years later, in 1977, Wisconsin judge Archie Simonson remarked, "Given the way women dress, rape is a normal reaction" (cited in Woliver 1990:111). "Even in open court we have…women appearing without bras and with the nipples fully exposed, and they think it is smart and they sit here on the witness stand with their dresses up over the cheeks of their butts, and we have this type of thing in the schools. … I can't go around walking exposing my genitals like they can the mammary glands" (cited in Griffin 1979:87). In 1982, another Wisconsin judge, William Reinecke, called a five-year-old sexual assault victim "an unusually sexually promiscuous young lady" (cited in *Columbus Citizen-Journal* 1983:171). These are the types of attitudes rape victims have confronted when they dared to bring their cases into the legal system. Their complaints have been discounted and trivialized. They have been accused of lying and of fabricating complaints to seek retribution against partners who have rejected them. In essence, they have experienced a "second assault" (Williams and Holmes 1981).

The chapters in this section focus on the criminal justice system and the legal criteria that govern state interventions in matters of sexual violation. Research on criminal justice processing of rape and sexual assault finds that cases of "classic" rape (i.e., those involving strangers who use weapons or other means of clearly identifiable force or who inflict clearly identifiable injury beyond the rape itself) are in general more likely to evoke a serious response by police, prosecutors, judges, and juries (Estrich 1987; LaFree 1989). When criminal justice officials are confronted with cases that deviate from "classic rape," their response is especially likely to be influenced by their assessment of the victim's credibility and by their concern with establishing that the sexual interaction was, in fact, nonconsensual. Often the veracity of a victim's complaint is judged in terms of the personal characteristics of the victim and offender and the interpersonal context of the incident (LaFree 1989; Rose and Randall 1982; Sanders 1980). For example, complaints by women whose moral character is questioned or whose perceived carelessness made them vulnerable to attack are greeted with more skepticism. Among those least likely to have their complaints treated seriously are prostitutes, juvenile runaways, and hitchhikers; females who were raped in situations involving alcohol and drug use; females who willingly entered the offender's home or apartment; and females considered to be "partiers," "pleasure seekers," or sexually promiscuous (LaFree 1989).

Beyond these observations, it is important to point out that factors that influence the processing of rape cases at each stage of the criminal justice system are quite complex (see LaFree 1989). For instance, arrests may be more likely for offenders who are prior acquaintances of the victim because they are easier than strangers to identify and locate. However, at later stages a prior relationship between the offender and victim may make prosecution and conviction more difficult because defendants often use this relationship to claim that the woman consented to sex or because a woman assaulted by a friend or relative may decline to cooperate as the case proceeds through the system.

In addition, although stereotypical and prejudicial attitudes toward rape victims are important factors in explaining case outcomes, so are constraints of legal criteria and pragmatic concerns regarding efficient allocation of scarce criminal justice resources (Stanko 1981–1982). Officials at each stage of the system are reluctant to pass on what they perceive to be "weak" cases that will not stand up at subsequent stages (LaFree 1989). For example, police officers may distinguish between "good victims" and "bad victims" on the basis of their perception of how well the case is likely to stand up in court (Sanders 1980). From a purely pragmatic point of view, officials may prefer cases where there is evidence of physical injury because such evidence may be helpful in swaying juries when the defendant claims that the woman consented to sex. Other factors such as the promptness of victims' reports, their ability to identify suspects, and their willingness to testify in court also influence case outcomes.

In the first chapter in this section, "Is It Rape?" Susan Estrich discusses cases that are often screened out by the criminal justice system even though they fit the legal definition of rape. These cases, which she calls "simple rape," involve sexual assaults "where a woman is forced to have sex without consent by only one man, whom she knows, who does not beat her or attack her with a gun." Criminal justice officials often justify excluding these cases, saying that since they treat sexual assault like any other (nonsexual) assault, their decisions are neutral. Estrich argues that this treatment is inappropriate and that these decisions are not neutral because there are important differences between sexual and nonsexual assaults that need to be considered in order to produce a fair outcome.

In the second chapter, "Jack and Ken," Timothy Beneke's interviews provide the viewpoints of two professionals who handle rape cases. Jack, a police sex-crimes investigator, discusses cases that he believes fall in the "grey area between consent and coercion," considers the issue of police insensitivity to rape victims, and offers advice on how women can avoid rape.[1] Ken, a public defender, explains that although he tries to be as ethical as possible, his job requires him to defend rapists to the best of his ability, even if that means suppressing evidence, suppressing a confession, or appealing to the sexism of the jury.

In "Discrediting Victims' Allegations of Sexual Assault: Prosecutorial Accounts of Case Rejections," Lisa Frohmann presents an ethnographic study of deputy district attorneys' decisions to accept or reject sexual assault cases for prosecution. Frohmann finds that prosecutors typically justify case rejections on the grounds that there are discrepancies in the victims' stories or ulterior motives in the victims' reports of assault. She argues that because prosecutors are motivated to avoid filing cases that are not likely to end in conviction, they tend to look for "holes" in cases that would justify rejection.

In "Rape, Racism, and the Law," Jennifer Wriggins offers a historical analysis of the racially biased legal treatment of rape in the United States from slavery to the present time. Wriggins argues that the legal system has consistently treated the rape of white women by African American men more harshly than any other kind of rape, has disproportionately targeted African American men for punishment for rape, and has discounted the victimization of African American women in spite of the fact that African American women are more likely than white women to be raped.[2]

Since the mid-1970s, rape legislation in the United States has undergone considerable reform as a result of attempts to eliminate the sexist assumptions and prejudicial practices associated with the traditional legal treatment of rape. Justice Hale's warning, for instance, is now after three centuries no longer a cautionary instruction that judges are required to read to juries. In the last chapter in this section, "Rape-Law Reform: Its Nature, Origins, and Impact," Ronald Berger, Patricia Searles, and W. Lawrence Neuman provide a succinct review of the literature. They argue that rape-law reforms passed by state legislatures were products of political coalitions and legislative compromises between feminist and nonfeminist interests and that in many states reforms were piecemeal and incomplete. Although instrumental goals have been far from fully realized, the symbolic impact of law reform has been considerable, and the authors remain hopeful that with vigilance, critique, and further reform, progress toward feminist goals will continue.

Notes

1. Despite a police reputation for insensitivity in handling rape cases, accounts of police indifference have become less frequent (Bart 1975). Departments are increasingly likely to educate officers about rape trauma, teach appropriate ways to interview complainants, and assign female officers to rape cases (Rose 1977). LaFree (1989:87) suggests that nowadays police behavior falls "somewhere between the popular television image of the unbiased champion of the crime victim and the image of the sexist, racist brute offered by some critics." Beneke's interview with Jack provides a good example of LaFree's characterization of the contemporary police officer.

2. According to Wyatt (1992), environmental and economic realities of many African American women's lives increase their vulnerability to assault. Compared to white women, African American women are more likely to be single, to have jobs with inflexible working hours, to be without means of private transportation, and to live in areas with high crime rates.

Is It Rape?

Susan Estrich

A MAN COMMITS RAPE when he engages in intercourse (in the old statutes, carnal knowledge) with a woman not his wife; by force or threat of force; against her will and without her consent. That is the traditional, common law definition of rape. ...

But many cases that fit this definition of "rape" are not treated as criminal by the criminal justice system, or even considered rape by their women victims. In the[se] cases ... , the man is not the armed stranger jumping from the bushes—nor yet the black man jumping the white woman, the case that was most likely to result in the death penalty prior to 1977, and the stereotype that may explain in part the seriousness with which a white male criminal justice system has addressed "stranger" rape. Instead the man is a neighbor, an acquaintance, or a date. The man and the woman are both white, or both black, or both Hispanic. He is a respected bachelor, a student, a businessman, or a professional. He may have been offered a ride home or invited in. He does not have a weapon. He acted alone. It is, in short, a simple rape.

The man telling me this particular story is an assistant district attorney in a large Western city. He is in his thirties, an Ivy League law school graduate, a liberal, married to a feminist. He's about as good as you're going to get making decisions like this. This is a case he did not prosecute. He considers it rape—but only "technically." This is why.

The victim came to his office for the meeting dressed in a pair of tight blue jeans. Very tight. With a see-through blouse on top. Very revealing. That's how she was dressed. It was, he tells me, really something. Something else. Did it matter? Are you kidding!

The man involved was her ex-boyfriend. And lover; well, ex-lover. They ran into each other on the street. He asked her to come up and see *Splash* on his new

VCR. She did. It was not the Disney version—of Splash, that is. It was porno. They sat in the living room watching. Like they used to. He said, let's go in the bedroom where we'll be more comfortable. He moved the VCR. They watched from the bed. Like they used to. He began rubbing her foot. Like he used to. Then he kissed her. She said no, she didn't want this, and got up to leave. He pulled her back on the bed and forced himself on her. He did not beat her. She had no bruises. Afterward, she ran out. The first thing she did was flag a police car. That, the prosecutor tells us, was the first smart thing she did.

The prosecutor pointed out to her that she was not hurt, that she had no bruises, that she did not fight. She pointed out to the prosecutor that her ex-boyfriend was a weightlifter. He told her it would be nearly impossible to get a conviction. She could accept that, she said: even if he didn't get convicted, at least he should be forced to go through the time and the expense of defending himself. That clinched it, said the D.A. She was just trying to use the system to harass her ex-boyfriend. He had no criminal record. He was not a "bad guy." No charges were filed.

Someone walked over and asked what we were talking about. About rape, I replied; no, actually about cases that aren't really rape. The D.A. looked puzzled. That was rape, he said. Technically. She was forced to have sex without consent. It just wasn't a case you prosecute.

This case is unusual in only one respect: that the victim perceived herself to be a victim of rape and was determined to prosecute. That is unusual. The prosecutor's response was not.

Much has been written about the incidence of rape and of rape reporting today. Some feminists have claimed that rape is at near epidemic levels, and that if the official statistics do not reflect this, it is because rape is the single most underreported crime. Defenders of the system claim that rape is relatively uncommon and that reporting rates are not atypical and are relatively high. In a sense everyone is right, since no one is defining terms.

The dimensions of the problem of rape in the United States depend on whether you count the simple, "technical" rapes. If only the aggravated cases are considered rape—if we limit our practical definition to cases involving more than one man, or strangers, or weapons and beatings—then "rape" is a relatively rare event, is reported to the police more often than most crimes, and is addressed aggressively by the system. If the simple cases are considered—the cases where a woman is forced to have sex without consent by only one man, whom she knows, who does not beat her or attack her with a gun—then rape emerges as a far more common, vastly underreported, and dramatically ignored problem.

...

Deciding to report a simple rape is a step most victims never take. If they do, it is only the first step. The road to conviction and sentencing is long. Simple rapes are not only far less likely to be reported than aggravated rapes; if they are reported, they are less likely to result in convictions.

The initial decisions are made by the police, in many cases without any review by prosecutors. Police exercise substantial discretion, and they do so almost invisibly. Judges sometimes are attacked publicly when a convicted defendant receives what appears to be an unduly lenient sentence, but police decide to abandon cases every day and no one knows. Police decide whether a woman's complaint is "founded" or "unfounded"; only "founded" complaints are forwarded for possible prosecution. They also decide whether and how much to investigate, a decision which affects the quality of evidence available for trial, or at least for plea bargaining with the defendant's lawyers.

Most jurisdictions do collect "unfounding" statistics for crimes, but numbers can be deceptive. What appear as "high" unfounding rates for rape are invoked by some as proof that police are unfairly skeptical of rape complainants, and by others as proof that rape complainants disproportionately lie. The problem with both approaches is that cases may be "unfounded" for reasons that have nothing to do with the merits of the complaint. Some complaints are unfounded because the police, rightly or wrongly, do not believe the victim. But some are unfounded because it emerges that the alleged offense took place outside the jurisdiction. And some are unfounded because the victim missed a subsequent appointment with the police. Different jurisdictions follow different policies in marking complaints as "founded" or "unfounded," and those differences make the national statistics almost meaningless. For example, in 1973 the FBI reported that nationally 15 percent of all rape complaints were unfounded by police. ... But that 15 percent includes city statistics ranging from 1.3 percent in Detroit to 54.1 percent in Chicago, with everything in between, making comparisons between cities, let alone serious reliance on the national numbers, virtually impossible.[1]

If the numbers themselves tell us little, individual studies of jurisdictions do shed light on some of the factors that lead police to decline certain complaints. Part of the problem, it appears, comes from a male evaluation of a woman's account: in New York and Philadelphia adding a woman to the police investigative team had the effect of substantially reducing the percentage of cases considered to be without merit.[2] But even in those jurisdictions, not all women rape victims are equally suspect: discretion to "unfound" is used more often in simple rape. In New York, for example, researchers studying police files found that 24 percent of the rape complaints in nonstranger cases were judged by the police to be without merit, compared with less than 5 percent in the stranger cases.[3] In Philadelphia a study of police files in the mid-1970s led researchers to conclude that "the police appear to endorse an extralegal victim precipitation logic, declaring unfounded those cases in which the circumstances of the victim-offender relationship are not wholly uncompromising."[4] An earlier study in Philadelphia pointed to race as well, along with the victim's "assumption of risk" (getting into a car, for example) and the promptness of her complaint, as factors influencing the exercise of police discretion.[5]

Even if the police do not unfound the complaint, and even if an arrest is made, conviction is not guaranteed. Arrests are certainly easiest where the victim knows the offender; convictions are another matter. Studies of individual jurisdictions have found that only 20 percent (Washington, D.C.) or 25 percent (New York City) or 34 percent (California) or 32 percent (Indiana) of felony arrests for rape result in convictions.[6]

Attrition of felony arrests, as it is called, is a seemingly unchangeable characteristic of the criminal justice system, and studies of different cities in the U.S. and in Europe in the 1920s and the 1970s have consistently found that from 40 to 60 percent of all felony arrests result in dismissal and acquittal.[7] Moreover, national statistics and statistics from some individual jurisdictions suggest that rape may be more typical than is sometimes claimed in the level of felony attrition compared to other crimes of violence. In California, between 1975 and 1981, rape ranked second (behind homicide) in the percentage of felony filings of all complaints, third (behind homicide and assault) in the average percentages of offenses cleared (solved) by arrest, and third (behind homicide and robbery) in the percentages of arrests resulting in the filing of a felony complaint, felony convictions of all felony complaints filed, and felony arrests resulting in institutional sentences.[8]

To the extent that "rapes" are screened more strictly by their victims and unfounded more often by police than other crimes, similar conviction rates are not proof of equally vigorous prosecution.[9] And, even if the conviction rates for rape are not atypical in some jurisdictions, the question remains whether the factors relied upon to produce them are.

Like police, prosecutors are not required to state reasons when they decide to dismiss or downgrade a case. In some district attorneys' offices, there may be internal guidelines for such decisions, but they tend to be jealously guarded so that defense attorneys cannot insist that they be applied to their clients. Still, studies have been done in a number of jurisdictions of the factors that determine which rape arrests result in felony convictions and which result in dismissal or acquittal. The findings of these studies suggest that my acquaintance's refusal to charge the "technical rape" is typical. The crime-related factors which influence the disposition of rape cases are those which distinguish the jump-from-the-bushes rape from the simple and suspect rape: a prior relationship between victim and offender; lack of force and resistance; and the absence of evidence corroborating the victim's account.

The relationship of victim and offender and the circumstances of their initial encounter appear key to determining the outcome of rape cases in virtually every study. A review of the case files in New York City's district attorney's office disclosed that one-third of the cases involving strangers, and only 7 percent of the nonstranger cases led to indictments; half the nonstranger cases were dismissed outright, compared to a third of the stranger cases.[10] These numbers are consistent with an almost systematic downgrading or dismissing of cases involving nonstrangers, a policy confirmed and defended in newspaper accounts for all crimes in that office.[11]

New York is not unique in this regard. A national survey of prosecutors conducted by the Battelle Memorial Institute found both the relationship of the victim to the suspect and the circumstances of their initial contact to be among the ten factors considered most important in screening rape cases and obtaining convictions.[12] In the state of Washington a 1980 study found the social interaction of victim and defendant to be the second most important factor, behind only the amount of force used, in predicting outcome.[13] In the District of Columbia researchers found that the relationship between victim and accused was substantially more important than the seriousness of the incident in explaining conviction rates: the closer the relationship, the lower the conviction rate.[14] In Austin, Texas, a researcher found that 58 percent of all stranger cases resulted in indictments, compared to 29 percent of the cases among acquaintances and 47 percent among friends. Even more revealing, where the initial encounter between the victim and the defendant was voluntary, only one-third of the cases resulted in indictment; where it was involuntary, the indictment rate was 62 percent.[15]

The second set of factors critical to conviction or dismissal relates to the amount of force used by the defendant and the level of resistance offered by the victim. In the Battelle survey use of physical force was rated by prosecutors as the single most important factor in screening and securing convictions; other key factors were injury to the victim, use of a weapon, and resistance by the victim.[16] In Washington force was the most important factor.[17] Similarly, in Texas both great force by the defendant and substantial resistance by the victim were among the five significant predictors of indictments. The existence of resistance was particularly critical in determining the outcome of cases where the initial encounter between the victim and her assailant was voluntary (she got into the car willingly, or invited him in). In voluntary encounter cases, the probability of indictment was only 13 percent where little victim resistance was used; it jumped to 53 percent where resistance was substantial. Where the initial encounter was involuntary, resistance was far less significant.[18]

The final set of factors predicting outcomes relates to the quality of the evidence itself: whether the prosecutor finds the victim's testimony plausible and whether her account can be corroborated. In Texas, where there was no medical corroboration (at least of penetration) only 12 percent of the arrests resulted in indictment.[19] Proof of penetration, certainty of victim identification, and the availability of witnesses were cited as among the ten most important factors in the Battelle study. Corroborative evidence was the third most important factor in the state of Washington study.[20] In Indiana researchers found that, despite the formal change in the law eliminating its necessity, corroboration remained an informal requirement, a conclusion reached as well by researchers who conducted interviews in Michigan.[21]

The factors emphasized by prosecutors are also considered significant by juries in the few cases that go to trial. In their landmark study of jury trials, Kalven and Zeisel found not only that juries tend to be prejudiced against the prosecution in rape cases, but that they will go to great lengths to be lenient with the defendants if there is any suggestion of "contributory behavior" on the part of the victim.[22] "Contributory behavior" warranting leniency includes the victim's hitchhiking, dating, and talking with men at parties.

Kalven and Zeisel divided their rape cases into two categories, aggravated and simple. ... "Aggravated" rape, according to them, includes cases with extrinsic violence, multiple assailants, or no prior relationship between victim and offender (strangers). "Simple" rape includes cases in which none of these "aggravating circumstances" is present. Jury conviction rates were nearly four times as high in the aggravated cases. Kalven and Zeisel asked judges if they agreed or disagreed with the jury's verdict in particular cases. The percentage of judges in disagreement with the jury jumped from 12 percent in the aggravated cases to 60 percent in the simple cases, with the bulk of the disagreement explained by the jury's absolute determination not to convict of rape if there was any sign of contributory fault by the woman, despite enough evidence of guilt to satisfy the judge.

The fact that juries distinguish among rape cases based on prior relationship and force and resistance provides a powerful defense for the reliance on these factors by police and prosecutors. But it is not necessarily determinative, if the factors are unjustifiable in their own right: that juries may consider race and class is no excuse for prosecutors to discriminate.

When I questioned (my word; he would doubtless describe it as a bit stronger) my acquaintance about his refusal to prosecute the "technical" rape, he barely paused in mounting his defense. He was smart enough not to mention the see-through blouse or the tight jeans. He did mention the likely response of juries. And he leaned heavily on the "neutrality" of his decision. In considering force and resistance and prior relationship and lack of corroboration, factors he termed critical, he was, he claimed, treating this case just like the assaults and robberies and drug deals that he screens and dismisses every day. Feminists might claim that rape is treated uniquely, but not by him. He, and most prosecutors, consider the same factors every day in every crime. Therefore, he concluded, he was beyond reproach. He was neutral.

Not by my standards. Because of the nature of the crime, rape is less likely to be supported by corroboration than these other crimes. Because of the sex and socialization of the victim, it may require less force and generate less resistance. To take into account prior relationship in rape in the same way as in other crimes communicates the message that women victims, particularly of simple rapes, are to blame for their victimization—precisely the sort of judgment that leads them to remain silent. Rape is different from assault or robbery or burglary. Ignoring these differences allow the exclusion of the simple "technical" rape from the working definition of the crime to appear neutral, when it is not.

Consider corroboration. Without question, rape victims, particularly in the nonstranger context, initially confront substantial skepticism from police and prosecutors. Corroboration is therefore that much more important to begin with. But corroborative evidence of rape is more difficult to secure than for many other crimes. In a street theft the requirement of corroboration may be easily met: the defendant is arrested with the stolen goods in his possession. In corruption it is routine to secure needed corroboration by sending in an informant with a tape recorder (if not the video cameras of Abscam) or by wiretapping telephone lines. In drug cases there is both physical evidence and, often, tape recordings.

These procedures cannot be applied to a rape. In most cases there are no witnesses. The event cannot be reenacted for the tape recorder, as bribes or drug sales are. There is no contraband—no drugs, no marked money, no stolen goods. Unless the victim actively resists, her clothes may be untorn and her body unmarked. Medical corroboration may establish the fact of penetration, but that proves only that the victim engaged in intercourse—not that it was nonconsensual or that this defendant was the man involved. Moreover, the availability of medical corroboration turns not only on prompt and appropriate treatment by police and medical personnel but also on the victim's *not* doing what interviews have found to be the most common immediate response of the rape victim, particularly in the nonstranger context: bathing, douching, brushing her teeth, gargling, let alone taking time to decide whether to report. In short, rape is a crime in which corroboration may be uniquely absent.

The same is true of force and resistance. In most crimes of violence the demographics of victim and offender tend to be nearly identical: young, male, center-city residents. Rape is different; its victims, even in jurisdictions with gender-neutral laws, are overwhelmingly female.[23] The reality of our existence is that it takes less force to overcome most women than most men.

Nor is it "neutral" to demand that women resist, as men might resist an assault. To expect a woman to resist an attacker who is likely to be larger and stronger than she is to expect her to do what she has probably been brought up and conditioned (and, if she has read some manuals, instructed) not to do. Women understand this. Many men do not. In one study where respondents were asked

to evaluate the seriousness of a rape, the male subjects overwhelmingly concluded that the rape was less serious where there was little resistance, but the female subjects had the exact opposite reaction. Seeking to explain this "startling
finding," the author concluded that most of the female subjects "identified with
the victim ... That the rapist in the no resistance case so terrified his victim that
she dared not resist apparently aroused more sympathy for her plight among female subjects. Perhaps they could more readily imagine themselves acting in a
similar fashion.[24]

Corroboration and force and resistance are not necessarily "neutral" factors
equally likely to be found in rape and assault cases and therefore entitled to
equal weight in both. Professor Susan Caringella-MacDonald's study of the
treatment of sexual and nonsexual assault cases (including robbery) in Kalama-
zoo County, Michigan, between 1981 and 1983 provides empirical evidence of the
differences. Caringella-MacDonald found that the mean number of witnesses
was more than twice as high in the nonsexual cases and that victim credibility
problems, including implausible account, inconsistent statements, and suspected ulterior motives, were noted by prosecutors in over a third of the sexual
and only 15 percent of the nonsexual assault cases. She also found that the sexual
assault victims, who were overwhelmingly female, offered less resistance and
sustained fewer injuries (apart from the sexual attack) than the nonsexual assault victims, who were predominantly male. The overall conviction probability
as rated by prosecutors was, not surprisingly, statistically higher for the nonsexual than for the sexual assault cases.[25]

Consideration of the prior relationship between the victim and the accused
and the circumstances of their initial contact presents the greatest problem.
Prior relationship cases often result in dismissal because of the withdrawal of
the complaining witness.[26] The reasons victims withdraw range from intimidation by the defendant to the private resolution of their dispute to the inadequacy
of either imprisonment or probation (which is all the criminal justice system can
offer) as a remedy for an individual who is dependent on her attacker (a battered
wife, for example). Vulnerability and dependence are not necessarily "neutral"
factors, equally applicable to all victims regardless of gender or age. Rape victims
are disproportionately young women, and, though they may enjoy the support
of family in stranger cases, support may be less forthcoming—and pressure from
the defendant far greater—when he is someone the victim knows.

Victim withdrawal in prior relationship cases is something of a self-fulfilling
prophecy; if that is so generally, it would seem particularly true in rape cases. If
the prosecutor believes the victim should withdraw—or that this is not a very serious case in any event—that message is unlikely to be lost on the victim. Pursu-
ing a rape complaint under the best of circumstances has unique costs; pursu-
ing it where the prosecutor seems to think that the crime is not serious or will

not result in serious punishment or does not deserve his attention may be more than most women can endure.

But lack of victim cooperation is not the only reason, or even the most important one, for downgrading or dismissing prior relationship cases. Apart from murder, prior relationship cases are simply viewed as less serious and less deserving of the attention of the system and of punishment.[27] At least four reasons are generally offered to support this systemic bias. Each, when applied to rape, incorporates the very notions of male power and entitlement and female contributory fault which make the exclusion of simple rape from prosecution damning for women victims.

First, prior relationship cases are described as truly "private" disputes which are not the business of the public prosecution system. I have no particular problem with this explanation when it is applied to two friends of relatively equal size and strength fighting over a bet or a baseball game. Leaving the two to their own devices is leaving them in a situation of rough equality. But if that is the case, it is unlikely that either will be pressing charges. It is quite a different matter when—and this is when one more often hears the explanation—the two are an estranged husband and wife or ex-boyfriend and girlfriend. To treat this relationship as private is to maintain the privilege of the more powerful (man) to rape or batter the less powerful (woman). The law claims to respect the privacy of a relationship by denying the request of one of the parties (the complaining witness) that it not treat the relationship as private and that it intervene to save her. To respect privacy in this context is to respect not voluntary relationships, but the abuse of greater power.

Second, prior relationship cases are said to be less serious (and the defendants less blameworthy) because they often involve a claim of right where attacks by strangers do not. The paradigmatic nonstranger theft, for example, is a case where underlying the taking of fifty dollars is a claim of right: the defendant asserts that he was legitimately owed the money and that when the victim refused to pay, he simply took it. If prosecutors want to view this case as less serious than a stranger theft or robbery, fine. But the same reasoning applied to rape cases is wholly unacceptable. The claim of right argument in this context means that if a woman has consented to sex in the past, as the victim of the "technical" rape did, then the man has a continuing right to sexual satisfaction; that her body might be his just entitlement in the same way the fifty dollars might.

Third, prior relationship cases often involve contributory fault by the complainant, while offenses by strangers do not. The paradigmatic nonstranger assault is the barroom fight. Both parties claim the other started it; both may even file complaints; and both will be dismissed. The same inquiry in the rape context conveys a very different message. There when we ask "who started it?" we imply that if the woman agreed to give the man a ride home, or to go to his office or apartment, she is to blame for her subsequent rape and should not complain. Indeed, Menachem Amir, a sociologist who studied Philadelphia rape cases in 1958 and 1960, adapted the concept of the "victim-precipitated" rape to describe, and implicitly ascribe blame for, just such cases. Amir considered rapes to be "victim precipitated" where the victim acted in a way that "could be taken as an invitation to sexual relations"—agreed to drinks, rides, or dates or failed to react strongly enough to sexual suggestions and overtures.[28]

Finally, it is said that an attack by a nonstranger—whether a rape or assault—is less terrifying, and therefore deserving of lesser (or no) punishment. As often as I have seen and heard this explanation, it continues to confound me. People are more afraid of stranger crime because they assume, often wrongly, that no one they know would victimize them. But once it happens, betrayal by someone you know may be every bit as terrifying, or more so, than random violence. That you know your attacker is no guarantee of better treatment: for robbery and assault (no equivalent figures are presented for rape) the most recent victimization survey finds a greater likelihood of physical injury from attacks by nonstrangers than by strangers.[29]

I would not be surprised if, someday, some study or studies definitively prove that there are substantial differences, more subtle than the categorization of factors or review of overall statistics suggest, in the way prosecutors treat rape cases. But we need not await that day to argue for change in the system. Sometimes the failure to discriminate is discriminatory; where there are real differences, failure to recognize and take account of them is the proof of unfairness. If the defenders of the system are right in saying rape cases are treated just like assault, and just like robbery and burglary, they are surely wrong in taking this as evidence of a fair and just system. The weight given to prior relationship, force and resistance, and corroboration effectively allows prosecutors to define real rape so as to exclude the simple case, and then to justify that decision as neutral, indeed inevitable, when it is neither.

Not long ago a young woman called me on the phone for advice. She had heard that I was an "expert" on rape. She had been raped by the man she used to date. The relationship had gone sour. This did not turn her into the vengeful female whom the law has so long feared. But it did, apparently, turn him into a vengeful attacker. He followed her and raped her brutally. She felt violated and betrayed. At first she did not know what to do. She talked to friends and relatives. She decided to report it to the police. She talked to the police and the assistant district attorney. She talked to the new victim-witness advocate. No one said that she was a liar, exactly. No one laughed at her, or abused her. They just said that they would not arrest him, would not file charges. It was all explained thoroughly, the way things are done these days by good district attorneys. She had not gone immediately to the doctor. By the time she did, some of the bruises had healed and the evidence of sperm had not been preserved. She had not complained to the police right away. She knew the man. They'd had a prior relationship of intimacy. He was a respected businessman. He had no criminal record. She couldn't believe their response. She had been raped. She called to ask me what she could do to make the prosecutors do something. Nothing, said I, the supposed expert. But I didn't tell her that it was all "neutral" and therefore fair. She knew better.

Notes

1. McCahill, Meyer, and Fischman, 1979.

2. Brownmiller, 1975, citing "Remarks of Laurence H. Cooke, Appellate Division Justice, Before the Association of the Bar of the City of New York" (January 16, 1974, p. 6); McCahill et al., 1979.

3. Chappell and Singer, 1977.

4. McCahill et al., 1979, p. 121.

5. *University of Pennsylvania Law Review*, 1968, p. 277.

6. Williams, 1978b, pp. 25–27, 43; Vera Institute of Justice, 1981, p. 8; Galvin and Polk, 1983; LaFree, 1980a.

7. Zeisel, 1982, pp. 22–24.

8. Galvin and Polk, 1983.

9. Lizotte, 1985.

10. Pfeffer, 1985.

11. *New York Times*, February 12, 1982, p. A1.

12. Battelle Memorial Institute, 1977.

13. Loh, 1980.

14. Williams, 1978b, p. 32.

15. Weninger, 1978.

16. Battelle Memorial Institute, 1977.

17. Loh, 1980, pp. 543, 604.

18. Weninger, 1978.

19. Weninger, 1978.

20. Battelle Memorial Institute, 1977, p. 19; Loh, 1980.

21. Myers and LaFree, 1982; Marsh, Geist, and Caplan, 1982.

22. Kalven and Zeisel, 1966, pp. 249–54.

23. See Caringella-MacDonald, 1985, p. 206.

24. Scroggs, 1976.

25. Caringella-MacDonald, 1985, pp. 206–22.

26. See Biderman et al., 1967; Davis et al., 1980.

27. Vera Institute of Justice, 1981, pp. 29–34; *University of Pennsylvania Law Review*, 1968, p. 280; Moore et al., 1984, p. 12.

28. Amir, 1971, pp. 259–76.

29. U.S. Department of Justice, 1984, pp. 44–45.

18

Jack and Ken

Timothy Beneke

Jack

IN HIS MID-FIFTIES, *he has been a policeman for twenty-five years and a sex crimes investigator for six.*

Most rape victims are very honest and frightened, and many of them have extended fears and apprehensions. The person who's frequently most shook up and difficult to deal with is the boyfriend. They are extremely emotional and defensive. I have one now that I'm working with who can't understand why the rapist isn't instantly caught. Everything possible has been done; there are no clues and the girl can't identify him. Boyfriends are frequently very angry and want to kill the guy. In their overly protective attitude, they are creating a problem. Frequently, the woman is made more upset because of the problems in their relationship.

A very lovely young lady was raped very violently and humiliatingly in front of her apartment house, and she was honestly and seriously upset. The boyfriend she was living with thought she was overexaggerating the seriousness of what happened, and insisted that she have sex with him. Technically, he raped her as vigorously as the suspect. Psychologically and physically she was not ready, and he demanded it and she gave in, for whatever reason. He raped her as forcibly as the guy who did before. He just held her down and took it. Now how does that man justify that? Some men give women a very low status in their lives. ...

In talking to rape victims, you have to find out exactly what happened. Sometimes they're reluctant to talk; sometimes you can't shut 'em up. Motive is always a point. Generally speaking, I believe something happened, I believe what the lady is saying happened to her. But I'm also aware that someone else looking at the incident may see it a little differently, and that's what the jury's going to be doing—examining the whole picture. There are times, we joke, that the rape occurred *after* the sexual intercourse. The cases where people meet, and she'll come into his motel room and they go to bed; the fellow's a little impatient and when he gets done with her, he says, "Bitch, get out of here!" That's when the rape occurred, not during the intercourse. If he'd been nice to her afterward, she probably wouldn't have reported the rape. She's hurt, there's a scuffle, she gets slapped—all the components of a rape are there. It's difficult to sort all this out.

To her, she was raped and she's very sincere about it; she didn't want to go in there, she admits she was wrong in going in to the guy's house or apartment or motel room. She shouldn't have had a couple of drinks with the guy, but she got raped. Probably, when she had sex, it was the gray area between consent and coercion. I advocate a misdemeanor rape law. All the do-gooders are saying every rapist should go to prison. That's not right; there's a lot of in-between in these things.

...

Those types of cases aren't unusual, maybe ten percent. You'll see it when somebody accepts a ride in a car or with a prostitute. They'll get dumped out without their clothes in an isolated area, and say, "I've been raped." The sex has been agreed upon and conducted with enthusiasm, but they'll holler rape and you have to be quite careful. Frequently, someone in an automobile will say, "Come on, I'll give you a ride, little girl," and he'll demand sex. Even after he's taken it, if he's got a little class she probably won't complain if he doesn't push her around. It's the degree of force; a little discretion afterward is as important as before sometimes. She'll go along with it once. She may be raped, but often how the man treats her afterward determines whether she makes a report. If he apologizes afterward that may make a difference.

Are policemen sometimes insensitive to rape victims?

Absolutely. We work hard to train our police officers to be sensitive but I'm sure not all of them are as sensitive as they could or should be. It is a problem and we're well aware of it, but it's a matter of changing personalities and ideas that go back generations, and it isn't going to be done easily. Some officers are immature and nervous and unable to handle a situation with any class. Some people have class, some people haven't. Some of our officers at twenty-four or twenty-five haven't got any class yet.

Recently I was out with a very experienced investigator and we were at a rape victim's workplace. We had some pictures and the man said he wanted her to identify the man who *raped* her. He said it loud enough so that other people could hear it; she may not have told the other people at work about it. It was obviously making her uncomfortable. Here's a man who's taught other officers not to do things like that. It made me wonder if sometimes I do things I shouldn't.

...

What should women do to keep from being raped?

It depends upon the circumstances. Usually the rape doesn't start when the rapist grabs a girl. If he jumps from the bushes and sticks a knife to your throat, your choices are few. If he comes up and he says, "Give me a dollar," the rape's starting right there. If she's fearful and submits and gives him the dollar, he's going to say, "Well, give me your wallet." If he takes her wallet, he's going to take her purse, and by the time he's taken her purse, he's going to take her body. It's a progressive thing. So the rape doesn't start when he touches her; it's the first approach. So a woman has to be continually alert that men are after her body. Some may take three months to get to the point, and some will take three minutes or three seconds, but that's the name of the boy/girl game. The boys want to get in bed with the girls.

Women have to be afraid and be alert. One way of looking at it is to imagine that you've just withdrawn $5,000 in cash from your savings account and you're going to deposit it in another bank. So you've got $5,000 dollars in your purse. How would you act differently? How would you park your car? If somebody were to approach you, would you act friendly or standoffish? If women were to act that way, there'd be a lot less rapes.

Some women get angry about having to constrict their lives.

Women and men like to trust and be trusted. Rapes have been going on for a long time, they're going to be going on for a long time—as long as there are boys and girls. There's a lot of strange people out there and boys are different from girls. I don't see any cure for it.

My job is secure.

Ken

He is a thirty-four-year-old public defender who is married to a feminist, and strongly supports the women's movement. At times, he finds himself in the position of defending rapists to the best of his ability, as he is bound to do, both by his personal ethics and the strictures of the bar association.

I always do the best I can for my client. When I get a case, I essentially have to dissociate myself from the morality of what someone may have done and focus on the legal issues. Sometimes a confession has to be suppressed, or the fruits of a search suppressed; sometimes I keep my clients from testifying and just argue the nonconvincing aspects of the prosecutor's case, even if I may know my client did it.

*In your zeal to get the best deal possible for your client do you ever, in rape cases,
appeal to the sexism of the jury?*

Let me pinpoint different types of rape cases. There are the cases where the
man jumps from the bushes with a knife, or crawls through a window at night,
and overpowers a woman. In that case, no jury's going to be sympathetic to the
rapist, even if the juror is sexist. In those cases, sexism will work to the woman's
favor because she's on a pedestal. Look at the sentences now for rape—they're
skyrocketing.

Another type of case where you *could* appeal to sexism is when the victim is a
prostitute. This is a typical case where the D.A.s will make jokes and offer the guy
a misdemeanor charge, even if the woman was beaten up.

I had a case in which an eighteen-year-old kid in high school picked up an attractive sixteen-year-old girl and offered her a ride to school. He drove her to a
dead-end street and said, "Okay, let's get down," and she said, "No! No! Take me
back to school!" And he took her back to school.

Somehow, this got up to felony court and he was charged with attempted
rape, although he only tried to lay her, was rebuffed, and drove her back to
school. I argued that you can totally disagree with this guy, he's an asshole, he
crudely attempted to have sex with this woman, but he didn't try to force her. I
argued that if *this* is attempted rape then half the men in fraternities have attempted rape and our prisons should be filled.

There are cases where a woman is raped who was wearing provocative
clothes—a miniskirt or no bra—and some attorneys will argue that she was asking for it; what man could resist; boys will be boys. They would argue the weakness of men, and that women are femme fatales. I can see somebody making
that work. I can see an attorney consciously selecting a jury with the idea that
these people will go for that and then appealing to those sentiments and getting
an acquittal. I don't think I could argue that convincingly because I don't believe
it. I'd know some jurors would be thinking it and the question is, would I leave
sexist jurors on the jury? In a sense, it's my job to keep sexist jurors, just as the
D.A. is trying to get feminists on the jury.

In a dating rape case where there's a consensual-type relationship up to a
point, and where force was used, if I honestly believed there was a chance the
woman was taunting the guy, was really being a prick-tease—and I realize that's
a stereotype—I would argue that side of it: that it was not unusual for this guy to
get angry and do what he did under the circumstances. I would argue that this is
a sexist society in which men are brought up to treat women as objects of desire
that they can dominate and treat as any other commodity, and that a woman
who acts coy or flirts is engaging herself in socially conditioned behavior. I'd talk
about my client, who's not a well-educated person, who probably had certain
notions about what the evening was going to be about. He's a victimizer/victim

of society. I'd try to show that he's not an autonomous person, that he's caught in this sexist configuration where he forced this woman to have sex either because he thought she owed it to him or he couldn't resist, because this sexual stereotype that she fell into was so overpowering for him that he couldn't control himself.

I may go so far as to say that what he did was wrong—all of us probably wouldn't do it that way, and sure, he's no great hero—but because of the interaction between them, and their cultural conditioning, his using force was somehow understandable. If the victim was very flip and casual on the stand I might say something like, "You saw her demeanor on the stand. She didn't appear extremely upset about the situation. Maybe she didn't particularly want to do it at the time, but you saw her demeanor." And I might argue that her flip, capricious manner might have led my client to believe she fits the old stereotype of the woman who really wants it but is saying no.

Isn't that just a sophisticated, sociological way of appealing to the classic rape-supporting myth that men can't control themselves in the presence of a sexy, provocative woman? Men have been saying for years that "if a woman is sexually provocative and gets raped, that's too bad," which I think is nonsense.

Now that you say it, I think you're right, I would be in the position of appealing to that stereotype. I try to be as ethical as I can while at the same time trying to do the best job I can for my client. I'm sure that by trying to do an objective social analysis of the problem, I'm justifying certain stereotypes and rationalizations that should be done away with in a utopian society. And the real problem is: a simple no should be enough for any man, no matter how much foreplay. It's always been enough for me.

How would your wife feel about your appeal to the jury? She's a feminist.

She'd hate it. She'd probably be outraged if she knew the cases I have. I don't even discuss them with her.

Postscript: Upon reading this interview, he wrote: "You have captured the contradictoriness (sophistry?) in the way we are forced to treat these cases, but that's what I said."

19

Discrediting Victims' Allegations of Sexual Assault: Prosecutorial Accounts of Case Rejections

Lisa Frohmann

CASE SCREENING IS THE GATEWAY to the criminal court system. Prosecutors, acting as gatekeepers, decide which instances of alleged victimization will be passed on for adjudication by the courts. A recent study by the Department of Justice (Boland et al. 1990) suggests that a significant percentage of felony cases never get beyond this point, with only cases characterized as "solid" or "convictable" being filed (Stanko 1981, 1982; Mather 1979). This paper will examine how prosecutors account for the decision to reject sexual assault cases for prosecution and looks at the centrality of discrediting victims' rape allegations in this justification.

A number of studies on sexual assault have found that victim credibility is important in police decisions to investigate and make arrests in sexual assault cases (LaFree 1981; Rose and Randall 1982; Kerstetter 1990; Kerstetter and Van Winkle 1990). Similarly, victim credibility has been shown to influence prosecutors' decisions at a number of stages in the handling of sexual assault cases (LaFree 1980, 1989; Chandler and Torney 1981; Kerstetter 1990).

Much of this prior research has assumed, to varying degrees, that victim credibility is a phenomenon that exists independently of prosecutors' interpretations and assessments of such credibility. Particularly when operationalized in terms of quantitative variables, victim credibility is treated statistically as a series of fixed, objective features of cases. Such approaches neglect the processes whereby prosecutors actively assess and negotiate victim credibility in actual, ongoing case processing.

An alternative view examines victim credibility as a phenomenon constructed and maintained through interaction (Stanko 1980). Several qualitative studies have begun to identify and analyze these processes. For example, Holmstrom and Burgess's (1983) analysis of a victim's experience with the institutional handling of sexual assault cases discusses the importance of victim credibility through the prosecutor's evaluation of a complainant as a "good witness." A "good witness" is someone who, through her appearance and demeanor, can convince a jury to accept her account of "what happened." Her testimony is "consistent," her behavior "sincere," and she cooperates in case preparation. Stanko's (1981, 1982) study of felony case filing decisions similarly emphasizes prosecutors' reliance on the notion of the "stand-up" witness—someone who can appear to the judge and jury as articulate and credible. Her work emphasizes the centrality of victim credibility in complaint-filing decisions.

In this article I extend these approaches by systematically analyzing the kinds of accounts prosecutors offer in sexual assault cases to support their complaint-filing decisions. Examining the justifications for decisions provides an understanding of how these decisions appear rational, necessary, and appropriate to decision-makers as they do the work of case screening. It allows us to uncover the inner, indigenous logic of prosecutors' decisions and the organizational structures in which those decisions are embedded (Garfinkel 1984).

I focus on prosecutorial accounting for case rejection for three reasons. First, since a significant percentage of cases are not filed, an important component of the case-screening process involves case rejection. Second, the organization of case filing requires prosecutors to justify case rejection, not case acceptance, to superiors and fellow deputies. By examining deputy district attorneys' (DDAs') reasons for case rejection, we can gain access to what they consider "solid" cases, providing further insight into the case-filing process. Third, in case screening, prosecutors orient to the rule—when in doubt, reject. Their behavior is organized more to avoiding the error of filing cases that are not likely to result in conviction than to avoiding the error of rejecting cases that will probably end in conviction (Scheff 1966). Thus, I suggest that prosecutors are actively looking for "holes" or problems that will make the victim's version of "what happened" unbelievable or not convincing beyond a reasonable doubt, hence unconvictable (see Miller [1970], Neubauer [1974], and Stanko [1980, 1981] for the importance of conviction in prosecutors' decisions to file cases). This bias is grounded within the organizational context of complaint filing.

Data and Methods

The research was part of an ethnographic field study of the prosecution of sexual assault crimes by deputy district attorneys in the sexual assault units of two branch offices of the district attorney's offices in a metropolitan area on the West

Coast.[1] Research was conducted on a full-time basis in 1989 for nine months in Bay City and on a full-time basis in 1990 for eight months in Center Heights. Three prosecutors were assigned to the unit in Bay City, and four prosecutors to the unit in Center Heights. The data came from 17 months of observation of more than three hundred case screenings. These screenings involved the presentation and assessment of a police report by a sexual assault detective to a prosecutor, conversations between detectives and deputies regarding the "filability"/reject status of a police report, interviews of victims by deputies about the alleged sexual assault, and discussions between deputies regarding the file/reject status of a report. Since tape recordings were prohibited, I took extensive field notes and tried to record as accurately as possible conversation between the parties. In addition, I also conducted open-ended interviews with prosecutors in the sexual assault units and with investigating officers who handled these cases. The accounts presented in the data below include both those offered in the course of negotiating a decision to reject or file a case (usually to the investigating officer [IO] but sometimes with other prosecutors or to me as an insider), and the more or less fixed accounts offered for a decision already made (usually to me). Although I will indicate the context in which the account occurs, I will not emphasize the differences between accounts in the analysis.

The data were analyzed using the constant comparison method of grounded theory (Glaser and Strauss 1967). I collected all accounts of case rejection from both offices. Through constant comparison of the data, I developed coding schema which provide the analytic framework of the paper.

The two branches of the district attorney's office I studied cover two communities differing in socioeconomic and racial composition. Bay City is primarily a white middle-to-upper-class community, and Center Heights is primarily a black and Latino lower-class community. Center Heights has heavy gang-drug activity, and most of the cases brought to the district attorney were assumed to involve gang members (both the complainant and the assailant) or a sex-drug or sex-money transaction. Because of the activities that occur in this community, the prior relationships between the parties are often the result of gang affiliation. This tendency, in connection with the sex-drug and sex-money transactions, gives a twist to the "consent defense" in "acquaintance" rapes. In Bay City, in contrast, the gang activity is much more limited and the majority of acquaintance situations that came to the prosecutors' attention could be categorized as "date rape."

The Organizational Context
of Complaint Filing

Several features of the court setting that I studied provided the context for prosecutors' decisions. These features are prosecutorial concern with maintaining a high conviction rate to promote an image of the "community's legal protector," and prosecutorial and court procedures for processing sexual assault cases.

The promotion policy of the county district attorney's (DA) office encourages prosecutors to accept only "strong" or "winnable" cases for prosecution by using conviction rates as a measure of prosecutorial performance. In the DA's office, guilty verdicts carry more weight than a conviction by case settlement. The stronger the case, the greater likelihood of a guilty verdict, the better the "stats" for promotion considerations. The inducement to take risks—to take cases to court that might not result in conviction—is tempered in three ways: First, a pattern of not-guilty verdicts is used by the DA's office as an indicator of prosecutorial incompetency. Second, prosecutors are given credit for the number of cases they reject as a recognition of their commitment to the organizational concern of reducing the case load of an already overcrowded court system. Third, to continually pursue cases that should have been rejected outright may lead judges to question the prosecutor's competence as a member of the court.

Sexual assault cases are among those crimes that have been deemed by the state legislature to be priority prosecution cases. That is, in instances where both "sex" and "nonsex" cases are trailing (waiting for a court date to open), sexual assault cases are given priority for court time. Judges become annoyed when they feel that court time is being "wasted" with cases that "should" have been negotiated or rejected in the first place, especially when those cases have been given priority over other cases. Procedurally, the prosecutor's office handles sexual assault crimes differently from other felony crimes. Other felonies are handled by a referral system; they are handed from one DDA to another at each stage in the prosecution of the case. But sexual assault cases are vertically prosecuted; the deputy who files the case remains with it until its disposition, and therefore is closely connected with the case outcome.

Accounting for Rejection Because of "Discrepancies"

Within this organizational context, a central feature of prosecutorial accounts of case rejection is the discrediting of victims' allegations of sexual assault. Below I examine two techniques used by prosecutors to discredit victim's complaints: discrepant accounts and ulterior motives.

Using Official Reports and Records to Detect Discrepancies

In the course of reporting a rape, victims recount their story to several criminal justice officials. Prosecutors treat consistent accounts of the incident over time as an indicator of a victim's credibility. In the first example two prosecutors are discussing a case brought in for filing the previous day.

> DDA Tamara Jacobs: In the police report she said all three men were kissing the victim. Later in the interview she said that was wrong. It seems strange because there are things wrong on major events like oral copulation and intercourse…, for example whether she had John's penis in her mouth. Another thing wrong is whether he forced her into the bedroom immediately after they got to his room or, as the police report said, they all sat on the couch and watched TV. This is something a cop isn't going to get wrong, how the report started. (Bay City)

The prosecutor questions the credibility of the victim's allegation by finding "inconsistencies" between the complainant's account given to the police and the account given to the prosecutor. The prosecutor formulates differences in these accounts as "discrepancies" by noting that they involve "major events"— events so significant no one would confuse them, forget them, or get them wrong. This is in contrast to some differences that may involve acceptable, "normal inconsistencies" in victims' accounts of sexual assault. By "normal inconsistencies," I mean those that are expected and explainable because the victim is confused, upset, or shaken after the assault.

The DDA also discredited the victim's account by referring to a typification of police work. She assumes that the inconsistencies in the accounts could not be attributed to the incorrect writing of the report by the police officer on the grounds that they "wouldn't get wrong how the report started." Similarly, in the following example, a typification of police work is invoked to discredit the victim's account. Below the DDA and IO are discussing the case immediately after the victim interview.

> DDA Sabrina Johnson: [T]he police report doesn't say anything about her face being swollen, only her hand. If they took pictures of her hand, wouldn't the police have taken a picture of her face if it was swollen? (Bay City)

The prosecutor calls the credibility of the victim's complaint into question by pointing to a discrepancy between her subsequent account of injuries received during the incident and the notation of injuries on the police reports taken at the time the incident was reported. Suspicion of the complainant's account is also expressed in the prosecutor's inference that if the police went to the trouble of photographing the victim's injured hand they would have taken pictures of her face had it also shown signs of injury.

In the next case the prosecutor cites two types of inconsistencies between accounts. The first set of inconsistencies is the victim's accounts to the prosecutor and to the police. The second set is between the account the victim gave to the prosecutor and the statements the defendants gave to the police. This excerpt was obtained during an interview.

> DDA Tracy Timmerton: The reason I did not believe her [the victim] was, I get the police report first and I'll read that, so I have read the police report which recounts her version of the facts but it also has the statement of both defendants. Both defendants were arrested at separate times and give[n] separate independent statements that were virtually the same. Her story when I had her recount it to me in the DA's office, the number of acts changed, the chronological order of how they happened has changed. (Bay City)

When the prosecutor compared the suspects' accounts with the victim's account, she interpreted the suspects' accounts as credible because both of their accounts, given separately to police, were similar. This rests on the assumption that if suspects give similar accounts when arrested together, they are presumed to have colluded on the story, but if they give similar accounts independent of the knowledge of the other's arrest, there is presumed to be a degree of truth to the story. This stands in contrast to the discrepant accounts the complainant gave to law enforcement officials and the prosecutor.

Using Official Typifications of Rape-Relevant Behavior

In the routine handling of sexual assault cases prosecutors develop a repertoire of knowledge about the features of these crimes.[2] This knowledge includes how particular kinds of rape are committed, post-incident interaction between the parties in an acquaintance situation, and victims' emotional and psychological reactions to rape and their effects on victims' behavior. The typifications of rape-relevant behavior are another resource for discrediting a victim's account of "what happened."

Typifications of Rape Scenarios. Prosecutors distinguish between different types of sexual assault. They characterize these types by the sex acts that occur, the situation in which the incident occurred, and the relationship between the parties. In the following excerpt the prosecutor discredits the victim's version of events by focusing on incongruities between the victim's description of the sex acts and the prosecutor's knowledge of the typical features of kidnap-rape. During an interview a DDA described the following:

> DDA Tracy Timmerton: [T]he only act she complained of was intercourse, and my experience has been that when a rapist has a victim cornered for a long period of time, they engage in multiple acts and different types of sexual acts and very rarely do just intercourse. (Bay City)

The victim's account is questioned by noting that she did not complain about or describe other sex acts considered "typical" of kidnap-rape situations. She only complained of intercourse. In the next example the DDA and IO are talking about a case involving the molestation of a teenage girl.

> DDA William Nelson: Something bothers me, all three acts are the same. She's on her stomach and has her clothes on and he has a "hard and long penis." All three times he is grinding his penis into her butt. It seems to me he should be trying to do more than that by the third time. (Center Heights)

Here the prosecutor is challenging the credibility of the victim's account by comparing her version of "what happened" with his typification of the way these crimes usually occur. His experience suggests there should be an escalation of sex acts over time, not repetition of the same act.

Often the typification invoked by the prosecutor is highly situational and local. In discussing a drug-sex-related rape in Center Heights, for example, the prosecutor draws on his knowledge of street activity in that community and the types of rapes that occur there to question whether the victim's version of events is what "really" happened. The prosecutor is describing a case he received the day before to an investigating officer there on another matter.

> DDA Kent Fernome: I really feel guilty about this case I got yesterday. The girl is 20 going on 65. She is real skinny and gangly. Looks like a cluckhead [crack addict]—they cut off her hair. She went to her uncle's house, left her clothes there, drinks some beers and said she was going to visit a friend in Center Heights who she said she met at a drug rehab program. She is not sure where this friend Cathy lives. Why she went to Center Heights after midnight, God knows? It isn't clear what she was doing between 12 and 4 a.m. Some gang bangers came by and offered her a ride. They picked her up on the corner of Main and Lincoln. I think she was turning a trick, or looking for a rock, but she wouldn't budge from her story. ... There are lots of conflicts between what she told the police and what she told me. The sequence of events, the sex acts performed, who ejaculates. She doesn't say who is who. ... She's beat up, bruises on face and a laceration on her neck. The cop and doctor say there is no trauma—she's done by six guys. That concerns me. There is no semen that they see. It looks like this to me—maybe she is a strawberry, she's hooking or looking for a rock, but somewhere along the line it is not consensual. ... She is [a] real street-worn woman. She's not leveling with me—visiting a woman with an unknown address on a bus in Center Heights—I don't buy it. ... (Center Heights)

The prosecutor questioned the complainant's reason for being in Center Heights because, based on his knowledge of the area, he found it unlikely that a woman would come to this community at midnight to visit a friend at an unknown address. The deputy proposed an alternative account of the victim's action based on his knowledge of activities in the community—specifically, prostitution and drug dealing—and questioned elements of the victim's account, particularly her insufficiently accounted for activity between 12 and 4 a.m., coming to Center Heights late at night to visit a friend at an unknown address, and "hanging out" on the corner.

The DDA uses "person-descriptions" (Maynard 1984) to construct part of the account, describing the complainant's appearance as a "cluckhead" and "street-worn." These descriptions suggested she was a drug user, did not have a "stable" residence or employment, and was probably in Center Heights in search of drugs. This description is filled in by her previous "participation in a drug rehab program," the description of her activity as "hanging out" and being "picked up" by gang bangers, and a medical report which states that no trauma or semen was found when she was "done by six guys." Each of these features of the account suggests that the complainant is a prostitute or "strawberry" who came to Center Heights to trade sex or money for drugs. This alternative scenario combined with "conflicts between what she told the police and what she told me" justify case rejection because it is unlikely that the prosecutor could get a conviction.

The prosecutor acknowledges the distinction between the violation of women's sexual/physical integrity—"somewhere along the line it wasn't consensual"—and prosecutable actions. The organizational concern with "downstream consequences" (Emerson and Paley 1992) mitigate against the case being filed.

Typifications of Post-Incident Interaction. In an acquaintance rape, the interaction between the parties after the incident is a critical element in assessing the validity of a rape complaint. As implied below by the prosecutors, the typical interaction pattern between victim and suspect after a rape incident is not to see one another. In the following cases the prosecutor challenges the validity of the victims' allegations by suggesting that the complainants' behavior runs counter to a typical rape victim's behavior. In the first instance the parties involved in the incident had a previous relationship and were planning to live together. The DDA is talking to me about the case prior to her decision to reject.

> DDA Sabrina Johnson: I am going to reject the case. She is making it very difficult to try the case. She told me she let him into her apartment last night because she is easily influenced. The week before this happened [the alleged rape] she agreed to have sex with him. Also, first she says "he raped me" and then she lets him into her apartment. (Bay City)

Here the prosecutor raises doubt about the veracity of the victim's rape allegation by contrasting it to her willingness to allow the suspect into her apartment after the incident. This "atypical" behavior is used to discredit the complainant's allegation.

In the next excerpt the prosecutor was talking about two cases. In both instances the parties knew each other prior to the rape incident as well as having had sexual relations after the incident. As in the previous instance, the victims' allegations are discredited by referring to their atypical behavior.

> DDA Sabrina Johnson: I can't take either case because of the women's behavior after the fact. By seeing these guys again and having sex with them they are absolving them of their guilt. (Bay City)

In each instance the "downstream" concern with convictability is indicated in the prosecutor's talk—"She is making it very difficult to try the case" and "By seeing these guys again and having sex with them they are absolving them of their guilt." This concern is informed by a series of common-sense assumptions about normal heterosexual relations that the prosecutors assume judges and juries use to assess the believability of the victim: First, appropriate behavior within ongoing relationships is noncoercive and nonviolent. Second, sex that occurs within the context of ongoing relationships is consensual. Third, if coercion or violence occurs, the appropriate response is to sever the relationship, at least for a time. When complainants allege they have been raped by their partner within a continuing relationship, they challenge the taken-for-granted assumptions of normal heterosexual relationships. The prosecutors anticipate that this challenge will create problems for the successful prosecution of a case because they think that judges and jurors will use this typification to question the credibility of the victim's allegation. They assume that the triers of fact will assume that if there is "evidence" of ongoing normal heterosexual relations—she didn't leave and the sexual relationship continued—then there was no coercive sex. Thus the certitude that a crime originally occurred can be retrospectively undermined by the interaction between complainant and suspect after the alleged incident. Implicit in this is the assumed primacy of the normal heterosexual relations typification as the standard on which to assess the victim's credibility even though an allegation of rape has been made.

Typifications of Rape Reporting. An important feature of sexual assault cases is the timeliness in which they are reported to the police (see Torrey 1991). Prosecutors expect rape victims to report the incident relatively promptly: "She didn't call the police until four hours later. That isn't consistent with someone who has been raped." If a woman reports "late," her motives for reporting and the sincerity of her allegation are questioned if they fall outside the typification of officially recognizable/explainable reasons for late reporting. The typification is characterized by the features that can be explained by Rape Trauma Syndrome (RTS). In the first excerpt the victim's credibility is not challenged as a result of her delayed reporting. The prosecutor describes her behavior and motives as characteristic of RTS. The DDA is describing a case to me that came in that morning.

> DDA Tamara Jacobs: Charlene was in the car with her three assailants after the rape. John (the driver) was pulled over by the CHP [California Highway Patrol] for erratic driving behavior. The victim did not tell the officers that she had just been raped by these three men. When she arrived home, she didn't tell anyone what happened for approximately 24 hours. When her best friend found out from the assailants (who were mutual friends) and confronted the victim, Charlene told her what happened. She then reported it to the police. When asked why she didn't report the crime earlier, she said that she was embarrassed and afraid they would hurt her more if she reported it to the police. The DDA went on to say that the victim's behavior and

reasons for delayed reporting were symptomatic of RTS. During the trial an expert in Rape Trauma Syndrome was called by the prosecution to explain the "normality" and commonness of the victim's reaction. (Bay City)

Other typical motives include "wanting to return home first and get family support" or "wanting to talk the decision to report over with family and friends." In all these examples, the victims sustained injuries of varying degrees in addition to the trauma of the rape itself, and they reported the crime within 24 hours. At the time the victims reported the incident, their injuries were still visible, providing corroboration for their accounts of what happened.

In the next excerpt we see the connection between atypical motives for delayed reporting and ulterior motives for reporting a rape allegation. At this point I focus on the prosecutors' use of typification as a resource for discrediting the victim's account. I will examine ulterior motives as a technique of discrediting in a later section. The deputy is telling me about a case she recently rejected.

> DDA Sabrina Johnson: She doesn't tell anyone after the rape. Soon after this happened she met him in a public place to talk business. Her car doesn't start, he drives her home and starts to attack her. She jumps from the car and runs home. Again she doesn't tell anyone. She said she didn't tell anyone because she didn't want to lose his business. Then the check bounces, and she ends up with VD. She has to tell her fiance so he can be treated. He insists she tell the police. It is three weeks after the incident. I have to look at what the defense would say about the cases. Looks like she consented, and told only when she had to because of the infection and because he made a fool out of her by having the check bounce. (Bay City)

The victim's account is discredited because her motives for delayed reporting—not wanting to jeopardize a business deal—fall outside those considered officially recognizable and explicable.

Typifications of Victim's Demeanor. In the course of interviewing hundreds of victims, prosecutors develop a notion of a victim's comportment when she tells what happened. They distinguish between behavior that signifies "lying" versus "discomfort." In the first two exchanges the DDA and IO cite the victim's behavior as an indication of lying. Below, the deputy and IO are discussing the case immediately after the intake interview.

> IO Nancy Fauteck: I think something happened. There was an exchange of body language that makes me question what she was doing. She was yawning, hedging, fudging something.
> DDA Sabrina Johnson: Yawning is a sign of stress and nervousness.
> IO Nancy Fauteck: She started yawning when I talked to her about her record earlier, and she stopped when we finished talking about it. (Bay City)

The prosecutor and the investigating officer collaboratively draw on their common-sense knowledge and practical work experience to interpret the yawns, nervousness, and demeanor of the complainant as running counter to behavior they expect from one who is "telling the whole truth." They interpret the victim's behavior as a continuum of interaction first with the investigating officer and then with the district attorney. The investigating officer refers to the victim's recurrent behavior (yawning) as an indication that something other than what the victim is reporting actually occurred.

In the next excerpt the prosecutor and IO discredit the victim's account by referencing two typifications—demeanor and appropriate rape-victim behavior. The IO and prosecutor are telling me about the case immediately after they finished the screening interview.

> IO Dina Alvarez: One on one, no corroboration.
>
> DDA William Nelson: She's a poor witness, though that doesn't mean she wasn't raped. I won't file a one-on-one case.
>
> IO Dina Alvarez: I don't like her body language.
>
> DDA William Nelson: She's timid, shy, naive, virginal, and she didn't do all the right things. I'm not convinced she is even telling the truth. She's not even angry about what happened to her. ...
>
> DDA William Nelson: Before a jury if we have a one on one, he denies it, no witnesses, no physical evidence or medical corroboration they won't vote guilty.
>
> IO Dina Alvarez: I agree, and I didn't believe her because of her body language. She looks down, mumbles, crosses her arms, and twists her hands.
>
> DDA William Nelson: ... She has the same mannerisms and demeanor as a person who is lying. A jury just won't believe her. She has low self-esteem and self-confidence. ... (Center Heights)

The prosecutor and IO account for case rejection by characterizing the victim as unbelievable and the case as unconvictable. They establish their disbelief in the victim's account by citing the victim's actions that fall outside the typified notions of believable and expected behavior—"she has the same mannerisms and demeanor as a person who is lying," and "I'm not convinced she is even telling the truth. She isn't even angry about what happened." They assume that potential jurors will also find the victim's demeanor and post-incident behavior problematic. They demonstrate the unconvictability of the case by citing the "holes" in the case—a combination of a "poor witness" whom "the jury just won't believe" and "one on one, [with] no corroboration" and a defense in which the defendant denies anything happened or denies it was nonconsensual sex.

Prosecutors and investigating officers do not routinely provide explicit accounts of "expected/honest" demeanor. Explicit accounts of victim demeanor tend to occur when DDAs are providing grounds for discrediting a rape allegation. When as a researcher I pushed for an account of expected behavior, the following exchange occurred. The DDA had just concluded the interview and asked the victim to wait in the lobby.[3]

> IO Nancy Fauteck: Don't you think he's credible?
>
> DDA Sabrina Johnson: Yes.

LF: What seems funny to me is that someone who said he was so unwilling to do this talked about it pretty easily.

IO Nancy Fauteck: Didn't you see his eyes, they were like saucers.

DDA Sabrina Johnson: And [he] was shaking too. (Bay City)

This provides evidence that DDAs and IOs are orienting to victims' comportment and could provide accounts of "expected/honest" demeanor if necessary. Other behavior that might be included in this typification are the switch from looking at to looking away from the prosecutor when the victim begins to discuss the specific details of the rape itself; a stiffening of the body and tightening of the face as though to hold in tears when the victim begins to tell about the particulars of the incident; shaking of the body and crying when describing the details of the incident; and a lowering of the voice and long pauses when the victim tells the specifics of the sexual assault incident.

Prosecutors have a number of resources they call on to develop typification related to rape scenarios and reporting. These include how sexual assaults are committed, community residents and activities, interactions between suspect and defendant after a rape incident, and the way victims' emotional and psychological responses to rape influence their behavior. These typifications highlight discrepancies between prosecutors' knowledge and victims' accounts. They are used to discredit the victims' allegation of events, justifying case rejection.

As we have seen, one technique used by prosecutors to discredit a victim's allegations of rape as a justification of case rejection is the detection of discrepancies. The resources for this are official documents and records and typifications of rape scenarios and rape reporting. A second technique prosecutors use is the identification of ulterior motives for the victim's rape allegation.

Accounting for Rejection by "Ulterior Motive"

Ulterior motives rest on the assumption that a woman consented to sexual activity and for some reason needed to deny it afterwards. These motives are drawn from the prosecutor's knowledge of the victim's personal history and the community in which the incident occurred. They are elaborated and supported by other techniques and knowledge prosecutors use in the accounting process.

I identify two types of ulterior motives prosecutors use to justify rejection: The first type suggests the victim has a reason to file a false rape complaint. The second type acknowledges the legitimacy of the rape allegation, framing the motives as an organizational concern with convictability.

Knowledge of Victim's Current Circumstances

Prosecutors accumulate the details of victims' lives from police interviews, official documents, and filing interviews. They may identify ulterior motives by drawing on this information. Note that unlike the court trial itself, where the rape incident is often taken out of the context of the victim's life, here the DDAs call on the texture of a victim's life to justify case rejection. In an excerpt previously discussed, the DDA uses her knowledge of the victim's personal relationship and business transactions as a resource for formulating ulterior motives. Drawing on the victim's current circumstances, the prosecutor suggests two ulterior motives for the rape allegation—disclosure to her fiance about the need to treat a sexually transmitted disease, and anger and embarrassment about the bounced check. Both of these are motives for making a false complaint. The ulterior motives are supported by the typification for case reporting. Twice unreported sexual assault incidents with the same suspect, a three-week delay in reporting, and reporting only after the fiance insisted she do so are not within the typified behavior and reasons for late reporting. Her atypical behavior provides plausibility to the alternative version of the events—the interaction was consensual and only reported as a rape because the victim needed to explain a potentially explosive matter (how she contracted venereal disease) to her fiance. In addition she felt duped on a business deal.

Resources for imputing ulterior motives also come from the specifics of the rape incident. Below, the prosecutor's knowledge of the residents and activities in Center Heights supply the reason: the type of activity the victim wanted to cover up from her boyfriend. The justification for rejection is strengthened by conflicting accounts between the victim and witness on the purpose for being in Center Heights. The DDA and IO are talking about the case before they interview the complainant.

> DDA William Nelson: A white girl from Addison comes to buy dope. She gets kidnapped and raped.
>
> IO Brandon Palmer: She tells her boyfriend and he beats her up for being so stupid for going to Center Heights. ... The drug dealer positively ID'd the two suspects, but she's got a credibility problem because she said she wasn't selling dope, but the other two witnesses say they bought dope from her. ...
>
> LF: I see you have a blue sheet [a sheet used to write up case rejections] already written up.
>
> IO Brandon Palmer: Oh yes. But there was no doubt in my mind that she was raped. But do you see the problems?
>
> DDA William Nelson: Too bad because these guys really messed her up. ... She has a credibility problem. I don't think she is telling the truth about the drugs. It would be better if she said she did come to buy drugs. The defense is going to rip her up because of the drugs. He is going to say, isn't it true you had sex with these guys but didn't want to tell your boyfriend, so you lied about the rape like you did about the drugs, or that she had sex for drugs. ... (Center Heights)

The prosecutor expresses doubt about the victim's account because it conflicts with his knowledge of the community. He uses this knowledge to formulate the ulterior motive for the victim's complaint—to hide from her boyfriend the "fact" that she was trading sex for drugs. The victim, "a white woman from Addison," alleges she drove to Center Heights "in the middle of the night" as a favor to a friend. She asserted that she did not come to purchase drugs. The DDA "knows" that white people don't live in Center Heights. He assumes that whites who come to Center Heights, especially in the middle of the night, are there to buy drugs or trade sex for drugs. The prosecutor's scenario is strengthened by the statements of the victim's two friends who accompanied her to Center Heights, were present at the scene, and admitted buying drugs. The prosecutor frames the ulterior motives as an organizational concern with defense arguments and convictability. This concern is reinforced by citing conflicting accounts between witnesses and the victim. He does not suggest that the victim's allegation was false—"there is no doubt in my mind she was raped"; rather, the case isn't convictable—"she has a credibility problem" and "the defense is going to rip her up."

Criminal Connections

The presence of criminal connections can also be used as a resource for identifying ulterior motives. Knowledge of a victim's criminal activity enables prosecutors to "find" ulterior motives for her allegation. In the first excerpt the complainant's presence in an area known by police as "where prostitutes bring their clients" is used to formulate an ulterior motive for her rape complaint. This excerpt is from an exchange in which the DDA was telling me about a case he had just rejected.

> DDA William Nelson: Young female is raped under questionable circumstances. One on one. The guy states it is consensual sex. There is no corroboration, no medicals. We ran the woman's rap sheet, and she has a series of prostitution arrests. She's with this guy in the car in a dark alley having sex. The police know this is where prostitutes bring their customers, so she knew she had better do something fast unless she is going to be busted for prostitution, so, lo and behold, she comes running out of the car yelling "he's raped me." He says no. He picked her up on Long Beach Boulevard, paid her $25 and this is "where she brought me." He's real scared, he has no record. (Center Heights)

Above, the prosecutor, relying on police knowledge of a particular location, assumes the woman is a prostitute. Her presence in the location places her in a "suspicious" category, triggering a check on her criminal history. Her record of prostitution arrests is used as the resource for developing an ulterior motive for her complaint: To avoid being busted for prostitution again, she made a false allegation of rape. Here the woman's record of prostitution and the imminent possibility of arrest are used to provide the ulterior motive to discredit her account. The woman's account is further discredited by comparing her criminal history— "a series of prostitution arrests" with that of the suspect, who "has no record," thus suggesting that he is the more credible of the two parties.

Prosecutors and investigating officers often decide to run a rap sheet (a chronicle of a person's arrests and convictions) on a rape victim. These decisions are triggered when a victim falls into certain "suspicious" categories, categories that have a class/race bias. Rap sheets are not run on women who live in the wealthier parts of town (the majority of whom are white) or have professional careers. They are run on women who live in Center Heights (who are black and Latina), who are homeless, or who are involved in illegal activities that could be related to the incident.

In the next case the prosecutor's knowledge of the victim's criminal conviction for narcotics is the resource for formulating an ulterior motive. This excerpt was obtained during an interview.

> DDA Tracy Timmerton: I had one woman who had claimed that she had been kidnapped off the street after she had car trouble by these two gentlemen who locked her in a room all night and had repeated intercourse with her. Now she was on a cocaine diversion [a drug treatment program where the court places persons convicted of cocaine possession instead of prison], and these two guys' stories essentially were that the one guy picked her up, they went down and got some cocaine, had sex in exchange for the cocaine, and the other guy comes along and they are all having sex and all doing cocaine. She has real reason to lie, she was doing cocaine, and because she has then violated the terms of her diversion and is now subject to criminal prosecution for her possession of cocaine charge. She is also supposed to be in a drug program which she has really violated, so this is her excuse and her explanation to explain why she has fallen off her program. (Bay City)

The prosecutor used the victim's previous criminal conviction for cocaine and her probation conditions to provide ulterior motives for her rape allegation—the need to avoid being violated on probation for the possession of cocaine and her absence from a drug diversion program. She suggests that the allegation made by the victim was false.

Prosecutors develop the basis for ulterior motives from the knowledge they have of the victim's personal life and criminal connections. They create two types of ulterior motives, those that suggest the victim made a false rape complaint and those that acknowledge the legitimacy of the complaint but discredit the account because of its unconvictability. In the accounts prosecutors give, ulterior motives for case rejection are supported with discrepancies in victims' accounts and other practitioners' knowledge.

Conclusion

Case filing is a critical stage in the prosecutorial process. It is here that prosecutors decide which instances of alleged victimization will be forwarded for adjudication by the courts. A significant percentage of sexual assault cases are rejected at this stage. This research has examined prosecutorial accounts for case rejection and the centrality of victim discreditability in those accounts. I have elucidated the techniques of case rejection (discrepant accounts and ulterior motives), the resources prosecutors use to develop these techniques (official reports and records, typifications of rape-relevant behavior, criminal connections, and knowledge of a victim's personal life), and how these resources are used to discredit victims' allegations of sexual assault.

This examination has also provided the beginnings of an investigation into the logic and organization of prosecutors' decisions to reject/accept cases for prosecution. The research suggests that prosecutors are orienting to a "downstream" concern with convictability. They are constantly "in dialogue with" anticipated defense arguments and anticipated judge and juror responses to case testimony. These dialogues illustrate the intricacy of prosecutorial decisionmaking. They make visible how prosecutors rely on assumptions about relationships, gender, and sexuality (implicit in this analysis, but critical and requiring of specific and explicit attention) in complaint filing of sexual assault cases. They also make evident how the processes of distinguishing truths from untruths and the practical concerns of trying cases are central to these decisions. Each of these issues, in all its complexity, needs to be examined if we are to understand the logic and organization of filing sexual assault cases.

The organizational logic unveiled by these accounts has political implications for the prosecution of sexual assault crimes. These implications are particularly acute for acquaintance rape situations. As I have shown, the typification of normal heterosexual relations plays an important role in assessing these cases, and case conviction is key to filing cases. As noted by DDA William Nelson: "There is a difference between believing a woman was assaulted and being able to get a conviction in court." Unless we are able to challenge the assumptions on which these typification are based, many cases of rape will never get beyond the filing process because of unconvictability.

Notes

1. To protect the confidentiality of the people and places studied, pseudonyms are used throughout this chapter.

2. The use of practitioners' knowledge to inform decisionmaking is not unique to prosecutors. For example, such practices are found among police (Bittner 1967; Rubenstein 1973), public defenders (Sundow 1965), and juvenile court officials (Emerson 1969).

3. Unlike the majority of rape cases I observed, this case had a male victim. Due to lack of data, I am unable to tell if this made him more or less credible in the eyes of the prosecutor and police.

Rape, Racism, and the Law

Jennifer Wriggins

THE HISTORY OF RAPE in this country has focused on the rape of white women by Black men. From a feminist perspective, two of the most damaging consequences of this selective blindness are the denials that Black women are raped and that all women are subject to pervasive and harmful sexual coercion of all kinds.

...

The Narrow Focus on
Black Offender/White Victim Rape

There are many different kinds of rape. Its victims are of all races, and its perpetrators are of all races. Yet the kind of rape that has been treated most seriously throughout this nation's history has been the illegal forcible rape of a white woman by a Black man. The selective acknowledgement of Black accused/white victim rape was especially pronounced during slavery and through the first half of the twentieth century. Today a powerful legacy remains that permeates thought about rape and race.

During the slavery period, statutes in many jurisdictions provided the death penalty or castration for rape when the convicted man was Black or mulatto and the victim white. These extremely harsh penalties were frequently imposed. In addition, mobs occasionally broke into jails and courtrooms and lynched slaves alleged to have raped white women, prefiguring Reconstruction mob behavior.

In contrast to the harsh penalties imposed on Black offenders, courts occasionally released a defendant accused of raping a white woman when the evidence was inconclusive as to whether he was Black or mulatto. The rape of Black women by white or Black men, on the other hand, was legal; indictments were sometimes dismissed for failing to allege that the victim was white. In those states where it was illegal for white men to rape white women, statutes provided less severe penalties for the convicted white rapist than for the convicted Black one. In addition, common-law rules both defined rape narrowly and made it a difficult crime to prove.

...

After the Civil War, state legislatures made their rape statutes race-neutral, but the legal system treated rape in much the same way as it had before the war. Black women raped by white or Black men had no hope of recourse through the legal system. White women raped by white men faced traditional common-law barriers that protected most rapists from prosecution.

Allegations of rape involving Black offenders and white victims were treated with heightened virulence. This was manifested in two ways. The first response was lynching, which peaked near the end of the nineteenth century. The second, from the early twentieth century on, was the use of the legal system as a functional equivalent of lynching, as illustrated by mob coercion of judicial proceedings, special doctrinal rules, the language of opinions, and the markedly disparate numbers of executions for rape between white and Black defendants.

Between 1882 and 1946 at least 4715 persons were lynched, about three-quarters of whom were Black.[1] Although lynching tapered off after the early 1950s, occasional lynch-like killings persist to this day. The influence of lynching extended far beyond the numbers of Black people murdered because accounts of massive white crowds torturing, burning alive, and dismembering their victims created a widespread sense of terror in the Black community.

The most common justification for lynching was the claim that a Black man had raped a white woman. The thought of this particular crime aroused in many white people an extremely high level of mania and panic. One white woman, the wife of an ex-Congressman, stated in 1898, "If it needs lynching to protect woman's dearest possession from human beasts, then I say lynch a thousand times a week if necessary.[2] The quote resonates with common stereotypes that Black male sexuality is wanton and bestial, and that Black men are wild, criminal rapists of white women.

Many whites accepted lynching as an appropriate punishment for a Black man accused of raping a white woman. The following argument made to the jury by defense counsel in a 1907 Louisiana case illustrates this acceptance:

> Gentlemen of the jury, this man, a nigger, is charged with breaking into the house of a white man in the nighttime and assaulting his wife, with the intent to rape her. Now, don't you know that, if this nigger had committed such a crime, he never would have been brought here and tried; that he would have been lynched, and if I were there I would help pull on the rope.[3]

It is doubtful whether the legal system better protected the rights of a Black man accused of raping a white woman than did the mob. Contemporary legal literature used the term "legal lynching" to describe the legal system's treatment of Black men. Well past the first third of the twentieth century, courts were often coerced by violent mobs, which threatened to execute the defendant themselves unless the court convicted him. Such mobs often did lynch the defendant if the judicial proceedings were not acceptable to them. A contemporary authority on lynching commented in 1934 that "the local sentiment which would make a lynching possible would insure a conviction in the courts."[4] Even if the mob was not overtly pressuring for execution, a Black defendant accused of raping a white woman faced a hostile, racist legal system. State court submission to mob pressure is well illustrated by the most famous series of cases about interracial rape, the Scottsboro cases of the 1930s.[5] Eight young Black men were convicted of what the Alabama Supreme Court called "a most foul and revolting crime," which was the rape of "two defenseless white girls." The defendants were summarily sentenced to death based on minimal and dubious evidence, having been denied effective assistance of counsel. The Alabama Supreme Court upheld the convictions in opinions demonstrating relentless determination to hold the defendants guilty regardless of strong evidence that mob pressure had influenced the verdicts and the weak evidence presented against the defendants. In one decision, that court affirmed the trial court's denial of a change of venue on the grounds that the mobs' threats of harm were not imminent enough although the National Guard had been called out to protect the defendants from mob executions. The U.S. Supreme Court later recognized that the proceedings had in fact taken place in an atmosphere of "tense, hostile, and excited public sentiment." After a lengthy appellate process, including three favorable Supreme Court rulings, all of the Scottsboro defendants were released, having spent a total of 104 years in prison.

In addition, courts applied special doctrinal rules to Black defendants accused of the rape or attempted rape of white women. One such rule allowed juries to consider the race of the defendant and victim in drawing factual conclusions as to the defendant's intent in attempted rape cases. If the accused was Black and the victim white, the jury was entitled to draw the inference, based on race alone, that he intended to rape her. One court wrote, "In determining the question of intention, the jury may consider social conditions and customs founded upon racial differences, such as that the prosecutrix was a white woman and defendant was a Negro man."[6] The "social conditions and customs founded upon racial differences" which the jury was to consider included the assumption that Black men always and only want to rape white women, and that a white woman would never consent to sex with a Black man.

The Georgia Supreme Court of 1899 was even more explicit about the significance of race in the context of attempted rape, and particularly about the motivations of Black men. It held that race may properly be considered "to rebut any presumption that might otherwise arise in favor of the accused that his intention was to obtain the consent of the female, upon failure of which he would abandon his purpose to have sexual intercourse with her."[7] Such a rebuttal denied to Black defendants procedural protection that was accorded white defendants.

...

The outcome of this disparate treatment of Black men by the legal system was often the same as lynching—death. Between 1930 and 1967, thirty-six percent of the Black men who were convicted of raping a white woman were executed.[8] In stark contrast, only two percent of all defendants convicted of rape involving other racial combinations were executed. As a result of such disparate treatment, eighty-nine percent of the men executed for rape in this country were Black. While execution rates for all crimes were much higher for Black men than for white men, the differential was most dramatic when the crime was the rape of a white woman.

The patterns that began in slavery and continued long afterwards have left a powerful legacy that manifests itself today in several ways. Although the death penalty for rape has been declared unconstitutional, the severe statutory penalties for rape continue to be applied in a discriminatory manner. A recent study concluded that Black men convicted of raping white women receive more serious sanctions than all other sexual assault defendants.[9] A recent attitudinal study found that white potential jurors treated Black and white defendants similarly when the victim was Black. However, Black defendants received more severe punishment than white defendants when the victim was white.[10]

The rape of white women by Black men is also used to justify harsh rape penalties. One of the few law review articles written before 1970 that takes a firm position in favor of strong rape laws to secure convictions begins with a long quote from a newspaper article describing rapes by three Black men, who at 3 a.m. on Palm Sunday "broke into a West Philadelphia home occupied by an eighty-year-old widow, her forty-four-year-old daughter and fourteen-year-old granddaughter," brutally beat and raped the white women, and left the grandmother unconscious "lying in a pool of blood."[11] This introduction presents rape as a crime committed by violent Black men against helpless white women. It is an image of a highly atypical rape—the defendants are Black and the victims white, the defendants and victims are strangers to each other, extreme violence is used, and it is a group rape. Contemporaneous statistical data on forcible rapes reported to the Philadelphia police department reveals that this rape case was virtually unique.[12] Use of this highly unrepresentative image of rape to justify strict rape laws is consistent with recent research showing that it is a prevalent, although false, belief about rape that the most common racial combination is Black offender and white victim.[13]

Charges of rapes committed by Black men against white women are still surrounded by sensationalism and public pressure for prosecution. Black men seem to face a special threat of being unjustly prosecuted or convicted. One example is Willie Sanders.[14] Sanders is a Black Boston man who was arrested and charged with the rapes of four young white women after a sensational media campaign and intense pressure on the police to apprehend the rapist. Although the rapes continued after Sanders was incarcerated, and the evidence against him was extremely weak, the state subjected him to a vigorous twenty-month prosecution. After a lengthy and expensive trial, and an active public defense, he was eventually acquitted. Although Sanders was clearly innocent, he could have been convicted; he and his family suffered incalculable damage despite his acquittal.

...

From slavery to the present day, the legal system has consistently treated the rape of white women by Black men with more harshness than any other kind of rape. ...

This selective focus is significant in several ways. First, since tolerance of coerced sex has been the rule rather than the exception, it is clear that the rape of white women by Black men has been treated seriously not because it is coerced sex and thus damaging to women, but because it is threatening to white men's power over both "their" women and Black men. Second, in treating Black offender/white victim illegal rape much more harshly than all coerced sex experienced by Black women and most coerced sex experienced by white women, the legal system has implicitly condoned the latter forms of rape. Third, this treatment has contributed to a paradigmatic but false concept of rape as being primarily a violent crime between strangers where the perpetrator is Black and the victim white. Finally, this pattern is perverse and discriminatory because rape is painful and degrading to both Black and white victims regardless of the attacker's race.

The Denial of the Rape of Black Women

The selective acknowledgement of the existence and seriousness of the rape of white women by Black men has been accompanied by a denial of the rape of Black women that began in slavery and continues today. Because of racism and sexism, very little has been written about this denial. Mainstream American history has ignored the role of Black people to a large extent; systematic research into Black history has been published only recently. The experiences of Black women have yet to be fully recognized in those histories, although this is beginning to change. Indeed, very little has been written about rape from the perspective of the victim, Black or white, until quite recently. Research about Black women rape victims encounters all these obstacles.

The rape of Black women by white men during slavery was commonplace and was used as a crucial weapon of white supremacy. White men had what one commentator called "institutionalized access" to Black women.[15] The rape of Black women by white men cannot be attributed to unique Southern pathology, however, for numerous accounts exist of northern armies raping Black women while they were "liberating" the South.

The legal system rendered the rape of Black women by any man, white or Black, invisible. The rape of a Black woman was not a crime. In 1859 the Mississippi Supreme Court dismissed the indictment of a male slave for the rape of a female slave less than 10 years old, saying:

> [T]his indictment can not be sustained, either at common law or under our statutes. It charges no offense known to either system. [Slavery] was unknown to the common law ... and hence its provisions are inapplicable. ... There is no act (of our legislature on this subject) which embraces either the attempted or actual commission of a rape by a slave on a female slave. ... Masters and slaves can not be governed by the same system or laws; so different are their positions, rights and duties.[16]

This decision is illuminating in several respects. First, Black men are held to lesser standards of sexual restraint with Black women than are white men with white women. Second, white men are held to lesser standards of restraint with Black women than are Black men with white women. Neither white nor Black men were expected to show sexual restraint with Black women.

After the Civil War, the widespread rape of Black women by white men persisted. Black women were vulnerable to rape in several ways that white women were not. First, the rape of Black women was used as a weapon of group terror by white mobs and by the Ku Klux Klan during Reconstruction. Second, because Black women worked outside the home, they were exposed to employers' sexual aggression as white women who worked inside the home were not.

The legal system's denial that Black women experienced sexual abuse by both white and Black men also persisted, although statutes had been made race-neutral. Even if a Black victim's case went to trial—in itself highly unlikely—procedural barriers and prejudice against Black women protected any man accused of rape or attempted rape. The racist rule which facilitated prosecutions of Black offender/white victim attempted rapes by allowing the jury to consider the defendant's race as evidence of his intent, for instance, was not applied where both persons were "of color and there was no evidence of their social standing."[17] That is, the fact that a defendant was Black was considered relevant only to prove intent to rape a white woman; it was not relevant to prove intent to rape a Black woman. By using disparate procedures, the court implicitly makes two assertions. First, Black men do not want to rape Black women with the same intensity or regularity that Black men want to rape white women. Second, Black women do not experience coerced sex in the sense that white women experience it.

These attitudes reflect a set of myths about Black women's supposed promiscuity which were used to excuse white men's sexual abuse of Black women. An example of early twentieth century assumptions about Black women's purported promiscuity was provided by the Florida Supreme Court in 1918. In discussing whether the prior chastity of the victim in a statutory rape case should be presumed subject to defendant's rebuttal or should be an element of the crime which the state must prove, the court explained that:

> What has been said by some of our courts about an unchaste female being a comparatively rare exception is no doubt true where the population is composed largely of the Caucasian race, but we would blind ourselves to actual conditions if we adopted this rule where another race that is largely immoral constitutes an appreciable part of the population.[18]

Cloaking itself in the mantle of legal reasoning, the court states that most young white women are virgins, that most young Black women are not, and that unchaste women are immoral. The traditional law of statutory rape at issue in the above-quoted case provides that women who are not "chaste" cannot be raped. Because of the way the legal system considered chastity, the association of Black women with unchastity meant not only that Black women could not be victims of statutory rape, but also that they would not be recognized as victims of forcible rape.

The criminal justice system continues to take the rape of Black women less seriously than the rape of white women. Studies show that judges generally impose harsher sentences for rape when the victim is white than when the victim is Black.[19] The behavior of white jurors shows a similar bias. A recent study found that sample white jurors imposed significantly lighter sentences on defendants whose victims were Black than on defendants whose victims were white. Black jurors exhibited no such bias.[20]

Evidence concerning police behavior also documents the fact that the claims of Black rape victims are taken less seriously than those of whites. A 1968 study of Philadelphia police processing decisions concluded that the differential in police decisions to charge for rape "resulted primarily from a lack of confidence in the veracity of Black complainants and a belief in the myth of Black promiscuity."[21]

The thorough denial of Black women's experiences of rape by the legal system is especially shocking in light of the fact that Black women are much more likely to be victims of rape than are white women.[22] Based on data from national surveys of rape victims, "the profile of the most frequent rape victim is a young woman, divorced or separated, Black and poverty stricken."[23]

...

Conclusion

The legal system's treatment of rape both has furthered racism and has denied the reality of women's sexual subordination. It has disproportionately targetted Black men for punishment and made Black women both particularly vulnerable and particularly without redress. It has denied the reality of women's sexual subordination by creating a social meaning of rape which implies that the only type of sexual abuse is illegal rape and the only form of illegal rape is Black offender/ white victim. Because of the interconnectedness of rape and racism, successful work against rape and other sexual coercion must deal with racism. Struggles against rape must acknowledge the differences among women and the different ways that groups other than women are disempowered. In addition, work against rape must go beyond the focus on illegal rape to include all forms of coerced sex, in order to avoid the racist historical legacy surrounding rape and to combat effectively the subordination of women.

Notes

1. Rose, 1948.

2. Reynolds, 1897–1898, p. 20.

3. State v. Petit, 119 La., 44 So. (1907).

4. Chadbourn, 1931, p. 330.

5. Patterson v. State, 224 Ala., 141 So. (1932); Weems v. State, 224 Ala., 141 So. (1932); Powell v. State, 224 Ala., 141 So. (1932); Powell v. Alabama, 287 U.S. (1932).

6. McQuirter v. State, 36 Ala., 63 So. 2d (1953).

7. Dorsey v. State, 108 Ga., 34 S.E. (1899).

8. Wolfgang, 1974.

9. LaFree, 1980a, p. 842.

10. Feild and Bienen, 1980.

11. Schwartz, 1968, p. 509.

12. Amir, 1971. Out of 343 rapes reported to the Philadelphia police, 3.3% involved Black defendants accused of raping white women; 42% involved complaints of stranger rape; 20.5% involved brutal beatings; 43% involved group rapes.

13. In answer to the question, "Among which racial combination do most rapes occur?" 48% of respondents stated Black males and white females, 3% stated white males and Black females, 16% stated Black males and Black females, 33% stated white males and white females (Feild and Bienen, 1980, p. 80). Recent victim survey data contradict this prevalent belief; more than four-fifths of illegal rapes reported to researchers were between members of the same race, and white/Black rapes roughly equaled Black/white rapes (Bowker, 1981, p. 172).

14. Suffolk Superior Court indictment (1980).

15. L. Curtis, 1974, p. 22.

16. George v. State, 37 Miss. (1859).

17. Washington v. State, 38 Ga., 75 S.E. (1912).

18. Dallas v. State, 76 Fla., 79 So. (1918).

19. LaFree, 1980a.

20. Feild and Bienen, 1980.

21. *University of Pennsylvania Law Review,* 1968, p. 277.

22. Recent data from random citizen interviews suggest that Black women are much more likely to be victims of illegal rape than are white women (Bowker, 1981).

23. Karmen, 1982, p. 188.

Rape-Law Reform: Its Nature, Origins, and Impact

Ronald J. Berger, Patricia Searles, and W. Lawrence Neuman

SOCIAL SCIENTISTS HAVE DRAWN attention to the centrality of social movements in the creation of law reform (Handler 1978).[1] Social movements focus attention on social problems, demand and propose solutions, mobilize resources, and negotiate with established institutions to achieve reform. Law reforms are aimed at achieving both the *instrumental* and *symbolic* goals of social movements. Instrumental goals focus on tangible results and include procedural mechanisms to implement change. Symbolic goals focus on changing attitudes and legitimizing the values and aspirations of social movements. Instrumental and symbolic goals are often intertwined, and the distinction between the two can be subtle.

The contemporary feminist movement has been the driving force behind a number of legal reforms aimed at changing women's roles and social status (Freeman 1975). Feminists have argued that the law has functioned as a symbol of male authority and as a means of maintaining women's subordinate social status (MacKinnon 1983; Polan 1982; Rifkin 1982). They have viewed law reform as a prerequisite for broader social change because of its capacity to influence public perceptions of women's problems and to provide visibility and legitimacy to feminist goals and values (Freeman 1975; Marsh, Geist, and Caplan 1982). Much of this feminist reform activity has focused on violence against women, particularly the problem of rape (Rose 1977; Tierney 1982). Rape-law reform was considered a highly visible place to begin to change the law and demand that women's "autonomy be protected by agents of social control" (Bienen 1980:213).

Traditionally, rape law regulated women's sexuality and protected male rights to possess women as sexual objects (Edwards 1981; Field 1983). The law contained sexist assumptions and reflected societal skepticism regarding the seriousness of rape and the veracity of women's accusations of rape. Images of women as seductive and untrustworthy were combined with sociolegal conceptions of women as the property of males, producing a wide range of prejudicial criminal justice system practices in the handling of rape cases (Field 1983; Robin 1977; Tong 1984).

These rules and procedures were not required for other violent crimes. For instance, special corroboration rules mandating that prosecutors produce evidence that verified the victim's testimony were considered necessary because of concern that women would deliberately lie about rape in order "to explain premarital intercourse, infidelity, pregnancy, or disease, or to retaliate against an ex-lover or some other man" (Spohn and Horney 1992:24). Successful prosecution also required that a rape victim demonstrate that she had attempted to resist her assailant to a degree beyond what was expected of victims of other violent crimes. Special cautionary instructions to juries were used to warn jurors that rape was a charge that was easily made but difficult for the defendant to disprove, even if innocent. Evidence of the victim's prior sexual history was admissible to impeach her testimony or show that she had consented to intercourse, for it was assumed that "chastity was a character trait" and that women with premarital or extramarital sexual experiences would have been more likely to have agreed to sexual relations with the defendant (p. 25). Spouses were granted immunity from prosecution on the assumption that when a woman married she impliedly and irrevocably consented to the sexual advances of her husband.

Since the mid-1970s, however, states have generally reformed their rape laws to eliminate or modify some or all of these practices (Berger, Searles, and Neuman 1988; Bienen 1980). From a feminist point of view, the reforms symbolize a movement away from the conception of women as inferior beings defined by family roles and male ownership toward a view of women as responsible, autonomous persons who possess the right to personal, sexual, and bodily self-determination (Schwendinger and Schwendinger 1983). Rape-law reforms "reflect and legitimate increasingly varied and independent roles ... for women ... [and] are part of a larger statement that [women's] activities deserve to be acknowledged and respected" (Marsh et al. 1982:3).

In addition to recognizing its symbolic function, feminists saw rape-law reform as a means of achieving specific instrumental goals. These included increasing the reporting of rape, enhancing prosecution and conviction in rape cases, improving the treatment of rape victims in the criminal justice system, prohibiting a wider range of coercive sexual conduct, and expanding the range of persons protected by law.

Areas of Rape-Law Reform

Although there is considerable diversity in the actual reforms that have been in-
stituted in the various states in the United States, reformers sought to implement the goals of rape-law reform through changes in four primary areas of law:
definition of the offense, evidentiary rules, statutory age offenses, and penalties.

Definition of the Offense

One reform redefined the crime of "rape" as "sexual assault," "sexual battery,"
and the like in order to emphasize the idea that rape was a violent crime and not
a crime of uncontrollable sexual passion. Semantic changes that likened rape to
other assaults were designed to divert attention from questions of the victim's
consent, for assault is, "by definition, something to which the victim does not
consent" (Bienen 1980:192; Tong 1984). Redefining rape as sexual assault also
broadened the definition of the crime beyond its traditional meaning, vaginal-
penile intercourse, to include oral and anal penetration as well as vaginal penetration, sexual penetration with objects, and in some statutes, touching of intimate body parts.

Another definitional reform included changes that reconstituted the offense
with a continuum of acts that specified varying degrees of seriousness based on
the amount of coercion, infliction of injury, age of the victim, and so on. This reform attempted to draw attention to the objective circumstances (e.g., presence
of a weapon, rape in the course of another crime) that indicated the absence of
consent, hence rendering unnecessary proof of the victim's resistance. Some
statutes reflected a "criminal circumstances" approach that eliminated the term
"consent" entirely on the assumption that the objective circumstances would
preclude a consent defense. Other statutes retained the "consent" terminology
but attempted to eliminate through evidentiary reforms (see further on) aspects
of the law that drew attention to the victim's rather than the offender's behavior
(Bienen 1980; Tong 1984).

Feminist reformers have been divided on the issue of consent terminology
(Tong 1984). Although reforms that remove the term "consent" from sex-offense
statutes make use of the consent defense more difficult, they are less consistent
with the feminist goal of criminalizing a wider range of nonconsensual sexual
contacts because the only illegal contacts are those associated with a particular
specified set of criminal circumstances. Statutes that criminalize nonconsensual
penetration or even nonconsensual touching without requiring the presence of
force, weapons, multiple assailants, and so on, attempt to prohibit a broader
spectrum of offensive acts.[2]

Finally, other reforms expanded the categories of persons to be held accountable or to be protected by law. For example, some reforms redefined the crime in
gender-neutral terms to protect victims from female offenders and to protect

male victims. Some removed or modified the spousal exemption that has traditionally given husbands immunity for rape of their wives. And some eliminated
exemptions for cohabitants and voluntary social companions (Berger et al.
1988).

Evidentiary Rules

Another set of reforms attempted to eliminate the prejudicial evidentiary rules
that made it more difficult to convict accused offenders. Special corroboration
and proof of resistance requirements, as well as cautionary jury instructions,
were abolished. Reform statutes also introduced "rape shield" provisions that
limited admissibility of evidence regarding the victim's prior sexual history
(Bienen 1980; Field 1983; Tong 1984).

Statutory Age Offenses

Traditionally, statutory age offenses were not aimed at prohibiting sexual exploitation of young girls but at protecting female virginity and regulating consensual
sexual conduct (Bienen 1980). These laws carried relatively low penalties in order to minimize the consequences to males for engaging in sex with unmarried
females. Reforms in this area were an attempt to move away from this moralistic
focus and double standard. Reformers sought to permit consensual teenage sex
while also providing increased protection for children. These goals may be
somewhat contradictory, as increasing protection for children requires relatively
high statutory ages, and permitting consensual sexual contact requires somewhat lower ages. Feminist reformers are divided on how to translate these goals
into law (see Bienen 1980; Olsen 1984), although a common approach is to identify a series of two or more graded offenses that prohibit sexual activity with
youths below specific ages (e.g., first-degree sexual assault if the youth is less
than twelve years, but second-degree sexual assault if the youth is greater than
twelve but less than sixteen years). Another type of reform was directed at eliminating the "mistake of age" defense, which has been used to assuage the guilt of
male defendants who claimed they thought the female was older than the specified age while subjecting young females (particularly those who appeared physically mature) to accusations of victim precipitation.

Penalty Structure

Reforms in the penalty structure included provisions for mandatory minimum
sentences as well as penalty gradations that based the severity of punishment on
the seriousness of the crime. Another reform reduced the penalties for rape on
the assumption that judges and juries would be more likely to convict if the punishment was less severe (Bienen 1980; Estrich 1987). Feminists disagree about the
appropriate prison term for rape, but many believe that certainty of punishment
has a stronger deterrent effect than severity of punishment (Tong 1984).

The Passage of Rape-Law Reform

The feminist movement has been viewed as the driving force behind the passage of rape-law reforms (Bienen 1980; Marsh et al. 1982; Rose 1977). Feminists have engaged in a variety of educational, social service, and lobbying efforts that have helped create public and political support for legislative change. Groups such as the National Organization for Women have developed rape task forces and lobbied for rape-law reform in state legislatures around the country. The influx of women into the legal and lawmaking professions has also facilitated reform efforts (Largen 1988). In this and other areas of feminist-oriented legal change, female attorneys have provided legal expertise and feminist legislators have sponsored legislation and worked to weaken resistance to women's lobbying activities (Boles 1979; Costain 1988).

In addition, opportunities for rape-law reform have been greater in states where women have been more successful in improving their economic and legal status. In these states women have had more resources to influence the legislative process and to build upon previous political accomplishments (Berger, Neuman, and Searles 1991). Moreover, states with relatively liberal political cultures or ideological climates have generally been more receptive to rape-law reforms, as well as to other feminist-oriented reforms such as the federal Equal Rights Amendment (Burris 1983; Call et al. 1991; Hill 1981; Volgy, Schwarz, and Gottlieb 1986; Wohlenberg 1980).

Feminists were not the only ones interested in rape-law reform, however. Law-and-order groups and victim rights groups also perceived the need for legal change, although they did not generally support all aspects of the feminist reform agenda. For instance, law-and-order advocates were less concerned than were feminists with women's issues per se. Their primary objectives were to increase the deterrent and punitive capabilities of the criminal justice system and to clean up statutory inconsistencies and systematize the hodgepodge of sex offense laws (Lawson 1984). Thus they favored reforms that provided criminal justice officials with clear guidelines and specific procedural mechanisms to increase the efficiency of the justice system and to make the system more rational and less arbitrary (Chappell 1984; Marsh et al. 1982).

Rape-law reforms that addressed these nonfeminist concerns were often incorporated into omnibus penal code bills (Bienen 1980). These reforms were generally more narrow than those favored by feminists, being limited, for example, to changes that created gender-neutral criteria for victims and offenders or that specified a continuum of offenses with graduated penalties. Conservative legislators often resisted changes designed to broaden rape statutes to criminalize offenses other than "classic rape" (see Williams 1984). Some feared, for instance, that removing the spousal exemption would invite false accusations by angry or vengeful wives, make reconciliation of estranged couples less likely, and give divorcing wives an unfair advantage in property settlements and custody disputes (Lawson 1984; Marsh et al. 1982). However, conservative political climates have been associated with attempts to protect female virtue and hence with laws that limit circumstances where consent to sex is implied. For example, Berger, Neuman, and Searles (1991) found political conservativism to be associated with legislative statutes that did not exempt cohabitants and voluntary social companions and that limited use of "mistake of age" as well as "mistake of incapacity" defenses.[3]

Thus rape-law reforms passed by state legislatures were the products of political coalitions and legislative compromises between feminist and nonfeminist interest groups. In order to achieve law reform, feminists had to offer a legal reform agenda attractive to legislators who held more traditional ideologies than they did. The coalitions have in many cases resulted in piecemeal reforms and a dilution or co-optation of feminist ideals and goals. As a result of the compromises, the reformed laws vary considerably from one state to another, differing in the degree to which they incorporate feminist-oriented elements. In many states reformed statutes still retain some traditional provisions (Berger, Neuman, and Searles 1988).

The Impact of Rape-Law Reform

A number of case studies of rape-law reform have been conducted in various jurisdictions throughout the country.[4] These studies allow for a partial assessment of the impact of the new legislation on the attitudes of criminal justice officials and on rape statistics. Interviews with criminal justice personnel, as well as with rape crisis center workers, suggest that officials' attitudes toward rape victims have improved and that, on the average, victims now experience less trauma during the criminal justice process (Marsh et al. 1982; Spohn and Horney 1991). However, studies have generally found little change that could be directly attributed to law reform in the number of crimes that citizens report to the police, in police arrest and clearance rates, and in conviction rates (see note 4). Although Marsh et al. (1982) found a slight increase in arrest rates following enactment of the reforms, the level of police "unfounding" of cases (i.e., complaint dismissals) remained stable. Largen (1988) reported that police believe that evidentiary reforms facilitate their investigations of rape and enhance their credibility with victims, but other researchers found that officers continue to rely on extralegal factors (e.g., the personal characteristics of the complainant, the relationship between the complainant and accused) in handling sexual assault cases (LaFree 1981; Rose and Randall 1982).

Studies found that the most improved criminal justice response has been an increase in convictions as charged, that is, a decrease in reductions to lesser offenses and to nonsexual assault offenses (Horney and Spohn 1991; Loh 1980; Marsh et al. 1982). Horney and Spohn (1991:146) also found some indication of an increase in the ratio of indictments to reports, which suggests that prosecutors may have been "more willing to file charges in borderline cases, ... [such as] cases involving acquaintances, cases involving sexually promiscuous men or women, [and] cases with little or no corroborating evidence." They hypothesized that the "greater willingness to prosecute might [have been] due in part to the fact that the definitions of the various degrees of criminal sexual conduct [were] much clearer than the old definition of rape." Overall, however, the primary beneficiaries of rape-law reform have been women who are raped by strangers (Spohn and Horney 1992). Marsh et al. (1982) found that prosecutors continued to distinguish cases of "real" or "classic" rape from "simple" rape insofar as they issued warrants primarily for what they considered more serious offenses. From a prosecutorial perspective, studies indicate "limited success" in reducing case attrition and in making prosecution and conviction of cases more feasible (Caringella-MacDonald 1984:72). However, since attrition rates are still quite high, "a conclusion of success is questionable" from a victim advocate's point of view (p. 78), and the probability of conviction for sexual assault cases remains lower than for nonsexual assault cases (Caringella-MacDonald 1985).

Researchers have also concluded that punishments for offenders convicted of sexual assault appear to be more certain, but not necessarily more severe, than in the prereform era (Loh 1980; Marsh et al. 1982). For instance, Loh reported a slight decrease in prison sentences and a substantial increase in commitment to sex-offender treatment programs. Polk (1985) found an increase in likelihood of incarceration but noted that this increase occurred for all serious offenses.

Importantly, the rape-law impact studies suggested that many criminal justice officials continue to operate on the basis of traditional assumptions and that they do not always comply with the statutes (Bienen 1980; Marsh et al. 1982; Spohn and Horney 1992). Decisions regarding sexual assault cases are still subject to a great deal of discretion, and the reforms do not necessarily affect the informal operations of the criminal justice system. For example, evidentiary reforms involving the victim's prior sexual history have been directed at the trial model of legal adjudication, although most cases are handled informally through plea bargaining (Caringella-MacDonald 1984). Moreover, these evidentiary reforms often contain loopholes that limit the admissibility of evidence regarding the complainant's past sexual conduct for some purposes (e.g., to prove the victim's consent) but continue to allow this evidence for other purposes (e.g., to challenge the victim's credibility) (Berger et al. 1988). Evidence involving the complainant's past sexual conduct with the accused continues to be allowed, and requirements for judicial review of evidence in closed (in-camera) hearings merely erect procedural barriers, as most judges eventually admit the evidence (Bienen 1980; Marsh et al. 1982).[5] In addition, sexual history evidence showing another possible source of semen or evidence of a complainant's motive to falsely accuse the defendant have a greater than 50–50 chance of being admitted at trial (Spohn and Horney 1991). And when evidence of the victim's past sexual conduct is admitted, juries continue to use it to mitigate the defendant's culpability (LaFree, Riskin, and Visher 1985).

Many of the rape-law reforms have also been based on untested assumptions regarding their potential impact. For instance, there is no reliable evidence that changing the definition of the offense from rape to sexual assault actually increases the perception that rape is a crime of violence rather than a crime of uncontrollable sexual passion (Chappell 1984; Osborne 1984). Nor is there evidence that lower sentences increase juries' propensity to convict (Feild and Bienen 1980).

Similarly, advocates of the "criminal circumstances" approach, which removes the term "consent" from the definition of sex offenses in order to preclude consent defenses, failed to anticipate that statutory silence on consent might allow defense attorneys to continue to use common law consent defenses or general definitions of criminal coercion that remained in other parts of the criminal code (Bienen 1980). As Loh (1981:45–46) observed, "As a practical matter a prosecutor must prove nonconsent ... [and] one cannot avoid the issue ... or pretend it no longer exists because of semantic changes in the law." The "criminal circumstance" approach also assumes that certain objective features of an act can easily be ascertained, when in fact, "unambiguous criminal circumstances are few and far between" (Tong 1984:111; Estrich 1987). And should such a statute fail to include a possible condition under which consent might be absent, no violation of the law could be claimed.

In spite of efforts to introduce a feminist perspective into the criminal justice system, the law continues to define the crime in terms of the accused's possession of criminal intent (i.e., mens rea) (MacKinnon 1983). Indices of closeness (e.g., dating, cohabiting, marriage) or of prior social interaction (e.g., the victim was acquainted with the accused or had agreed to interact socially with him) are still used by defendants to persuade judges and juries that they believed the woman had consented. According to MacKinnon (1983:652), although "the injury of rape lies in the meaning of the act to its victims, ... the standard for its criminality lies in the meaning of the same act to the assailants." The law merely attempts to adjudicate "the level of acceptable force starting just above the level set by what is seen as normal male sexual behavior" (p. 649). In a society where men are socialized to be the sexual aggressors, to expect women to be coy and reluctant, and even to dismiss women's protests, it is indeed difficult to distinguish forced acquiescence from freely given consent. As MacKinnon said, "The distance between most sexual violations of women and the legally perfect rape measures the imposition of someone else's definition upon women's experiences. Rape, from women's point of view, is not prohibited, it is regulated. ... [While] many women are raped by men who know the meaning of their acts to women and proceed anyway, ... women are also violated ... by men who have no idea of the meaning of their acts to women. To them, it is sex. Therefore, to the law it is sex" (pp. 651–653).[6]

Conclusion

The results of the impact studies indicate that the goals of rape reform legislation have not been fully realized. Some reform advocates continue to suggest that desired goals can eventually be achieved through further modification of existing laws, experimentation with alternative legislative strategies, and elimination of the gap between the "law on the books" and the "law in action" (Caringella-MacDonald 1985; Polk 1985). Some sociolegal scholars have characterized this view as a form of legal liberalism that promises "efficacy and justice" in spite of research that "repeatedly reveals instances of ineffectiveness and injustice" (Abel 1980:829; Sarat 1985). However, Horney and Spohn (1991) argued that the symbolic message of rape-law reform may be even more important than the anticipated instrumental changes. The law not only gives commands and issues sanctions for violation of rules but also educates people by providing information about an issue and conferring legitimacy on new social norms (Kidder 1983). Indeed, the educational and consciousness-raising efforts associated with the antirape movement's campaign for law reform (Rose 1977) may have helped change some male's perceptions of appropriate sexual conduct, making them somewhat less inclined to engage in sexual aggression. Even if males do not accept feminist definitions of sexual assault as normatively valid, they may be deterred by an awareness that criminal justice jurisdiction is now mandated over a broadened range of offenses or by a perception that women are more likely to define certain sexual actions as intolerable and more motivated to report them as crimes (see Bachman, Paternoster, and Ward 1992; Orcutt and Faison 1988). Thus, as Caringella-MacDonald (1988:139) observed, "Even reforms that fail in meeting objectives can serve a constructive purpose. ... Failures may beget new waves of change to rectify problems ... and to address areas previously overlooked by reform efforts. In this way, liberal reforms, coupled with vigilance and critique, may build incrementally towards future progress."

Notes

1. Parts of this chapter are derived from our previous work that appears in Berger, Neuman, and Searles (1988, 1991) and Searles and Berger (1987a).

2. For example, Wisconsin's sexual assault law defines "consent" as "words or overt actions by a person who is competent to give informed consent indicating a freely given agreement to have sexual intercourse or sexual contact" (see Berger, Neuman, and Searles 1988).

3. "Mistake of incapacity" defenses have been used to assuage the guilt of defendants who claimed they did not know the victim lacked the capacity to consent to sexual contact (e.g., due to mental defect or unconsciousness).

4. See Caringella-MacDonald (1984, 1985), Horney and Spohn (1991), Largen (1988), Loh (1981), Marsh et al. (1982), Polk (1985), and Spohn and Horney (1991, 1992). For a discussion of reforms in other countries, see Chappell (1984) and Goldberg-Ambrose (1992).

5. Particularly disturbing to many feminists was a pretrial ruling in the well-publicized Glen Ridge, New Jersey, sexual assault case involving a young woman with an IQ of 64. The ruling lifted the state's rape-shield law to allow testimony about the woman's sexual history (Hanley 1993). Defense lawyers contended that the woman, seventeen years old at the time of the assault, was "a promiscuous temptress throughout her teen-age years" and, in the case in question, "an oversexed aggressor" who knew what she was getting into when she followed the defendants to their basement (p. B4). The jury, however, was convinced that the young woman fit the legal definition of "mentally defective" and found three of the four defendants guilty of aggravated sexual assault on the grounds that they should have known the woman was not capable of giving informed consent to sexual acts, in this case, vaginal penetration with a baseball bat, broom handle, and stick.

6. In attempting to determine whether a sexual act was in fact nonconsensual, the courts have always scrutinized the accuser's conduct. This scrutiny takes a bizarre twist, however, in the age of AIDS. In a 1992 case, a Texas woman had the presence of mind to insist her knife-wielding attacker use a condom to protect against disease (Milloy 1992). Not only did the defense argue that this action implied the woman's consent, but the first grand jury to investigate the assault refused to indict the man because some jurors felt the woman's provision of a condom may have suggested her complicity in the encounter. After a public outcry, the case was brought before another grand jury and eventually to trial, and the accused was convicted of aggravated sexual assault.

Part Five

Surviving and Preventing Rape

ANN BURGESS AND LYNDA HOLMSTROM FIRST documented rape trauma syndrome in 1974 after observing a consistent pattern of symptoms in ninety-two adult women who had been subjected to forced sexual penetration. These women were initially interviewed within thirty minutes of arrival at a city hospital emergency ward and were reinterviewed at various intervals afterward. Burgess and Holmstrom labeled the observed cluster of symptoms "rape trauma syndrome" and argued that it was composed of two phases, acute and long term. Subsequent research has documented that most victims experience acute symptoms for three or four months, but the long-term reaction has been found to be more variable in length (i.e., one to six or more years) and not as universal (Ellis 1983). Rape is now listed in the American Psychiatric Association's diagnostic manual (DSM-III-R) as a traumatic event (i.e., stressor) known to precipitate post–traumatic stress disorder.

In the first chapter in this section, "Rape Trauma Syndrome," Ann Burgess discusses the stress-response patterns of rape victims and outlines a crisis-intervention model of issue-oriented treatment, now the most typical model of intervention used by rape crisis centers. According to a survey of rape crisis centers across the United States, crisis intervention and supportive services (medical, legal, and psychological) are being provided to women immediately following sexual assault, but follow-up counseling in the acute period, and especially longer-term counseling, are less often offered despite the acknowledged need for these services (King and Webb 1981).[1]

Because the acute phase of rape trauma syndrome has been widely documented, expert testimony on this syndrome is increasingly accepted by the courts (Cling 1988). Rape trauma syndrome evidence has been successfully used in civil litigation cases to testify to the psychological injuries of rape. It is also generally accepted to rebut defense claims that the victim's postrape behavior

233

was not typical. For instance, "If the victim goes into shock, and seems not to react emotionally following the assault, evidence of post–traumatic stress symptoms, such as recurrent nightmares and phobias, can disabuse the jury of the notion that she was emotionally unreactive because nothing happened to her, i.e., she wasn't raped" (p. 250). The courts have been divided, however, on the issue of using rape trauma syndrome evidence as proof of rape, that is, proof that intercourse was nonconsensual. When evidence has not been admitted as proof of rape, it has been argued that "the research on rape trauma syndrome was based on diagnosis for treatment, not for cause of symptoms" (p. 258). Some feminists have pointed out, however, that battered child syndrome has been allowed as evidence of proof of battering and that not allowing rape trauma syndrome as evidence of proof of rape is inconsistent and unfair.

Although research on rape trauma syndrome has been useful to rape survivors in the courtroom and has helped crisis workers and other counselors provide supportive and effective interventions, the positivistic methodology of this body of research has been criticized. Liz Kelly (1988:187) argued that many who research the impact of sexual violence attempt to isolate and study via psychological tests the "effects" of violence, conceptualizing effects as "negative changes in women's feelings and behaviour." She encouraged us to recognize the "complexity of women's experience," to locate the consequences of violence "in the context of the active process of coping," which all survivors engage in (p. 186). Rather than separate "the 'effects' from how women cope with them," we should recognize that in the process of coping, women frequently "make choices and come to understandings which they value positively" (p. 187). All too often, Kelly said, women's "resistance, strength, and coping strategies" are pathologized, that is, "transformed into an abstract pattern of negative reactions: problems to be resolved through expert intervention" via various therapeutic methods (p. 189).

For example, much research that notes the impact sexual violation often has on women's attitudes toward men and toward sex implicitly assumes this impact is negative and that women should be "helped" to overcome these reactions, "to readjust to 'normal' heterosexuality. ... The possibility that incest survivors might choose lesbian relationships and see this as a positive choice which was influenced, but not determined by, their experience of abuse is ignored" (p. 187). Similarly, Kelly suggested that rather than seeing women as "frigid," we might see them as choosing to be celibate for a time; rather than seeing women as "promiscuous," we might see them as choosing not to make emotional commitments to men. She reminds us that "women's coping strategies are directed towards both controlling the impact of sexual violence and protecting themselves from further abuse. Distrust of men and conflicts about sexuality are not 'dysfunctional' reactions but part of women's active and adaptive attempts to cope with the reality of sexual violence" (p. 216). Given the prevalence of sexual violence, Kelly said, it is in women's interest to insist that trust be earned, not given automatically. "It is the reality of men's violence which creates the necessity of women's distrust" (p. 216).

The importance of Kelly's message becomes clear when we read "When You Grow Up an Abused Child ... ," Christina Glendenning's moving account of her struggle to make sense of her past, her struggle to heal and grow. We see here the active coping, the spirited resistance of a child who knew her "parameters were being violated." We see the strength and tenacity of an adult coming to terms with her anger and allowing herself to have emotional needs. We see the integrity of a woman learning to accept herself and coming to understand her lesbianism as a means to reclaim her boundaries and "the light in [her] eyes." This story is a testament to the strength and courage of survivors everywhere.

Fred Pelka is also a survivor. In the next chapter, "Raped: A Male Survivor Breaks His Silence," Pelka recounts the brutal victimization he experienced at the hands of another man. He shows us how destructive societal myths (e.g., *men* don't get raped—at least not *real* men) translate into insensitive treatment that compounds the suffering of male survivors. He argues that victimization marks men "as traitors to [their] gender," and he challenges the sexism and homophobia that serve to keep men silent. Pelka, who did receive a supportive response from a rape crisis center, notes that it is "ironic ... that what little acknowledgement there is of male victimization generally comes from the *women's* stop-rape movement."

The establishment of rape crisis centers was a key component of the women's antirape movement that emerged in the 1970s. Initially composed of volunteer feminist activists, this grassroots self-help movement gave birth to a wide range of community services such as hot lines and other crisis intervention, short- and long-term counseling, and information, advocacy, and support services. Rape crisis center activists pressed for and achieved significant improvements in the treatment of rape survivors by the criminal justice system and by medical and mental health professionals. They also initiated a variety of educational programs aimed at rape prevention, including self-defense and rape-avoidance training and efforts to change rape-supportive beliefs and attitudes. These programs are now available in a variety of settings (e.g., schools, religious institutions, and the workplace) (Rose 1977; Koss and Harvey 1991).

The rape crisis center movement has been quite successful in attracting government and private funding. Koss and Harvey (1991:122) argued that the formerly grassroots movement has now "realized the formation of more enduring and in many ways more influential organizations and coalitions ... [that] enhance communication and coordinate rape awareness and victim advocacy efforts among ... [various] groups." In addition, specialized services designed to meet the needs of diverse populations (e.g., children, males, minorities, gays and lesbians, and the elderly) have also been developed, although outreach to underserved groups is still much in need (Matthews 1989; Yoshihama, Parekh, and Boyington 1991).[2]

The antirape movement has also spawned a number of victim-prevention strategies aimed at improving the safety of the environment for women. Examples of these environmental modifications include improvements in public lighting, the construction of "brightway paths," the institution of women's nighttime safety transit systems, the installation of emergency police-alert telephones, and the expansion of police services. Environmental modifications such as these may help reduce crime, but by themselves they are insufficient, for no environment can be made completely safe. Thus strategies aimed at strengthening individual capacities and decreasing individual vulnerabilities have been pursued as well. These efforts include educational strategies such as assertiveness training; the dissemination of information about crime, crime prevention, and available safety systems; programs to develop defense consciousness and specific prevention behaviors; and instruction in self-defense (Burgess and Holmstrom 1979; Searles and Berger 1987b).

Traditionally, the victim prevention information given to women, particularly white middle class women,[3] has encouraged them to limit their mobility and to depend upon men, large barking dogs, chemical sprays, whistles, and other external agents for their protection. In the event of attack, women have often been advised not to resist but to submit to rape to avoid further harm or, at most, to plead or reason with their assailants (Hazelwood and Harpole 1986; Storaska 1975). Increasingly, feminists have critiqued those messages and encouraged women to fight back (Delacoste and Newman 1981).

In the last chapter in this section, "And He Turned Around and Ran Away," Gail Groves, a rape hot-line worker and self-defense instructor, argues that successful self-defense is possible—and common. In this inspiring piece, she states that "there are always options for the defender—ways she can damage the attacker, verbal points she can gain through negotiation, strategies that will work. Self-defense means looking for these openings, having the faith that there will be one at some point, ... trying something, and not giving up."

Groves's conviction comes from years of experience in the antirape movement. Others, not content with subjective personal accounts, have looked to research for an evaluation of the effectiveness of different responses to assault. There are now many studies, using a variety of data sources, that indicate that immediate active resistance (e.g., yelling, fighting, and running away) and especially the use of multiple-resistance strategies reduce the likelihood that an attempted rape will be completed.[4] Pleading, threatening, and arguing seem to be less effective unless used in combination with other verbal strategies such as yelling and calling for help (Cohen 1984).

The research is less clear regarding the question of whether resistance increases the likelihood of additional injury (i.e., injury beyond the rape itself).

McDermott (1979) found that resisters received greater additional injury than nonresisters, but most of these injuries were of a relatively unserious nature, such as bruises, cuts, and scratches. Similarly, Bart and O'Brien (1984:94) found that resistance increased women's chances of receiving "rough treatment." However, in both these studies, women who experienced completed rape reported more serious injury than women who experienced attempted rape, and women who resisted were much less likely to have rape completed.

Other data indicate that the connection between resistance and additional injury may be related to the type of resistance employed. Sanders (1980:145), for example, found that those who "struggled" (e.g., attempted to push the attacker away) were more likely than those who fought (e.g., hit, bit, or kicked) or those who ran away to incur serious additional injury. Kleck and Sayles (1990) found weaponless forceful resistance associated with increased injury but noted the likelihood that resistance followed rather than preceded injury. They pointed out that ancilliary evidence on nonsexual "assaults and robberies indicates that resistance rarely precedes injury" (p. 149). They noted that some advice-givers counsel nonresistance because a small proportion of "rapists are indeed incited to further violence by victim resistance" (p. 160). But Kleck and Sayles concluded:

> The flaw in this reasoning is that it depends on an unstated, but false, premise that nonresistance does not entail any risks of its own. ... Advice to not resist depends on the belief that the nonresisting rape victim trades off an increased likelihood of rape completion for a reduced likelihood of injury. Such a trade-off makes sense only if one assumes the additional injury is in some sense a more serious harm to the victim than the completion of the rape itself. (p. 160)

It is clearly not appropriate for anyone to give women blanket advice about what they *should* do if attacked, as if all attack situations are the same, or to criticize what a woman *did* or *did not* do in a stressful and frightening situation. But teaching girls and women both psychological and physical self-defense skills and nurturing in them a strong sense of self-worth broadens the range of options they have in threatening situations, and it increases the likelihood that they will have the self-confidence and presence of mind to evaluate their options and act in what *they see* to be their own best interests.

Regrettably, as Rozee, Bateman, and Gilmore (1991:351) noted, sexual interventions that are "aimed primarily at behavioral change among women place an unwarranted responsibility on individual women for their own safety. To live a life free of the fear of sexual assault ought to be a right afforded to us by the society in which we live." Nevertheless, given the omnipresence of violence against women in contemporary society, many women may decide that the wisest strategy involves choosing to make personal behavioral changes while also "working for the social change that will make" such personal remedies unnecessary.

Notes

1. In the age of AIDS, rape crisis counseling is especially complicated. The process of dealing with the possibility of exposure to HIV (i.e., the virus that causes AIDS) and other sexually transmitted diseases may compound and prolong the victim's rape-trauma response. In addition, the necessity of repeated testing for HIV may activate the victim's memory of the assault and exacerbate the symptoms experienced (Lazlo, Burgess, and Grant 1991). Depending on the particular hospital's protocol or the state's legislation, HIV testing may be a standard part of the emergency department's procedures, or it may require the special consent of the assault victim.

2. African American rape survivors are less likely than white women to report rape to crisis centers as well as to police. When they do seek counseling, they often discontinue it because the programs ignore or are unable to change aspects of their environment that make them especially vulnerable (see Part 4, note 2). African American women are also less likely to disclose sexual assault at the time of the incident to anyone at all, and one important reason for this is their anticipation of a "lack of community and societal support" (Wyatt 1992:86). As Monica Williams, director of a rape crisis program, said, "I think our image has always been of strong and persevering and you can take it all, and it doesn't make a difference, and I started to notice that most of the women who were assaulted, that it wasn't a priority for them, that they couldn't see that they were hurting, too. And that usually their first concern was their children, or their home or their husband, or how'm I going to make ends meet" (quoted in Matthews 1989: 525–26). Since women in crisis are "most likely to feel comfortable and use services if they [are] provided by someone like themselves," racially and ethnically homogeneous organizations are often more effective, and increasingly women of color are developing services for survivors in their communities (Matthews 1989:523). (See Yoshihama et al. [1991] for suggestions for designing culturally sensitive educational, outreach, and support services for Asian Pacific teen survivors.)

3. Bart and O'Brien (1985) found that African American women were more likely to have acquired "street smarts," to have been advised by their families to fight back, and to resist when attacked.

4. See Bart and O'Brien (1984, 1985), Block and Skogan (1986), Gibson, Linden, and Johnson (1980), Griffen and Griffen (1981), Kleck and Sayles (1990), Lizotte (1986), McDermott (1979), Prentkey, Burgess, and Carter (1986), Queens Bench (1976), Quinsey and Upfold (1985), Sanders (1980), Scully (1990), and Siegal et al. (1989).

22

Rape Trauma Syndrome

Ann Wolbert Burgess

RAPE AFFECTS THE LIVES of thousands of people each year. ...

The legal definition of rape varies from state to state; however, the issues generally addressed include lack of consent, force or threat of force, and sexual penetration. The clinical definition of rape trauma—the focus of this paper— is the stress response pattern of the victim following forced, non-consenting sexual activity. This rape trauma syndrome of somatic, cognitive, psychological, and behavioral symptoms is an active stress reaction to a life-threatening situation.

Parallel with the increase in rape reporting has been the positive institutional response to rape victims through the establishment of sex crime units by law enforcement agencies, victim advocates in rape crisis centers, victim specialists in prosecutors' offices and victim counselors in emergency departments of general hospitals. Rape rehabilitation services are also being covered by some insurance companies under workers' compensation policies, thus placing a value on early intervention to expedite emotional and physical recovery of victims and assist in return to work.

Recognition of rape as a significant trauma and life event capable of disrupting normal life patterns is clearly being addressed by clinicians in the treatment setting. Concurrently, the admissibility of expert testimony on rape trauma syndrome is being tested both in criminal and civil litigation cases. This paper describes rape trauma syndrome within the new category of Post-Traumatic Stress Disorder of the DSM-III (American Psychiatric Association, 1980), acute, chronic and delayed. ...

...

In a 1973 hospital-based study using a convenience sample of all (N = 146) persons admitted to the emergency department with the complaint of rape, Burgess, a psychiatric nurse, and Holmstrom, a sociologist, ... analyzed data from

239

109 child, adolescent and adult victims, ages 5–73, who had been subjected to forced sexual penetration. Discovering similarities in responses that seemed to qualify as a clinical entity, they termed this acute traumatic reaction the rape trauma syndrome, in which the nucleus of the anxiety was a subjective state of terror and overwhelming fear of being killed. Rape trauma triggers intrapsychic disequilibrium with a resultant crisis state for the victim.

The rape trauma syndrome (Burgess and Holmstrom, 1974) is divided into two phases which can disrupt the physical, psychological, social or sexual aspects of a victim's life. The acute or disruptive phase can last from days to weeks and is characterized by general stress response symptoms. During the second phase— the long-term process of reorganization—the victim has the recovery task of re- storing order to his or her lifestyle and re-establishing a sense of control in the world. This phase is characterized by rape-related symptoms and can last from months to years.

Rape-Related Post-Traumatic Stress Disorder

The early conceptualizations of the stress response patterns of rape victims are consistent with the diagnostic criteria of Post-Traumatic Stress Disorder (PTSD) of the DSM-III within the major category of Anxiety Disorders. The four cardinal criteria will be discussed with documentation from clinical research data.

The primary feature of PTSD is that the stressor be of significant magnitude as to evoke distinguishable symptoms in almost everyone. PTSD is defined by symptoms which have a temporal and presumably causal relationship to a stressor beyond usual human experience (Ochburg and Fojtik-Stround, 1982). The stressor under review is rape.

The contemporary view of rape sees it as an act of violence expressing power, aggression, conquest, degradation, anger, hatred, and contempt. ... Bard and Ellison (1974) have emphasized the significance of the personal violation for the rape victim. Hilberman (1976) characterizes rape as the "ultimate violation of the self, short of homicide, with the invasion of one's inner and most private space, as well as loss of autonomy and control." Hilberman argues that it is the person's self, not an orifice, that has been invaded and that the core meaning of rape is the same for a virgin, a housewife, a lesbian, and a prostitute.

Notman and Nadelson (1976) observe how a rape attack heightens a woman's sense of helplessness, intensifies conflicts about dependence and indepen- dence, generates self-criticism and guilt that devalue her as an individual, and interferes with partner relationships. Burgess and Holmstrom (1976) noted that for almost all victims, the rape was something far out of the ordinary that seri- ously taxed their adaptive resources.

...

The second major diagnostic criteria is re-experiencing of the trauma, which is most frequently evidenced by recurrent and intrusive recollection of the event ("It is the first thing I think of when I wake up in the morning"). Day images are common ("Something will trigger in my head and it all comes back"). The victim may feel as though the traumatic event was recurring ("I panicked at work when two people came into the store and acted suspicious"). Or the impact may be so intense that the victim will not report remembering anything initially ("I was in constant fear; crying ... just had to be led around ... the panic was unbelievable") and then be reminded constantly of the event. The victim may report seeing the assailant everywhere ("I see his face on every man") as well as searching him out ("I walk next to walls and look at every face and think: Is he the one?").

Dreams and nightmares are common and very upsetting. Dreams include people chasing the victim and revictimizing the victim. Dreams may be of three types: (1) replication of the state of victimization and helplessness ("I use my mace and it turns to water"); (2) symbolic dreams which include a theme from the rape, as in one case in which a victim pleaded unsuccessfully her fear of pregnancy and had recurrent dreams of eggs pouring out of her and babies rolling down the hill and dying; and (3) mastery dreams in which the victim is powerful in assuming control ("I took the knife and stabbed him over and over"). Non-mastery dreams dominate until the victim is recovered. ...

The third major diagnostic criteria is a numbing of responsiveness to or reduced involvement with the environment. Victims talk of being in a "state of shock," or "feeling numb," or state "it doesn't feel real." They say they can't believe it happened. Sometimes this phenomenon is observed through the demeanor of the victim as in an expressed style where the feelings the victim had were visible (e.g., anxiety, fear, shame, sobbing, relief, anger, paranoia) or a controlled style where the victim appeared calm and controlled externally. This latter style is more common reflecting denial, shock or exhaustion (Burgess and Holmstrom, 1974; Horowitz, 1976; Soules et al., 1978). This psychic numbing may be observed through the victim's reduced interests in former activities ("I used to enjoy sketching in the park but now am terrified of going out alone"). Victims will talk of previously taking long walks but now feel constrained in their activities; of feeling isolated and estranged from others ("Stay in my own little world by myself now"). Victims may be immobilized and refuse to venture out of their apartment except for work or, if attacked inside the home, may feel less anxious at work or outside. There may be constricted affect. People will comment on the sudden change in the victim's behavior, as one husband who said, "She used to be the spark plug in the family." Victims may become defensive and rigid in demeanor; may refuse to attend social functions; may stop work or school and withdraw from their family ("I live by myself now and prefer that. I can retreat; I have my own loaded gun"). Victims talk of how easily one can become a victim

("He was in the door in seconds"). One 52-year-old woman became socially isolated from her friends, less patient with her grandchildren and found it exceedingly difficult to attend to the health needs of her elderly parents. The terror
holds the affect of the victim ("I feel like a dead woman") and the behavior following the rape is in the service of survival ("I sleep fully clothed so this time I
can run out of the house if he comes back to get me").

The fourth criteria states that there be two of the following list of symptoms
that were not present prior to the rape:

Exaggerated startle response or hyperalertness. Victims report feeling moody,
irritable, experiencing crying spells, often when crying was not a common behavior. Victims report feeling paranoid ("I keep thinking I am being followed");
search their house before feeling safe; feel there are "eyes" everywhere; believe
people can tell by looking that they have been raped. They may act on their
hyperalertness ("I scream when I hear footsteps behind me"). Victims may
change residence and telephone number in order to feel safe and anonymous.

Disturbance in sleep pattern. In the acute disruptive phase there can be a wide
range of somatic complaints that frequently includes headaches as well as sleep
pattern disturbance. Victims are either not able to fall asleep or fall asleep only
to wake and not be able to return to sleep. Victims who have been suddenly
awakened from their sleep by the assailant may find themselves waking each
night at the same time the attack occurred. Partners of victims report that the
victim may cry or scream out during sleep.

Guilt about surviving or behavior employed during the rape. Victims may express a self-blame reaction to the rape because of their socialization to the attitude of "blame the victim" (Ryan, 1971). Or victims may feel guilty about not reporting. In cases in which the same assailant rapes a second person, such as in
the same work place or apartment complex, the first victim may feel guilty for
not reporting initially. Or in cases in which a partner or parent is present, there
may be guilt for not being able to prevent the rape of the partner or child.

Impairment of memory and/or power of concentration. The intrusive imagery,
in part, is responsible for the victim's not being able to concentrate on school
work (Schuker, 1979) or usual activities. Victims may have memory lapses ("I
couldn't remember the names of my customers"); or have decreased energy
levels ("I found doing the laundry was too exhausting"). Students have difficulty
writing papers and examinations ("I failed my final tests").

Avoidance of activities that arouse recollection. Fears and phobias develop as a
defensive reaction to the circumstances of the rape. Rado (1948), in describing
war victims, used the term traumatophobia to define the phobic reaction to a
traumatic situation. Some of the common phobic responses noted in rape victims include: fears of indoors if the rape occurred inside; fears of outdoors if the
rape occurred outside the home; fear of being alone ("I can't take a shower if my
husband isn't home"); fear of crowds ("I panic when there are people around");

fear of elevators or stairs or people behind them ("I left my clothes in the dryer for four days because I was too scared to go to the cellar"). There are a wide variety of activities that can trigger a flashback ("My stomach gets into a big knot when anything reminds me of it"). Victims try to avoid memories by throwing out clothes they were wearing during the rape or the furniture from their room if attacked inside.

Increased symptoms to event that symbolize or resemble the event. One of the more common rape-related symptoms that resemble the rape occurs when the victim is confronted with sexual activity. Many victims experienced disruption in the sexual life area and developed a wide range of symptoms including change in sexual frequency (abstention, decreased activity as well as increased); flashbacks to the rape; vaginismus; change in orgasmic response; and worries about partner reaction to the rape. Some women terminated primary relationships; there could be a change in gender preference for a sexual partner. Other symbolic events where linkage was noted between some idiosyncratic aspect of the rape included the following: difficulty swallowing, singing or speaking after forced oral sexual penetration; repetition of symptoms from a prior victimization following the second victimization; anniversary reaction due to the day or time of the month (e.g., full moon; during the victim's menstrual period; date of the month).

Treatment

The prototype of crisis responses is the acute grief reaction (Notman and Nadelson, 1976; Ochburg and Fojtik-Stroud, 1982; Parad, 1965; Rado, 1948; Tyhurst, 1951). Lindemann (1944) first described the grieving process after interviewing survivors and relatives of a community disaster involving fire. Response to loss was characterized by distorted, prolonged or delayed reactions.

Crisis Intervention

Crisis intervention is clearly the treatment of choice when a rape is disclosed immediately after it has occurred (Burgess and Holmstrom, 1974; Forman, 1980; Fox and Scherl, 1975; McCombie, 1980). The basic assumptions underlying this type of intervention include: (1) the rape represents a crisis in that the victim's style of life is disrupted; (2) the victim is regarded as "normal" or functioning adequately prior to the external stressor; (3) crisis intervention aims to return the victim to his or her previous level of functioning as quickly as possible. The crisis model is issue-oriented treatment designed to ameliorate the target symptom of anxiety, fear, depression, loss of control and decreased assertiveness. The most favorable prognosis for treatment of acute rape trauma occurs if the victim is seen immediately following the rape; the speed of the intervention is crucial. The use of the term "crisis intervention" provides a non-threatening term that avoids labeling the treatment in psychiatric terms. Other crisis services to offer the victim include advocacy services, especially regarding legal matters, work with the victim's support system and victim mutual support groups.

Within the acute period, issues unique to the crisis need to be resolved and integrated or the victim will fail to return to a pre-crisis level of functioning. Rape work—the term used by Bassuk (1980)—refers to the content specific to rape which needs to be addressed. Three factors pathognomic of the crisis response to rape, and which comprise the rape work, include: (1) resolution of the threatened sense of safety in the world or confrontation with one's vulnerability and helplessness—one's potential victim status; (2) reworking of body image and body boundaries connected with self-esteem; and (3) confrontation with power relations between men and women. The aim of rape work is to regain a sense of safety and a valued sense of self and to re-establish sharing, altruistic, mutually satisfying partner relationships in a world where rape remains a threat to all women.

...

Subtypes of Rape Trauma and Special Treatment Needs

The DSM-III lists three types of PTSD. The *acute disorder* may start immediately after the rape and continue with symptoms up to six months. Symptoms that last longer than the six month period may be aggravating other issues and concerns of the victim and a subtype of chronic-post-traumatic stress disorder is usually diagnosed. A third category of delayed post-traumatic stress response is given to persons who suddenly exhibit symptoms either when there has been a quiescent period following the rape or when the rape has not been disclosed. These two additional subtypes have been discussed as compounded rape trauma and unresolved rape trauma.

Compounded reaction to rape trauma. There will be some victims who also have a history of past or current physical, psychiatric or social difficulties along with the acute rape trauma. This group may develop additional symptoms such as depression, psychotic behavior, psychosomatic disorders, suicidal behavior, and acting out behavior associated with alcoholism, drug use, and marked change in sexual activity. The victim needs to be referred back to a previous therapist or physician and negotiations initiated for treatment in addition to crisis intervention for the rape. Prognosis in such cases is guarded and contingent upon the amount of progress or regression that occurs specific to the aggravation of the previous psychiatric or social problems.

Unresolved sexual trauma. A delayed response to rape trauma, e.g., an unresolved sexual trauma, occurs in the victim who experienced the rape long before contact with the clinician. This victim has not told anyone of the rape, has not settled or integrated his or her thoughts, feelings or behaviors on the issue, and is carrying a tremendous psychological burden. Very often a second sexual trauma, crisis or flashback will reactivate the person's reaction to the prior experience. Psychotherapy is the treatment of choice. ...

When a diagnosis of unresolved sexual trauma is made, the person has three therapeutic tasks: (1) to talk of the previous assault in terms of the details, feelings, beliefs and thoughts; (2) to identify the reasons as to why the assault was never revealed; (3) to talk of the current traumatic situation in order to look at the similarities and differences. The prognosis for resolving an unresolved sexual trauma is favorable if the person is able to spend therapy sessions fully reviewing the experience and putting it into perspective with his or her current life situation.

...

When You Grow Up
an Abused Child …

Christina Glendenning

WHEN YOU GROW UP an abused child your vocabulary is one of objects, of images. Words such as incest or violence no longer carry personal impact. Too often they've been used to rationalize feelings too painful and overwhelming to accept. But those feelings live, buried in objects as common as a wicker clothes hamper. The white wicker hamper in which I hid from my father, a small child covering herself with soiled bed linens. Those objects invade our peace like a strap wielded by a violent hand, leaving bright red welts on the prism of memory.

I don't suffer nightmares like some: it is the mundane encounter with a white wicker hamper that shakes me. Forcing me to relive a childhood that seems so unfair, so destructive. I'm thirty-one now, living far away from my family, but so often I am that same vulnerable little girl peering through the strands of woven wicker.

Our family lived in Pittsburgh. When my parents weren't separated my father drove a truck out of state. Either way, he was a stranger to my life. My mother and I and her two maiden aunts formed an extended family. From them I received a strong sense of who I was. Those first five years of life were an idyll where my individuality was encouraged. My father moved back home about the time I was ready to start school and with him came a change of atmosphere. It was both a feeling, dark and oppressive, and a physical presence that I can only compare to a volcano. I sensed I could no longer argue the appropriateness of my bedtime or plead my case during meals. I went directly to bed at eight and no longer argued about eating certain foods. There were rules that I had to obey. I was glad, initially, to be like my friends and have a father at home. But there was a price to pay. The freedoms I had taken for granted ended with the return of my father and for the first time I knew authority. I did not question my father's rights over me. All of my friends' fathers behaved like that but until then it hadn't affected my life. Where once I was thought independent, my father now called me willful. I began to resent this new oppression and the man who returned to my life not as a suppliant but as an owner.

I clearly remember the evening my father first kissed me. My mother had gone to the store and I was playing with my doll house. The kiss was unexpected, full on the lips and warm, very warm. "I love you," he said.

For a child needing parental love those words are important. I couldn't understand why they made me uneasy. That this authoritative, temperamental man loved me brought a promise of better times to come. I should have been happy but I was only confused.

Each time my mother left us alone I felt an expectation from my father that I should sit with him by the television and we would kiss. During and after those sessions he was always very kind. His heavyhanded manners relaxed and I saw glimpses of freedoms I thought I had lost. But I was still uneasy and more and more I hoped my mother would not let me alone with him. I begged to go along or pretended I was ill. Looking back, I know it was his need I feared. His love was only a thinly disguised neediness that threatened to overwhelm me. My instincts knew what my child's mind couldn't know: I was right to be afraid. It was then I discovered the clothes hamper.

It stood outside my parents' bedroom close to the front door. After crouching among the laundry I'd close the cover and wait for my mother's footsteps on the stairs. A trip to the store took about thirty minutes. I would wait and mark time by the programs on the television set. I remember a time or two when he walked past the hamper into my bedroom and called my name. My fear was palpable inside those wicker walls. I expected myself to respond but I couldn't. What would he do if he found me? What explanation could I give that wouldn't betray my distaste for being alone with him? Sometimes I left the hamper early and would go and sit with him, knowing she'd be back before too long. Before he could start our "game."

The more I hid in the hamper the meaner he became. My withdrawal brought little punishments or the loss of already dwindling privileges. But the more I kissed him the more intolerable my inner world became. There are two pictures I keep locked away in my grandmother's cedar chest. The first is of me taken on the first day of kindergarten, proud and spirited. The second is my school picture at the end of first grade. The spark in my eyes had gone and a limpness had replaced it. Those pictures mean a lot because twenty-seven years later I am still rekindling the light in my eyes.

When I was ten we moved to my great-aunts' house. My parents had been having marital problems again, so I had been staying over there on weekends.

Their home meant protection for me; my father and I would never be alone to-gether. There wouldn't be time for our "game." I was growing older and knew the facts of life. My father's advances were odious and I knew consciously that his needs were inappropriate. I was angry and began to avoid him. My rejection turned his neediness into violence.

One morning I slept through my alarm. Afraid of being late for school, I quickly dressed and headed for the front door. There he stood waiting for me. In my haste I hadn't made my bed and this infuriated him. He grabbed my hair and started to hit me on the back and shoulders until I ran out the door. Any small in-fraction of the "rules" was enough to set him off. As I sat in class I could feel the bruises forming, turning purple beneath my clothing. A few years before I had tried to tell my mother and a school counselor what was happening. Both re-fused to hear me and I felt shamed for saying things that obviously should have been left secret. I never mentioned it again and I lived that way until I left for col-lege in Minnesota when I was eighteen.

Perhaps I'm most bitter about how my father's and my relationship affected my own concept of myself as a parent. I became pregnant when I was twenty-three and after much deliberation I decided to abort. The reasons I gave for my decision were lack of money and a lot of confusion about my affectional prefer-ence. But my innermost fear was that I was emotionally incapable of being a good parent; the fear that I would imitate the man I've tried to disown in my soul. I had to come to terms with my own anger and know that it won't over-whelm me. It is very difficult to consciously denounce what I consider negative "masculine" behavior, to deny the patriarchy only to have to confront those very same feelings in myself. Perhaps that is not all bad. But it would be much easier to say those behaviors only exist "out there."

Allowing myself to have emotional needs has been another difficult task. My personal belief is that Lesbians, especially those of us raised without the benefits of community, have a difficult time with our needs, anyway. Not only because they are different from the norm but because they are so traumatic to accept let alone try to fulfill. Added to that was my inner belief that to have needs is a weakness. You will either suffocate others close to you or be suffocated in turn by their needs. I am still awkward, still learning to accept my own needs as normal. Still learning to meet those needs in ways that are healthy.

Naturally, the inevitable question arises. Did my father's behavior "make" me a Lesbian? Back in the days when I thought myself abnormal I leant an ear to that tired chestnut. Now I have different thoughts. I prefer women because it is in their company that I blossom, just like when I thrived with my mother and her aunts before my father reentered our lives. By the age of five I had been permit-ted more of a sense of myself than most women acquire in middle life—if they're fortunate. I was a female child who had defined her own space: I knew when those perimeters were being violated.

My being a Lesbian means reclaiming my boundaries, reclaiming the light in my eyes. It seems more appropriate to say that my lesbianism, my childhood strength, made my father violent. I could have played our "game." I could have pleased and supplicated my father: perhaps sexual intercourse would not have been required—only a posture of feminine passivity. But I knew I had been violated and I fought. It cost me my childhood, it cost me my child and it scarred me in places where I'm the most vulnerable—but I preserved an integrity that heals.

24

Raped: A Male Survivor Breaks His Silence

Fred Pelka

THE MAN WHO RAPED ME had a remarkable self-assurance which could only have come from practice. He picked me up just outside Cleveland, heading east in a van filled with construction equipment. That early morning in May I'd already spent a sleepless 24 hours trying to hitchhike from Oxford, Mississippi to Buffalo, New York, so it felt good when I was offered a ride through the western fringe of Pennsylvania. First, though, the driver told me he needed to stop along the way, to pick up some building supplies. We drove to a country club undergoing renovation, where I hung out with his co-workers while he signed for several boxes of equipment which we carried back to his van. Getting back onto the turnpike he told me about one more stop he had to make.

As a man, I've been socialized never to admit to being vulnerable, to discuss those moments when I wasn't in control. I know also how women and children are routinely punished when they speak out about abuse, how they are blamed for their own victimization. The examples are endless: Witness the contempt with which Anita Hill was treated. For these reasons and more I'm still reticent, years after it happened, to recount what happened to me that day in Ohio. This article marks the first time in 15 years I have publicly discussed it under my own name.

The second building seemed deserted. We went up a flight of stairs, down a corridor into a side room. I looked around for the equipment he'd mentioned, and noticed him locking the door behind us. He slugged me before I could react, forced me down with his hands around my throat. As I began to lose consciousness I heard him say, "If you scream, if you make one wrong move, I'll kill you."

The police told me later that the man who raped me was a suspect in the rapes of at least six other young men. During the assault his mood swung from vicious, when he promised to strangle me or break my neck, to self-pity, when he wept because we were both among "the wounded ones." In that enormous calm that comes after the acceptance of death, I wondered who would find my body.

Most rapes don't happen like this. Most victims know their attacker(s)—he is a neighbor, friend, husband, or father, a teacher, minister or doctor. The vast majority of rapes are committed by men against women and children, and the FBI estimates that anywhere from 80 to 90 percent go unreported. Rape is an integral part of our culture, and fully one third of all women in this country will be raped at some point in their lives. But this sexist violence does occasionally spill over onto boys and men. The National Crime Survey for 1989 estimated that one in 12 rape survivors is male.

For all this, nobody really knows how many men are raped each year, or how many boys are sexually abused. One study at the University of New Hampshire found that one in 11 young men surveyed had been sexually abused before their 18th birthday. I've seen articles which speculate that anywhere from one in nine to one in seven men will be raped or sexually abused in their lifetime, most often by other males, but these are little more than guesses.

"Since rape is generally misconstrued to be a sexually motivated crime," write Dr. A. Nicholas Groth and Anne Wolbert Burgess, "it is generally assumed that males are unlikely targets of such victimization, and then when it does occur, it reflects a homosexual orientation on the part of the offender. However, the causes of male rape that we have had an opportunity to study do not lend much support to either assumption." Groth and Burgess interviewed men in the community who had been raped, and men who admitted to raping other men, and published their findings in the *American Journal of Psychiatry.* In half the cases they studied, the gender of the victim "did not appear to be of specific significance" to the rapist. "Their victims included males and females, adults and children," and "may symbolize ... something they want to conquer or defeat. The assault is an act of retaliation, an expression of power, and an assertion of their strength or manhood."

In their article, Burgess and Groth dispute some of the prevalent myths about male rape. The first is that men simply don't get raped, at least not outside prison. Of course, if men don't get raped then what happened to me either wasn't rape (the police asking, "Did you come?"), or I'm not a man (my male friends wanting to know how I could "let something like this" happen to me). The second myth—that all men who are raped or rape other men are gay—is a product of our culture's homophobia, and our ignorance of the realities of sexual violence. Most people find it difficult to understand why a straight man would rape another straight man. But if you see rape as a way of exerting control, of confirming your own power by disempowering others, then it makes perfect sense. If it makes you feel powerful and macho to force sex on a woman or child, think of how much more powerful you feel raping another man.

"I have a special place," the man who raped me said after a long while. "It's out in the country, where we can make all the noise we want." It seemed obvious what would happen to me once we arrived at "his special place," but I knew there was no hope for my survival as long as we stayed in that room. So I agreed to go with him to "the country." I promised not to try to escape. It is perhaps an indication of his fragile hold on reality that he believed me.

We walked back to his van and drove away. I waited until I saw some people, then jumped as we slowed to make a turn, rolling as I hit the pavement. I ran into the nearest building—a restaurant—just as patrons were finishing their lunch. Conversation stopped, and I was confronted by a roomful of people, forks raised in mid-bite, staring.

"I think you'd better call the police," I told the waitress. This was all I could say, placing my hands flat on the counter between us to control their trembling. She poured me a cup of black coffee. And then the police arrived.

The two detectives assigned to my case conformed to the standard good cop/bad cop archetype. The good cop told me how upset he'd seen "girls" become after being raped. "But you're a man, this shouldn't bother you." Later on he told me that the best thing to do would be to pull up my pants "and forget it ever happened." The bad cop asked me why my hair was so long, what was I doing hitchhiking at seven o'clock in the morning? Why were my clothes so dirty? Did I do drugs? Was I a troublemaker?

I used to be puzzled at how the bad cop obviously didn't believe me, in spite of the fact that, by his own account, in the months before my assault six other men had come to him with similar stories. Then I heard of the Dahmer case in Milwaukee, how in May 1991 Dahmer's neighbors saw him chasing a naked 14-year-old boy, bleeding from the anus, through the alley behind their building. The responding officers returned the boy to Dahmer's apartment, where Dahmer explained that this was just a lover's spat, which the police believed in spite of the youth's apparent age, and the photos scattered on Dahmer's floor of murdered and mutilated boys and men. The police reassured a neighbor who called again, saying that everything was all right—this at the very moment Dahmer was murdering Konerak Sinthasomphone. Afterwards Dahmer dismembered Sinthasomphone's body.

Sinthasomphone was one of at least 17 boys and men raped and murdered by Dahmer, their body parts stored in vats and freezers in his apartment. It was reported that his first assaults were committed in Ohio, so I had to brace myself before I could look at Jeffrey Dahmer's photo in the paper. At first I was relieved to find that he was not the man who raped me. Then I thought how this meant my assailant is likely still out there, looking for more "wounded ones."

Because I gave them such detailed information—the country club, the name painted on the side of his van—the detectives were able to locate my assailant not too many hours after I was brought into their precinct. The good cop asked, after I identified the rapist, whether I wanted to press charges. He explained how I'd have to return to Ohio to appear before a grand jury, and then return again for the trial, how the newspapers would publish my name, how little chance there was of a conviction.

"He says you seduced him," the good cop said. "So it's your word against his."

The bad cop glared at me when I told them there was no way I wanted any of this to be made public. "You mean," he fumed, "I wasted my whole afternoon on this shit?" Standing in front of me with an expression of disgust, he asked, "How do you think this makes me feel?"

By then it was getting dark. I hitchhiked the remaining 200 miles home, studying every movement of every man who offered me a ride. I arrived at my apartment after midnight, walking the last 10 miles.

In the weeks that followed the assault, every stupid, insensitive thing I'd ever said about rape came back to haunt me. A friend of mine had been attacked several months earlier, also while hitchhiking. She told me just a few hours after it happened how she'd missed her bus, and didn't want to be late to work. She said the man offering her a lift seemed normal enough, even "nice."

"You should've waited for the next bus," I lectured. Today I cringe at my arrogance. Hitchhiking, like walking alone after dark, or feeling safe on a date, at work, at home, is another perquisite to which only men are entitled. How dare she not understand the limits of her freedom?

While women tell me that the possibility of rape is never far from their minds, most men never give it a first, let alone a second, thought. This may explain why they react so negatively to accounts by male survivors. To see rape as "a women's issue" is a form of male privilege most men would prefer not to surrender. They would rather believe that they can move with immunity through the toxic atmosphere of violence and fear they and their compatriots create. Being a male survivor meant I'd lost some of that immunity. No wonder I felt as if I'd been poisoned, as if I were drowning.

For years I pretended, as per the good cop's recommendation, that nothing had happened, secretly feeling that I was somehow responsible, somehow less masculine. The turning point came with the media storm that swirled up around the Big Dan rape in New Bedford, Massachusetts. The movie "The Accused" is based on that incident—a woman assaulted in a bar while other men looked on and cheered. Naive as I was, I figured this was a pretty clear-cut case. Where the police might have doubted my will to resist (no broken bones, no massive lacerations), here was a victim overpowered by half a dozen men. How could anyone doubt that she had been brutalized? Yet, during the trial, *The Boston Herald* ran the front page headline "SHE LED US ON!" I realized then that, even had I been murdered, someone would have inevitably questioned my complicity: "He probably liked rough sex."

It's just this sort of victim-blaming that discourages survivors from reporting their trauma, or seeking treatment, but there are other factors which may discourage males in particular. Homophobia for one: The sort of gender McCarthyism that labels any man a faggot who cannot or will not conform to accepted norms of masculine feeling or behavior. Men who rape other men capitalize on this, knowing that straight victims don't want to appear gay, and gay victims might fear coming out of the closet. Groth and Burgess report, for instance, that "a major strategy used by some offenders ... is to get the victim to ejaculate." This "strategy" was attempted in roughly half the cases they studied, and in half of those the rapist succeeded in ejaculating his victim. This confuses the victim, who often misidentifies ejaculation with orgasm. It confirms for the rapist the old canard about how victims "really want it." And, as Groth and Burgess say, it leaves the survivor "discouraged from reporting the assault for fear his sexuality may be suspect."

For male survivors of child sexual abuse there is also the unfortunate theory that boys who are abused inevitably grow up to be men who rape. One survivor told me it was for this reason he had decided never to be a father. Not that he'd ever wanted to abuse children, nor was there any evidence he ever would. He eventually came to realize that because some rapists are themselves survivors doesn't mean that all male survivors of child sexual abuse turn out to be rapists.

Finally, rape crisis centers, the only institutions in our society founded expressly to help rape survivors, are identified by some men as hotbeds of feminism, and many men take "feminist" to mean "man-hating." It's true that the vast majority of rape crisis counselors are women, that the entire stop-rape movement is an extension of the women's movement. For the record, though, I have never felt any hostility in response when calling a rape crisis center, this in spite of the fact that RCCs are often plagued by "hotline abusers"—men who call to masturbate to the sound of a female voice.

On the other hand, I've run across a good deal of hostility towards women from male survivors with whom I've talked. One man told me how certain he was that the counselors at his local RCC hated men, even though, by his own admission, he'd never called, and knew no one who had. A while back I attended a survivors' conference organized by a Boston women's group, attended by several hundred women and maybe a dozen men. One of these men stood up during a plenary session to shout at the women on the podium. As an incest survivor, he said, he felt "marginalized" and "oppressed' by the way the conference was run, despite the fact that a number of the workshops were specifically geared toward males, and that a keynote speaker received a standing ovation when he described his work with boys and men. Some male survivors even blame women for the denial and homophobia they encounter after their assault. They openly resent the (pitifully few) resources available to female survivors, as if any help women receive is at the expense of men. Even Geraldo has picked up this theme: His show on male survivors ended with an attack on rape crisis centers for their alleged refusal to acknowledge male victimization.

This hostility has been exacerbated by the so-called men's movement, the Robert Bly/mythopoetic crowd, with their "Wild Man" and "Inner Warrior" archetypes. These men say a lot of absurd things about sexual violence, not the least of which is that "just as many men get raped as women." This last statement is often repeated by Chris Harding, editor of *Wingspan,* which *The Boston Globe* calls "the bible of the new men's movement." Harding is generally quick to add that most of these rapes "occur in prison"—a statement which is as inaccurate as it is pernicious, assuming as it does that a disproportionate number of male rapes are committed by working-class and minority men. The men's movement claims that rape is a "gender-neutral issue," and thus has nothing to do with sexism.

What is ironic about all this is that what little acknowledgement there is of male victimization generally comes from the *women's* stop-rape movement. To the extent that male survivors *can* tell their stories, it is because of the foundation laid by feminists. So this woman-bashing is an ungrateful as it is gratuitous.

One source of confusion appears to be the distinction between victimization and oppression. Male survivors charge that feminists see rape as a "man vs. woman" issue, emphasizing the central role male violence plays in stunting and destroying women's lives, and they're right. The distinction is that while many women, and some men, are victimized by rape, all women are oppressed by it, and any victimization of women occurs in a context of oppression most men simply do not understand. Rape for men is usually a bizarre, outrageous tear in the fabric of reality. For women, rape is often a confirmation of relative powerlessness, of men's contempt for women, and its trauma is reinforced every day in a thousand obvious and subtle ways.

For myself, I don't need for rape to be gender neutral to feel validated as a male survivor. And I certainly don't need to denigrate women, or to attack feminists, to explain why I was abused by the (male) police, ridiculed by my (male) friends, and marginalized by the (male dominated) society around me. It is precisely because we have been "reduced" to the status of *women* that other men find us so difficult to deal with. It was obvious to me at the police station that I was held in contempt because I was a *victim*—feminine, hence perceived as less masculine. Had I been an accused criminal, even a rapist, chances are I would have been treated with more respect, because I would have been seen as more of a man. To cross that line, to become victims of the violence which works to circumscribe the lives of women, marks us somehow as traitors to our gender. Being a male rape survivor means I no longer fit our culture's neat but specious definition of masculinity, as one empowered, one always in control. Rather than continue to deny our experience, male survivors need to challenge that definition.

As Diana E.H. Russell says in *The Politics of Rape,* "Women must start talking about rape: Their experiences, their fears, their thoughts. The silence about rape must be broken."

The same must be true for men. And so I offer this article as my first contribution to that effort.

...

25

And He Turned Around and Ran Away

Gail Groves

FOR SIX YEARS I WORKED on a rape hotline in Santa Cruz, a small California central-coast town with an activist spirit. Santa Cruz Women Against Rape, the collective that runs the hotline, is known for propagating the idea that direct confrontation of rapists is a way to exert community control over men's behavior. The group prides itself on its political, rather than service, orientation. The rape calls we got were not unusual, from what I know about rape hotlines in the state and the nation. One year, the hotline received six hundred calls, while local police got only seventeen.

One of the most surprising aspects of these calls was the fact that so many women got away without being raped. Over the years, a consistent picture began to emerge of women effectively resisting, paying attention to clues about a potential attack, and escaping by many different means. We told each other success stories at our group meetings, partly to bolster ourselves for another night of waiting for the phone to ring.

I had been working the hotline for six months, when one day, at a meeting, someone was talking about her boyfriend in high school pressuring her to have sex. Suddenly, I remembered that I had been raped once and had fought off a second rape attempt by the time I was twenty—both times by acquaintances in "social" situations. I had blocked them entirely out of my memory. As you read this book [*Her Wits About Her: Self-Defense Success Stories by Women,* edited by Denise Caignon and Gail Groves (Harper & Row, 1987)] you may find yourself remembering incidents you wish you had forgotten, too, but perhaps, you will also remember how you got away.

The knock on the glass apartment door startled me. It was late: it wasn't my house. Strains of the Jefferson Airplane and my quiet thoughts were disturbed by this person at the door. It was a foggy San Francisco night, and my boyfriend had already taken a bus back to his mother's house across town.

The clear glass door revealed a large man in his mid-thirties, with a beard and bushy dark hair.

"Who are you?" I said.

"I'm a friend of Cherri's," he said, smiling at me with large, perfect teeth. Cherri Black, my friend who rented this flat, was across the bay at the time with her boyfriend. I felt uneasy, confused by conflicting values and messages. I knew I should not let the man in.

"What's your name?" I asked.

"I'm T. J. Broderick. See?" There, on his expensive patchwork corduroy shirt, were his embroidered initials: T. J. An expansive, egocentric man, he was sure I wanted him to come in.

"Why don't you let me in, and we can talk for a few minutes?" he said.

"Cherri isn't here right now," I said suspiciously. And not likely to come back after 11:00 P.M. either, I thought. But I had been raised to be polite, and he was a very smooth talker, very nice. Why not, after all, let him in? What if I was a scared seventeen-year-old who had never had sex. He just wanted to talk. After a few more of his persuasive assurances, I let him in.

We walked into the living room. My body stiffened. I knew this wasn't right, but my upbringing had not prepared me to rebuff the friendly approach. We talked, or rather I listened and nodded.

"I write scripts for television. Cherri has known me for years. I'm surprised she never told you—I drop in on her all the time. What's your name?"

"Gail," I said numbly. This man wanted me to trust him. What was I going to do? I was slight next to his huge man's body. He talked on and on. I felt uncomfortable, aware of sexual overtones, afraid of rape.

"Here, come sit over here with me." He planted himself on Cherri's couch-bed, leaning back against the pseudo-Victorian wallpaper.

"No, I don't want to," I said, sitting across the room. But he hadn't hurt me yet. He had only talked me into passivity.

"What's the matter? I won't hurt you. I just want to talk. Come on over here." Unconsciously, he mimicked my thoughts. I got up woodenly, walked to where he sat, and sat down at the far end of the settee, near his legs. I allowed him to manipulate by body into a half-lying position at his side. He tried to kiss me. I fended him off. My entire body was stiff, unyielding.

I kept thinking over and over, You can do this, but I am not going to feel anything. You can touch me, but you can't really get to me. My only defense was this unfeeling rigidity.

He stroked my back, kept talking.

"There now, that's not so bad. Look, I won't hurt you. A pretty little girl like you should have a boyfriend." I wouldn't tell him how old I was, and contemplated telling him my boyfriend would be right back, but didn't. I didn't want him to think I had had sex.

He kept stroking my back, over and over again. Lost in my thoughts, trying to absent myself, I fought to stay stiff. Then, for a crucial moment, I relaxed. I have always hated myself for that "guilty" moment. I shocked myself back into awareness, and finally began to react.

"I want you to go away," I said tentatively. "I don't want to do this." We talked a little while longer. I began to feel shaky, tired of resisting. Finally, he let me go. I got up, moved away, and since his only weapon was persuasion, he could not force me back. Finally, hours after I answered the door, when I was obviously, if passively, continuing to resist, he left.

"Give Cherri my best regards," he finished amiably as I shut the door in his face. He could have raped me. At that moment, I had no idea why he hadn't. I looked out the window, watched him leave, began to shake, still feeling numb. I called my boyfriend's house. His mother answered.

"May I speak to Tim?" I asked.

"He's gone to bed." His mother never slept. She was a suspicious, prudish woman who had raised Tim alone after his father abandoned them.

"Look, Mrs. Drummond, I was almost raped, and I want to talk to your son," I gasped angrily at her.

He came to the house. I told him what had happened, cried, made tea. It was over.

But I never forgave myself for that moment in which I relaxed; I felt in that moment I gave in and betrayed myself. Now, I see that I also successfully avoided rape.

Eight years later, I took an eight-week self-defense class, wanting to finally break free from some of the fear that gripped me whenever I walked alone, that compelled me to look in all the closets whenever I came home to an empty house. These were my private nightmares then. Now I see them as common to the everyday terror of having been born female. I began to question limits I had previously accepted.

I was fascinated by self-defense. After years of living in a cage, I had been given a key—skills and attitudes that could change my approach to life. My teacher, Kathy Quinn, helped me see that I had power, and that I could learn to use my mind and body to sense an impending attack and to detect it. I *could* fight back effectively, no holds barred.

I apprenticed myself to her, and within a year found myself studying joshi (women's) judo, and teaching one-day self-defense workshops for women and girls at the YWCA.

Part of my motivation for learning to teach self-defense was fear. I was afraid to walk home from the bus stop. I was afraid of someone breaking in through my bedroom window. I was furious at the restrictions that had been put on me and other women.

When I felt it safe to do so, I began to experiment. On my way home, instead of running breathlessly with blinders on down the long road by the ocean to my house, I would stop. I would stand still by the side of the road, or sometimes in the middle of it, and listen in the dark. I would look to see how far away someone was when I could first sense they were there. The first thing I learned was that I was not afraid of the dark. If I was alone in the dark, I was fine. I was afraid of people in the dark.

My limit was about twenty yards. If people were out there and I was listening and looking for them, even if they stood relatively still, I could still tell where they were. If they made any sound at all, I could spot them immediately. This was a revelation. After all, I too had seen all the movies in which the woman walks down the street while the rapist lurks in the (rustling!) bushes, then suddenly jumps out, and, wham, it's all over, she's been raped. The more I studied rape, the more I concluded that this thirty-second fantasy was born out of the necessities of half-hour TV shows and two-hour movies.

Most rapes in real life take longer than that. In real life, for someone to get close enough to rape you, he must first be far away. Then either he sneaks over the last twenty yards, or he runs them, giving you lots of warning. Or the person is an acquaintance and you let him come near, even if you feel uncomfortable. Paying attention to, rather than ignoring, those uncomfortable feelings became the norm for me rather than the exception. I began to enjoy my nighttime walks a great deal more.

Fear plays a special role in learning about self-defense. One of the most effective ways to teach self-defense is to have students act out situations they are afraid of, using other students—telling the "attacker" what to do, and then seeing what the defender's options are. Now fear is a tool for me—it helps me see areas of my life where I need more skills to handle situations.

One way to deal with particular fears and to learn realistic self-defense is through dreams. I used to be extremely afraid of someone breaking in through my bedroom window. Early in my second year of teaching, I had a series of nine dreams about this. In the first dream, I was paralyzed, and somehow the attacker disappeared by magic. In the second dream, I struggled and pushed him out the door. In the third dream, I picked up a flowerpot and hit him over the head. During my waking life, I began to look around my room for available weapons. I practiced throwing someone off me while I was under the covers, and I learned how to deal with a knife from that position. Finally, in the ninth dream, after each previous dream's defense had become more effective and realistic, I killed the man. That was the end of the dreams, and signaled some resolution of this particular fear.

Fear becomes more and more a pointer to areas where I need to learn skills, and thus a useful tool. Many students tell of dream sequences in which they cannot scream or move, but as the class goes on, they find their dreams changing to include more effective, skilled responses.

Contrary to images on TV and in movies, when you make a situation real in your mind, there are always options for the defender—ways she can damage the attacker, verbal points she can gain through negotiation, strategies that will work. Self-defense means looking for these openings, having the faith that there will be one at some point, and then trying something, and not giving up.

The more I taught, the more self-defense stories I heard. Initially, I found that women in classes and workshops used me as a place to dump all the horror stories they had ever heard. After some workshops, I would need to go have a good cry, staggered by the ugly, brutal violence against women I heard about. I think my students assumed that because I was a self-defense teacher, it was all right to talk to me about all the terrible things they were afraid of, about all the stories they had heard on television. They thought I could handle it. More and more, I found I couldn't. The stories upset me and brought down the positive mood of an empowerment workshop. I found I had to shield myself from the stories, to cut myself off from the pain associated with them. My empathy was working against me.

In an effort to focus on the positive in these classes, I began to collect success stories informally. All self-defense teachers have them. These were stories of both the simplest and the most convoluted escapes. The woman who rolled out of a car going fifty miles per hour to escape a kidnapping. The woman who, hearing two men talking behind her about what they were going to do to her, began punching air, only to see them turn and run. The man who pulled his frightened face back from me when I stuck a fistful of keys in it to stop him from approaching. The woman who took care of her attacker with one hand and her knee while not breaking the cookies she was taking home for her children in the other hand. The woman at the bus stop who answered the man who said he was going to rape her with "No, you're not!" He turned away, mumbling vaguely, "I guess you're right."

These were not the kind of stories I saw on the nightly news. The crime report in the local paper abounded with stories of women brutally raped. Regional and national news were excruciating with their tales of horrors done to women. Santa Cruz itself had been named "Murder Capital of the World" by the media, for a series of rape-murders that Edmund Kemper committed here in 1971 and 1972. Later would come David Carpenter, the "Trailside Killer."

During the time I worked on the rape line, I stopped watching television and rarely learned about world events. When you hear the real stories on the phone every night, the sensationalized versions are overkill.

At best, the media would report on spectacular defenses, like the woman in Berkeley, California, who pulled a bayonet out of her closet and stabbed her attacker with it. But these unusual stories did nothing to alleviate the fears of the average woman on the street.

Few people believed that women could protect themselves or stop an attacker. Instead, they believed that women lied about rape, that all men were stronger than all women, and that no woman ever got away. Gradually, through my involvement with self-defense and the rape hotline, the belief began to build in me that these ideas simply were not true. Women did get away before rapes were completed. They did fight back—and they did win. In fact, most of the women I talked to on the phone had done something to stop the rape, or to make the situation safer for themselves. They were not paralyzed by fear. They acted.

Most women who are attacked remember feeling a hunch, an intuition, a nonverbal perception before something physical happens—the feeling that something is wrong. The sooner women act on this intuition, the more likely they are to be safe in the end. Ninety percent of an effective defense is the recognition that yes, this person is attacking me. This feeling is especially important with people we have reason to trust, but who take advantage of that trust. Over 75 percent of all attacks on women are committed by men who know them, at least on a first-name basis. Acquaintance rape and rape in marriage are not uncommon.

One in three girls and one in six boys are attacked sexually in this country by the age of eighteen; the majority of these are attacked by a family member or friend. Yet even very small children, like those who have been trained by the Child Assault Prevention Program in Columbus, Ohio, can learn to defend themselves.

Dr. Pauline Bart, a renowned sociologist from the University of Illinois, began to publish the results of her studies about effective rape avoidance in 1980. Bart established that women who fight back get away more often than women who are passive. For the first time, a reputable scientist was contradicting the advice of the police "not to resist, you'll just get hurt." Too many women had gone into court after following that advice, only to be told that it was not rape if they didn't fight back.

Dr. Bart's results were extremely interesting. She found that the more strategies a woman uses, the more likely she is to escape with minimal injuries. Strategies include yelling, fleeing, reasoning with the attacker, pleading, and physically fighting back—kicking, hitting, biting, using the body as a weapon. Verbal strategies alone were not particularly effective unless used with other strategies. Pleading and acting passive actually seemed to *increase* chances that the rape would be completed. Her reports included exciting stories, many about women who had escaped from armed attackers.

Dr. Bart's findings were borne out by the stories we collected. These women used their wits and their incredible nerve, even when terrified, to figure out what to do in life-threatening situations. Even in some of the most brutal attacks we heard about, women tried strategy after strategy until something worked. They used their wits to negotiate with or outwit their attackers. At times carrying out split-second physical decisions, these women fought back physically, ran, reasoned, and yelled with vigor until their attackers gave up. They have made true the maxim: Your own will to defend yourself is stronger than the attacker's will to hurt you. Dr. Bart's results were recently published in *Stopping Rape: Successful Survival Strategies* (co-authored by Patricia O'Brien, New York: Pergamon Press, 1985), which we recommend.

Women Who Resist: The Self-Defense Success Story Project is the result of my work with Denise Caignon, first in studying judo together, then in teaching self-defense as founding members of the Santa Cruz Women's Self-Defense Teaching Cooperative, and now in writing and editing this book.

The conviction has grown in us that many women do successfully defend themselves. Furthermore, we believe that women use success stories and their knowledge of other women's strategies to create new defenses in unknown situations. This project comes out of our joint desire to share the stories we knew existed with as many women as possible.

There are not ten easy steps to perfect self-defense. Good self-defense is whatever works. The defenses women use are as varied as the women themselves. Each woman uses intuition not only to gauge the danger of the situation, but also to plan her own unique response, geared to her perceptions and abilities. No one can teach you exactly what to do in every possible situation. But in a self-defense class you can learn skills and attitudes that you can combine, should the situation arise, in appropriate ways. The idea is to give women more control and more options. Part of this means unlearning inappropriate responses, originally modeled by actresses on television or in movies—like panic, helplessly screaming with your head thrown back, or pounding on someone's chest, which happens to be one of the strongest parts of the body.

Sometimes the most unexpected strategies work. One woman, guessing that her attacker was Catholic, told him that the Baby Jesus would hate him if he did this to her, and that Mother Mary would condemn him and hate him. He burst into tears and took her home.

Another woman said, yes, it sounded fine with her, but she needed to get her sweater and purse inside at the party first, and then they could go somewhere comfortable. Inside, she screamed and got help.

Two young girls were being followed by two men in a car. When one of the men got out of the car to lure them in, they began to beat him up. The other attacker jumped out of the car to help his buddy escape. The girls' parents, both karate teachers, had taught them some good blows and kicks.

One woman, trapped between two men in the backseat of a car, grabbed the knife one attacker was holding and broke it over her knee. She cut her hands badly, but the attackers apparently thought she was crazy and let her out.

The women that get away are as diverse as their stories. Black women, Latinas, Asian-Americans, white women, fat women, young girls, teens, women in wheelchairs, women with canes, deaf women, married women, mothers, women with cerebral palsy, lesbians, old women. I think of the eighty-six-year-old woman who told me she grabbed and pulled on a man's testicles after he dropped his pants and began to assault her. He ran away crying.

Many attackers can be discouraged verbally at the outset. Lots of assailants begin with a verbal attack, asking personal questions, or becoming obscene. If the woman seems intimidated, or goes along with them, the attack may become physical. The verbal attack is a form of testing, like teasing, that is aimed at the weak points in a woman's self-esteem.

Attackers are not looking for equal partners to fight with when they pick women to attack. Men do not begin an attack on a woman thinking, I'm going to attack her, and then she's going to hurt me. Rather, they see women and girls as easy targets, weak and helpless. There is some evidence, from interviews with rapists in prison, that they look for women who exhibit little confidence, who use minimal eye contact, and who are hunched in posture and taking relatively small steps. They often choose to attack women who seem physically infirm in some way, or who react in passive rather than self-respecting ways.

Most of us women have been taught to be polite, to smile at everyone so that people will like us. Girls learn that they should be seen but not heard, and that they should truthfully answer questions put to them by adults, even strangers. Many of us have been told not to talk to strangers, but were not taught what to do when we don't want to talk to people we know, or if a stranger tries to talk to us or to touch us. These passive patterns make women and girls less likely to resist and easier to rape. And the patterns are often cemented through years of reinforcement and are difficult to unlearn.

Women have been seen for years as weak, helpless *victims*. I used to cringe every time I heard someone in the rape crisis movement say that word, which literally means "sacrifice unto death." In the past few years, many groups in the rape crisis movement have begun to question the use of that word to describe a woman who was raped. I have changed my vocabulary. I now refer to women who have been attacked, whether a rape was completed or not, as *survivors*.

Perhaps as more and more men are injured by the women they have attacked, another truth about women's strength, determination, and will to survive will begin to emerge and spread. Maybe women and girls, after reading these stories of success, will feel encouraged and be determined to fight back should they ever be attacked. Certainly the interest is there: over two hundred women from all over the United States responded in writing to our call for stories.

Although these are subjective personal accounts, it is clear that women do succeed in influencing the behavior of their attackers. In fact, one of the most common and most satisfying endings for the stories we have heard is "and he turned around and ran away."

26

Conclusion

SUSAN GRIFFIN (1979) WROTE OF GROWING UP at a time when women did not speak out about rape, when it was assumed that a woman raped was a woman damaged, complicit, shamed. No one questioned this assumption then or even seemed to recognize that this *was* an assumption, not an inevitability, not a natural state of affairs. Griffin recalled living in a city permeated with fear as a serial rapist moved from one neighborhood to the next. She recalled the silence, so horrible and disheartening, and how each woman struggled privately with her own fear and with the shame of every woman's taintability. And then a reporter who had been raped by this man came forward, broke this silence. As Griffin said,

> How can I tell you what it felt like to hear Carolyn Craven speak out about this rape. This terror, this subjection, this humiliation and torture, she said, we will not bear. I remember him, she said. I hold this man accountable. I hold this city accountable. I do not bear this act alone. We do not. We do not accept this state of being of submission and trembling and fear for our lives, of locking the door against brutality and sleeping uneasily, of our lives on edge, we do not accept this. (p. 29)

Perhaps it is hard for us today to imagine such an atmosphere of *silent* terror hanging over a city, of no one speaking out. But in that atmosphere, heavy and stifling as it was, the courage of Carolyn Craven was an "opening of the field… , a healing… , a feat…herald[ing] more to come" (Griffin 1979:29–30).

Indeed it was. Since then many survivors have spoken out. And women and men, moved by these testimonies, this horror, have

- done research
- conducted interviews
- written poetry, essays, books
- staged skits, plays, protests
- organized boycotts, speak-outs, "take back the night" marches

- raised money
- built shelters
- started hot lines, crisis centers, support groups
- provided counseling
- taught defense consciousness, assertiveness training, self-defense
- developed treatment programs for offenders
- designed "Feel Safe, Be Safe" lessons for children
- demanded police-alert telephones, better lighting, safer streets
- organized "buddy" systems, escort services, women's safety transit
- created rape-awareness days (or weeks)
- started sexual assault and harassment programs in schools, work-places, community centers
- written legislators
- reformed laws
- recalled judges
- critiqued sexist stereotypes, media imagery, rape myths
- educated reporters, police officers, emergency room personnel, school officials, their partners, themselves.

The mobilization of this energy, this tremendous effort, is also " a feat ... [that] heralds more to come" (Griffin 1979:30). Because in making these changes, we were transformed—our consciousness, our pride and dignity, our sense of purpose, of what is possible.

But much work still lies before us. Rape is not an isolated phenomenon. It is deeply woven in the fabric of our social order. Eliminating violence against women requires radical social structural and cultural change (hooks 1984; Klein 1981). Our rape-prevention strategies must be comprehensive, multifaceted, and societal-wide, and they must involve us all—men, women, and children. We must redesign our sex-education programs so as not to continue to "rear our sons and daughters in such ignorance of their sexuality that many confuse pleasure with pain and domination" (Buchwald, Fletcher, and Roth 1993:2). We must develop and expand educational programs that confront rape-supportive beliefs and attitudes, that challenge traditional notions of masculinity and femininity, that facilitate communication and mutual respect between men and women. We must continue to conduct research that investigates the ways in which "social and economic institutions sustain and multiply the kinds of violence women experience" (Fine 1989:556). We must persist in our efforts to uproot these "dense institutional supports." We must advocate and create social and economic reforms designed to promote gender equality and improve the overall condition of women in society (e.g., policies that promote pay equity; make available quality low-cost child care; and provide access to contraception, abortion services, prenatal and maternal care). And since violence against women is significantly related to the general level of violence in society, we must address the socioeconomic causes of crime and seek to reduce unemployment, poverty, and racial discrimination (Schwendinger and Schwendinger 1983).[1]

Yes, there is much work to do. Transforming rape culture requires no less than "a revolution of values" (Buchwald et al. 1993:2). As Griffin (1979:67) asked,

> Would not ... the recognition of sacredness in the other, of the spirit in the other, and this cherishing of woman's body need to spring from a whole weave that must also include a different notion of power; one that acknowledges the power in each being, but eschews power over another being as a lower order of behavior? Would not this weave have to include the erasing of the possibility of other kinds of cruelties for which rape might be a metaphor? Could theft of food from the mouths of children exist in this world, or any murder of body or soul?

Could war exist? Is not the penetration and domination of a woman by a man intimately tied to the penetration and domination of one nation by another? Are they not part of the same weave?

Indeed they are. Violence against women and children "is part of a culture in which violence to life [itself] is condoned" (Bass 1983:42). As our very earth is polluted, raped, so are women and children. Beneath the willingness to violate the trust and security of another human being, beneath the willingness to desecrate our world and the possibility of life itself, lies a profound selfishness.

We must, as Griffin implored, try to imagine the "kind of mind that finds rape unimaginable" (1979:67). We must nurture that mind, its sensibility, its sensitivity. We must "envision a world without rape" (p. 25), for envisioning that world is the first step toward its realization. As Griffin said, "I know the world has changed before and the seemingly unchangeable has become different. And if I am asked to be cynical because of facts and numbers and probabilities, or defeats or imperfections in our efforts to change, or because of weapons which can destroy the earth or time and space which grow too precious, I answer that what I feel, even in the face of all this, is a joy in the possibility I see" (p. 68).

If it is our anger, our outrage, at the horror of rape that provokes us to take up the fight against rape, perhaps it is our "joy in the possibility" of a different world that will sustain us in our efforts. We close this book with the beautiful, inspiring poem of Ellen Bass, a poem that summons us to gather our power for the task that lies ahead. "Our numbers are grand," Bass writes. And so will be "our stunning harvest."

Notes

1. For further discussion of rape-prevention programs and strategies, see Bateman (1982), Buchwald et al. (1993), Fonow, Richardson, and Wemmerus (1992), Levy (1991), Lundberg-Love and Geffner (1989), Parrot and Bechhofer (1991), Searles and Follansbee (1984).

Our Stunning Harvest

Ellen Bass

I.

She recognizes miner's lettuce
nibbles its round leaf.
Her father asks *Do you know*
not to eat the other plants?
and she nods solemnly.
We have taught her not to swallow pits
of cherries or olives.
She spits them out bald
and repeats *Could make a child sick.*
and walking, when we hear a car
she runs to the side of the road
stands, stationary, until it passes.
But how do I protect her
from men who rape children?
from poison in the air?
from nuclear holocaust?

I walk this road—oak trees, eucalyptus
blackberry bushes in white flower
the hard green fruit pushing out behind the blossoms—
the first time I have walked here alone
since that day almost two years ago
when I carried her in my belly,
the morning before her birth.
It was dustier then, drought
the smell of hot clay and stillness
in the tall Queen Anne's lace.
Today the breeze is cool.

But the dread, the urgency
etch my pleasure like acid.

I clean house, shove socks and shirts
in the washer, speed through the grocery,
type, fold, staple—
but what good are dishes stacked in the cupboard,
peaches and avocadoes in the basket, envelopes
stamped in the dark mailbox?

At night I lie in bed imagining what I will do if attacked—
alone, I could run
or fight
but with her—in the stroller, holding my hand
on this country road?
A mother bird flutters and distracts.
She risks her life, but the babies are protected.
I could not even protect her.
She is too small to run. If I whispered *run*
she would not go. And if I tried to carry her
we would be overcome. I could not fight with her
not far from help. I am prey.
With her as hostage
I am blackmailed.
And if I am not enough? if they want her too?

My husband sleeps by my side
his regular sleep breath. I
lean closer, try to absorb
the calm. But the possibilities do not stop.
I don't let them. I keep trying scenarios,
get as far as convincing the rapist to let me take her to a neighbor
then rushing into the house, locking him out.
But he may not even speak English
I sober myself, and besides …

I am sick in the night, sick the next day.
My stomach won't digest food, it runs through me
foul, waste.
By noon I fall asleep, she sleeps in the crook of my arm.
We sleep for hours. For these few hours
we are safe.

I know we have been safe
afterward.

II.

Yesterday I read they tried to kill Dr. Rosalie Bertell,
a nun who researched radiation-caused cancer. Here,
the resource center for nonviolence is shot up,
tires slashed.

My husband is limiting his practice
so he can work against nuclear destruction.
He says *We may be in danger, you know.*
If the steering on the car ever feels funny
pull right over.
He's had the lug nuts loosened before.

But we both know that is not the greater danger.
Radiation from Lovecreek, Churchrock, Rocky Flats,
Three Mile Island, West Valley, Hanford—
we live near the San Andreas Fault—
an earthquake
and the Diablo Canyon plant
could kill millions—
and bombs, Trident, the draft beginning again.
Who are these madmen
whose lives are so barren, so desperate
they love nothing?

What will it take to make them change?
What will it take?

What will it take to make *me* change?
I still use plastic bags from Dow Chemical.
When am I
going to stop?

I ask my friend. She smiles.
Polyvinylchloride poisons your food she says.

What do you do with your lettuce? I ask.

Glass jars, or a pot with a lid.

I smile.
I have a pot with a lid.

What good will one woman never again using plastic bags do
in the face of tons of plutonium, recombinant DNA
a hundred thousand rapists?
What good does it do that I feed my daughter organic rice
purple beets, never sugar?
What good that I march with other women
and we yell *WOMEN UNITED*
WILL NEVER BE DEFEATED
banshees into the night?

These things will not save my daughter.
I know. I know that.
But unless I do them
she will not be saved

and I want to save her.
Oh Mother of us all, I am a mother too
I want to save her.

III.

I want to talk to the president.
I want to go with other mothers
and meet with the president.
And I want mothers from Russia there.
And the head of Russia.
And Chinese mothers
and the head of China
and mothers from Saudi Arabia and Japan and South Africa
and all the heads of state and the families of the heads of state
and the children, all the children of the mothers.
I want a meeting.

I want to ask the president, *Is there nothing*
precious to you?

And when the president explains how it's the
Russians, I want the Russian women to say *We don't*
want war. I want all the women to scream *We don't want war, we,*
the people, do not want war.

And I want the president to admit he wants war,
he wants power and money and war more
than he wants the lives of his children.
I want to see him turn to his children and tell them
they will not live, that
no one will live,
that with one computer error all life on this planet can be
annihilated, that two men could go mad and push one button
in a silo, in a plane, that these men do go mad,
the men with access to the buttons go mad all the time,
are replaced, that one
might not be replaced soon enough.

I want each head of state to tell his children what will happen
if any country sends a thermonuclear bomb.
I want each head of state, with his own tongue, to tell his children
how the computers of the other country would pick up the signal,
how they would fire back, how the bombs would hit.
I want each president and prime minister and king
to tell his children how firestorms would burn, vaporizing people,
animals, plants, and then as days passed,
how the millions would die of radiation sickness,
their skin sloughing off, the nausea, hair falling out,
hemorrhage, infection, no hospitals, no clean water,
the stench of dead and decaying bodies, bacteria and virus rampant,
insects rampant, and the radiation ticking, ticking
as millions more die over the next years, leukemia, cancer,
    and no hope
for the future, birth deformity, stillbirth, miscarriage, sterility,
millions and billions.

I want them to watch the faces of their children.
I want them to watch their eyes pale
the flecks of light fading,
and when their children ask *Why?*
I want them to point to the other heads of state
and the others to point back
and I want the mothers screaming.
I want the mothers of the children of the heads of state screaming.
I want them to scream until their voices are hoarse whispers
raw as the bloody rising of the sun, I want them to hiss
    How dare you?

How dare you?
Kill them yourself, then.
Kill them here, now, with your own hands.
Kill all these children, clench
your hands around their necks, crunch their spines.
Kill one
two, three, kill hundreds. If you are going to kill
then kill.

I want to see the faces of the president, the premier, the prime
   minister, the chancellor, the king.
I want to see their faces tremble.
I want to see them tremble like a still lake under wind.
I want to see them weep.

I must be crazy myself.
My mother is an optimist. She believes in a survival instinct.
She has read the statistics, knows
plutonium is poison for 500,000 years.
But she does not think of these things.
It depresses her, she says.

I say she is naive.
But I write poems in which presidents and premiers weep
at the voices of raging mothers, I write
they weep.
I must be crazy. I am crazy.
And I want this meeting like a crazy woman wants.

I want to go myself.
I want my daughter to ride her four-wheeled horse around the carpeted room
fast, steering with her red sneakered feet through
   potted plants and filing cabinets,
precise, dauntless.
I want her spirit to inspire us.
I don't want to hear about numbers.
I don't want to hear one number about how many bombs or how much money
or dates or megatons or anything else.
I want to hear *No more.*
I want to hear *My child will not be murdered.*
My child will live.

I want to dance victorious, to dance and dance
ring around the rosie, with no one falling down.
No ashes, no ashes.
I want no ashes from my child's tender head.
I want to dance. I want to sing. I want to kiss all the heads of state,
all the mothers, every child.
I want to kiss them all and dance the hora, dance the mazurka,
   the waltz, the tribal dances, bare feet on red clay
                 on white sand
                 on black earth.
dancing, kissing, singing
dancing, dancing until our legs are strong
our arms strong, our thighs, lungs, bellies strong,
until our voices are loud, clear, and vibrate with the wind
until we ride the wind
until we ride home, with the wind, flying, flying
laughing, kissing, singing, cackling, our children
tucked under our wings, safe.
Safe. We are safe. We are so strong.
We can protect our children.

IV.

No you won't, the young, composed woman taunts us
slowly, from the stage.
She is our teacher. She is teaching us our power.

Yes we will, We yell back.

No you won't.

Yes we will.

No you won't.

We are roaring, *YES WE WILL. YES WE WILL.*

Now she pauses *Say, Yes I will.*
Yes I will, I yell.
AGAIN, she bellows.
Yes I will, my eyes fill with tears. I am trembling.

YES I WILL. YES I WILL. YES I WILL.

I will.
I will protect my daughter.
How
will I protect my daughter?

Even if we dismantle the bombs, cement the power plants,
ban 2, 4, 5-T, men are still raping women.

Men raped women before they split the atom
before they concocted herbicides in their stainless steel laboratories.
They raped in war and they raped in what they called peace,
they raped in marriage,

they raped in groups, they raped old women, young women,
they raped when they were angry,
    they raped when they were scorned,
they raped when they got drunk, got high, got a weekend pass,
got on the Dean's list, got fired. They still do.

They rape women asleep, children asleep—
    fathers have easy access to children asleep.
They rape babies—
    doctors treat three month old babies for gonorrhea
    of the throat.

They rape women getting into their cars after late night shifts,
they rape old women washing up their breakfast dishes,
they call on the phone and threaten rape, they write songs like
your lips tell me no no, but there's yes yes in your eyes,
they design high heeled sandals so we can't run away,
they invent the pill—easy sex and we die from cancer when they're done.

They use knives and guns when subtler coercion is not enough,
sometimes they use the knives and guns anyway, afterward.

And how shall I protect her?
How shall we protect each other?

I can warn her not to talk to strangers
I can forbid her to go out at night

I can nag her to press her knees together
    and button her blouses to her neck,
but none of that will assure her safety
or even her survival.

I can enroll her in self-defense, judo, karate.
I can practice with her in our yard. We can grow
quick and deft, together.
And that will help, but it is not enough.
Three boys with razor blades, a man with a 45 ...

We can castrate rapists. My mother suggested that.
She thinks simply, and I like the idea.
But the damage is already done, and the next time
they can use a broken bottle, it's not sex they want.
So what's enough? what's enough?

Only
to gather,
to gather as our foremothers gathered.
Wild plants, berries, nuts—they were gatherers
they gathered together, their food, their sustenance
reeds for weaving baskets, feathers, raven and flamingo
dyes, ochre and vermilion,
they gathered flat stones for pounding
scooped stones for grinding, they gathered rocks, they gathered
shells and the meat of the shells—conch, mussel, clam, they
gathered wood for fire, they gathered clay from the riverbank
they kneaded the clay, they pinched and pressed it with their fingers
they shaped bowls and jars, they baked the vessels
in the coals of the fire, they gathered water, they gathered rain
they gathered honey, they gathered the stories of their mothers
their grandmothers, they gathered under moonlight
they danced, the feel of cool packed dirt under feet
they sang praises, they cried prayers.
When attacked, they knew how to gather their fingers into a fist
they could jab with sharpened sticks, they could hurl rock.
They gathered their strength, they gathered together
they gathered the blessings of the goddess, their faith
in the turning of the earth, the seasons bleeding into each other
        leaves crumbled into earth, earth
        sprouting water-green leaves

they gathered leaves, chickweed, comfrey, plantain, nettles
they worked together, they fought together
they fed, they bathed, they suckled their young,
they gathered stars into constellations
and their reflections into shallow bowls of water,
they gathered an acknowledged, familiar harmony
one I have never known, one I long for
long to gather
with all you women.

V.

Women, I want
to gather with you.
Our numbers are grand.
Our hands are capable, practised,
our minds know pattern, know
relationship, how the tree
pulls water up through root
through trunk, through branch, stem
into leaf, how the surface stomata release
water vapor into the air, the air cooled. We know
to honor trees. We know
the chrysalis, the grub, the earthworm.
We have handled baby poop and vomit
the incontinence of the old and sick.
We smell menses every month
from the time we are young girls.
We do not faint.
We do not titter
at mice.
We have handled horses, tractors
scalpels, saws.
We have handled money
and the lack of it
and we have survived

poverty, puerperal fever
forceps, scopolamine
footbinding, excision, infibulation
beatings, thorazine, diet pills
rape, witch burning, valium, chin lifts

female infanticide, child molestation
breast x-rays, suttee.

Some of us have died. Millions, millions
have been killed, murdered. We
mourn, we mourn
their courage, their innocence
their wisdom often lost to us.
We remember.
We are fierce
like a cornered animal.
Our fury spurts like geysers
like volcanoes, brilliant lava, molten gold
cascading in opulent plumes.

And every morning we gather eggs from the chickens
we milk the goat
or drive to the Safeway and push our cart
under fluorescent lights.
We feed our children.

We feed them blood from our womb
milk at our breast.
Our bodies create and nourish life.

We create. Alone
we are able to create.
Parthenogenesis. Two eggs unite. It happens.
It has always happened.
One woman, alone, can create life.
Think what all of us could do

if we gather
gather like the ocean gathers for the wave
the cloud gathers for the storm
the uterus gathers for contraction
the pushing out, the birth.

We can gather.
We can save our earth.
We can labor like we labored
to birth our babies,

laboring past thirst, past the rising and the setting of the sun
past distraction, past demands
past the need to pee, to cry, or even to live
into the consuming pain
        pain
pain beyond possibility,
until there is nothing but the
inevitable gathering
gathering, gathering
and
the new is born,
relief spreading through us
like the wave after cresting
spreads over sand in a shush of foam, grace
our saving grace.

VI.

NO touch bee
BITE my finger
my daughter explains to me
pulling back her hand from the wild radish blossoms
        buzzing with furry bees.

My child
with your neck still creased in slight folds
the tiny white hairs of your back stemming up your spine
fanning out over shoulders like a fern,
you *may* live
you *may,* you *may,* oh I want to believe it is possible
that you may live
to handle bees, pick miner's lettuce
eat black olives in the sun,
    to gather,
        with me
            with your daughters
                with all the world's life-sweet women,
                    our stunning harvest.

References

Abel, R. 1980. "Redirecting Social Studies of Law." *Law and Society Review* 14:805–29.

Abel, G., J. Becker, and J. Cunningham-Rather. 1984. *The Treatment of Child Molesters*. New York: New York State Psychiatric Institute.

Abel, G., J. Becker, and L. Skinner. 1980. "Aggressive Behavior and Sex." *Psychiatric Clinics of North America* 3:133–51.

———. 1983. "Treatment of the Violent Sex Offender." In L. Roth (ed.), *Clinical Treatment of the Violent Person*. Washington, DC: NIMH Monograph Series.

Abel, G., J. Mittelman, and J. Becker. 1983. "The Characteristics of Men Who Molest Young Children." Paper presented at the World Congress of Behavior Therapy, Washington, DC.

———. 1985. "Sex Offenders: Results of Assessment and Recommendations for Treatment." In H. Ben-Aron, S. Hucker, and C. Webster (eds.), *Clinical Criminology: Current Concepts*. Toronto: M & M Graphics.

Abel, G., J. Rouleau, and J. Cunningham-Rather. 1985. "Sexually Aggressive Behavior." In A. McGarry and S. Shah (eds.), *Modern Legal Psychiatry and Psychology*. Philadelphia: Davis.

Adams, A., and G. Abarbanel. 1988. *Sexual Assault on Campus: What Colleges Can Do*. Santa Monica, CA: Rape Treatment Center.

Ageton, S. 1983. *Sexual Assault Among Adolescents*. Lexington, MA: Lexington Books.

Albuquerque Tribune. 1984. "Blood Trail Ends: Brother Says He's Glad Wilder's Killing Is Over" (April 14):2.

Allgeier, E. 1986. "Coercive Versus Consensual Sexual Interactions." G. Stanley Hall Lecture at American Psychological Association Meeting, Washington, DC, August.

American Psychiatric Association. 1980. *Diagnostic and Statistical Manual of Mental Disorders*, third edition. Washington, DC: U.S. Department of Justice.

Amir, M. 1971. *Patterns in Forcible Rape*. Chicago: University of Chicago Press.

Athens, L. 1977. "Violent Crime: A Symbolic Interactionist Study." *Symbolic Interaction* 1:56–71.

Bachman, R., R. Paternoster, and S. Ward. 1992. "The Rationality of Sex Offending: Testing a Deterrence/Rational Choice Conception of Sexual Assault." *Law and Society Review* 26:343–72.

Baldwin, M. 1984. "The Sexuality of Inequality: The Minneapolis Pornography Ordinance." *Law and Inequality* 2:636.

Bard, M., and K. Ellison. 1974. "Crisis Intervention and Investigation of Rape." *Police Chief* 16:68–74.

Baron, L., and M. Straus. 1987. "Four Theories of Rape: A Macrosociological Perspective." *Social Problems* 34:467–89.

Barry, K., C. Bunch, and S. Castley (eds.). 1984. *International Feminism: Networking Against Female Sexual Slavery.* New York: International Women's Tribune Center.

Bart, P. 1975. "Rape Doesn't End With a Kiss." *Viva* 11:39–42, 100–1.

———. 1979. "Rape as a Paradigm of Sexism in Society—Victimization and Its Discontents." *Women's Studies International Quarterly* 2:347–57.

———. 1983. "Why Men Rape." *Western Sociological Review* 14:46–57.

———. 1986. "Pornography: Hating Women and Institutionalizing Dominance and Submission for Fun and Profit: Response to Alexis M. Durham III." *Justice Quarterly* 3:103–5.

Bart, P., and P. O'Brien. 1984. "Stopping Rape: Effective Avoidance Strategies." *Signs* 10:83–101.

———. 1985. *Stopping Rape: Successful Survival Strategies.* New York: Pergamon.

Bass, E. 1983. "Introduction: In the Truth Itself There Is Healing." In E. Bass and L. Thornton (eds.), *I Never Told Anyone: Writings by Survivors of Child Sexual Abuse.* New York: Harper and Row.

Bass, E., and L. Thornton (eds.). 1983. *I Never Told Anyone: Writings by Women Survivors of Child Sexual Abuse.* New York: Harper and Row.

Basuk, E. 1980. "A Crisis Theory Perspective on Rape." In S. McCombie (ed.), *The Rape Crisis Intervention Handbook.* New York: Plenum.

Bateman, P. 1982. *Acquaintance Rape: Awareness and Prevention.* Seattle: Alternatives to Fear.

Battelle Memorial Institute, Law and Justice Center. 1977. *Forcible Rape: A National Survey of the Responses by Prosecutors.* Washington, DC: U.S. Department of Justice.

Becker, J. 1985. "Behavioral Treatment of Sex Offenders." Workshop presented at the Massachusetts Department of Mental Health, Conference on Child Sexual Abuse, Boston.

Becker, J., and G. Abel. 1985. "Adolescent Sex Offenders: Issues in Research and Treatment." ADM85-1396, Washington DC: U.S. Department of Health and Human Services.

Becker, J., J. Cunningham-Rather, and M. Kaplan. 1986. "Adolescent Sexual Offenders: Demographics, Criminal and Sexual Histories, and Recommendations for Reducing Future Offenses." *Journal of Interpersonal Violence* 1:431–45.

Benard, C., and E. Schlaffer. 1984. "The Man in the Street: Why He Harasses." In A. Jaggar and P. Rothenberg (eds.), *Feminist Frameworks.* New York: McGraw-Hill.

Beneke, T. 1982. *Men on Rape.* New York: St. Martin's Press.

Berger, J. 1984. "Traits Shared by Mass Killers Remain Unknown to Experts." *New York Times* (August 27):1.

Berger, R., W. Neuman, and P. Searles. 1991. "The Social and Political Context of Rape Law Reform: An Aggregate Analysis." *Social Science Quarterly* 72: 221–38.

Berger, R., P. Searles, and C. Cottle. 1991. *Feminism and Pornography.* New York: Praeger.

Berger, R., P. Searles, and W. Neuman. 1988. "The Dimensions of Rape Reform Legislation." *Law and Society Review* 22:329–57.

Berger, R., P. Searles, R. Salem, and B. Pierce. 1986. "Sexual Assault in a College Community." *Sociological Focus* 19:1–26.

Berk, S., and D. Loseke. 1981. "Handling Family Violence: Situational Determinants of Police Arrest in Domestic Disturbances." *Law and Society Review* 15:315–46.

Berlin, F. 1983. "Sex Offenders: A Biomedical Perspective and a Status Report on Biomedical Treatment." In J. Greer and I. Stuart (eds.), *The Sexual Aggressor: Current Perspectives in Treatment.* New York: Van Nostrand Reinhold.

Biderman, A., et al. 1967. *Report on a Pilot Study in the District of Columbia on Victimization and Attitudes Toward Law Enforcement.* Washington, DC: U.S. Department of Justice.

Bienen, L. 1980. "Rape III—National Developments in Rape Reform Legislation." *Women's Rights Law Reporter* 6:170–213.

Bittner, E. 1967. "The Police on Skid-Row: A Study of Peace Keeping." *American Sociological Review* 32:699–715.

Black, D. 1970. "Production of Crime Rates." *American Sociological Review* 35:733–48.

———. 1983. "Crime as Social Control." *American Sociological Review* 48:34–45.

Blanchard, W. 1959. "The Group Process in Gang Rape." *Journal of Social Psychology* 49:259–66.

Block, R., and W. Skogan. 1986. "Resistance and Nonfatal Outcomes in Stranger-to-Stranger Predatory Crime." *Violence and Victims* 1:241–53.

Blumberg, R. 1979. "A Paradigm for Predicting the Position of Women: Policy Implications and Problems." In J. Lipman-Blumen and J. Bernard (eds.), *Sex Roles and Social Policy.* London: Sage Studies in International Sociology.

Bogal-Allbritten, R., and W. Allbritten. 1985. "The Hidden Victims: Courtship Violence Among College Students." *Journal of College Student Personnel* 43:201–4.

Bohmer, C. 1974. "Judicial Attitudes Toward Rape Victims." *Judicature* 57: 303–7.

Bohrnstedt, G. 1969. "Conservatism, Authoritarianism and Religiosity of Fraternity Pledges." *Journal of College Student Personnel* 27:36–43.

Boland, B., C. Conly, P. Mahanna, L. Warner, and R. Sones. 1990. *The Prosecution of Felony Arrests, 1987.* Washington, DC: Bureau of Justice Statistics, U.S. Department of Justice.

Boles, J. 1979. "Systematic Factors Underlying Legislative Responses to Woman Suffrage and the Equal Rights Amendment." *Women and Politics* 2:5–22.

Bonavoglia, A. 1992. "The Sacred Secret." *Ms.* (March-April):40–45.

Boostrom, R., and J. Henderson. 1983. "Community Action and Crime Prevention: Some Unresolved Issues." *Crime and Social Justice* 19:24–30.

Bowker, L. (ed.). 1981. *Women and Crime in America.* New York: Macmillan.

Boxall, B. 1989. "Prostitutes: Easy Prey for Killers." *Los Angeles Times* (March 21):1, 23.

Bradford, M. 1986. "Tight Market Dries Up Nightlife at University." *Business Insurance* (March 2):2, 6.

Brecher, E. 1978. *Treatment Programs for Sex Offenders.* Washington, DC: U.S. Department of Justice.

Briere, J., S. Corne, M. Runtz, and N. Malamuth. 1984. "The Rape Arousal Inventory: Predicting Actual and Potential Sexual Aggression in a University Population." Paper presented at meeting of the American Psychological Association.

Broude, G., and S. Greene. 1976. "Cross-Cultural Codes on Twenty Sexual Attitudes and Practices." *Ethnology* 15:409–28.

Brownmiller, S. 1975. *Against Our Will: Men, Women, and Rape.* New York: Simon and Schuster.

Buchwald, E., P. Fletcher, and M. Roth (eds.). 1993. *Transforming a Rape Culture.* Minneapolis: Milkweed Editions.

Bureau of Justice Statistics. 1984. *Criminal Victimization in the United States, 1982.* Washington, DC: U.S. Department of Justice.

Burgess, A., and L. Holmstrom. 1974. "Rape Trauma Syndrome." *American Journal of Psychiatry* 131:981–86.

———. 1976. "Coping Behavior of the Rape Victim." *American Journal of Psychiatry* 133:413–18.

———. 1979. *Rape Crisis and Recovery.* Bowie, MD: Robert Brady.

Burgess, A., A. Groth, and M. McCausland. 1981. "Child Sex Initiation Rings." *American Journal of Orthopsychiatry* 51:110–19.

Burkhart, B., 1989. Comments in Seminar on Acquaintance/Date Rape Prevention: A National Video Teleconference (February 2).

Burkhart, B., and A. Stanton. 1985. "Sexual Aggression in Acquaintance Relationships." In G. Russell (ed.), *Violence in Intimate Relationships.* Englewood Cliffs, NJ: Spectrum.

Burnham, J. 1968. "New Perspectives on the Prohibition 'Experiment' of the 1920s." *Journal of Social History* 2:51–68.

Burris, V. 1983. "Who Opposed the ERA? An Analysis of the Social Bases of Antifeminism." *Social Science Quarterly* 64:307–17.

Burstyn, V. (ed). 1985. *Women Against Censorship.* Vancouver: Douglas and McIntyre.

Burt, M. 1980. "Cultural Myths and Supports for Rape." *Journal of Personality and Social Psychology* 38:217–30.

Butler, S. 1978. *Conspiracy of Silence: The Trauma of Incest.* New York: Bantam.

Byington, D., and K. Keeter. 1988. "Assessing Needs of Sexual Assault Victims on a University Campus." In *Student Services: Responding to Issues and Challenges.* Chapel Hill: University of North Carolina Press.

Caignon, D., and G. Groves (eds.). 1987. *Her Wits About Her: Self-Defense Success Stories by Women.* New York: Harper and Row.

Caldicott, H. 1981. *Nuclear Madness.* New York: Bantam.

Call, J., D. Nice, and S. Talarico. 1991. "An Analysis of State Rape Shield Laws." *Social Science Quarterly* 72:774–88.

Cameron, D. 1988. "That's Entertainment? Jack the Ripper and the Celebration of Sexual Violence." *Trouble and Strife* 13:17–19.

Cameron, D., and E. Frazer. 1987. *The Lust to Kill: A Feminist Investigation of Sexual Murder.* New York: New York University Press.

Caputi, J. 1987. *The Age of Sex Crime.* Bowling Green, OH: Bowling Green State University Press.

———. 1989. "Stranger than Fiction." Review of *Waverly Place. Women's Review of Books* 6(May):10–11.

Caringella-MacDonald, S. 1984. "Sexual Assault Prosecution: An Examination of Model Rape Legislation in Michigan." *Women and Politics* 4:65–82.

———. 1985. "The Comparability in Sexual and Nonsexual Assault Case Treatment: Did Statute Change Meet the Objective?" *Crime and Delinquency* 31:206–22.

———. 1988. "Marxist and Feminist Interpretations on the Aftermath of Rape Reforms." *Contemporary Crises* 12:125–44.

Carmen, E., P. Rieker, and T. Mills. 1984. "Victims of Violence and Psychiatric Illness." *American Journal of Psychiatry* 141:378–83.

Carnes, P. 1983. *The Sexual Addiction.* Minneapolis: CompCare.

Centers for Disease Control. 1985. "Adolescent Sex Offenders—Vermont, 1984." *Morbidity and Mortality Weekly Report* 34:738–41.

Chadbourn, J. 1931. "Plan for Survey of Lynching and the Judicial Process." *North Carolina Law Review* 9:330–36.

Champion, C. 1986. "Clinical Perspectives on the Relationship Between Pornography and Sexual Violence." *Law and Inequality* 4:22–27.

Chancer, L. 1987. "New Bedford, Massachusetts, March 6, 1983–March 22, 1984: The 'Before and After' of a Group Rape." *Gender and Society* 1:239–60.

Chandler, S., and M. Torney. 1981. "The Decision and the Processing of Rape Victims Through the Criminal Justice System." *California Sociologist* 4:155–69.

Chappell, D. 1984. "The Impact of Rape Legislation Reform: Some Comparative Trends." *International Journal of Women's Studies* 7:70–80.

Chappell, D., and S. Singer. 1977. "Rape in New York City: A Study of Material in the Police Files and Its Meaning." In D. Chappell, R. Geis, and G. Geis (eds.), *Forcible Rape: The Crime, the Victim, and the Offender.* New York: Columbia University Press.

Clark, L., and D. Lewis. 1977. *Rape: The Price of Coercive Sexuality.* Toronto: Canadian Women's Educational Press.

Cleaver, E. 1970. *Soul on Ice.* London: Panther Books.

Cling, B. 1988. "Rape Trauma Syndrome: Medical Evidence of Non-Consent." *Women's Rights Law Reporter* 10:243–59.

Cohen, P. 1984. "Resistance During Sexual Assaults: Avoiding Rape and Injury." *Victimology* 9:120–29.

Cohn, E. S., L. Kidder, and J. Harvey. 1981. "Criminal Prevention vs. Victimization Prevention: The Psychology of Different Reactions." *Victimology* 3:285–96.

Columbus Citizen-Journal. 1983. "Judge Faces Recall." In L. Richardson and V. Taylor (eds.), *Feminist Frontiers: Rethinking Sex, Gender, and Society.* Reading, MA: Addison-Wesley.

Commission on Obscenity and Pornography. 1970. *The Report of the Commission on Obscenity and Pornography.* New York: Bantam Books.

Conklin, M. 1992. "Sins of Our Fathers." *Isthmus* 17 (November 13–19):1, 8–11.

Connell, N., and C. Wilson (eds.). 1974. *Rape: The First Sourcebook for Women.* New York: New American Library.

Costain, A. 1988. "Representing Women: The Transition from Social Movement to Interest Group." In E. Boneparth and E. Stoper (eds.), *Women, Power and Policy: Toward the Year 2000.* New York: Pergamon.

Curtis, L. 1974. *Criminal Violence: National Patterns and Behavior.* Lexington, MA: Lexington Books.

Daly, M. 1973. *Beyond God the Father: Toward a Philosophy of Women's Liberation.* Boston: Beacon Press.

_____. 1978. *Gyn/Ecology.* Boston: Beacon Press.

Davis, A. 1981. *Women, Race and Class.* New York: Random House.

Davis, R., V. Russell, and F. Kunreuther. 1980. *The Role of the Complaining Witness in an Urban Criminal Court.* New York: Vera Institute of Justice.

Delacoste, F., and F. Newman (eds.). 1981. *Fight Back: Feminist Resistance to Male Violence.* Minneapolis: Cleis Press.

Diamond, I. 1980. "Pornography and Repression: A Reconsideration." In C. Stimpson and E. Person (eds.), *Women: Sex and Sexuality.* Chicago: University of Chicago Press.

Dietz, P., and B. Evans. 1982. "Pornographic Imagery and Prevalence of Paraphilia." *American Journal of Psychiatry* 139:1493–95.

Dobash, R., and R. Dobash. 1979. *Violence Against Wives.* New York: Free Press.

Donnerstein, E. 1984. "Pornography: Its Effects on Violence Against Women." In N. Malamuth and E. Donnerstein (eds.), *Pornography and Sexual Aggression.* New York: Academic Press.

————. 1986. "Pornography and the First Amendment: What Does the Social Science Research Say?" *Law and Inequality* 4:17–22.

Dworkin, A. 1981. *Pornography: Men Possessing Women.* New York: Perigee.

————. 1984. "Pornography: The New Terrorism." Lecture presented at the conference "Pornography: Through the Eyes of Women." Madison, WI.

————. 1985. "Against the Male Flood: Censorship, Pornography, and Equality." *Harvard Women's Law Journal* 8:1–30.

Earls, C., and W. Marshall. 1983. "The Current State of Technology in the Laboratory Assessment of Sexual Arousal Patterns." In J. Greer and I. Stuart (eds.), *The Sexual Aggressor: Current Perspectives in Treatment.* New York: Van Nostrand Reinhold.

Edwards, S. 1981. *Female Sexuality and the Law.* Oxford: Martin Robertson.

Egger, S. 1984. "A Working Definition of Serial Murder and the Reduction of Linkage Blindness." *Journal of Police Science and Administration* 12:348–57.

Ehrhart, J., and B. Sandler. 1985. *Campus Gang Rape: Party Games?* Washington, DC: Association of American Colleges.

Eigenberg, H. 1990. "The National Crime Survey and Rape: The Case of the Missing Question." *Justice Quarterly* 7:655–71.

Einsiedel, E. 1986. "Social Science Report." Prepared for the Attorney General's Commission on Pornography, U.S. Department of Justice, Washington, DC.

Ellis, E. 1983. "A Review of Empirical Rape Research: Victim Reactions and Response to Treatment." *Clinical Psychology Review* 3:473–90.

Emerson, R. 1969. *Judging Delinquents: Context and Process in Juvenile Court.* Chicago: Aldine.

Emerson, R., and B. Paley. 1992. "Organizational Horizons and Complaint-Filing." In K. Hawkins (ed.), *The Uses of Discretion.* Oxford: Oxford University Press.

Estrich, S. 1987. *Real Rape.* Cambridge: Harvard University Press.

Farr, K. 1988. "Dominance Bonding Through the Good Old Boys Sociability Network." *Sex Roles* 18:259–77.

Federal Bureau of Investigation. 1986–1987. *Uniform Crime Reports.* Washington DC: U.S. Government Printing Office.

Feild, H., and L. Beinen. 1980. *Jurors and Rape: A Study in Psychology and Law.* Lexington, MA: Lexington Books.

Field, M. 1983. "Rape: Legal Aspects." In S. Kadish (ed.), *Encyclopedia of Crime and Justice,* Volume 4. New York: Free Press.

Fine, B. 1989. "The Politics of Research and Activism: Violence Against Women." *Gender and Society* 3:549–58.

Finkelhor, D. 1979. *Sexually Victimized Children.* New York: Free Press.

Finkelhor, D., and I. Lewis. 1987. "An Epidemiologic Approach to the Study of Child Molestation." Paper presented to the New York Academy of Sciences.

Finkelhor, D., and K. Yllo. 1985. *License to Rape: Sexual Abuse of Wives.* New York: Holt, Rinehart, and Winston.

Fisher, G., and E. Rivlin. 1971. "Psychological Needs of Rapists." *British Journal of Criminology* 11:182–85.

Florida Flambeau. 1988. "Pike Members Indicted in Rape" (May 19):1, 5.

Fonow, M., L. Richardson, and V. Wemmerus. 1992. "Feminist Rape Education: Does It Work?" *Gender and Society* 6:108–21.

Forman, B. 1980. "Psychotherapy with Rape Victims." *Psychotherapy: Theory, Research, and Practice* 17:304–11.

Fox, E., C. Hodge, and W. Ward. 1987. "A Comparison of Attitudes Held by Black and White Fraternity Members." *Journal of Negro Education* 56:521–34.

Fox, S., and D. Scherl. 1972. "Crisis Intervention with Victims of Rape." *Social Work* 17:37–42.

Freeman, J. 1975. *The Politics of Women's Liberation.* New York: David McKay.

Freud, S. 1973. "Femininity: New Introductory Lectures on Psychoanalysis." In *The Complete Works.* London: Edn. Hogarth.

Freund, K., C. McKnight, R. Langevin, and S. Cibiri. 1972. "The Female Child as a Surrogate Object." *Archives of Sexual Behavior* 2:119–33.

Frieze, I. 1980. "Causes and Consequences of Marital Rape." Paper presented at conference of American Psychological Association, Montreal.

Gagnon, J., and W. Simon. 1974. *Sexual Conduct.* London: Hutchinson.

Galvin, J., and K. Polk. 1983. "Attrition in Rape Case Processing: Is Rape Unique?" *Journal of Research in Crime and Delinquency* 20:126–56.

Garfinkel, H. 1984. *Studies in Ethnomethodology.* Cambridge, England: Polity Press.

Gebhard, P., J. Gagnon, W. Pomeroy, and C. Christenson. 1965. *Sex Offenders: An Analysis of Types.* New York: Harper and Row.

Geis, G. 1971. "Group Sexual Assaults." *Medical Aspects of Human Sexuality* 5:101–13.

Gelman, D. 1993. "Mixed Messages." *Newsweek* (April 12):28–29.

George, L., I. Winfield, and D. Blazer. 1992. "Sociocultural Factors in Sexual Assault: Comparison of Two Representative Samples of Women." *Journal of Social Issues* 48:105–25.

Gershel, M. 1985. "Evaluating a Proposed Civil Rights Approach to Pornography: Legal Analysis as if Women Mattered." *William Mitchel Law Review* 11:41.

Giaretto, H. 1982. *Integrated Treatment of Child Sexual Abuse.* Palo Alto, CA: Science and Behavior Books.

Gibson, L., R. Linden, and S. Johnson. 1980. "A Situational Theory of Rape." *Canadian Journal of Criminology* 22:51–65.

Glaser, B. 1978. *Theoretical Sensitivity: Advances in the Methodology of Grounded Theory.* Mill Valley, CA: Sociology Press.

Glaser, B., and A. Strauss. 1967. *The Discovery of Grounded Theory.* Chicago: Aldine.

Goldberg-Ambrose, C. 1992. "Unfinished Business in Rape Law Reform." *Journal of Social Issues* 48:173–85.

Goldstein, M., H. Kant, and J. Hartman. 1974. *Pornography and Sexual Deviance.* Berkeley: University of California Press.

Goodchilds, J., and G. Zellman. 1984. "Sexual Signaling and Sexual Aggression in Adolescent Relationships." In N. Malamuth and E. Donnerstein (eds.), *Pornography and Sexual Aggression.* New York: Academic Press.

Goodwin, J. 1986. "Post-Traumatic Symptoms in Incest Victims." In R. Pynoos and S. Eth (eds.), *Post-Traumatic Syndromes in Children.* Washington, DC: American Psychiatric Press.

Grant, J. 1988a. "Who's Killing Us? Part One." *Sojourner: The Women's Forum* (June):20–21.

———. 1988b. "Who's Killing Us? Part Two." *Sojourner: The Women's Forum* (July):16–18.

Greely, A., and W. McReady. 1980. *Ethnic Drinking Subcultures.* New York: Praeger.

Green, A. 1983. "Child Abuse: Dimensions of Psychological Trauma in Abused Children." *Journal of the Academy of Child Psychiatry* 22:231–37.

Greer, G. 1970. *The Female Eunuch.* London: Paladin.

Griffen, B., and C. Griffen. 1981. "Victims in Rape Confrontation." *Victimology* 6:59–75.

Griffin, S. 1971. "Rape: The All-American Crime." *Ramparts* 10:26–35.

———. 1979. *Rape: The Power of Consciousness.* New York: Harper and Row.

———. 1981. *Pornography and Silence: Culture's Revenge Against Nature.* New York: Harper and Row.

———. 1983. "Rape: The All-American Crime." In *Made from the Earth: An Anthology of Writings.* New York: Harper and Row.

Groth, A. 1979. *Men Who Rape: The Psychology of the Offender.* New York: Plenum Press.

Groth, A., and W. Hobson. 1983. "The Dynamics of Sexual Assault." In L. Schlesinger and E. Revitch (eds.), *Sexual Dynamics of Anti-Social Behavior.* Springfield, IL: Charles Thomas.

Groth, A., W. Hobson, and T. Gary. 1982. "The Child Molester: Clinical Observations." In J. Conte and D. Shore (eds.), *Social Work and Child Sexual Abuse.* New York: Haworth.

Groth, A., R. Longo, and J. McFadin. 1982. "Undetected Recidivism Among Rapists and Child Molesters." *Crime and Delinquency* 28:102–6.

Haggard, H., and E. Jellinek. 1942. *Alcohol Explored.* New York: Doubleday.

Hammer, E., and I. Jacks. 1955. "A Study of Rorschack Flexnor and Extensor Human Movements." *Journal of Clinical Psychology* 11:63–67.

Handler, J. 1978. *Social Movements and the Legal System: A Theory of Law Reform and Social Change.* New York: Academic Press.

Hanley, R. 1993. "Four Are Convicted of Sexual Abuse of Retarded New Jersey Woman." *New York Times* (March 17):A1, B4.

Harlow, C. 1991. *Female Victims of Violent Crime.* Washington, DC: U.S. Department of Justice.

Harney, P., and C. Muehlenhard. 1991. "Factors That Increase the Likelihood of Victimization." In A. Parrot and L. Bechhofer (eds.), *Acquaintance Rape: The Hidden Crime.* New York: Wiley.

Hazelwood, R., and J. Harpold. 1986. "Rape: The Dangers of Providing Confrontational Advice." *FBI Law Enforcement Bulletin* (June):1–5.

Heise, L. 1989. "The Global War Against Women." *Washington Post* (April 9):B1.

Henn, F. 1978. "The Aggressive Sexual Offender." In I. Kutash, S. Kutash, and S. Schlesinger (eds.), *Violence: Perspectives on Murder and Aggression.* San Francisco: Jossey-Bass.

Hepburn, J. 1978. "Race and the Decision to Arrest." *Journal of Research in Crime and Delinquency* 15:54–73.

Herman, D. 1984. "The Rape Culture." In J. Freeman (ed.), *Women: A Feminist Perspective.* Palo Alto: Mayfield.

Herman, J. 1981. *Father-Daughter Incest.* Cambridge: Harvard University Press.

Herschberger, R. 1970. *Adam's Rib.* New York: Harper and Row.

Hilberman, E. 1976. *The Rape Victim.* Washington, DC: American Psychiatric Association.

Hill, D. 1981. "Political Culture and Female Political Representation." *Journal of Politics* 43:159–68.

Hirschi, T. 1969. *Causes of Delinquency.* Berkeley: University of California Press.

Hoebel, E. 1954. *The Law of Primitive Man.* Boston: Harvard University Press.

Holloway, W. 1981. "'I Just Wanted to Kill a Woman.' Why? The Ripper and Male Sexuality." *Feminist Review* 9:33–40.

Holmstrom, L., and A. Burgess. 1978. *The Victim of Rape: Institutional Reactions.* New York: Wiley-Interscience.

――――. 1983. *The Victim of Rape: Institutional Reactions.* New Brunswick, NJ: Transaction Books.

Hood, J. 1989. "Why Our Society Is Rape-Prone." *New York Times* (May 16).

hooks, b. 1984. *Feminist Theory: From Margin to Center.* Boston: South End Press.

Horney, J., and C. Spohn. 1991. "Rape Law Reform and Instrumental Change in Six Jurisdictions." *Law and Society Review* 25:117–53.

Horowitz, M. 1976. *Stress Response Syndromes.* New York: Jason Aronson.

Hughes, M., and R. Winston. 1987. "Effects of Fraternity Membership on Interpersonal Values." *Journal of College Student Personnel* 45:405–11.

Jackson, S. 1978. "The Social Context of Rape: Sexual Scripts and Motivation." *Women's Studies International Quarterly* 1:27–38.

Jensen, G., and M. Karpos. 1993. "Managing Rape: Exploratory Research on the Behavior of Rape Statistics." *Criminology* 31:363–84.

Johnson, A. 1980. "On the Prevalence of Rape in the United States." *Signs* 6:136–46.

Jones, J., and T. Wood. 1989. "Sheriff's Deputy Held in Prostitute's Killings." *Los Angeles Times* (February 25):1.

Justice, B., and R. Justice. 1979. *The Broken Taboo.* New York: Human Sciences Press.

Kalvin, H., and H. Zeisel. 1966. *The American Jury.* Boston: Little, Brown.

Kanin, E. 1957. "Male Aggression in Dating-Courtship Relations." *American Journal of Sociology* 63:197–204.

――――. 1965. "Male Sex Aggression and Three Psychiatric Hypotheses." *Journal of Sex Research* 1:227–29.

――――. 1967. "Reference Groups and Sex Conduct Norm Violations." *Sociological Quarterly* 8:495–504.

――――. 1969. "Selected Dyadic Aspects of Male Sex Aggression." *Journal of Sex Research* 5:12–28.

Kanin, E., and S. Parcell. 1977. "Sexual Aggression: A Second Look at the Offended Female." *Archives of Sexual Behavior* 6:67–76.

Kantrowitz, B. 1991. "Naming Names." *Newsweek* (April 29):26–32.

Karacon, I., R. Williams, and M. Guerraro. 1974. "Nocturnal Penile Tumescence and Sleep of Convicted Rapists and Other Prisoners." *Archives of Sexual Behavior* 3:19–26.

Karmen, A. 1982. "Women Victims of Crime: Introduction." In B. Price and N. Sokoloff (eds.), *The Criminal Justice System and Women: Women Offenders, Victims, Workers.* New York: Clark Boardman.

Kasinsky, R. 1975. "Rape: A Normal Act?" *Canadian Forum* (September):18–22.

Katz, S., and M. Mazur. 1979. *Understanding the Rape Victim: A Synthesis of Research Findings.* New York: Wiley.

Kaufman, J., and E. Zigler. 1987. "Do Abused Children Become Abusive Parents?" *American Journal of Orthopsychiatry* 57:186–92.

Kelly, L. 1987. "The Continuum of Sexual Violence." In J. Hanmer and M. Maynard (eds.), *Women, Violence and Social Control*. Atlantic Highlands, NJ: Humanities International Press.

———. 1988. *Surviving Sexual Violence*. Minneapolis: University of Minnesota Press.

Kempe, R., and C. Kempe. 1978. *Child Abuse*. Cambridge: Harvard University Press.

Kerstetter, W. 1990. "Gateway to Justice: Police and Prosecutorial Response to Sexual Assaults Against Women." *Journal of Criminal Law and Criminology* 81:267–313.

Kerstetter, W., and B. Van Winkle. 1990. "Who Decides? A Study of the Complainant's Decision to Prosecute in Rape Cases." *Criminal Justice and Behavior* 17:268–83.

Kidder, L., J. Boell, and M. Moyer. 1983. "Rights Consciousness and Victimization Prevention: Personal Defense and Assertiveness Training." *Journal of Social Issues* 39:155–70.

Kidder, R. 1983. *Connecting Law and Society: An Introduction to Research and Theory*. Englewood Cliffs, NJ: Prentice-Hall.

Kilpatrick, D., L. Veronen, and C. Best. 1984. "Factors Predicting Psychological Distress Among Rape Victims." In C. Figley (ed.), *Trauma and Its Wake: The Study and Treatment of Post–Traumatic Stress Disorder*. New York: Brunner/Mazel.

Kilpatrick, D., et al. 1985. "Mental Health Correlates of Criminal Victimization: A Random Community Survey." *Journal of Consulting and Clinical Psychology* 53:866–73.

Kimmel, M. (ed.). 1987. *Changing Men: New Directions in Research on Men and Masculinity*. Newbury Park, CA: Sage.

King, H., and C. Webb. 1981. "Rape Crisis Centers: Progress and Problems." *Journal of Social Issues* 37:93–103.

Kirkpatrick, C., and E. Kanin. 1957. "Male Sex Aggression on a University Campus." *American Sociological Review* 22:52–58.

Kirshenbaum, J. 1989. "Special Report, An American Disgrace: A Violent and Unprecedented Lawlessness Has Arisen Among College Athletes in All Parts of the Country." *Sports Illustrated* (February 27):16–19.

Kleck, G., and S. Sayles. 1990. "Rape and Resistance." *Social Problems* 37:149–62.

Klein, D. 1981. "Violence Against Women: Some Considerations Regarding Its Causes and Its Elimination." *Crime and Delinquency* 27:64–80.

Knight, R., R. Rosenberg, and B. Schneider. 1985. "Classification of Sex Offenders: Perspectives, Methods, and Validation." In A. Burgess (ed.), *Rape and Sexual Assault: A Research Handbook*. New York: Garland.

Knopp, F. (ed.). 1982. *Remedial Intervention in Adolescent Sex Offenses: Nine Program Descriptions*. Syracuse, NY: Safe Society Press.

———. 1984. *Retraining Adult Sex Offenders: Methods and Models*. Syracuse, NY: Safe Society Press.

Kollias, K. 1979. "Class Realities: Create a New Power Base." In E. Shapiro and B. Shapiro (eds.), *The Women Say, The Men Say: Women's Liberation and Men's Consciousness*. New York: Dell.

Koss, M. 1985. "The Hidden Rape Victim: Personality, Attitudinal, and Situational Characteristics." *Psychology of Women Quarterly* 9:193–212.

Koss, M., and B. Burkhart. 1986. "Clinical Treatment of Rape." Unpublished manuscript.

Koss, M., and C. Gidycz. 1985. "Sexual Experiences Survey: Reliability and Validity." *Journal of Consulting and Clinical Psychology* 53:422–23.

Koss, M., and M. Harvey. 1991. *The Rape Victim: Clinical and Community Interventions,* second edition. Newbury Park, CA: Sage.

Koss, M., and K. Leonard. 1984. "Sexually Aggressive Men: Empirical Findings and Theoretical Implications." In N. Malamuth and E. Donnerstein (eds.), *Pornography and Sexual Aggression.* New York: Academic Press.

Koss, M., and C. Oros. 1982. "Sexual Experiences Survey: A Research Instrument Investigating Sexual Aggression and Victimization." *Journal of Consulting and Clinical Psychology* 50:455–57.

Koss, M., C. Gidycz, and N. Wisniewski. 1987. "The Scope of Rape: Incidence and Prevalence of Sexual Aggression in a National Sample of Higher Education Students." *Journal of Consulting and Clinical Psychology* 55: 162–70.

Koss, M., K. Leonard, D. Beezley, and C. Oros. 1985. "Nonstranger Sexual Aggression: A Discriminant Analysis of the Psychological Characteristics of Undetected Offenders." *Sex Roles* 12:981–92.

Lacy, S. 1982–1983. "In Mourning and in Rage." *Ikon* (Fall-Winter):60–67.

LaFree, G. 1980a. "The Effect of Social Stratification by Race on Official Reactions to Rape." *American Sociological Review* 45:842–54.

———. 1980b. "Variables Affecting Guilty Pleas and Convictions in Rape Cases." *Social Forces* 58:833–50.

———. 1981. "Official Reactions to Social Problems: Police Decisions in Sexual Assault Cases." *Social Problems* 28:582–94.

———. 1982. "Male Power and Female Victimization: Towards a Theory of Interracial Rape." *American Journal of Sociology* 88:311–28.

———. 1989. *Rape and Criminal Justice: The Social Construction of Sexual Assault.* Belmont, CA: Wadsworth.

LaFree, G., B. Riskin, and C. Visher. 1985. "Jurors' Response to Victims' Behavior and Legal Issues in Sexual Assault Trials." *Social Problems* 32:389–407.

Lamar, J. 1989. "'I Deserve Punishment.'" *Time* (February 6):34.

Largen, M. 1988. "Rape-Law Reform: An Analysis." In A. Burgess (ed.), *Rape and Sexual Assault II: A Research Handbook.* New York: Garland.

Larsen, R. 1980. *Bundy: The Deliberate Stranger.* Englewood Cliffs, NJ: Prentice-Hall.

Laszlo, A., A. Burgess, and C. Grant. 1991. "HIV Counseling Issues and Victims of Sexual Assault." In A. Burgess (ed.), *Rape and Sexual Assault III: A Research Handbook.* New York: Garland.

Law Enforcement Assistance Administration. 1974. *Crimes and Victims: A Report on the Dayton–San Jose Pilot Survey of Victimization.* Washington, DC: National Criminal Justice Information and Statistics Service.

———. 1975. *Criminal Victimization Surveys in 13 American Cities.* Washington, DC: U.S. Government Printing Office.

Laws, D., and J. O'Neil. 1981. "Variations on Masturbatory Conditioning." *Behavioral Psychotherapy* 9:111–36.

Laws, D., and C. Osborne. 1983. "How to Build and Operate a Behavioral Laboratory to Evaluate and Treat Sexual Deviance." In J. Greer and I. Stuart (eds.), *The Sexual Aggressor: Current Perspectives on Treatment.* New York: Van Nostrand Reinhold.

Lawson, K. 1984. "Sex Crimes: Revised." *Illinois Issues* 6 (February):6–11.

Lederer, L. (ed.). 1980. *Take Back the Night: Women on Pornography.* New York: William Morrow.

Leidholdt, D., and D. Russell (eds.). Forthcoming. *No Safe Place for Women: Feminists on Pornography.* Oxford: Pergamon.

Lemire, D. 1979. "One Investigation of the Stereotypes Associated with Fraternities and Sororities." *Journal of College Student Personnel* 37:54–57.

Lender, M., and J. Martin. 1982. *Drinking in America.* New York: Free Press.

Leo, J. 1989. "Crime: That's Entertainment." *U.S. News and World Report* (February 6):53.

Letchworth, G. 1969. "Fraternities Now and in the Future." *Journal of College Student Personnel* 10:118–22.

Levy, B. (ed.). 1991. *Dating Violence: Young Women in Danger.* Seattle: Seal Press.

Lewis, H. 1976. *Psychic War in Men and Women.* New York: New York University Press.

Lindemann, E. 1944. "Symptomatology and Management of Acute Grief." *American Journal of Psychiatry* 101:141–46.

Lindsey, R. 1984. "Officials Cite Rise in Killers Who Roam U.S. for Victims." *New York Times* (January 21):1.

Lisak, D. 1991. "Sexual Aggression, Masculinity, and Fathers." *Signs* 16: 238–62.

Lisak, D., and S. Roth. 1990. "Motives and Psychodynamics of Self-Reported, Unincarcerated Rapists." *Journal of Orthopsychiatry* 60:268–80.

Lizotte, A. 1985. "The Uniqueness of Rape: Reporting Assaultive Violence to the Police." *Crime and Delinquency* 31:169–90.

_____. 1986. "Determinants of Completing Rape and Assault." *Journal of Quantitative Criminology* 2:203–17.

Llewellyn, K., and E. Hoebel. 1941. *The Cheyenne Way: Conflict and Case Law in Primitive Jurisprudence.* Norman: University of Oklahoma Press.

Loh, W. 1980. "The Impact of Common Law and Reform Rape Statutes on Prosecution: An Empirical Study." *Washington Law Review* 55:543–652.

_____. 1981. "Q: What Has Reform of Rape Legislation Wrought? A: Truth in Criminal Labeling." *Journal of Social Issues* 37:28–52.

Longino, C., and C. Kart. 1973. "The College Fraternity: An Assessment of Theory and Research." *Journal of College Student Personnel* 31:118–25.

Longino, H. 1980. "What Is Pornography?" In L. Lederer (ed.), *Take Back the Night.* New York: William Morrow.

Lovelace, L. 1980. *Ordeal.* New York: Berkeley Books.

Luckenbill, D. 1977. "Criminal Homicide as a Situated Transaction." *Social Problems* 25:176–87.

Lundberg-Love, P., and R. Geffner. 1989. "Date Rape: Prevalence, Risk Factors, and a Proposed Model." In M. Pirog-Good and J. Stets (eds.), *Violence in Dating Relationships: Emerging Social Issues.* New York: Praeger.

Lutheran Social Services of Minnesota. 1982. "Personal Socio-Awareness Program." In F. Knopp (ed.), *Remedial Intervention in Adolescent Sex Offenses: Nine Program Descriptions.* Syracuse, NY: Safe Society Press.

MacIntyre, K. 1981. "The Role of Mothers in Father-Daughter Incest: A Feminist Analysis." *Social Work* 26:462–66.

MacKinnon, C. 1982. "Feminism, Marxism, Method, and the State: An Agenda for Theory." *Signs* 7:515–44.

———. 1983. "Feminism, Marxism, Method, and the State: Toward Feminist Jurisprudence." *Signs* 8:635–58.

———. 1986. "Pornography as Sex Discrimination." *Law and Inequality* 4:38–49.

———. 1993. "Turning Rape into Pornography: Postmodern Genocide." *Ms.* (July-August):24–30.

MacKinnon, C., and A. Dworkin. 1984. *City Council General Ordinance No. 35*, Indianapolis, IN.

MacPherson, M. 1989. "The Roots of Evil." *Vanity Fair* (May):140–48, 188–98.

Malamuth, N. 1981. "Rape Proclivity Among Males." *Journal of Social Issues* 37:138–57.

———. 1984. "Aggression Against Women: Cultural and Individual Causes." In N. Malamuth and E. Donnerstein (eds.), *Pornography and Sexual Aggression*. New York: Academic Press.

———. 1985. "The Mass Media and Aggression Against Women: Research Findings and Prevention." In A. Burgess (ed.), *Rape and Sexual Assault: A Research Handbook*. New York: Garland.

Malamuth, N., and E. Donnerstein. 1982. "The Effects of Aggressive-Pornographic Mass Media Stimuli." In L. Berkowitz (ed.), *Advances in Experimental Social Psychology*, Volume 15. New York: Academic Press.

Malamuth, N., and E. Donnerstein (eds.). 1984. *Pornography and Sexual Aggression*. Orlando, FL: Academic Press.

Malamuth, N., S. Haber, and S. Feshback. 1980. "Testing Hypotheses Regarding Rape: Exposure to Sexual Violence, Sex Difference, and the 'Normality' of Rapists." *Journal of Research in Personality* 14:121–37.

Malamuth, N., M. Heim, and S. Feshback. 1980. "Sexual Responsiveness of College Students to Rape Depictions: Inhibitory and Disinhibitory Effects." *Social Psychology* 38:399–408.

Malcolm, A. 1989. "New Efforts Developing Against the Hate Crime." *New York Times* (May 12):A12.

Mann, C. 1993. *Unequal Justice: A Question of Color.* Bloomington: Indiana University Press.

Marlowe, A., and D. Auvenshine. 1982. "Greek Membership: Its Impact on the Moral Development of College Freshmen." *Journal of College Student Personnel* 40:53–57.

Marsh, J., A. Geist, and N. Caplan. 1982. *Rape and the Limits of Law Reform*. Boston: Auburn House.

Martin, D. 1976. *Battered Wives*. San Francisco: Glide Publications.

Martin, P., and B. Turner. 1986. "Grounded Theory and Organizational Research." *Journal of Applied Behavioral Science* 22:141–57.

Mather, L. 1979. *Plea Bargaining or Trial? The Process of Criminal-Case Disposition*. Lexington, MA: Lexington Books.

Matthews, N. 1989. "Surmounting a Legacy: The Expansion of Racial Diversity in a Local Anti-Rape Movement." *Gender and Society* 3:518–32.

Matza, D. 1964. *Delinquency and Drift*. London: Wiley.

Maynard, D. 1984. *Inside Plea Bargaining: The Language of Negotiation*. New York: Plenum Press.

McCahill, T., L. Meyer, and A. Fischman. 1979. *The Aftermath of Rape*. Lexington, MA: Lexington Books.

McCall, M. 1966. "Courtship as Social Exchange." In B. Farber (ed.), *Kinship and Family Organization*. London: Wiley.

McCombie, S. (ed.). 1980. *The Rape Crisis Intervention Handbook*. New York: Plenum.

McConahay, S., and J. McConahay. 1977. "Sexual Permissiveness, Sex-Role Rigidity, and Violence Across Cultures." *Journal of Social Issues* 33:134–43.

McCord, J., and W. McCord. 1960. *Origins of Alcoholism*. Stanford, CA: Stanford University Press.

McDermott, J. 1979. *Rape Victimization in 26 American Cities*. Washington, DC: U.S. Government Printing Office.

McDonough, J. 1984. "I Can Teach You How to Read the Book of Life." *Bill Landis' Sleazoid Express* 3 (7):3–5.

Mead, M. 1963. *Sex and Temperament in Three Primitive Societies*. New York: William Morrow.

Medea, A., and K. Thompson. 1974. *Against Rape*. New York: Farrar, Straus, and Giroux.

Merton, A. 1985. "On Competition and Class: Return to Brotherhood." *Ms.* (September):60–65, 121–22.

Messner, M. 1989. "Masculinities and Athletic Careers." *Gender and Society* 3:71–88.

Meyer, T. 1984. " 'Date Rape': A Serious Problem That Few Talk About." *Chronicle of Higher Education* (December 5).

———. 1986. "Fight Against Hazing Rituals Rages on Campuses." *Chronicle of Higher Education* (March 12):34–36.

Michaud, S., and H. Aynesworth. 1983. *The Only Living Witness*. New York: Linden Press.

Miller, F. 1970. *Prosecution: The Decision to Charge a Suspect with a Crime*. Boston: Little, Brown.

Miller, L. 1973. "Distinctive Characteristics of Fraternity Members." *Journal of College Student Personnel* 31:126–28.

Millett, K. 1970a. "Sexual Politics in Literature." In R. Morgan (ed.), *Sisterhood Is Powerful*. New York: Random House.

———. 1970b. *Sexual Politics*. Garden City, NY: Doubleday.

———. 1972. *Sexual Politics*. London: Abacus.

Milloy, R. 1992. "Furor over a Decision Not to Indict in a Rape Case." *New York Times* (October 25):B4.

Mills, C. W. 1940. "Situated Actions and Vocabularies of Motives." *American Sociological Review* 5:439–52.

Moore, M., S. Estrich, D. McGillis, and W. Spelman. 1984. *Dangerous Offenders*. Cambridge, MA: Harvard University Press.

Morgan, R. 1980. "Theory and Practice: Pornography and Rape." In L. Lederer (ed.), *Take Back the Night: Women on Pornography*. New York: William Morrow.

———. 1989. *The Demon Lover: On the Sexuality of Terrorism*. New York: Norton.

Muehlenhard, C., and M. Linton. 1987. "Date Rape and Sexual Aggression in Dating Situations: Incidence and Risk Factors." *Journal of Counseling Psychology* 34:186–96.

Myers, M. 1985. "A New Look at Mothers of Incest Victims." *Journal of Social Work and Human Sexuality* 3:47–58.

Myers, M., and G. LaFree. 1982. "Sexual Assault and Prosecution: A Comparison with Other Crimes." *Journal of Criminal Law and Criminology* 73:1300.

Neubauer, D. 1974. *Criminal Justice in Middle America.* Morristown, NJ: General Learning Press.

Neuman, W. 1992. "Gender, Race, and Age Differences in Student Definitions of Sexual Harassment." *Wisconsin Sociologist* 29:63–75.

New York Radical Feminists. 1974. *Rape: The First Sourcebook for Women.* New York: New American Library.

Nordheimer, J. 1978. "All-American Boy on Trial." *New York Times Magazine* (December 10):46ff.

Notman, M., and C. Nadelson. 1976. "The Rape Victim: Psychodynamic Considerations." *American Journal of Psychiatry* 133:408–13.

Ochberg, F., and K. Fojtik-Stroud. 1982. "A Comprehensive Mental Health Clinical Service Program for Victims." Unpublished manuscript.

Office of Civil Rights. 1980. *Fall Enrollment and Compliance Report of Institutions of Higher Education.* Washington, DC: U.S. Department of Education.

Ohio Revised Code. 1980. 2907.01A,2907.02.

Olsen, Frances. 1984. "Statutory Rape: A Feminist Critique of Rights Analysis." *Texas Law Review* 633:387–432.

Orcutt, J., and R. Faison. 1988. "Sex-Role Attitude Change and Reporting of Rape Victimization, 1973–1985." *Sociological Quarterly* 29:589–604.

Osborne, J. 1984. "Rape Law Reform: The New Cosmetic for Canadian Women." *Women and Politics* 4:49–64.

Osman, A., and R. Ford. 1981. "Lost Chances, Bad Luck and Malice of the Tapes Foiled Untiring Search." *Times* (May 23):5.

Pagelow, M. 1980. "Double Victimization of the Battered Woman: Victimized by Spouses and the Legal System." Paper presented at the conference of the American Society of Criminology, San Francisco.

————. 1984. *Family Violence.* New York: Praeger.

Papandreou, M. 1988. "Feminism and Political Power: Some Thoughts on Strategies for the Future." In E. Boneparth and E. Stoper (eds.), *Women, Power, and Policy: Toward the Year 2000.* New York: Pergamon.

Parad, H. 1965. *Crisis Intervention: Selected Readings.* New York: Family Service Association.

Parrot, A., and L. Bechhofer (eds.). 1991. *Acquaintance Rape: The Hidden Crime.* New York: Wiley.

Penrod, S., and D. Linz. 1984. "Using Psychological Research on Violent Pornography to Inform Legal Change." In N. Malamuth and E. Donnerstein (eds.), *Pornography and Sexual Aggression.* New York: Academic Press.

Pfeffer, M. 1985. "Where Have All the Sex Crimes Gone?" Unpublished paper, Harvard Law School.

Pithers, W., J. Marques, and C. Gibat. 1983. "Relapse Prevention with Sexual Aggressives: A Self-Control Model of Treatment and Maintenance of Change." In J. Greer and I. Stuart (eds.), *The Sexual Aggressor: Current Perspectives in Treatment.* New York: Van Nostrand Reinhold.

Pittman, D., and C. Synder. 1962. *Society, Culture and Drinking Patterns.* New York: Wiley.

Pleck, E. 1987. *Domestic Tyranny: The Making of American Social Policy Against Family Violence from Colonial Times to the Present.* New York: Oxford University Press.

Polan, D. 1982. "Toward a Theory of Law and Patriarchy." In D. Kairys (ed.), *The Politics of Law.* New York: Pantheon.

Polk, K. 1985. "Rape Reform and Criminal Justice Processing." *Crime and Delinquency* 31:191–205.

Pope, B. 1993. "In the Wake of Tailhook: A New Order for the Navy." In E. Buchwald, P. Fletcher, and M. Roth (eds.), *Transforming a Rape Culture.* Minneapolis: Milkweed Editions.

Prentky, R., A. Burgess, and D. Carter. 1986. "Victim Response by Rapist Type: An Empirical and Clinical Analysis." *Journal of Interpersonal Violence* 1:73–98.

Pressley, S. 1987. "Fraternity Hell Night Still Endures." *Washington Post* (August 11):B1.

Queen's Bench Foundation. 1976. *Rape: Prevention and Resistance.* San Francisco: Queen's Bench Foundation.

Quinsey, V., and W. Marshall. 1983. "Procedures for Reducing Inappropriate Sexual Arousal: An Evaluation Review." In J. Greer and I. Stuart (eds.), *The Sexual Aggressor: Current Perspectives in Treatment.* New York: Van Nostrand Reinhold.

Quinsey, V., and D. Upfold. 1985. "Rape Completion and Victim Injury as a Function of Female Resistance Strategy." *Canadian Journal of Behavioral Science* 17:40–50.

Rada, R. 1978. *Clinical Aspects of Rape.* New York: Grune and Stratton.

Rada, R., R. Kellner, D. Laws, and W. Winslow. 1978. "Drinking, Alcoholism, and the Mentally Disordered Sex Offender." *Bulletin of the American Academy of Psychiatry and Law* 6:296–300.

Rado, S. 1948. "Pathodynamics and Treatment of Traumatic War Neurosis." *Psychosomatic Medicine* 4:362–68.

Rapaport, K., and B. Burkhart. 1984. "Personality and Attitudinal Characteristics of Sexually Coercive College Males." *Journal of Abnormal Psychology* 93:216–21.

Ressler, R., A. Burgess, and J. Douglas. 1983. "Rape and Rape-Murder: One Offender and Twelve Victims." *American Journal of Psychiatry* 140:36–40.

Reynolds, W. 1897–1988. "The Remedy for Lynch Law." *Yale Law Journal* 7:20–25.

Rifkin, J. 1982. "Toward a Theory of Law and Patriarchy." In P. Beirne and R. Quinney (eds.), *Marxism and Law.* New York: Wiley.

Roark, M. 1987. "Preventing Violence on College Campuses." *Journal of Counseling and Development* 65:367–70.

Robin, G. 1977. "Forcible Rape: Institutionalized Sexism in the Criminal Justice System." *Crime and Delinquency* 23:136–53.

Robins, L., and E. Smith. 1980. "Longitudinal Studies of Alcohol and Drug Problems: Sex Differences." In O. Kalant (eds.), *Alcohol and Drug Problems in Women.* New York: Plenum.

Rose, A. 1948. *The Negro in America.* New York: Harper.

Rose, V. M. 1977. "Rape as a Social Problem: A By-Product of the Feminist Movement." *Social Problems* 25:75–89.

Rose, V. M., and S. Randall. 1982. "The Impact of Investigator Perceptions of Victim Legitimacy on the Processing of Rape/Sexual Assault Cases." *Symbolic Interaction* 5:23–36.

Rosen, E. 1985. "The New Bedford Rape Trial." *Dissent* 32:207–11.

Rosenfeld, A. 1982. "Sexual Abuse of Children: Personal and Professional Reponses." In E. Newberger (ed.), *Child Abuse*. Boston, Little, Brown.

Rozee, P., P. Bateman, and T. Gilmore. 1991. "The Personal Perspective of Acquaintance Rape Prevention: A Three-Tier Approach." In A. Parrot and L. Bechhofer (eds.), *Acquaintance Rape: The Hidden Crime*. New York: Wiley.

Rubinstein, J. 1973. *City Police*. New York: Farrar, Straus and Giroux.

Rule, A. 1980. *The Stranger Beside Me*. New York: New American Library.

Rush, F. 1980. *The Best Kept Secret: Sexual Abuse of Children*. Englewood Cliffs, NJ: Prentice-Hall.

Russell, D. 1975. *The Politics of Rape: The Victim's Perspective*. New York: Stein and Day.

———. 1982. *Rape in Marriage*. New York: Macmillan.

———. 1984. *Sexual Exploitation: Rape, Child Sexual Abuse, and Workplace Harassment*. Newbury Park, CA: Sage.

———. 1986. *The Secret Trauma: Incest in the Lives of Girls and Women*. New York: Basic Books.

———. 1988. "Pornography and Rape: A Causal Model." *Political Psychology* 9:41–73.

Rutter, P. 1989. *Sex in the Forbidden Zone*. New York: Ballantine.

Ryan, W. 1972. *Blaming the Victim*. New York: Random House.

St. Petersburg Times. 1988. "A Greek Tragedy" (May 29):1F, 6F.

Sanday, P. 1979. *The Socio-Cultural Context of Rape*. Washington, DC: United States Department of Commerce, National Technical Information Service.

———. 1981a. "The Socio-Cultural Context of Rape: A Cross-Cultural Study." *Journal of Social Issues* 37:5–27.

———. 1981b. *Female Power and Male Dominance: On the Origins of Sexual Inequality*. London: Cambridge University Press.

———. 1986. "Rape and the Silencing of the Feminine." In S. Tomaselli and R. Porter (eds.), *Rape*. Oxford: Basil Blackwell.

Sanders, W. 1980. *Rape and Woman's Identity*. Beverly Hills, CA: Sage.

Sato, I. 1988. "Play Theory of Delinquency: Toward a General Theory of 'Action.'" *Symbolic Interaction* 11:191–212.

Scroggs, J. 1976. "Penalties for Rape as a Function of Victim Provocativeness, Damage, and Resistance." *Journal of Applied Social Psychology* 6:360–68.

Scheff, T. 1966. *Being Mentally Ill: A Sociological Theory*. Chicago: Aldine.

Schuker, E. 1979. "Psychodynamics and Treatment of Sexual Assault Victims." *Journal of American Academy of Psychoanalysis* 7:553–73.

Schwartz, B. 1968. "The Effect of Pennsylvania's Increased Penalties for Rape and Attempted Rape." *Journal of Criminal Law, Criminology, and Police Science* 59:509–15.

Schwartz, M., and W. Masters. 1985. "Treatment of Paraphiliacs, Pedophiles, and Incest Families." In A. Burgess (ed.), *Rape and Sexual Assault: A Research Handbook*. New York: Garland.

Schwendinger, J., and H. Schwendinger. 1983. *Rape and Inequality*. Newbury Park, CA: Sage.

Scully, D. 1990. *Understanding Sexual Violence: A Study of Convicted Rapists*. New York: Unwin Hyman.

Scully, D., and J. Marolla. 1984. "Convicted Rapists' Vocabulary of Motives: Excuses and Justifications." *Social Problems* 31:530–44.

————. 1985a. "Rape and Psychiatric Vocabulary of Motive: Alternative Perspectives." In A. Burgess (ed.), *Rape and Sexual Assault: A Research Handbook*. New York: Garland.

————. 1985b. " 'Riding the Bull at Gilley's': Convicted Rapists Describe the Rewards of Rape." *Social Problems* 32:251–63.

Searles, P., and R. Berger. 1987a. "The Current Status of Rape Reform Legislation: An Examination of State Statutes." *Women's Rights Law Reporter* 10:25–43.

————. 1987b. "The Feminist Self-Defense Movement: A Case Study." *Gender and Society* 1:61–83.

Searles, P., and P. Follansbee. 1984. "Self-Defense for Women: Translating Theory into Practice." *Frontiers: A Journal of Women Studies* 8:65–70.

Seghorn, T., T. Boucher, and M. Cohen. 1983. "Sexual Abuse in the Life Histories of Sexual Offenders: A Retrospective Longitudinal Analysis." Paper presented at the Sixth World Congress for Sexology, Washington, DC.

Serrano, R. 1989. "S.D. Serial-Killer Probe Mimics 'Error' Pattern of Green River Slayings." *Los Angeles Times* (February 26):Part 2, 1.

Sheffield, C. 1989. "The Invisible Intruder: Women's Experiences of Obscene Phone Calls." *Gender and Society* 3:483–88.

Shields, N., and C. Hanneke. 1981. "Battered Wives' Reactions to Marital Rape." Paper presented at the National Conference on Family Therapy, Durham, NH.

Siegal, J., S. Sorenson, J. Golding, M. Burnam, and J. Stein. 1989. "Resistance to Sexual Assault: Who Resists and What Happens?" *American Journal of Public Health* 79:27–31.

Silver, S. 1976. "Outpatient Treatment for Sex Offenders." *Social Work* 21:134–40.

Smart, C. 1976. *Women, Crime and Criminology*. London: Routledge.

Smith, B. 1981. "Introduction to 'Twelve Black Women: Why Did They Die?' " In F. Delacoste and F. Newman (eds.), *Fight Back: Feminist Resistance to Male Violence*. Minneapolis: Cleis Press.

Smith, D. 1976. "The Social Context of Pornography." *Journal of Communications* 26:16–24.

Smith, J. 1982. "Getting Away with Murder." *New Socialist* (May-June):10–12.

Smith, T. 1964. "Emergence and Maintenance of Fraternal Solidarity." *Pacific Sociological Review* 7:29-37.

Smithyman, S. 1978. "The Undetected Rapist." Unpublished Ph.D. dissertation, Claremont Graduate School.

Sokoloff, N., and B. Raffel Price. 1982. "The Criminal Law and Women." In B. Raffel Price and N. Sokoloff (eds.), *The Criminal Justice System and Women*. New York: Clark Boardman.

Soules, M., S. Stewar, K. Brown, and A. Pollard. 1978. "The Spectrum of Alleged Rape." *Journal of Reproductive Medicine* 20:33–39.

Spohn, C., and J. Horney. 1991. " 'The Law's the Law, But Fair is Fair': Rape Shield Laws and Officials' Assessment of Sexual History Evidence." *Criminology* 29:137–60.

————. 1992. *Rape Law Reform: A Grassroots Revolution and Its Impact*. New York: Plenum.

Stanko, E. 1980. "These Are the Cases That Try Themselves: An Examination of the Extra-Legal Criteria in Felony Case Processing." Paper presented at the annual meeting of the North Central Sociological Association, Buffalo, NY, December.

_____. 1981–1982. "The Impact of Victim Assessment on Prosecutor's Screening Decisions: The Case of the New York District Attorney's Office." *Law and Society Review* 16:225–39.

_____. 1982. "Would You Believe This Woman? Prosecutorial Screening for 'Credible' Witnesses and a Problem of Justice." In N. Rafter and E. Stanko (eds.), *Judge, Lawyer, Victim, Thief.* Boston: Northeastern University Press.

_____. 1985. *Intimate Intrusions: Women's Experience of Male Violence.* London: Routledge and Kegan Paul.

Starr, M. 1984. "The Random Killers." *Newsweek* (November 26):106.

Storaska, F. 1975. *How to Say No to a Rapist and Survive.* New York: Warner.

Strong, B., and C. DeVault. 1992. *The Marriage and Family Experience,* fifth edition. St. Paul: West.

Sudnow, D. 1965. "Normal Crimes: Sociological Features of the Penal Code in a Public Defender's Office." *Social Problems* 12:255–76.

Summers, A. 1989. "The Hedda Conundrum." *Ms.* (April):54.

Summit, R., and J. Kryso. 1978. "Sexual Abuse of Children: A Clinical Spectrum." *American Journal of Orthopsychiatry* 48:237–51.

Sykes, G., and D. Matza. 1957. "Techniques of Neutralization: A Theory of Delinquency." *American Sociological Review* 22:667–70.

Szasz, T. 1973. *The Manufacture of Madness.* London: Paladin.

Tallahassee Democrat. 1988a. "FSU Fraternity Brothers Charged" (April 27):1A, 12A.

_____. 1988b. "FSU Interviewing Students About Alleged Rape" (April 24):1D.

_____. 1989. "Woman Sues Stetson in Alleged Rape" (March 19):3B.

Tampa Tribune. 1988. "Fraternity Brothers Charged in Sexual Assault of FSU Coed" (April 27):6B.

Tash, G. 1988. "Date Rape." *The Emerald of Sigma Pi Fraternity* 75(4):1–2.

Telander, R., and R. Sullivan. 1989. "Special Report: You Reap What You Sow." *Sports Illustrated* (February 27):20–34.

Terr, L. 1983. "Chowcilla Revisited: The Effects of Psychic Trauma Four Years After a School Bus Kidnapping." *American Journal of Psychiatry* 140:1543–50.

Terris, M. 1967. "Epidemiology of Cirrhosis of the Liver: National Mortality Data." *American Journal of Public Health* 57:2076–88.

Tierney, K. 1982. "The Battered Women Movement and the Creation of the Wife Beating Problem." *Social Problems* 29:207–20.

The Tomahawk. 1988. "A Look Back at Rush: A Mixture of Hard Work and Fun" (April-May):3D.

Thyfault, R. 1980. "Sexual Abuse and the Battering Relationship." Paper presented at conference of Rocky Mountain Psychological Association, Tucson, AZ.

Toner, B. 1977. *The Facts of Rape.* London: Arrow Books.

Tong, R. 1984. *Women, Sex, and the Law.* Totowa, NJ: Rowman and Allanheld.

Torrey, M. 1991. "When Will We Be Believed? Rape Myths and the Idea of a Fair Trial in Rape Prosecutions." *U.C. Davis Law Review* 24:1013–71.

Tyhurst, J. 1951. "Individual Reaction to Community Disaster: The Habitual History of Psychic Phenomenon." *American Journal of Psychiatry* 107:764–69.

Uehling, M. 1986. "The LA Slayer." *Newsweek* (June 9):28.

University of Pennsylvania Law Review. 1968. "Police Discretion and the Judgment That a Crime Has Been Committed—Rape in Philadelphia" 117:277–322.

U.S. Bureau of Census. 1980. *Current Population Reports, 1980–1981.* Washington, DC: U.S. Government Printing Office.

U.S. Department of Justice. 1981. *Federal Bureau of Investigation, Uniform Crime Reports (1977–1980).* Washington, DC: Government Printing Office.

_____. 1984. *Criminal Victimization in the United States: 1982.* Washington, DC: Government Printing Office.

Vaillant, G. 1983. *The Natural History of Alcoholism: Causes, Patterns, and Paths to Recovery.* Cambridge: Harvard University Press.

Vera Institute of Justice. 1981. *Felony Arrests: Their Prosecution and Disposition in New York City's Courts,* revised edition. New York: Longman.

Volgy, T., J. Schwarz, and H. Gottlieb. 1986. "Female Representation and the Quest for Resources: Feminist Activism and Electoral Success." *Social Science Quarterly* 67:156–68.

Waegel, W. 1981. "Case Routinization in Investigative Police Work." *Social Problems* 28:263–75.

Walker, A. 1982. *The Color Purple.* New York: Harcourt Brace Jovanovich.

Walkowitz, J. 1982. "Jack the Ripper and the Myth of Male Violence." *Feminist Studies* 8:543–74.

Walsh, C. 1989. Comments in Seminar on Acquaintance/Date Rape Prevention: A National Video Teleconference (February 2).

Weis, K., and S. Borges. 1973. "Victimology and Rape: The Case of the Legitimate Victim." *Issues in Criminology* 8:71–115.

Weninger, R. 1978. "Factors Affecting the Prosecution of Rape: A Case Study of Travis County, Texas." *Virginia Law Review* 64:386.

West, D. 1983. "Sex Offenses and Offending." In M. Tonry and N. Morris (eds.), *Crime and Justice: An Annual Review of Research.* Chicago: University of Chicago Press.

West, R. 1987. "U.S. Prostitutes Collective." In F. Delacoste and P. Alexander (eds.), *Sex Work: Writings by Women in the Sex Industry.* Pittsburgh: Cleis Press.

Wheeler, H. 1985. "Pornography and Rape: A Feminist Perspective." In A. Burgess (ed.), *Rape and Sexual Assault: A Research Handbook.* New York: Garland.

Wilder, D., A. Hoyt, D. Doren, W. Hauck, and R. Zettle. 1978. "The Impact of Fraternity and Sorority Membership on Values and Attitudes." *Journal of College Student Personnel* 36:445–49.

Wilder, D., A. Hoyt, B. Surbeck, J. Wilder, and P. Carney. 1986. "Greek Affiliation and Attitude Change in College Students." *Journal of College Student Personnel* 44:510–19.

Williams, J., and K. Holmes. 1981. *The Second Assault: Rape and Public Attitudes.* Westport, CT: Greenwood Press.

Williams, K. 1978a. *The Role of the Victim in the Prosecution of Violent Crimes.* Washington, DC: Institute for Law and Social Research.

_____. 1978b. *The Prosecution of Sexual Assaults.* Washington, DC: Institute for Law and Social Research.

Williams, L. 1984. "The Classic Rape: When Do Victims Report?" *Social Problems* 31:459–67.

Wilson, G., and D. Lawson. 1976. "Expectancies, Alcohol, and Sexual Arousal in Male Social Drinkers." *Journal of Abnormal Psychology* 85:587–94.

Wohlenberg, E. 1980. "Correlates of Equal Rights Amendment Ratification." *Social Science Quarterly* 60:676–84.

Wolfgang, M. 1974. "Racial Discrimination in the Death Sentence for Rape." in W. Bowers (ed.), *Executions in America*. Lexington, MA: Lexington Books.

Woliver, L. 1990. "Feminism at the Grassroots: The Recall of Judge Archie Simonson." *Frontiers: A Journal of Women Studies* 11:111–19.

Wyatt, G. 1992. "The Sociocultural Context of African American and White American Women's Rape." *Journal of Social Issues* 48:77–91.

Yoshihama, M., A. Parekh, and D. Boyington. 1991. "Dating Violence in Asian/Pacific Communities." In B. Levy (ed.), *Dating Violence: Young Women in Danger*. Seattle: Seal Press.

Zeisel, H. 1982. *The Limits of Law Enforcement*. Chicago: University of Chicago Press.

Credits

Part One: Feminist Foundations for the Study of Rape and Society

"Rape Poem," from *Circles on the Water* by Marge Piercy, copyright © 1982 by Marge Piercy. Reprinted by permission of Alfred A. Knopf, Inc.

Chapter 1: "The Trauma of Rape: The Case of Ms. X," from Diana E.H. Russell, *The Politics of Rape* (Briarcliff Manor, N.Y.: Stein and Day, 1975), pp. 17–24. Reprinted by permission of the author.

Chapter 2: Stevi Jackson, "The Social Context of Rape: Sexual Scripts and Motivation," reprinted with permission from *Women's Studies International Quarterly* 1 (1978): 27–38, Elsevier Science Ltd., Pergamon Imprint, Oxford, England.

Chapter 3: "Sex and Violence: A Perspective," reprinted by permission of the publishers from *Feminism Unmodified: Discourses on Life and Law* by Catharine A. MacKinnon, Cambridge, Mass.: Harvard University Press, copyright © 1987 by the President and Fellows of Harvard College.

Chapter 4: Mary Koss, "Hidden Rape: Sexual Aggression and Victimization in a National Sample of Students in Higher Education," in A. Burgess, ed., *Rape and Sexual Assault* 2 (1988): 3–25. Reprinted by permission.

Part Two: Why Men Rape

Chapter 5: "Jay: An 'Armchair' Rapist," from *Men on Rape* by Timothy Beneke, copyright © 1982 by Timothy Beneke, St. Martin's Press, Inc., New York, N.Y. Reprinted by permission.

Chapter 6: Diana Scully and Joseph Marolla, " 'Riding the Bull at Gilley's': Convicted Rapists Describe the Rewards of Rape," copyright © 1985 by the Society for the Study of Social Problems. Reprinted from *Social Problems* 32, 3 (1985): 251–253, by permission.

Chapter 7: Judith Lewis Herman, "Considering Sex Offenders: A Model of Addiction," *Signs* 13 (1988): 695–724. Reprinted by permission of The University of Chicago Press and the author.

Chapter 8: Catharine A. MacKinnon, "Pornography as Sex Discrimination," *Law & Inequality* 4, 17 (1986): 38–49. Reprinted by permission.

Part Three: Varieties of Rape and Sexual Assault

Chapter 9: "Child Sexual Abuse," excerpted from "Introduction" by Ellen Bass from *I Never Told Anyone: Writings by Women Survivors of Child Sexual Abuse* by Ellen Bass and Louise

Thornton. Copyright © 1983 by Ellen Bass, Louise Thornton, Jude Brister, Grace Hammond, and Vicki Lamb. Reprinted by permission of HarperCollins Publishers, Inc.

Chapter 10: Maggie Hoyal, "These Are the Things I Remember," excerpted from *I Never Told Anyone: Writings by Women Survivors of Child Sexual Abuse* by Ellen Bass and Louise Thornton. Copyright © 1983 by Ellen Bass, Louise Thornton, Jude Brister, Grace Hammond, and Vicki Lamb. Reprinted by permission of HarperCollins Publishers, Inc.

Chapter 11: "White Man Wants a Black Piece: The Case of Sonia Morrell," from Diana E.H. Russell, *The Politics of Rape* (Briarcliff Manor, N.Y.: Stein and Day, 1975), pp. 129–139. Reprinted by permission of the author.

Chapter 12: Patricia Yancey Martin and Robert A. Hummer, "Fraternities and Rape on Campus," *Gender and Society* 3, 4 (1989): 457–473. Reprinted by permission of Sage Publications, Inc.

Chapter 13: "Types of Marital Rape," from Chapters 2 and 3 of David Finkelhor and Kersti Yllo, *License to Rape: Sexual Abuse of Wives* (New York: Holt, Rinehart and Winston). Copyright © 1985 by David Finkelhor and Kersti Yllo. Reprinted by permission of Henry Holt and Co., Inc.

Chapter 14: Jane Caputi, "The Sexual Politics of Murder," *Gender and Society* 3, 4 (1989): 437–456. Reprinted by permission of Sage Publications, Inc.

Chapter 15: Susan Brownmiller, "Making Female Bodies the Battlefield," *Newsweek* (Jan. 4, 1993): 37. Reprinted by permission of the author.

Chapter 16: Nina Kadić, "Dispatch from Bosnia-Herzegovina: A Seventeen-Year-Old Survivor Testifies to Systematic Rape," *Ms.* (Jan.-Feb. 1993): 12–13. Reprinted by permission of Ms. Magazine, copyright © 1993.

Leslie A. Donovan, "For a Paralyzed Woman Raped and Murdered While Alone in Her Own Apartment," *Women Studies Quarterly* 17 (1985). Reprinted by permission.

Part Four: Rape and the Legal System

Chapter 17: "Is It Rape?" reprinted by permission of the publishers from *Real Rape* by Susan Estrich, Cambridge, Mass.: Harvard University Press, copyright © 1987 by the President and Fellows of Harvard College.

Chapter 18: "Jack and Ken," from *Men on Rape* by Timothy Beneke, copyright © 1982 by Timothy Beneke, St. Martin's Press, Inc., New York, N.Y. Reprinted by permission.

Chapter 19: Lisa Frohmann, "Discrediting Victims' Allegations of Sexual Assault: Prosecutorial Accounts of Case Rejections," copyright © 1991 by the Society for the Study of Social Problems. Reprinted from *Social Problems* 38, 2 (1991): 213–226, by permission.

Chapter 20: Jennifer Wriggins, "Rape, Racism, and the Law," *Harvard Women's Law Journal* 6 (Spring 1983): 103–141. Reprinted by permission.

Chapter 21: Ronald J. Berger, Patricia Searles, and W. Lawrence Neuman, "Rape-Law Reform: Its Nature, Origins, and Impact," original chapter.

Part Five: Surviving and Preventing Rape

Chapter 22: Ann Wolbert Burgess, "Rape Trauma Syndrome," *Behavioral Sciences and the Law* 1 (1983): 97–113. Copyright © 1983 by John Wiley and Sons. Reprinted by permission of John Wiley and Sons Limited.

Chapter 23: Christina Glendenning, "When You Grow Up an Abused Child ... ," in Toni A. McNaron and Yarrow Morgan, eds., *Voices in the Night* (Pittsburgh, Pa.: Cleis Press, 1982). Reprinted by permission.

Chapter 24: Fred Pelka, "Raped: A Male Survivor Breaks His Silence," *On the Issues: The Progressive Women's Quarterly* 22 (Spring 1992): 10–11, 40. Reprinted by permission.

Chapter 25: Gail Groves, "And He Turned Around and Ran Away," from the Preface from *Her Wits About Her,* edited by Denise Caignon and Gail Groves. Copyright © 1987 by Denise Caignon and Gail Groves. Reprinted by permission of HarperCollins Publishers, Inc.

Ellen Bass, "Our Stunning Harvest," in Pam McAllister, ed., *Reweaving the Web of Life: Feminism and Nonviolence* (Philadelphia: New Society Publishers, 1982), pp. 63–77. Reprinted by permission of New Society Publishers, 4527 Springfield Avenue, Philadelphia, Pa., 19143, (800) 333-9093.

About the Book and Editors

In the 1970s rape became the point of departure for an ongoing feminist examination of the subordination and sexual victimization of women. More recently, domestic violence, prostitution, sexual harassment, and pornography have come to the forefront of investigators' concerns. *Rape and Society* returns to the original focus on rape while also illuminating the interconnections among the many forms of violence against women.

The book provides a comprehensive treatment of the subject, drawing on writers and researchers from across a range of social and behavioral sciences and the humanities and representing the experiences of women of diverse backgrounds and lifestyles. From the private torment of a child abused by her father to the horror of mass rape and ethnic cleansing in the former Yugoslavia, the authors analyze rape as a tool of humiliation, control, and terror.

Rape and Society is an essential resource for academics and professionals and for anyone wanting to come to grips with the magnitude of the problem of sexual violence. Because the selections are moving as well as thought-provoking and varied in approach (theoretical, empirical, literary, and experiential), this interdisciplinary anthology is a superb text for undergraduate and graduate courses in women's studies, psychology, sociology, and criminology. It offers incisive analyses and carefully designed research to help us understand and explain rape while sensitizing us to the personal dimensions of sexual victimization and the emotional toll of living in a violent society. There are hopeful voices here too, helping readers envision a safer and more humane world, offering concrete suggestions for social change, and encouraging us all to gather the power and courage to take on the work that lies before us.

Patricia Searles is professor of sociology and women's studies at University of Wisconsin–Whitewater. **Ronald J. Berger** is professor of sociology and coordinator of the Criminal Justice Program at University of Wisconsin–Whitewater. They have published widely on a number of criminological and gender-related topics.